THE EPHEMERAL EIGHTEENTH CENTURY

Often regarded as trivial and disposable, printed ephemera, such as tickets, playbills, and handbills, was essential in the development of eighteenth-century culture. In this original study, richly illustrated with examples from across the period, Gillian Russell examines the emergence of the cultural category of printed ephemera, its relationship with forms of sociability, the history of the book, and ideas of what constituted the boundaries of literature and literary value. Russell explores the role of contemporary collectors such as Sarah Sophia Banks in preserving such material, arguing for 'ephemerology' as a distinctive strand of popular antiquarianism. Multi-disciplinary in scope, *The Ephemeral Eighteenth Century* reveals new perspectives on the history of theatre, the fiction of Maria Edgeworth and Jane Austen, and on the history of bibliography, as well as highlighting the continuing relevance of the concept of ephemerality to how we connect through social media today.

GILLIAN RUSSELL is Professor of English at the University of York. A Fellow of the Australian Academy of the Humanities, she is internationally renowned for her innovative interdisciplinary research which began with *The Theatres of War: Performance, Politics and Society, 1793–1815* (1995). She has pioneered field-changing new directions in scholarship – on war and theatre and on the study of sociability. Her books include *Romantic Sociability: Social Networks and Literary Culture 1770–1840* (Cambridge, 2002), co-edited with Clara Tuite; *Women, Sociability and Theatre in Georgian London* (Cambridge, 2007); and *Tracing War in British Enlightenment and Romantic Culture*, co-edited with Neil Ramsey (2015).

CAMBRIDGE STUDIES IN ROMANTICISM

Founding Editor
MARILYN BUTLER, *University of Oxford*

General Editor
JAMES CHANDLER, *University of Chicago*

Editorial Board
JOHN BARRELL, *University of York*
PAUL HAMILTON, *University of London*
MARY JACOBUS, *University of Cambridge*
CLAUDIA JOHNSON, *Princeton University*
ALAN LIU, *University of California, Santa Barbara*
JEROME MCGANN, *University of Virginia*
DAVID SIMPSON, *University of California, Davis*
DEIDRE LYNCH, *Harvard University*

This series aims to foster the best new work in one of the most challenging fields within English literary studies. From the early 1780s to the early 1830s, a formidable array of talented men and women took to literary composition, not just in poetry, which some of them famously transformed, but in many modes of writing. The expansion of publishing created new opportunities for writers, and the political stakes of what they wrote were raised again by what Wordsworth called those 'great national events' that were 'almost daily taking place': the French Revolution, the Napoleonic and American wars, urbanization, industrialization, religious revival, an expanded empire abroad, and the reform movement at home. This was an enormous ambition, even when it pretended otherwise. The relations between science, philosophy, religion, and literature were reworked in texts such as *Frankenstein* and *Biographia Literaria*; gender relations in *A Vindication of the Rights of Woman* and *Don Juan*; journalism by Cobbett and Hazlitt; and poetic form, content, and style by the Lake School and the Cockney School. Outside Shakespeare studies, probably no body of writing has produced such a wealth of commentary or done so much to shape the responses of modern criticism. This indeed is the period that saw the emergence of those notions of literature and of literary history, especially national literary history, on which modern scholarship in English has been founded.

The categories produced by Romanticism have also been challenged by recent historicist arguments. The task of the series is to engage both with a challenging corpus of Romantic writings and with the changing field of criticism they have helped to shape. As with other literary series published by Cambridge University Press, this one will represent the work of both younger and more established scholars on either side of the Atlantic and elsewhere.

See the end of the book for a complete list of published titles.

THE EPHEMERAL EIGHTEENTH CENTURY

Print, Sociability, and the Cultures of Collecting

GILLIAN RUSSELL

University of York

Shaftesbury Road, Cambridge CB2 8EA, United Kingdom

One Liberty Plaza, 20th Floor, New York, NY 10006, USA

477 Williamstown Road, Port Melbourne, VIC 3207, Australia

314–321, 3rd Floor, Plot 3, Splendor Forum, Jasola District Centre, New Delhi – 110025, India

103 Penang Road, #05–06/07, Visioncrest Commercial, Singapore 238467

Cambridge University Press is part of Cambridge University Press & Assessment, a department of the University of Cambridge.

We share the University's mission to contribute to society through the pursuit of education, learning and research at the highest international levels of excellence.

www.cambridge.org
Information on this title: www.cambridge.org/9781108720663

DOI: 10.1017/9781108767347

© Gillian Russell 2020

This publication is in copyright. Subject to statutory exception and to the provisions of relevant collective licensing agreements, no reproduction of any part may take place without the written permission of Cambridge University Press & Assessment.

First published 2020
First paperback edition 2025

A catalogue record for this publication is available from the British Library

ISBN 978-1-108-48758-0 Hardback
ISBN 978-1-108-72066-3 Paperback

Cambridge University Press & Assessment has no responsibility for the persistence or accuracy of URLs for external or third-party internet websites referred to in this publication and does not guarantee that any content on such websites is, or will remain, accurate or appropriate.

To Harry Morrow and Jennifer FitzGerald

Contents

List of Figures	*page* viii
Acknowledgements	xi
Introduction: 'All the Ephemera of Our Lives'	1
1 Accidental Readings and Diurnal Historiographies: The Invention of Ephemera	30
2 Making Collections: Enlightenment Ephemerology	60
3 The Natural History of Sociability: Sarah Sophia Banks and Her Ephemera Collections	98
4 Sarah Sophia Banks's 'Magic Encyclopedia'	126
5 'Announcing Each Day the Performances': Playbills as Theatre/Media History	153
6 Transacting Hospitality: The Novel Networks of the Visiting Card	186
7 England in 1814: Frost Fairs, Peace, and *Persuasion*	214
Conclusion	251
Bibliography	255
Index	281

Figures

1. Anonymous handbill encouraging a public celebration of the second year of Gallic Liberty, 1791. Permission The National Archives, HO 42/19 (138). *page* 47
2. 'The Tall *Indian*-King', handbill advertisement with annotations by Anthony Wood 1678. The Bodleian Libraries, The University of Oxford. MS. Wood Diaries 16. Fol. 8r. 76
3. 'Sir, FOR the Continuance of mutual Society', ticket with annotations by Anthony Wood 1686. The Bodleian Libraries, The University of Oxford. MS. Wood Diaries 30, Item 61. 79
4. 'Oxford-Shire. 1662.', ticket. The Bodleian Libraries, The University of Oxford. Wood 276 B (119), Item 119. 80
5. 'Sawney in the Boghouse'. Etching 1745. © The Trustees of the British Museum. 82
6. Frost fair tickets of John Forde which are pasted inside folio volume of 'The Holy Bible' (formerly owned by John Forde). Permission University of Cambridge Library BSS.201.D06.2. 87
7. 'Great BRITAINS Wonder: Or LONDONS Admiration' with annotations by Nicholas Luttrell (1684). © The Trustees of the British Museum. 89
8. Bookplate of Anne Seymour Damer. Collection of Sarah Sophia Banks D,3.162. © The Trustees of the British Museum. 117
9. Lady's ticket to a ball in Norwich; with delicately drawn butterfly on blade of grass; Lady's ticket to a ball in Norwich; with hand-drawn vase of flowers, and red ribbon; Lady's ticket to a ball in Norwich; with hand drawn wreath with red flowers and blue bow. Collection of Sarah Sophia Banks J,9.237–239. © The Trustees of the British Museum. 118

List of Figures

10 Second page of a folded sheet, twenty-one undecorated visiting cards, one MS note, and three newspaper cuttings 1779–1815. Collection of Sarah Sophia Banks C,1.2401–2426. © The Trustees of the British Museum. 122

11 Sticklers tickets (c. 1807). Collection of Sarah Sophia Banks D,3.501–504. © The Trustees of the British Museum. 127

12 Ticket to a Ball at Ranelagh on 1 June 1803. Collection of Sarah Sophia Banks C,2.1915. © The Trustees of the British Museum. 133

13 Ticket to a Ball at Ranelagh on 1 June 1803. Collection of Sarah Sophia Banks C, 2.1913. © The Trustees of the British Museum. 134

14 Fourteen admission tickets and two newspaper cuttings relating to ballooning events; dated 1783–96. Collection of Sarah Sophia Banks C,2.11–28. © The Trustees of the British Museum. 140

15 Edinburgh Fire Balloon. Collection of Sarah Sophia Banks C,2.23. © The Trustees of the British Museum. 141

16 'L'experience de cette Figure …'. A collection of broadsides, cuttings from newspapers, engravings, etc., of various dates, formed by Miss S. S. Banks. Bound in nine volumes. © The British Library Board. L. R. 301.h.3 f. 45r. 146

17 Theatre-Royal Liverpool … This present SATURDAY will be performed August 21, 1830, Rowe's celebrated Tragedy of Jane Shore. [Liverpool: Melling and Co., 1830]. Ashford collection of theatre playbills from English theatres between 1796 and 1905. National Library of Australia. Permission National Library of Australia. 158

18 For the benefit of J. Butler and W. Bryant: at the Theatre, Sydney on July 30, 1796, will be performed Jane Shore … [Sydney: George Hughes, Govt. Printer for Theatre, Sydney, 1796]. National Library of Australia F692 RBRS N 686.2099441. Permission National Library of Australia. 178

19 For the benefit of J. Butler and W. Bryant: at the Theatre, Sydney on July 30, 1796, will be performed Jane Shore … [Sydney: George Hughes, Govt. Printer for Theatre, Sydney, 1796]. National Library of Australia F692 RBRS N 686.2099441, recto. Permission National Library of Australia. 182

20 Mr. Omai Presents his Compliments to Miss Banks. Visiting card 1776. Collection of Sarah Sophia Banks, C,1.2225. © The Trustees of the British Museum. 194
21 Where little wherries once did use to ride ... [London: Printed at Holme's and Broad's Booth, at the sign of the Ship, against Old Swan-Stairs, where is the only real Printing-Press on the frozen Thames. January the 14th, 1715/6]. © The British Library Board. 840.m.271, facing p. 20. 218
22 *Frostiana: or a History of the River Thames, in a Frozen State, with an Account of the Late Severe Frost* (London: G. Davis, 1814). © The British Library Board. 840.m.27(3) title page. 221
23 The Grand Jubilee. Hand-coloured etching. [Southwark: G. Smith, 1814]. Collection of Sarah Sophia Banks. J, 10.8. © The Trustees of the British Museum. 232
24 John Bexley, Fifty-Four Years the Canterbury News-Carrier. Engraving. [Rochester and Chatham: Gillman, 1788]. © The Trustees of the British Museum. 245

Acknowledgements

The Ephemeral Eighteenth Century has been a long time in the making. I was privileged to receive a professorial research fellowship from the Australian Research Council in 2010 which gave my ideas valuable time to grow and develop. This project had its genesis in the return from Canada in 2007 to the National Library of Australia, Canberra, of the playbill for a production of the tragedy *Jane Shore* in Sydney in 1796, the earliest printed document in Australian history to be so far discovered. I am grateful to the former Director General of the National Library of Australia, Jan Fullerton, for inviting me to participate in events associated with the playbill's return. The project also grew out of a period of shared teaching and research in Australia with Sarah Lloyd, whose pioneering work on the ticket has been invaluable. I have benefited immensely from the work of two outstanding research assistants, David Free and latterly Kate Horgan, whose expertise, as well as kindness and patience, has sustained me throughout. I would particularly like to thank Kate for her invaluable help in compiling the index.

In the course of writing *The Ephemeral Eighteenth Century* I moved institutions twice – to the University of Melbourne from the Australian National University (ANU), and most recently to the University of York. Particular colleagues and friends have been with me through thick and thin: Deirdre Coleman, Jon Mee, Neil Ramsey, Russell Smith, Daniel O'Quinn, and Clara Tuite. Monique Rooney's intellectual example, as well as wisdom, has influenced my work in profound ways and produced a better book. I am grateful for a visiting research fellowship at the University of Warwick in 2012, for which I particularly thank Karen O'Brien, and I also thank Theresa Kelley for inviting me to participate in the extremely useful workshop on archives and agentic life at the University of Wisconsin-Madison in 2013. Kevin Gilmartin has been supportive in very many ways, including an invitation to the conference 'Sociable Spaces' at the Huntington Library in 2012 and to an MLA panel in

2013 in honour of the late Jane Moody. An invitation to give a keynote in Wellington, New Zealand, in 2017 helped me develop ideas about the handbill, for which I thank Nikki Hessell and Ingrid Horrocks. Chawton House Library was a congenial environment in which to write the conclusion of the book in 2017: I was honoured to be the recipient of the Marilyn Butler fellowship there and thank the Library's director, Gillian Dow, and also my companions in the Stables for showing interest in ephemera on a memorable afternoon bus trip to Winchester. I thank Sarah Comyn and Porscha Fermanis for the opportunity to talk about ephemera at University College Dublin in 2017.

Other colleagues and friends whose support I would like to acknowledge include, at the ANU, Julieanne Lamond, Lucy Neave, Roald Maliangkay, Caroline Stevenson, Rex Stevenson, and Wei Shuge; in Melbourne, Trevor Burnard, Sarah Balkin, Susan Conley, Tom Ford, Eoin Hahessy, Joe Hughes, and Jimmy Yang; and at the University of York Centre for Eighteenth-Century Studies, Catriona Kennedy, Mary Fairclough, Alison O'Byrne, Jane Rendall, Jim Watt, Joanna Wharton, and Chloe Wigston-Smith. John Barrell and Harriet Guest were generous and welcoming on numerous occasions of visits to York.

I am grateful to staff in many libraries and research institutions, particularly the National Library of Australia, Canberra. Michela Bonardi at the British Museum and Deborah Horner at the British Library were particularly helpful in acquiring images. At Cambridge University Press I would like to thank Linda Bree for her support and encouragement over many years, and her successor Bethany Thomas (as well as Tim Mason) for skilfully shepherding the book through the Press in its final stages. The advice of the anonymous readers was extremely helpful in honing the argument and also in drawing attention to how I was beguiled by the collecting practices of Sarah Sophia Banks. I would also like to acknowledge the editorial support of Victorian Parrin at the Press and Elizabeth Stone. I thank James Chandler, not only for his role as general editor in this instance but also for the support he gave me while I was at the University of Melbourne. Iain McCalman was similarly ready to give advice and support which I greatly appreciated at the time.

Finally, as always, my greatest debt is to Benjamin Penny and our son, Tom Russell-Penny, for their faith and encouragement. This book is dedicated to two important teachers: Harry Morrow, who set me on the path to academia in Northern Ireland in the 1970s, and Jennifer FitzGerald for showing how to be a scholar, a feminist, and a good friend.

Introduction
'All the Ephemera of Our Lives'

In the late 1920s in Old Headington outside Oxford, a woman called Lilian Gurden, who was working in the garden of the home of Mrs Dorothea Johnson, was invited inside by her employer for a cup of coffee. Mrs Johnson was the wife of John de Monins Johnson (1882–1956), Printer to the University of Oxford from 1925 to 1946 and the most significant English ephemerist of the twentieth century.[1] Interviewed in 1986 by another important ephemerist, Maurice Rickards, Lilian Gurden (later Thrussell) recalled Dorothea Johnson telling her that she was unable to take a bath because it was 'full of soaking album pages'.[2] These albums contained printed ephemera from which John Johnson was extracting material for his collection, the 'Sanctuary of Printing', housed in an upper room of the printery of the Oxford University Press. Johnson's interest in paper scraps had been inspired by his early experience as an Egyptologist, 'digging the rubbish-mounds of Graeco-Roman cities in Egypt for the written materials – the waste paper of those ages'.[3] Encountering long queues outside cinemas in 1920s Oxford as he travelled home from work, Johnson was led to contemplate the relationship between twentieth-century visual media, the cityscape, and advertising as a form of graphic and visual art. His not inconsiderable ambition was to document 'the miscellany of the world ... Trivial things like the development of advertisements on our hoardings ... all the ephemera of our lives'.[4] Lilian Gurden would be recruited to what she called Johnson's 'marvellous adventure':

---

[1] See Charles Batey, 'Johnson, John de Monins (1882–1956)', rev. Julie Anne Lambert, *Oxford Dictionary of National Biography*, Oxford University Press, 2004 [www.oxforddnb.com/view/article/34203, accessed 25 January 2017].
[2] Maurice Rickards, 'The Girl Who Came in from the Garden', *The Ephemerist*, 53 (June 1986), 148–9 (148).
[3] Johnson quoted in *The John Johnson Collection: Catalogue of an Exhibition* (Oxford: Bodleian Library, 1971), 7.
[4] Johnson quoted in *The John Johnson Collection*, 8.

It was through those album pages, and Dr. Johnson asking me to have a go at soaking the bits off while he was busy, that I got drawn in. It was an awful mess – but I managed to cope with them. Before long I got quite good at it, and soon it was a case of coming in part-time, collecting holly for wreaths in the morning, say, and floating, sorting and mounting ephemera in the afternoon.[5]

Lilian Gurden later moved full-time to the Press, acting as an informal assistant curator of the collection, and was in charge of it after Johnson's retirement; a working-class woman with no qualifications, she was, as she said, 'just – ordinary'.[6] From the late 1920s to his death in 1956 Johnson amassed an astonishing 1.5 million items of ephemera.[7] Housed unofficially in the Oxford University Press buildings, close to the machinery and the labour of printing, the collection was moved to the Bodleian Library in 1968. Partial digitisation of the collection on the Bodleian website and a commercial database, published in collaboration with the Library by ProQuest in 2008, mean that some of its contents are more accessible: like the Johnsons' bathtub though, even the resources of the World Wide Web seem inadequate to containing all the trivial paper things that Lilian Gurden was employed to float and sort.[8]

John Johnson was not alone in his fascination with ephemera, the albums that he recycled to make his collections being a sign that many others had made 'books' out of tickets, cards, and labels. This book is a study both of what Johnson collected – the print products grouped under the elusive category of 'ephemera' – and the significance of the field of knowledge which the collecting practices of Johnson and many others represented, what I am calling, following Michael Twyman, 'ephemerology'.[9] Deriving from the Greek 'epi' (on, at, or around) and 'hemeris' (a day), via the medieval Latin 'ephemera', and used in entomology to classify insects that live for a day and in medicine to refer to a temporary fever, ephemera

---

[5] Rickards, 'The Girl', 148–9.   [6] Rickards, 'The Girl', 149.
[7] John Johnson Collection of Printed Ephemera, Bodleian Libraries, University of Oxford, About the Collection [www.bodleian.ox.ac.uk/johnson/about, accessed 25 January 2017].
[8] *The John Johnson Collection: An Archive of Printed Ephemera*, Chadwyck-Healey-ProQuest [http://johnjohnson.chadwyck.co.uk, accessed 25 January 2017].
[9] Michael Twyman has argued that it would be 'helpful to have a word to describe the study of [printed ephemera], if only to stress the distinctiveness of this particular category of printing ... I tentatively offer the term "ephemerology" to define a parallel branch of knowledge or study comparable to bibliography, cartography, and musicology (in its graphic aspects)': Twyman, 'The Long Term Significance of Printed Ephemera', *RBM: A Journal of Rare Books, Manuscripts and Cultural Heritage*, 9:1 (2008), 19–57 (31).

Introduction: 'All the Ephemera of Our Lives'

describes printed artefacts that were not designed to endure.[10] 'Ephemera' refers to forms of print that are ubiquitous and familiar but which occupy a marginal, even buried, place in institutions and disciplinary formations. Resistant to classification and organisation because it cannot be filed easily or stood up like a book, or because there is simply too much of it, ephemeral print is often to be found literally in the 'too hard basket' – box files in the corners of bookshops or the deepest recesses of libraries. 'Ephemera studies' is not widely recognised as an academic discipline (though it is growing) and the interest in ephemera is still regarded as the amateurish preoccupation (or obsession) of the hobbyist.[11] The investments of literary studies and bibliography in the codex-form book as a vehicle for authorial genius and the pre-eminent genres of drama, poetry, and prose fiction, to the extent of subordinating the materiality of the book itself to the intangibility of the 'work', have similarly entailed the marginalisation of ephemera.[12] Indeed, in this sense ephemera represents the antithesis of the literary: in her 2011 book *The Use and Abuse of Literature*, addressed to 'our culture in crisis', Marjorie Garber deploys ephemera to define 'what isn't literature'.[13]

The rise of Anglophone book history since the 1980s has had the effect of rematerialising the book in literary studies. At the same time, however, book history has itself reinforced the status of the book as the object of study, even though many proponents of the discipline from its early stages were conscious that the codex-form book was contingent on and circulated with many

---

[10] See *Oxford English Dictionary* entry on ephemera which notes that the in medieval Latin 'ephemera was neuter plural' but that early English practice treated the word as feminine singular. The term 'ephemera' thus tends to oscillate between the one and the many. For convenience I will use it as a collective singular. For a useful discussion of the derivation of ephemera (and its pronunciation), see Maurice Rickards, *This is Ephemera: Collecting Printed Throwaways* (London: David & Charles, 1977), 7–8. Rickards also claimed that the word 'ephemera' has a 'battered history' and was 'never a word for the man on the street': Rickards, *Collecting Printed Ephemera* (Oxford: Phaidon/Christie's, 1988), 13.

[11] For recent work on early modern and Enlightenment printed ephemera see e.g. Michael Twyman, 'Printed Ephemera', in *The Cambridge History of the Book in Britain, Volume V: 1695–1830*, eds. Michael F. Suarez, S. J. and Michael L. Turner (Cambridge, UK: Cambridge University Press, 2009), 66–82; Paula McDowell, 'Of Grubs and Other Insects: Constructing the Categories of "Ephemera" and "Literature" in Eighteenth-Century British Writing', *Book History*, 15 (2012), 48–70; Kevin Murphy and Sally O'Driscoll (eds.), *Studies in Ephemera: Text and Image in Eighteenth-Century Print* (Lewisburg, PA: Bucknell University Press, 2013); Richard Taws, *The Politics of the Provisional: Art and Ephemera in Revolutionary France* (Philadelphia University of Pennsylvania Press, 2013).

[12] See e.g. N. Katherine Hayles's comment that 'the long reign of print made it easy for literary criticism to ignore the specificities of the CODEX book when discussing literary texts. With significant exceptions, print literature was widely regarded as not having a body, only a speaking mind': Hayles, *Writing Machines* (Cambridge, MA: MIT Press, 2002), 32.

[13] Marjorie Garber, *The Use and Abuse of Literature* (New York: Pantheon Books, 2011), 84–6.

other forms of printed matter. In his seminal essay, 'The Book as an Expressive Form', D. F. McKenzie argued that 'a sociology of texts' should be concerned with how 'forms affect meaning' and the 'social processes of their transmission', accounting for 'a history of the book and, indeed, of all printed forms including *all textual ephemera* as a record of cultural change'.[14] The introductory statement to the journal *Book History*, established in 1998, declared a similar catholicity of focus: 'Our field of play is *the entire history of written communication*: the creation, dissemination, and uses of script and print in any medium, including books, newspapers, periodicals, manuscripts, and ephemera'.[15] Yet in spite of the fact that many book historians remain uneasy about the hegemony of the codex-form book, this most interdisciplinary of disciplines remains deeply invested in attachment to the book. The universal aspirations of book history are often difficult to achieve, meaning that though the boundaries and pre-eminence of the 'book' are frequently challenged theoretically, in practical terms they tend to remain in place. An exception is the chapter on printed ephemera by Michael Harris in *The Oxford Companion to the Book* in which he draws attention to the 'dialectic of ephemera and books' that condescends to ephemera as 'the great sea of flimsy print continuously washing up against the sturdy breakwaters of the book'.[16] Harris even goes so far as to assert that 'the separation of books from the printed archive and the privileging of the codex … seem increasingly untenable' and that the book should have a 'modest place' in the spectrum of print. Book history's interest in the reception and social context of print, according to Harris, should make 'the issue of daily experience – and therefore, of ephemerality – an integral part of its remit'.[17]

The Ephemeral Eighteenth Century takes up Harris's challenge by making printed ephemera and ephemerality a central focus of inquiry, not with the aim of diminishing the status or significance of the codex-form book, but in order to explore how the categories of the book and ephemera as we know them created each other in the long eighteenth century. Samuel Johnson's description, dating from 1751, of 'the papers of the day' (referring to newspapers and pamphlets) as the '*Ephemerae* of learning', has been cited as the earliest example of the application of 'ephemera',

---

[14] D. F. McKenzie, *Bibliography and the Sociology of Texts* (London: British Library, 1986), 13 (my emphasis).
[15] Ezra Greenspan and Jonathan Rose, 'An Introduction to Book History', *Book History*, 1 (1998), ix–x (my emphasis).
[16] Michael Harris, 'Printed Ephemera', in *The Oxford Companion to the Book*, eds. Michael F. Suarez, S. J. and M. R. Woudhuysen, 2 vols. (Oxford: Oxford University Press, 2010), I: 120–8 (120).
[17] Harris, 'Printed Ephemera', 128.

meaning something that has a fleeting existence, to printed matter.[18] However, the currency of the term does not necessarily begin with Johnson, important though the historical moment of that coinage was. 'Ephemerality' in both its material and conceptual senses was a constitutive feature of the age of print that began in the mid-fifteenth century. Not only were printed single-sheet indulgences designed for short-term uses the earliest products of the printing press, but ephemerality was also implicated in ideas of the reach, impact, and durability of print after Johannes Gutenberg's invention of mechanical movable type.[19] What distinguished 'print culture' from scribal publication, according to the seminal arguments of Elizabeth Eisenstein, was the capacity of print to preserve the written word: '[o]f all the new features introduced by the duplicative powers of print, preservation is possibly the most important'.[20] Though paper as a support for the printed word was in many respects less durable than parchment or vellum, the advantage of print was that many copies of a particular text could potentially be produced, thereby enhancing the possibility of that text's survival. Critiques of Eisenstein have tended to focus on her concept of 'typographic fixity' – the idea of print as producing a stable and thus reliably reproducible text that could be deemed authoritative, a precondition for the emergence of modern authorship – at the expense of her emphasis on the 'duplicative powers' of print as an insurance or hedge against the loss of the written word.[21] It was the effect of

---

[18] *The Rambler*, no. 145, in Samuel Johnson, *The Works of Samuel Johnson, Volumes III–V: The Rambler*, eds. W. J. Bate and Albrecht B. Strauss (New Haven, CT: Yale University Press, 1969), III: 11; 'ephemera, n.2.', *Oxford English Dictionary*, Oxford University Press, June 2014 [www.oed.com, accessed 22 July 2014].

[19] For the indulgence see Maurice Rickards and Michael Twyman, *The Encyclopedia of Ephemera: A Guide to the Fragmentary Documents of Everyday Life, for the Collector, Curator and Historian* (London: British Library, 2000), 181.

[20] Elizabeth L. Eisenstein, *The Printing Revolution in Early Modern Europe*, 2nd edn (Cambridge, UK: Cambridge University Press, 2005; first pub. 1983), 87. The concept of 'print culture' has been subject to much debate though it continues to be used in a variety of ways. For a useful summary of its applications see the introduction to Frances Robertson, *Print Culture: From Steam Press to Ebook* (Abingdon: Routledge, 2013), 1–15; also Paula McDowell, 'Mediating Media Past and Present: Toward a Genealogy of "Print Culture" and "Oral Tradition"', in *This is Enlightenment*, eds. Clifford Siskin and William Warner (Chicago: University of Chicago Press, 2010), 229–46.

[21] For the most influential critique of 'typographic fixity' see Adrian Johns, *The Nature of the Book: Print and Knowledge in the Making* (Chicago: University of Chicago Press, 1998), esp. 28–33 and the subsequent debate between Johns and Eisenstein: Elizabeth L. Eisenstein, 'An Unacknowledged Revolution Revisited', *The American Historical Review*, 107:1 (2002), 87–105; Adrian Johns, 'How to Acknowledge a Revolution', *The American Historical Review*, 107:1 (2002), 106–25; Elizabeth L. Eisenstein, 'Reply', *The American Historical Review*, 107:1 (2002), 126–8. See also David McKitterick, *Print, Manuscript and the Search for Order, 1450–1830* (Cambridge, UK: Cambridge University Press, 2003), 151–64.

scale – the sheer number of texts that could be manufactured – that made the printing press a more powerful technology of preservation than the work of the scribe. However, the ever-increasing scale of the production and dissemination of print information, especially after the late seventeenth century, inevitably raised the question of the limits of what could, and should, survive. As Eisenstein notes,

> When written messages are duplicated in such great abundance that they can be consigned to trash bins or converted into pulp, they are not apt to prompt thoughts about prolonged preservation. Manuscripts guarded in treasure rooms, wills locked in vaults, diplomas framed behind glass do appear to be less perishable than road maps, kitchen calendars, or daily newspapers.[22]

The 'duplicative powers' of print, especially after 1700, were such that they potentially preserved too much, making visible and retainable traces of human experience such as the daily life marked on kitchen calendars. Such documents existed in contingency with others deemed more important by acts of preservation. The idea of the ephemeral text that could be consigned to the 'trash' of history, was therefore deeply embedded in what Eisenstein termed 'print culture' in so far as it defined the limits of print's 'preservative' powers, thereby constituting the limits of 'print culture' itself.

The success of the codex-form book as a building block of Enlightenment knowledge, commerce, and cultural life, and subsequently the institutions associated with the arts and sciences in the nineteenth century, was contingent on the 'ephemeralisation' of other kinds of print and the social and cultural experiences such print facilitated and recorded, experiences that would come to be objectified and studied under the rubric of 'everyday life'. So powerful has been the triumph of the book in this respect that the historical specificity of the process of ephemeralisation has been obscured, 'ephemera' and 'ephemerality' being taken-for-granted categories in academic and general discourse that are rarely scrutinised in their own right. Moreover, the triumph of the book can be seen not as a conclusive teleological outcome but as a particular, if tremendously significant, phase in the history of the print media that began in Britain in the late 1600s, with the suspension of the Licensing Act in 1695, and only started to wane with the rise of electronic media in the late twentieth century. Though the 'death' of the printed, codex-form book has been

---

[22] Eisenstein, *Printing Revolution*, 88–9.

greatly exaggerated in recent years, it is undoubtedly the case that the book's pre-eminence as a vehicle of knowledge and culture has been challenged by the greater relativisation of media forms as a result of the rise of the electronic media.[23] One of the effects of this change has been that other forms of print media, such as ephemera, hitherto invisible, have 'floated' to the surface, like the items in Mrs Johnson's bathtub, in a way that highlights the contingent status the codex always had, how it was produced, circulated, read, and preserved with many other kinds of print.

Ephemerality is increasingly constitutive of the emergent post-print age too, playing a distinctive role in the study and theorisation of digital media. The work of Matthew Kirschenbaum, Wendy Hui Kyong Chun, Lisa Gitelman, and others has drawn attention to the fact that the digital text cannot be said to 'exist' in the same way as printed words on paper because it is the result of multiple layers of coded instructions that are constantly in process.[24] As Andrew Piper notes, 'The digital page ... is a fake, a simulation called up from distributed data. It is not *really* there.'[25] Computer memory thus represents what Chun terms the 'enduring ephemeral', in the sense, firstly, that what we thought was deleted or obsolete leaves a digital trace that is forensically recoverable, and secondly, that we are aware of the accessing and creation of digital information as transitory ephemeral processes. As Chun states, 'the experiences of using [computers] – the exact paths of execution – are ephemeral. Information is "undead": neither alive nor dead, neither quite present nor absent'.[26] Chun's concept of the 'enduring ephemeral' can be said to be reflected in contemporary concerns about, on the one hand, the evanescence of ever proliferating digital information and, on the other, its persistence and potential recovery by,

---

[23] See e.g. James Mussell, 'The Passing of Print', *Media History*, 18:1 (2011), 77–92; Anthony Grafton, 'Codex in Crisis: The Book Dematerializes', *Worlds Made By Words: Scholarship and Community in the Modern West* (Cambridge, MA: Harvard University Press, 2009), 288–324; also Andrew Piper, *Book Was There: Reading in Electronic Times* (Chicago: University of Chicago Press, 2012). Related to the discourse surrounding the 'death' of the book are the many books and articles addressing the cultural condition of imaginative literature and the very viability of the reading habits and affective bonds engendered by the book, particularly the novel, in the digital age; e.g. Rachel Ablow, *The Feeling of Reading: Affective Experience and Victorian Literature* (Ann Arbor: University of Michigan Press, 2010); Deidre Lynch, *Loving Literature: A Cultural History* (Chicago: University of Chicago Press, 2014); see also Garber, *Use and Abuse of Literature*.

[24] Matthew G. Kirschenbaum, *Mechanisms: New Media and the Forensic Imagination* (Cambridge, MA: MIT Press, 2008); Wendy Hui Kyong Chun, 'The Enduring Ephemeral, or the Future is a Memory', *Critical Inquiry*, 35 (2008), 148–71; Lisa Gitelman, *Paper Knowledge: Towards a Media History of Documents* (Durham, NC: Duke University Press, 2014).

[25] Piper, *Book Was There*, 54.

[26] Wendy Hui Kyong Chun, *Programmed Visions: Software and Memory* (Cambridge, MA: MIT Press, 2011), 133.

for example, potential employers or government agencies. The fear inspired by the ephemerality of digitised information is not that words and images will be obliterated but, rather, the prospect that they will never go away, representing a nightmarish haunting of the present by an 'undead' past. As I will show in Chapter 1, this aspect of ephemerality is not actually new but is also discernible in the category's formation in the eighteenth century.

Ephemerality as a constitutive element of 'print culture' broadly conceived has thus always been with us, at least since the mid-fifteenth century, and seems set to make the transition from print to the digital age and, indeed, to become more urgent than ever before. The term 'ephemera' is notable for how it occurs in promiscuous and diverse contexts in which it is often used unreflexively and rarely, if ever, theorised. The history of ephemera must therefore take account of how the category has been so successful in functioning anachronistically and discursively. There was 'ephemera' before 'ephemera', in other words. However, while ephemera resonates transhistorically, both backwards into the medieval past and forwards into the digital future, in this book I argue that its reach across time can only be properly understood in the context of the historical moment of its formation in the long eighteenth century.

'This Is Ephemera': The 1960s and After

Before I discuss these contexts, however, it is important to consider the institutional and disciplinary frameworks as well as the 'amateur' circles that have shaped the category of printed ephemera in the twentieth century. The slipperiness of the term is reflected in its currency in a range of domains, some of which also have a marginal status within the academy. An example is printing history for which ephemera has always been important, apparent in the work of eighteenth-century collectors such as John Bagford (1650/1–1716) who acquired and was a broker of title pages, advertisements, and other forms of printed 'scrap' which he dedicated to a never-realised history of printing (though Bagford did not identify what he was collecting as 'ephemera').[27] John Johnson's collecting of ephemera also derived from an interest in it as evidence of the development of printing,

---

[27] On Bagford see Milton McC. Gatch, 'John Bagford, Bookseller and Antiquary', *British Library Journal*, 12 (1986), 150–71; T. A. Birrell, 'Anthony Wood, John Bagford and Thomas Hearne as Bibliographers', in *Pioneers in Bibliography*, eds. Robin Myers and Michael Harris (New Castle, DE: Oak Knoll Press, 1996), 25–39.

though this dimension of the collection became increasingly absorbed in his preoccupation with ephemera as a potential 'museum' of everyday life.[28] A seminal text in the history of the emergence of 'printed ephemera' as a cultural category in the twentieth century was John Lewis's *Printed Ephemera* of 1962. Subtitled 'The Changing Uses of Type and Letterforms in English and American Printing', Lewis's book interpreted ephemera through the lens of printing history.[29] A striking design artefact in its own right, *Printed Ephemera* both informed and reflected innovations in mid-twentieth-century graphic design, as well as stimulating interest in printed ephemera per se.

While declaring its relationship to printing history, Lewis's *Printed Ephemera* also appealed to the ephemera collector. The 1960s was the decade when ephemera collectors began to organise, creating a new visibility for ephemera that was influential on the development of ephemera studies in the academy and also on the collecting policies of major public and university libraries. In the 1960s and 1970s it was still possible to find collections of ephemera from the nineteenth century, the kind of albums that were a major resource for John Johnson. In June 1969, for example, Sotheby's auction house advertised, under the headline, 'Printed Ephemera', 'a collection of eighteenth and nineteenth century pamphlets, and books from the library of Sara Coleridge [daughter of S. T. Coleridge]; chapbooks; juvenile drama; a collection of playing cards; valentine and greetings cards; scrapbooks and albums'.[30] The publicising of this material as 'printed ephemera' was designed to whet the appetite of a growing market. In the 1960s and 1970s ephemera was mainly associated with individual collectors and commercial interests, ranging from Sotheby's to small antique dealers. These individuals and businesses

---

[28] For Johnson's framing of his collecting in terms of the history of printing see John Johnson, 'The Development of Printing, Other than Book-Printing', *The Library*, Ser. 4, 17 (1936), 22–35.

[29] John Lewis, *Printed Ephemera: The Changing Uses of Type and Letterforms in English and American Printing* (Ipswich: W. S. Cowell 1962). Lewis's book was published in the context of a wider interest in media and communication in the early 60s, inspired partly by the work of Marshall McLuhan (*The Gutenberg Galaxy* appeared in 1962) and manifested in the exhibition 'Printing and the Mind of Man', which took place at Earl's Court in London in July 1963. See John Carter and Percy H. Muir (eds.), *Printing and the Mind of Man: Descriptive Catalogue Illustrating the Impact of Print on the Evolution of Western Civilization during Five Centuries* (New York: Holt, Rinehart, and Wilson, 1967). The attentiveness to the ephemeral text as an artefact of print encouraged a particular focus on and appreciation of what later became known as graphic design, reflected in the evolution of the Centre for Ephemera Studies at the University of Reading (established in 1992) that had its origins in printing, specifically typographic, history, latterly developing into a focus on 'graphic communication' in general [see www.reading.ac.uk/typography/research/typ-research centres.aspx, accessed 29 July 2014].

[30] *The Times*, 10 June 1969.

formed informal knowledge and sociable networks that later organised themselves as societies producing literature on ephemera in the form of newsletters and journals and also book-length studies. Maurice Rickards (1919–98) was an important figure in this development, responsible for the much-cited definition of printed ephemera as 'the minor transient documents of everyday life'.[31] Rickards's basement flat in Fitzroy Square in London, so crowded with books and ephemera that he could not find space for a bed and had to sleep on six chairs, was the meeting place for the group that would later form the Ephemera Society. The Society held its first exhibition in November 1975, 'This is Ephemera', in the showrooms of the paper manufacturers Wiggins Teape in Soho, a sign of its links with the commercial world of print.[32] (It is also notable that the exhibition took place very close to the site of no. 32 Soho Square, the home of Sir Joseph Banks and the repository until 1818 of the ephemera collections of his sister, Sarah Sophia). Maurice Rickards was involved in the formation of the Centre for Ephemera Studies at the University of Reading, for which his collection of ephemera was foundational. He also devoted twenty years to writing the definitive reference guide, *The Encyclopedia of Ephemera*, published posthumously by the British Library in 2000.[33]

The academic and institutional visibility of ephemera since the 1990s has therefore been largely due to the work of 'private' ephemerists in the 1960s and 1970s. The associational and commercial networks linked with ephemera as a collectible continue to thrive, the Internet representing a global shop-meet for ephemerists and a resource for ephemera-based research. The cultural 'space' of ephemera in Britain since the 1960s is therefore a distinctive one: it is neither properly 'in' nor 'out', incorporated in both a material and a metaphorical sense within dominant institutions of public culture but never fully assimilated by them. Printed ephemera is a guest in the house of hegemonic cultural formations, like a room bulging with 'stuff' which the householder tolerates but for most of the time tries to ignore. As we shall see, these spatial and material metaphors are not just

---

[31] Rickards, *Collecting Printed Ephemera*, 7.
[32] *The Times*, 18 November 1975. Similar associations dedicated to the collection and study of ephemera have a longer history in France. The 'Vieux Papier' society was established in 1900 [see www.levieuxpapier-asso.org/, accessed 6 November 2014]; see also Nicolas Petit, *L'éphémère, l'ocasionnel et le non livre à la bibliothèque Sainte-Geneviève* (Paris: Klincksieck, 1997).
[33] Patrick Hickman Robertson, 'Obituary: Maurice Rickards', *The Independent*, 20 February 1998 [www.independent.co.uk/news/obituaries/obituary-maurice-rickards-1145817.html, accessed 11 November 2011]; Rickards and Twyman, *Encyclopedia of Ephemera*.

applicable to the late twentieth century but are also relevant to the formation of the category of ephemera in the Georgian period.

The role of individual collectors and private societies in promoting awareness of ephemera in the 1960s and 1970s parallels and in some cases intersects with the increased attention paid to ephemera by library science during this period. This development reflected the expansion of higher education and public library provision in the post-war period and the rise and diversification of the social sciences, particularly 'history from below' and cultural studies. In the late 1960s the British government commissioned from John E. Pemberton a report on 'the national provision of printed ephemera in the social sciences': its recommendations included the establishment of a register of ephemera collections in the UK and the creation of a repository specifically devoted to ephemera, a 'National Document Library'.[34] While the former has been incompletely realised, the latter now seems a utopian impossibility, a sign of the confidence of that era in the role of the state, as well as a belief in the manageability of information in a totalising way.[35] Librarians continue to wrestle with the meaning of ephemera and what can be done with it, in order to classify, store and make it accessible to the general public. In 1981 Alan Clinton quoted from Pemberton's report to represent the librarian's view of ephemera in the following way:

> A class of printed or near-printed or near-print documentation which escapes the normal channels of publication, sale and bibliographical control. It covers both publications which are freely available to the general public and others which are intended for a limited and specific circulation only. For librarians, it is in part defined by the fact that it continues to resist conventional treatment in acquisition, arrangement and storage and it may not justify full cataloguing.[36]

The 'problem' of ephemera is starkly posed here as one of difference or estrangement from normative codes and practices of information acquisition, storage, and access provision implicitly identified with the book. Ephemera 'escapes' 'bibliographical control' and the 'normal channels' of

---

[34] John E. Pemberton, *The National Provision of Printed Ephemera in the Social Sciences: A Report Prepared for the Social Science and Government Committee of the Social Science Research Council* (Coventry: University of Warwick Library, 1971), 47.

[35] *Register of Ephemera Collections in the United Kingdom, excluding those in the major national collections and others not normally available to the public* (Reading: Centre for Ephemera Studies, 2003).

[36] Alan Clinton, *Printed Ephemera: Collection Organisation and Access* (London: Clive Bingley, 1981), 15; see also Chris E. Makepeace, *Ephemera: A Book on Its Collection, Conservation and Use* (Aldershot: Gower, 1985).

dissemination, 'normal' being defined in terms of the commercial print trade. It is implied that in order to count as 'normal' a printed text must itself be a commodity: otherwise it 'resists' the disciplinary apparatus of 'conventional treatment' and 'escapes' assimilation.

Clinton himself proposes an alternative approach to ephemera which, rather than seeking to define it in specific terms, considers it in relationship to other kinds of documents. He suggests that ephemera 'can be located somewhere on a continuum between printed and bound volumes at one end and small scraps of manuscript at the other'.[37] I want to return later to the relevance of Clinton's idea of a continuum of print for the conceptualisation of eighteenth-century ephemera: its value lies in the recognition that a definition of ephemera must refer to the totality of printed matter, and indeed writing on paper as a whole, and that the location of ephemera on such a spectrum is shifting and uncertain.

The status and meaning of ephemera continues to be problematic for library science, a point elaborated by Timothy G. Young in a 2003 article, 'Evidence: Toward a Library Definition of Ephemera'. 'Material that falls in the very broad category of ephemera', Young states, 'continues to vex us'.[38] He ascribes to the ephemeral text a perverse anthropomorphic agency: ephemera has the tendency to 'just show up' in library collections, acting as 'awkward also-rans', in contrast to the uniformity of sturdy books.[39] Pamphlets have a 'hard time standing up', and are effete, 'limp pages unprotected from wear'.[40] Even when ephemera doesn't just 'show up', the librarian is always aware of the possibility of private collections existing somewhere out there, old broadsheets lining the walls of country houses, hidden but making their presence felt under layers of wallpaper: 'left alone enough, they literally become the fabric of existence'.[41] Quoting Clinton's reference to ephemera escaping 'the normal channels of ... bibliographical control', Young comments, in a remarkable gesture of personification: 'not only are outward appearances different, but something innate [in ephemera] is skewed, uncontrollable, as well'.[42] Young's essay confronts the intractability (and appeal) of ephemera head on, by endowing it with a kind of life, an innate vulnerability-cum-recalcitrance that books are too dumb to have. Ultimately Young concedes that 'the

---

[37] Clinton, *Printed Ephemera*, 15–16.
[38] Timothy G. Young, 'Evidence: Toward a Library Definition of Ephemera', *RBM: A Journal of Rare Books, Manuscripts and Cultural Heritage*, 4 (2003), 11–26 (12).
[39] Young, 'Evidence', 18, 16.   [40] Young, 'Evidence', 16.   [41] Young, 'Evidence', 19.
[42] Young, 'Evidence', 16.

word *ephemera* ... is intended to describe substantives but, instead, functions as an abstract'.[43] In grappling with the question of ephemera because of the practical task of organising and classifying such material, library science has therefore been the domain which has come closest to acknowledging the polarities contained by the category – how it is both substantive *and* abstract and how it has the capacity to make the substantive abstract and vice versa.

'Non-book' History

While the question 'what is ephemera?' inevitably includes the question 'what is the book?', in this study I aim to give an account of ephemera that, following the advice of Peter Stallybrass and Ann Blair, tries to avoid being 'held in thrall to the concept of the book'.[44] Book history has tended to frame the question of ephemera in terms of the centrality of books surrounded by concentric circles of relative ephemerality radiating out into the oblivion or deep space of the truly disposable or meaningless text, what might be termed 'absolute' ephemerality. An alternative approach is one that adapts Alan Clinton's idea of a 'continuum' between printed and bound books and paper 'scrap', implicitly linking the domains of the library and the archive.[45] Thinking of ephemera in terms of a linear model of a spectrum of paper also reminds us that paper has uses beyond the print trade. In *Paper Machine* Jacques Derrida emphasised that in addition to paper as a support for writing, 'there is also wrapping paper, wallpaper, cigarette papers, toilet paper, and so on. Paper for writing on (notepaper, printer or typing paper, headed paper) may lose this intended use or this dignity'.[46] As a substrate of writing, paper always has the potential to be used in a variety of ways:

---

[43] Young, 'Evidence', 24.
[44] Ann Blair and Peter Stallybrass, 'Mediating Information, 1450–1800', in *This is Enlightenment*, eds. Clifford Siskin and William Warner (Chicago: University of Chicago Press, 2010), 139–63: 'The broadening of the "history of the book" to include all textual forms is counterproductive to the extent that it is still held in thrall to the concept of the book' (140).
[45] See also Robert Darnton's observation that a 'peculiar paper consciousness existed in early modern Europe ... people looked at the material substratum of books, not merely at their verbal message': Darnton, '"What Is the History of Books?" Revisited', *Modern Intellectual History*, 4:3 (2007), 499–508 (498).
[46] Jacques Derrida, *Paper Machine*, trans. Rachel Bowlby (Stanford, CA: Stanford University Press, 2005), 43. The primary application of paper in the eighteenth century was as wrapping paper: D. C. Coleman, *The British Paper Industry 1495–1860: A Study in Industrial Growth* (Oxford: Clarendon Press, 1958), 4.

on the one hand there is the condition of a priceless archive, the body of an irreplaceable copy, a letter or painting, an absolutely unique event (whose rarity can give rise to surplus value and speculation). But there is also paper as support or backing for printing ... for reproducibility, replacement, prosthesis, and hence also for the industrial commodity, use and exchange value, and finally for the throwaway object, the abjection of litter.[47]

Printed ephemera can run the gamut of the possibilities of paper, ranging from the 'abjection' of paper as waste, the condition of absolute ephemerality, to paper's role in constituting a 'priceless archive', as we shall see in relation to the long history of ephemera collecting. As Clinton indicated in 1981, ephemera cannot be fixed in a particular place within the multiple uses or 'dignities' of print and paper but, like a dial on a radio, can be tuned into anywhere on that spectrum. Every individual text, every bit of paper, also includes its own ephemera 'wavelength': as Derrida remarks, the 'hierarchy' of the 'priceless archive' at the top and the 'throwaway object' at the bottom is 'always unstable': '"fine paper" in all its forms can become something thrown out'.[48]

Derrida's emphasis on the differing uses of paper, and the 'dignities' they represent, opens up the field of inquiry in relation to printed ephemera. Modes of literary interpretation that focus on textual content are not easily applicable to printed ephemera in which meaning is communicated primarily by material signifiers, such as typography or intaglio engraving, the quality of the underlying paper, or if the document is used or not (often indicated by a signature and other material signs). Also relevant is the significance of printed ephemera as tokens of value, comparable to coins and forms of paper credit that can be circulated and accumulated as forms of cultural and social 'capital'. Such documents have virtual representativeness: they do not have a commodity value in their own right but signify the 'good' or specie to which they give access or facilitate. As Derrida suggests, these forms of paper are also 'prosthetic': they stand for or extend the body and the subjecthood of the bearer, particularly when they are tendered by hand as part of the process of social exchange. This prosthesis of paper documentation has political and social dimensions as a means of legitimating identity, apparent now in the global reliance on papers to control population movement and to police the boundaries of nation states. As Derrida notes, 'identity, the social bond, and the forms of solidarity (interpersonal, media-based, and institutional) go through filters

---

[47] Derrida, *Paper Machine*, 43. [48] Derrida, *Paper Machine*, 43.

made of paper'.[49] In this study, I want to explore a formative period of this 'filtering' of identity, bonds, and solidarity in the ephemeral print culture of the eighteenth century.

Conceptualising ephemera in terms of the paper continuum does not mean thinking less of books but rather is a way of situating the book within what D. F. McKenzie influentially called a 'sociology of texts', specifically 'the full range of social realities which the medium of print had to serve, from receipt blanks to bibles'.[50] As I have noted already, however, the book continues to maintain its centrality in book history, in part due to the success of the codex. Developed between the second and fourth centuries AD, the codex was a technology whereby written matter in the form of a sequence of wax tablets, and subsequently leaves made of parchment and vellum and ultimately paper, was fastened together on one side to create a single artefact. The codex-form book not only had an internal spatiality, as something that could be opened and closed, (and imaginatively entered), but was also a highly efficient way of transmitting and organising knowledge, particularly by means of the device of the spine that holds the book together and is the main way of organising books as knowledge. As Andrew Piper suggests, 'books are essentially vertebral, contributing to our sense of human uniqueness that depends upon bodily uprightness'.[51] The vertebral quality of the book contrasts with the spinelessness of the most common form of printed ephemera, the broadside or broadsheet. A broadside was a sheet of paper printed on one side only that, particularly in the form of the poster, pasted to a wall, militantly faced the world in an analogous way to the broadsides of naval ships. These two kinds of print media thus oriented themselves towards the world in fundamentally different ways. A book is something that is three-dimensional, that is entered, that opens and closes, and acts as a container: a broadside, like a single page, a photograph, or indeed a screen, is two- or at most thinly three-dimensional. The broadside demands to be looked at, not looked into.

The book and the library, according to Derrida, 'point up the act of *putting*, depositing, but also the act of immobilizing, of giving something over to a stabilizing immobility', acts which, also have legalistic, institutional, and political meanings.[52] The idea of rendering the mobile immobile, of gathering together, or standing up that which was loose, scattered, or insecure is relevant to ephemerality, because intrinsic to

---

[49] Derrida, *Paper Machine*, 55. [50] McKenzie, *Bibliography and the Sociology of Texts*, 13, 15.
[51] Piper, *Book Was There*, 2. [52] Derrida, *Paper Machine*, 7.

ephemerality is an idea of texts not only disappearing but also escaping regimes of control. Derrida's ideas suggest new ways of conceptualising ephemera in relation to the book and vice versa. Firstly, as a form of support for writing, the ephemeral text itself is capable of constituting a kind of 'book', one that is different from the codex-form book but a book nonetheless; secondly, to view the codex as a gathering together or immobilising of paper not only makes the book more porous to other kinds of print media but also suggests that it contains within it the capacity for its constituent elements to become mobile again. There is therefore a deeply embedded tension or controlled fissiparous energy within the very idea of the codex-form book. Thirdly, the idea of 'gathering together' and rendering immobile can be applied to other cultural practices not primarily related to the book or the library such as the work of collectors in amassing, organising, and housing ephemeral texts. The making of ephemera 'collections' can therefore be seen in a Derridean sense as a form of 'book' making. Indeed, it is possible to regard the category 'ephemera' itself as functioning discursively in a book-like sense, in that it always entails the attempt to gather together, to sift, differentiate, and 'immobilise' ephemeral texts, if not in their totality then in relation to the book or to different degrees or kinds of ephemerality.

Ephemera and Its Relationship to the Print 'Job'

Beginning in the 1970s, the British Library initiated a project of national bibliography entitled the Eighteenth-Century Short Title Catalogue (E-CSTC), later the English Short Title Catalogue (ESTC), that uncovered a vast range of printed material beyond the codex-form book, raising questions of how to describe and categorise such material and what should be included or excluded in the E-CSTC.[53] In an essay entitled 'The Eighteenth-Century Non-Book: Observations on Printed Ephemera', R. C. Alston, a leading figure in the development of the E-CSTC, was

---

[53] The E-CSTC began as a collaboration between the British Library and the American Society for Eighteenth-Century Studies in 1976. The first phase of the catalogue appeared in microfiche in 1983 and led to the publication in microform of imprints by Research Publications under the title *The Eighteenth Century* and, ultimately, the database Eighteenth Century Collections Online. Due to issues of scale and limitations of funding it was decided to exclude from the ESTC, '[e]phemeral publications such as: trade cards, labels, tickets, visiting cards, invitations, bookplates and currency; playbills, concert and theatre programmes, playing cards, games, and puzzles': see *Factotum Occasional Paper 4. The First Phase: An Introduction to the Catalogue of the British Library Collections for ESTC* (London: British Library, 1984), 16.

the first to recognise the importance of such print in transforming eighteenth-century society. The genres, formats, and purposes of non-book print, according to Alston, included:

> advertisements of every kind ... lists of goods imported and exported ... inventories; company accounts and reports; prospectuses of books and insurance companies; notices of lectures, exhibitions, converts, race meetings, tournaments, and fights; petitions to Parliament; lists of witnesses and juries in trials; hundreds of locally printed acts; rules and regulations of clubs, societies, and hospitals; ... lists of goods for auction; almanacs and pocket books; bills of mortality; chapbooks and garlands; games and puzzles; song-sheets; genealogies and pedigrees; recipes, both culinary and medicinal; lists of schoolbooks and curricula; abstracts of grammar for use of schools; dying speeches of notorious malefactors; lists of prisoners; notices of goods stolen.[54]

But how should this diversity of print be classified and described? Alston hedges his bets by describing his subject as both 'non-book' and as 'printed ephemera' in the title of his essay. Another possible label is 'jobbing print', discussed by Michael Twyman in his chapter on printed ephemera in the fifth volume of *The Cambridge History of the Book in Britain*. 'Jobbing' refers to how the print trade distinguished the production of single-sheet letterpress items from books, William Savage's *Dictionary of the Art of Printing* of 1841 defining a print 'job' as 'any thing which printed does not exceed a sheet'. A 'job house' was a business that concentrated on the 'printing of Jobs; namely, cards, shop bills, bills for articles stolen or lost, play bills, lottery bills, large posting bills, and all other things of a similar description'.[55] A defining characteristic of such print is that it was bought from the printer to be freely distributed, usually for the purposes of advertising. According to Twyman, 'ephemera' is a much less specific category than jobbing, designating 'the brief life such documents were designed, or likely to have, [and] tends to be used retrospectively'.[56] He thus distinguishes 'jobbing print' as more empirically 'real' than 'ephemera' which is concerned with the transitory 'life' of texts, their

---

[54] R. C. Alston, 'The Eighteenth-Century Non-book: Observations on Printed Ephemera', in *The Book and Book Trade in Eighteenth-Century Europe*, eds. Giles Barber and Bernhard Fabian (Hamburg: Dr. Ernst Hauswedell & Co, 1981), 343–60 (349).
[55] William Savage, *A Dictionary of the Art of Printing* (London: Longman, Brown, Green and Longmans, 1841), 428. See also Peter Stallybrass, '"Little Jobs": Broadsides and the Printing Revolution', in *Agent of Change: Print Culture Studies after Elizabeth L. Eisenstein*, eds. Sabrina Alcorn Baron, Eric N. Lindquist, and Eleanor F. Shevlin (Amherst: University of Massachusetts Press, 2007), 315–41.
[56] Twyman, 'Printed Ephemera', 66.

historicity, and implicitly their value: in Timothy Young's terms, 'jobbing print' deals with 'substantives' rather than the 'abstract'. Some single-sheet publications such as songs and ballads were designed to be sold, however, complicating the identification of ephemera with jobbing print, as do other non-book formats that might be considered ephemeral, such as the tract, the pamphlet, or the newspaper.[57] Job printing, in the strict sense of the term, was integrated with other kinds of 'non-book' production that would be classified as 'ephemeral', particularly in the provinces, where printers catered to diverse needs and interests. Writing about eighteenth-century Exeter, Ian Maxted identified a wide range of single-sheet items produced by particular printers, including job printing in the strict sense of the term such as forms (e.g. indenture forms) and invitation cards for use by local councils, as well as a range of different genres of 'bills', such as playbills, political broadsheets (squibs, songs, and addresses), last dying speeches, and ballads, patters, and penny histories, the latter being sold by a network of peddlers and hawkers.[58]

James Raven also favours 'jobbing printing' rather than ephemera in his study of non-book publishing and the infrastructure of commerce in the eighteenth century.[59] He argues that the period between 1695 and the beginning of the industrialisation of printing after 1814 represented a second printing revolution that was notable for the explosion of 'jobs', the kind of texts that Alston contemplated as 'endless' in their scope and uses. Jobbing printing was transformative in providing the infrastructure of communicative transactions in all aspects of social life, but particularly in business. The issuing of bills and receipts, recording of accounts, advertising of goods and services, the development of paper currency, even the labelling of goods, were dependent on jobbing printing, in ways moreover that often blurred the distinction between the printed and the written text, many 'jobs' such as blank forms or tickets being designed for

---

[57] For a challenge to the usefulness of the category of 'jobbing print', see Harris, 'Printed Ephemera': 'Ephemeral print cannot be defined through the character of the organization or business through which it was produced' (122).

[58] Ian Maxted, 'Single Sheets from a County Town: The Example of Exeter', in *Spreading the Word: The Distribution Networks of Print 1550–1850*, eds. Robin Myers and Michael Harris (Winchester: St Paul's Bibliographies, 1990), 109–29. 'Patters' were 'humorous songs in which a large number of words are fitted to a few notes and sung rapidly' (*Oxford English Dictionary*).

[59] James Raven, *Publishing Business in Eighteenth-Century England* (Woodbridge: Boydell Press, 2014); subsequent page references in parentheses in text. Dror Wahrman has described this second printing revolution as 'Print 2.0', (the Gutenberg revolution being Print 1.0), noting that 'the key to the qualitative difference of Print 2.0 was ephemerality': see Wahrman, *Mr. Collier's Letter Racks: A Tale of Art & Illusion at the Threshold of the Modern Information Age* (New York: Oxford University Press, 2012), 20.

inscription. Consistency in the design and layout of jobbing print, what Raven describes as 'typographical assuredness', gave the public confidence in what they were buying and in turn encouraged commercial entities to enhance the visual appeal of these documents (267). The reach of commerce, both nationally and internationally, was enhanced by familiarity, a trade card for a business in London being essentially similar in its design conventions and purpose to one produced in Cork or Philadelphia. Jobbing printing also underpinned the growth of and sophistication of local and central government administration throughout Europe in the eighteenth century, producing the forms, ledgers, dockets, and other forms of stationery by which the bureaucratic apparatus and the associated phenomenon of 'paperwork' emerged.[60] Rather than being incidental to the production of books, jobbing printing, Raven argues, was much more significant than has been hitherto recognised in book history, constituting the field's 'hidden history' (262). Not only did jobbing printing sustain many printers and booksellers, it also had a commensurate impact on society, being crucial to the 'social construction of knowledge' (262). While Raven's focus is primarily on how jobbing printing facilitated the development of Georgian business, he also acknowledges that the 'knowledge' it produced had wider implications: 'As much as books, it was the diverse jobbing work of the printers that recast the production, material form and reception of everyday knowledge. Small pieces of printed paper ... reshaped intimate, private worlds and human relationships' (258).

Jobbing printing was to be of enduring importance, as media historian Lisa Gitelman shows in her analysis of its impact after 1870. Gitelman proposes an even more 'catholic' sociology of texts for the digital age, extending to the development of contemporary digital media such as the PDF (portable document format). She situates job printing as a subgenre of the document in order to avoid the tendency to conceive digital media via print, particularly the codex-form book. 'Documents have existed longer than books, paper, printing, or the public sphere, and certainly longer than the literary has been described as such', she writes. 'Thinking about documents helps in particular to adjust the focus of media studies away from grand catchall categories like "manuscript" and "print" and toward an embarrassment of material forms that have together supported such a varied and evolving scriptural economy'.[61] It is noteworthy,

---

[60] See Ben Kafka, *The Demon of Writing: Powers and Failures of Paperwork* (New York: Zone Books, 2012).
[61] Gitelman, *Paper Knowledge*, 6.

however, that both Gitelman and Raven, writing in the 2010s, prefer jobbing printing to 'printed ephemera'. Gitelman describes jobbing printing as being hitherto 'encountered if at all in that most unglamorous and miscellaneous of bibliographical and archival designations, ephemera', while Raven claims that the term ephemera is of little use to the study of jobbing printing because it represents little more than 'an archival deposit status' in library science, a kind of 'too hard basket' for cataloguers, rather than a viable hermeneutic tool (43).[62] In other words, 'ephemera' evokes much more than the print job: it is a sign for what cannot be properly described or known, what is 'unglamorous', or what endures in perverse persistence, even when it was supposed to be thrown away or disappear.

'Ephemera' as applied to print is thus an enduringly slippery and imprecise concept. Printed ephemera is a form of bibliographical description that includes more than job printing in the strict sense of the term, encompassing single-sheet ballads, pamphlets, and newspapers that were commodities in their own right. Moreover, ephemera also functions discursively as a sign of an overarching poetics of print, responding to how print was able to document new kinds of temporality and historicity, focused in particular on the dialectic of loss and preservation and, ultimately, the meaning of documentation per se. The possibility of ephemerality can therefore be said to haunt all kinds of documentation: the category of 'printed ephemera' as it developed in the eighteenth century, became an object of attention by modernists in the nineteenth and twentieth century, was revived in the 1960s and 1970s, and is now being reconfigured in the digital age represents various historical responses to that condition. The codex-form book, as both a technology and an ideology, has been particularly successful in countering evanescence, hence the stigma attached to the destruction of books or their de-acquisition from libraries. As I shall argue, the emergence of the category of ephemera in the eighteenth century served to uphold the integrity of the book as a durable, preservable object by 'othering' the possibility of its own disappearance in the form of the category of 'ephemera'.

Ephemerality not only concerns the durability of the documentary trace itself but also the event to which the ephemeral document refers, enables, or makes visible in a performative sense. Documents can 'do' things but certain kinds of documents 'do' more than others. According to Jean-Luc Nancy, for example, 'manifestoes, squibs, broadsheets' are *works* that 'militate', that 'are engaged in' and 'carry demands' 'in the world of

[62] Gitelman, *Paper Knowledge*, 26.

theoretical or practical action', whereas the book theoretically 'has no end outside of itself, neither is it in itself the end of any operation whatsoever'.[63] The performative force of such '*works*' is exemplified by the ticket that enables admission to an event or the classic example of documentality, the passport, that defines an individual's citizenship and rights to travel. Sociologists of documentation have argued that written records were developed as a means of countering the evanescence of verbal communication, functioning as more durable repositories of memory. However, some forms of documentation, such as tickets, do not merely record or memorialise a speech act or transaction but are also performative 'acts' in their own right, virtually transparent to the event that they were making. Some forms of jobbing print were thus both ephemeral in a qualitative sense, being of limited use and less significance than the book, and also because they were deeply embedded in the myriad, transient occurrences and transactions of the everyday world: in other words they have the effect/affect of seeming to 'be', ontologically speaking, the event to which they are referring.

Ephemeral mediality which, I shall argue, has a long history, is thus concerned with anxieties that the present is too much with us, with documents that cannot be assimilated to or persistently evade the totalising reach of library science, with forms of connection or sociality that are close and immediate, with what is always already lost rather than what can be immobilised and preserved for all time, and with what surrenders to rather than takes time. The mutual investments of the literary field and the codex-form book as they developed in the Romantic period and after can be seen as a response to ephemeral mediality, the novel in particular being a genre/book technology whereby the quotidian, heteroglossic, constantly-renewing-itself excess of the world could be encompassed, assimilated, and objectified. Risking identification as 'ephemeral productions', novels by Maria Edgeworth and Jane Austen, as I shall explore later, were profoundly indebted to new 'social media' of the eighteenth century such as the ticket, the timeliness of which they remediated in ways that made their own fiction capable of surviving as timeless. The waning of the dominance of the book thus has significant implications for the idea of the literary as, to paraphrase Garber, 'what isn't ephemera', and also for the very parameters and continuing viability of the discipline of literary studies itself. Two major responses to this change have come from Romanticists:

---

[63] Jean-Luc Nancy, *On the Commerce of Thinking: Of Books and Bookstores* (New York: Fordham University Press, 2008), 5. I am grateful to Monique Rooney for drawing my attention to this.

Clifford Siskin and William Warner on the one hand and Jerome McGann on the other.

Siskin and Warner have influentially argued for a reconfiguration of Enlightenment and in particular Romantic studies in terms of a 'history of mediations'. Their manifesto, articulated at conferences, in articles and books, and the 'Re:Enlightenment' website, was compelled by what they called the 'vertigo' entailed by the new and possibly precarious position of institutions, disciplines, and writing in general on the 'platform' of the digitisation of knowledge.[64] A 'history of mediations' would, they suggest, coalesce around four 'cardinal mediations': the development of 'infrastructure' such as the postal system and improved roads enabling the dissemination of information and new spaces for sociality such as the coffeehouse or tavern; new 'genres and formats', primarily the newspaper, that acted both as a source of information and an 'interface' whereby networking could be conceived and practised; and new 'associational practices' exemplified by political clubs and scientific societies. Siskin and Warner's fourth cardinal mediation is 'protocols' – the habits, rituals, and regulations that influenced what could be spoken about, published, and circulated such as 'the postal system, public credit, and the regime of copyright'.[65] In *The Ephemeral Eighteenth Century* I follow Siskin and Warner's lead by proposing the essential importance of printed ephemera and ephemerality to a history of Enlightenment mediations. Printed ephemera criss-crosses all four of the 'cardinal points': as a sub-infrastructure of printed communication more generally; as a multiplicity of genres in addition to the newspaper but playing a similar role; as enabling the new associational culture; and finally as a protocol. The latter is exemplified by the protocols surrounding the ticket that ritualised and made visible the myriad threshold dramas of the new associational culture, determining who could come and go, and who could never be admitted in any circumstance. The ticket and other forms of printed ephemera are also notable for not being easily commodifiable or recognisable as property in the terms of 'regimes of copyright'; ephemeral mediation in this sense shadows or escapes normative protocols of a commercial society. As an infrastructure of an infrastructure, printed ephemera made visible the importance of sociability to the Enlightenment, the (daily) performances, transactions, and affects of

---

[64] Clifford Siskin and William Warner, 'If This Is Enlightenment Then What Is Romanticism?', *European Romantic Review*, 22:3 (2011), 281–91 (290); also Clifford Siskin and William Warner (eds.), *This Is Enlightenment* (Chicago: University of Chicago Press, 2010); The Re:Enlightenment Project [www.reenlightenment.org, accessed 28 January 2017].

[65] Siskin and Warner, 'If This Is Enlightenment', 284–5.

which were similarly fleeting and intangible. In Georg Simmel's memorable formulation, sociability consists of 'the innumerable forms of social life, all the with-one-another, for-one-another, in-one-another, against-one-another, and through-one-another, in state and commune, in church and economic associations, in family and clubs': printed ephemera was essential to the dynamic energy of those hyphenations, their momentariness, and their binding force.[66]

Recognition of the stratum of printed ephemera linking the 'cardinal points' of mediation also requires broadening the parameters of periodisation. Siskin and Warner follow a conventional model of periodisation for their proposed history of mediations, according to which the 'event' of the Enlightenment takes place between the 1730s and 1780s, followed by the 'eventuality' of the Romantic period (the 1780s to the 1830s), and the 'variation' of the Victorian era.[67] The ephemeral Enlightenment, as I shall go on to argue, has its genesis earlier than the 1730s in the print revolution triggered by the English Civil Wars in the 1640s and only begins to end around 1814 with the accelerated industrialisation of printing leading to the eclipse of the hand press. Arguably, though, the ephemeral Enlightenment is still with us or, rather, it keeps resurfacing during periods of rapid media change and heightened awareness of the power and uncontrollability of communication – such periods would be the 1640s, the 1790s, the 1920s when the impact of media such as the cinema on print was recognised by John Johnson, the 1960s when media studies begins with the work of Marshall McLuhan and the term 'printed ephemera' gains currency and visibility, and our own present moment of rapid media flux, particularly in the wake of Facebook and Twitter. Hence, while focusing on the period of the 1740s to the early 1800s as crucial to the formation of the category of printed ephemera, the scope of this book is defined by a very capacious long eighteenth century that begins in the 1640s and is not necessarily over.

Jerome McGann shares with Siskin and Warner the view that it is only by conceiving our present moment as continuous with the Enlightenment and Romanticism, rather than a radical rupture, that new futures for humanities scholarship can be secured. Describing literature as 'an institutional system of cultural memory – a republic of letters', McGann argues for a renewal of philology as the base discipline of the humanities,

---

[66] Georg Simmel, 'The Sociology of Sociability', in *Simmel on Culture: Selected Writings*, eds. David Frisby and Mike Featherstone (London: Sage, 1997), 120–30 (120).
[67] Siskin and Warner, 'If This Is Enlightenment', 289.

philology being '*to* preserve, monitor, investigate, and augment our cultural inheritance, including all the material means by which it has been realized and transmitted'.⁶⁸ McGann's reference to 'all the material means' also potentially extends the scope of his philology beyond the written word, taking into account the materiality of media which some media archaeologists have argued has autonomous agentic force, and the capacity of all material things to act as substrates of writing, what Bill Brown describes as 'textual materialism'.⁶⁹ Echoing the totalising aspirations of book history, McGann's philology 'in a new key' recognises the need for a science, inclusive of literary studies, that would enable a grounding of the profound relativisation of textuality since the 1970s, paying attention to the 'call' to history of both 'Sappho and Shakespeare' on the one hand and of 'the smallest datum' on the other.⁷⁰ In this book I argue that McGann's philology in a new key and the idea of the scholar as disinterestedly open to the preservation and transmission of the totality of our cultural inheritance has its genealogy in the collecting, preservation, and systematisation of the products of the spectrum of print in its broadest sense, the science of ephemerology, of which John Johnson was a twentieth-century exemplar. Not formally institutionalised, or even recognisable to its own practitioners, eighteenth-century ephemerology was foundational in philology, bibliography, and ultimately literary history as they would develop in the nineteenth and twentieth centuries, but it is only now, with the waning of the dominance of the book, that this science of the ephemeral is becoming more visible.

Marilyn Butler recognised the significance of such practices as early as 1984 in a chapter entitled 'Popular Antiquities', published posthumously in 2015, in which she argued that the work of antiquarian collectors and scholars such as Francis Douce and Joseph Ritson made visible the culture of 'the people', and indeed 'the people' as a conceptual category, influencing the development of literary Romanticism. In 1984 Butler described Douce and Grose as 'early social historians and social scientists, comparable in different ways to their contemporaries, the emerging political

---

⁶⁸ Jerome McGann, *A New Republic of Letters: Memory and Scholarship in the Age of Digital Reproduction* (Cambridge, MA: Harvard University Press, 2014), ix, 33.

⁶⁹ For media archaeology see e.g. the work of Friedrich Kittler and Wolfgang Ernst, esp. the latter's *Digital Memory and the Archive*, ed. Jussi Parikka (Minneapolis: University of Minnesota Press, 2013); on 'textual materialism' see Bill Brown, 'Introduction: Textual Materialism', *PMLA*, 125:1 (2010), 24–8.

⁷⁰ Jerome McGann, *The Scholar's Art: Literary Studies in a Managed World* (Chicago: University of Chicago Press, 2006), ix.

economists and natural scientists'. Situating popular antiquarianism in the context of Baconian empiricism she also sought to recuperate the methodologies of the antiquarians as more than 'mere spadework, compared with the higher, gentlemanly task of formulating propositions and constructing the wider view'.[71] In a subsequent essay Butler notes the presence of 'ephemera' as part of the range of material collected by Douce and Grose. The latter was, she says, an 'ex-army captain, draughtsman, historian, lexicographer, satirist, jester, and collector of ephemera' while Douce amassed 'a great collection of illustrated books, manuscripts, and ephemera': both men thus heeded the call of the 'smallest datum' as well as of the folios of Shakespeare.[72] *The Ephemeral Eighteenth Century* seeks to elucidate the meaning of the 'ephemera' that men such as Grose and Douce collected, situating them as part of a network of like-minded tillers in the highly stratified, diverse, and fertile terrain of Georgian print culture. Men such as Douce and Ritson were not just literary and cultural historians but also archivists and sociologists of print communication more broadly. John Guillory has asserted that the 'dominion of the document is a feature of modernity' and what the ephemerologists were doing, as Marilyn Butler perceived, was scouting the outer reaches of that dominion and thus the boundaries of modernity itself.[73]

Chapter Overview

The Ephemeral Eighteenth Century begins with a discussion of Joseph Addison's alignment of fugitive print with the idea of 'accidental reading' in *The Spectator*, as an important context for Samuel Johnson's later theorisation of fugitive literature and *ephemerae* in the mid-eighteenth-century. The second part of the chapter explores the importance of the new medium of the handbill and in particular its role in paper wars of the 1790s which, I argue, is a crucial decade for the application of ephemera to print and related concepts of ephemerality.

While the application of the term 'ephemera' to printed matter begins in the mid-1750s, interest in this kind of textuality and the archiving of it dates from the seventeenth century. Chapter 2 explores the interest of figures such

---

[71] Marilyn Butler, *Mapping Mythologies: Countercurrents in Eighteenth-Century British Poetry and Cultural History* (Cambridge, UK: Cambridge University Press, 2015), 124.
[72] Marilyn Butler, 'Antiquarianism (Popular)', in *An Oxford Companion to the Romantic Age: British Culture 1776–1832*, ed. Iain McCalman (Oxford: Oxford University Press, 1999), 328–38 (330, 333).
[73] John Guillory, 'The Memo and Modernity', *Critical Inquiry*, 31:1 (2004), 108–32 (113 n.).

as George Thomason, Anthony Wood, and Narcissus Luttrell in the paraphernalia of texts that subsequently became classified as ephemera: single-sheet ballads, advertisements, pamphlets, and tickets. I link this interest to the development of early Enlightenment associational culture and the importance of such kinds of print in catering to and archiving the quotidian, sociable life of the developing public sphere, epitomised above all by the phenomenon of frost fairs on the river Thames. Printing presses were set up on the frozen river in 1683 (also in 1715 and 1739) to sell souvenir tickets recording names of those present on the ice. I discuss how such material was archived and preserved in the form of 'collections' and in the last section of the chapter outline how such ephemera books were important in literary history, Romantic-period bibliography, and also the idea of a repository of the archives of the nation, a public records office, as represented by William Godwin's interest in the Thomason tracts.

A central figure for this study as a whole is Sarah Sophia Banks (1744–1818), who is crucial to my broader claim about the significance of the collecting of ephemera as the Enlightenment's 'other' science. I explore Banks's archiving of fashionable life in relation to the significance of No. 32 Soho Square, where she lived with her brother Sir Joseph Banks, as a hub of Enlightenment scientific inquiry, knowledge and social networks, and flows of documentary information. The chapter that follows explores the methodologies and significance of her collections, firstly in relation to her brother, and secondly as an archive of fashionable sociability and public culture after 1760, with particular reference to her interest in ballooning from the 1780s.

One of the items that Sarah Sophia Banks sought to acquire (without success) was a playbill from a theatre in the British penal colony in Sydney, New South Wales. One such playbill from 1796, the earliest example of printing in Australia, was discovered in National Library of Canada in the 2000s and gifted with much fanfare to the National Library of Australia in 2007. This example of fugitive literature is now listed on the UNESCO Memory of the World register. The story of the Sydney playbill frames a discussion of the importance of the playbill in general in Romantic-period culture. Playbills represent by far the largest body of ephemeral texts that have survived and this chapter explores the history of their interest to collectors and how the theatre, as part of the category of 'public amusements' was integrated into ephemera collecting as a whole. The history of the playbill also focuses a discussion of changes in printing technology around 1800 – mainly the introduction of larger typefaces that could be read from a distance – which led to the emergence of the poster and the increasing colonisation of urban space by print. One of the writers to take account of this change was William Wordsworth in Book VII of *The Prelude*. I argue for the importance of ephemera and ephemerality to Romantic-period media history and also to the genealogy of theatre history as a discipline.

Another important ephemera genre of the eighteenth century is the visiting card, collected in the thousands by Sarah Sophia Banks. In Chapter 6 I discuss the visiting card as a new form of social media, anticipating the text messaging of today, and explore how its novelty caught the attention of Horace Walpole and Samuel Johnson. As a genre that was particularly invested in the representation of social life, the novel is one of the most important sources for understanding the complexities of visiting in eighteenth-century social life and textual media that facilitated and recorded it. With reference to the novels of Jane Austen and, in particular, Maria Edgeworth's *The Absentee* (1812), I discuss how prose fiction adapted the capacity of the visiting card and other kinds of ephemeral texts in order to realise the affective power of the intimate social encounter entailed in handing over one's card. I argue that *The Absentee* is exceptional as a fiction that not only utilises the visiting card but also emulates ephemerology as the Enlightenment's other science.

While referring to how a number of major figures in the literary canon, such as Samuel Johnson, Horace Walpole, Maria Edgeworth, William Godwin, Samuel Taylor Coleridge, William Wordsworth, and Jane Austen, engaged with ephemera and ephemerality, I aim to place ephemeral genres and the history of ephemera and ephemeral collecting front and centre, on the ground that such genres and histories have been largely invisible in literary studies. I therefore read literary texts such as *Persuasion* through the hitherto neglected prism of the history of printed ephemera with the goal of laying the groundwork for how other canonical literary works could be interpreted in the same way. Similarly, though I argue that the Romantic period, roughly 1780–1830, is pivotal in the emergence of the category of ephemera in relation to literary genres and the disciplines of bibliography and literary history, such developments need to be contextualised within the parameters of a very capacious eighteenth century, beginning in the early Enlightenment of the seventeenth century and continuing to at least the 1840s. In so far that ephemera and ephemerality (though not these terms) can be located at the very beginning of the invention of the printing press and are still vital to the speed and apparent evanescence of the media universe of today, a study of these phenomena inevitably complicates strict period chronologies and temporalities. In its methodology this study aims to account for ephemera and ephemerality in historical and transhistorical ways, as loose, mobile, often eluding or escaping from being tied down by definition, time, systematisation, and where it is placed (whether in the British Museum or a shoebox under a bed).

The concluding substantive chapter of *The Ephemeral Eighteenth Century* focuses on the year 1814 to argue for the importance to Romantic-period culture of an ephemeral historicism. The year 1814 was notable for ephemeral public events, beginning with the February frost fair on the Thames and the extensive celebrations of the premature peace in the summer, culminating in the Jubilee Fair in the royal parks of London. Both occasions produced a wide range of ephemeral print – tickets, handbills, and prints – collected and arranged from very different political perspectives by Sarah Sophia Banks and the radical reformer Francis Place. These events, which have rarely been considered in accounts of this period, can be said to constitute an ephemeral, forgotten history of 1814. I focus on 1814 in order to trace how ideas of ephemerality as developed in the eighteenth century mutated into the category of the everyday in the nineteenth. The year 1814 is also significant in literary history as the year in which Jane Austen set her posthumously published *Persuasion*. I relate that novel to the significance of 1814 as a particularly 'ephemeral' year, with reference to Austen's acknowledgement of the presence of 'flying' literature in the form of the newsmen of Bath.

My approach in *The Ephemeral Eighteenth Century* is indebted to a number of disciplinary frameworks – to literary studies, book history and bibliography as 'the sociology of texts', media history, the history of cultural politics, library science, and textual materialism – while being alert to where and how the study of ephemera challenges these frameworks. I explore how printed ephemera as a category was formative in defining how literary value became invested in the codex-form book, while I also attempt to assimilate printed ephemera to literary studies in a number of ways. Is ephemera amenable to the close reading we associate with literary texts? Is reading a handbill, a playbill, or a ticket in any way comparable with reading a poem (in a newspaper or a book)? Simon Eliot has claimed the 'most common reading experience, by the mid-nineteenth century at latest' was 'the advertising poster, all the tickets, handbills and forms generated by an industrial society, and the daily or weekly paper'.[74]

---

[74] Simon Eliot, 'The Reading Experience Database; or, What Are We to Do about the History of Reading?', The Reading Experience Database (RED), 1450–1945 [www.open.ac.uk/Arts/RED/redback.htm, accessed 21 February 2017].

This kind of reading has been neglected, Eliot suggests, because it was 'too much a part of the fabric of everyday life to be noticed' but what if we try to unpick that fabric or become aware that it was already noticed by the ephemerologists? How do we account for reading that was accidental, fleeting, part of the virtually invisible fabric of the everyday, and what were the aesthetic or affective dimensions, if any, of such reading? The importance of cheap printed ephemera in modernity was that unlike the majority of books it was accessible to all. It was on the walls, handed out as advertisements or as tickets: words were everywhere and comprehending them opened up the possibility of being able to read the world. Reading printed ephemera was thus potentially as affectively meaningful as other forms of reading, making the appreciation of ephemera not marginal to the love of books but a connection to the experiences that made reading universally possible in the first place.

Ephemerality, the third term that I invoke in this book, in addition to printed ephemera and ephemerology, also represents a poetics: an intensified sense of presentness and the evanescence or quickness of time; of the difficulty of holding on to and preserving what we momentarily know and experience; and of the data constituting human knowledge as infinitely diverse, unfathomable, and possibly overwhelming. An enduring legacy of the age of print, the poetics of ephemerality was formative in literary Romanticism and in twentieth-century modernism and continues to feature in cultural debates today.[75] This book is an account of why ephemerality came to matter in this way, of the men and women who devoted their lives to documenting what John Johnson called the 'miscellany of the world', and why, though marginal, their efforts were ultimately not ephemeral.

---

[75] For continuities of the focus of this study with twentieth-century modernist poetry see Bartholomew Brinkman, *Poetic Modernism in the Culture of Mass Print* (Baltimore, MD: Johns Hopkins University Press, 2016).

CHAPTER I

Accidental Readings and Diurnal Historiographies
The Invention of Ephemera

As I noted in the Introduction, modern understandings of printed ephemera derive ultimately from Samuel Johnson's reference to 'the papers of the day' as the '*Ephemerae* of learning'. Johnson explored and in a sense theorised ephemerality in a number of occasional pieces published in the 1740s and 1750s, some of which were ephemeral in their own right but have received little attention in this context.[1] A similarly neglected and in many ways foundational text for eighteenth-century ephemerality is *Spectator* no. 85 (7 June 1711), now best known for its reference to the broadside ballad 'Two Children in the Wood' (also known as 'The Babes in the Wood') as one of the 'Darling Songs of the Common People'.[2] Addison's claim that he had first encountered the song pasted on the wall of a 'House in the Country' is part of a wider discussion of similar 'accidental Readings' which he introduces by alluding to the practice of the '*Mahometans'* in scrutinising any discarded piece of paper on the grounds that it might contain part of the Koran (361). Mr. Spectator describes himself as a compulsive scavenger of such paper scraps:

> I must confess I have so much of the *Mussulman* in me, that I cannot forebear looking into every Printed Paper which comes in my way, under whatsoever despicable Circumstances it may appear; for as no Mortal Author, in the ordinary Fate and Vicissitude of Things, knows to what use his Works may, some time or other, be applied ... (360–1)

Such uses include enclosing a wad of tobacco, forming a spill to light a pipe, recycling the 'Essays of a Man of Quality' into a 'Fringe for ... Candlesticks', or lining a pie plate with pages from the book of a Puritan divine:

---

[1] An exception is McDowell, 'Of Grubs and Other Insects', 61–4.
[2] *The Spectator*, ed. Donald F. Bond, 5 vols. (Oxford: Clarendon Press, 1965), I: 362; subsequent page references in parentheses in text.

> I once met with a Page of Mr. *Baxter* under a *Christmas* Pye. Whether or no the Pastry-Cook had made use of it through Chance or Waggery, for the defence of that Superstitious *Viande*, I know not; but, upon the Perusal of it, I conceived so good an idea of the Author's Piety, that I bought the whole Book. (361)[3]

The extreme example of the vicissitudes besetting paper 'Things' in *Spectator* no. 85 is a 'Poem of an Eminent Author on a Victory' which Addison describes encountering 'in several Fragments' after it had been used to light 'Squibs and Crackers', thereby celebrating its 'Subject in a double Capacity' (361). The double meaning of squib, referring to both a firecracker and a short, explosive work of satire, accentuates the idea of an occasional poem as an evanescent, even combustible, medium. The poem that is also a firework puts print and, in this case, imaginative literature, at the centre of the evanescence of a social event.

Spectator no. 85 therefore evokes the full spectrum of the paper economy of the early eighteenth century, ranging from the sacral meanings of writing in the allusion to the Koran, suggestive of Derrida's 'priceless archive', to other more mundane forms of paper support and, ultimately, to paper as a 'throwaway object', the 'abjection of litter'. In its fascination with the recycling of the printed text as tobacco papers and lining for piecases, Addison's essay is an early example of the convergence of concepts of ephemerality with those of the everyday, a link popularised in Maurice Rickards's twentieth-century definition of ephemera as 'the minor transient documents of everyday life'. If the academic study of ephemera has barely begun, the same cannot be said of the everyday, which became the focus of extensive interdisciplinary inquiry in the twentieth century and has been influential in, for example, humanist Marxism, philosophy, history, and the development of feminism and cultural studies.[4] One of

---

[3] Such uses were not uncommon and pre-date the expansion of print culture and the paper trade in the seventeenth and eighteenth centuries: see Elizabeth Yale, 'With Slips and Scraps: How Early Modern Naturalists Invented the Archive', *Book History* 12 (2009), 1–36; also her *Sociable Knowledge: Natural History and the Nation in Early Modern Britain* (Philadelphia: University of Pennsylvania Press, 2016), chap. 6. For later Victorian practices involving the recycling of paper see Leah Price, 'Getting the Reading Out of It: Paper Recycling in Mayhew's London', in *Bookish Histories: Books, Literature, and Commercial Modernity, 1700–1900*, eds. Ina Ferris and Paul Keen (Basingstoke: Palgrave Macmillan, 2009), 148–66; see also William Noblett, 'Cheese, Stolen Paper, and the London Book Trade, 1750–99', *Eighteenth-Century Life*, 38:3 (2014), 100–10.

[4] Seminal works on everyday life are Henri Lefebvre, *Critique of Everyday Life* [1947–1958], trans. John Moore, 3 vols. (London: Verso, 1991–2005) and Michel de Certeau, *The Practice of Everyday Life*, trans. Steven Rendall (Berkeley: University of California Press, 1984). For surveys of approaches to everyday life see Michael Gardiner, *Critiques of Everyday Life: An Introduction* (London: Routledge, 2000); Michael Sheringham, *Everyday Life: Theories and Practices from Surrealism to the Present*

the most frequently cited accounts of the everyday is Maurice Blanchot's 1962 essay 'Everyday speech' ('La Parole Quotidienne').[5] For Blanchot the everyday is an indeterminate state of adverbial being – 'ourselves, ordinarily' – that escapes definition (12). The everyday is platitudinous, being associated with 'the residual life with which our trash cans and cemeteries are filled: scrap and refuse'; it is banal because it 'brings us back to existence in its very spontaneity and as it is lived – in the moment when, lived, it escapes every speculative formation, perhaps all coherence, all regularity' (13). The anonymity and inchoateness of the everyday – its state of perpetual becoming – is realised most powerfully in the urban out of doors, particularly in the fluidity of the street. The medium that comes closest to the street's capacity to 'render public' is the newspaper, which represents the 'everyday transcribed ... informed, stabilized, put forth to advantage' but which is nonetheless incapable of capturing the elusiveness of everyday life (17, 18). The everyday is ultimately to be feared, Blanchot argues, because it represents the 'corrosive force of human anonymity', the 'hero' being the person who is able to confront its 'power of dissolution'. The embrace of that power enables a kind of freedom because it is inaccessible to religious, moral, and political authority but this is also a dead-end freedom, a 'radical nihilism' that goes nowhere (19).

Blanchot's characterisation of the everyday – as that which escapes or is fugitive, as a state of perpetual becoming or presentness, as being manifested by the anonymous sociality of the street, as imperfectly mediated by the newspaper, and as constantly disappearing into the banality or vacuity of rubbish – suggests the congruence of twentieth-century theories of the everyday with the category of printed ephemera and related concepts of ephemerality. Genres of printed ephemera such as the ticket stub, the junk mail flyer, or the newspaper tend to recur as substrates of philosophical and literary encounters with the everyday. However, the link between the two concepts of ephemerality and the everyday has rarely if ever been explicitly historicised or theorised, which is remarkable in the light of the enormous scholarly attention given to the everyday (a sign of the taken-for-grantedness of ephemera, and consequently its invisibility). To address Rickards's definition of ephemera as 'the minor transient documents of everyday life', we might ask: what came first, the 'everyday' or 'ephemera'? To what extent

---

(Oxford: Oxford University Press, 2006). See also Barry Sandywell, 'The Myth of Everyday Life: Toward a Heterology of the Ordinary', *Cultural Studies*, 18:2–3 (2004), 160–80 and John Brewer, 'Microhistory and the History of Everyday Life', *Cultural and Social History*, 7 (2010), 87–109.

[5] Maurice Blanchot and Susan Hanson, 'Everyday Speech', *Yale French Studies*, 73 (1987), 12–20; subsequent page references in parentheses in text.

are these concepts and the textual and material artefacts to which they refer, predicated on each other? In other words, can you have an 'everyday life' without ephemera and ephemerality (and vice versa)? – a question to which I will return in the final chapter. In this chapter I outline the genealogy of the association between printed ephemera and everyday life in *The Spectator* and later, Samuel Johnson's articulation of the importance of *ephemerae* within the natural order of literature, before addressing the 1790s as the decade when printed ephemera becomes consolidated and visible as a discursive category. Particularly important in this latter respect is the format of the handbill, which in the 1790s becomes a potent instrument in the paper wars of radicalism and counter-revolution, with long-term consequences for how the relationship between the codex-form book and the spectrum of the print media came to be conceived.

Band-Boxes and the Paper Scrap

Spectator no. 85 is historically important in articulating an association between as yet inchoate concepts of ephemerality and the penetration of paper into the mundane activities of everyday life, such as lighting pipes or decorating candlesticks. Addison's essay adumbrates ephemerality without explicitly naming it: he does not need to define a particular kind of text as 'ephemera' because all printed texts are ephemeral, including the codex-form book itself. To this end, Mr. Spectator highlights the presence in his library, 'upon the shelf of Folio's' of 'two long Band-boxes standing upright among my Books' (361). Band-boxes were containers for collars, hats, and other forms of millinery, dating from the seventeenth century when they housed 'bands' or ruffs; they were often made of cardboard and lined with paper to protect their contents. It is this paper lining which Mr. Spectator praises as a fund of 'deep Erudition and abstruse Literature'. Standing upright and 'vertebral', like the folios with which they are ranked, the band-boxes are a kind of book in the sense of the meaning which Derrida ascribes to the etymology of the book in 'biblion', that is, a support for writing; they are reminders of the book's place within the wider economy of paper, commerce, and fashion and also of the book's status as a material object, a textual 'thing'.[6] The band-box, as a paper support, makes the flimsy ephemeral scrap 'stand up', giving it 'spine' or backbone.

[6] '(so derived from *biblos*, which in Greek names the internal bark of the papyrus and thus of the paper, like the Latin word liber, which first designated the living part of the bark before it meant "book") ... *biblion* can also, by metonymy, mean any writing support ...': Derrida, *Paper Machine*, 6.

While for later nineteenth-century bibliophiles the dismemberment of books was condemned as acts of violence, perversions of a book's integrity, in *Spectator* no. 85 the scrap has its own intrinsic value and can even enable the reconstitution of the book.[7] Mr. Spectator's discovery of a fragment of Baxter under his Christmas pie, which ultimately led him to buy the book, resembles William Hone's later account of the importance of the printed scrap in his informal childhood education. Like Mr. Spectator, Hone was an assiduous collector of paper waste, being at age eleven 'in the habit of making my own every scrap of printed and written paper, whether from cheesemongers' or other shops'. His discovery of an 'old printed leaf' led eventually to its identification as part of *The Trial of John Lilburne* which he claimed 'riveted' him like no other book, with the exception of *Pilgrim's Progress*.[8] This mode of reading, reconstituting the book by means of its scrap or fragment, challenges the idea that the printed word can ever be truly obsolescent or 'dead'. The diverse printed products of the eighteenth-century press, even their fragments, could constitute 'books' to be read. Moreover, the polarity implied by the purity of 'fine paper' at one end of the print spectrum and the throwaway, debased paper remnant at the other, here takes the form of a circularity, the scrap being metonymic of the book, indeed being the means through which the book lives again, the aperture through which the totality of the book can be perceived.

In *Spectator* no. 85 the location of the codex-form book within a broader print and paper economy, including more mundane uses of paper such as wrapping paper, also entails an acknowledgement of how the commercialisation of culture was creating new kinds of print literacies. Reading was less a matter of choice and a sign of privilege but increasingly an inescapable part of engagement with the urban environment and the fabric of daily commerce: food came in readable texts while walls, and even the ground itself, were being colonised by words and print; hence the fact that Addison draws attention to the new phenomenon of accidental reading, when reading is compelled rather than sought. This form of ephemeral textuality had a distinctive kind of materiality, closer to the concrete world and the stuff, even the detritus of everyday life, but it was also, as the allusion to practice of the 'Mahometans' suggested, still capable of connecting the accidental reader to other, more profound, things.

---

[7] E.g. William Blades's attack on John Bagford as a 'wicked old biblioclast' in *The Enemies of Books* (London: Elliot Stock, 1896), 105–6.

[8] Frederick Wm. Hackwood, *William Hone: His Life and Times* (New York: Augustus M. Kelley, 1970; first pub. 1912), 40.

The printed word, even in its most mundane manifestations, carried a vestigial power. The fascination with printed ephemera of later collectors such as Sarah Sophia Banks or John Johnson can be seen as residual traces or a reconfiguration of the attachment to the latent sacrality of the word, confounding the later identification of printed ephemera with a banal or asacral everyday.

'Accidental readings' as a theme of *Spectator* no. 85 is also important in contextualising Addison's discussion of the ballad of 'Two Children in the Wood'. This ballad is located both specifically in that Addison accidentally encounters it pasted on the walls of a house in the country and generally in terms of other single sheets and kinds of paper support such as the poem-firework and pie-wrappings. This filiation can even be said to be extend to *The Spectator* itself which was published initially as a single folio half sheet, printed on both sides.[9] Circulating in coffeehouses, conspicuous on drawing room tables, or even recycled as tobacco paper, the unbound *The Spectator* was itself implicated in the full spectrum of the paper economy that Addison describes.[10] It too was liable to casual, 'accidental readings' (and also to being thrown away as rubbish). As adumbrated in *Spectator* no. 85, therefore, ephemerality was not just a matter of the transitoriness of texts, the latent sacrality of the word, and the possibility of reading the book via the scrap, but was also concerned with modes of textuality (and their reception) that evaded or exceeded bookish modes of dissemination and reception to produce 'accidental readings'. As is well known, the book gained ascendancy in the eighteenth century as a commodity that was sought out by the reader in particular commercial, institutional, and cultural contexts such as the bookshop and the library. One found the book; the book did not normally accidentally find you. By the end of the century the book was increasingly legitimated and reified as the intellectual property of an identifiable author, with whom the reader entered into a kind of contractual relationship. If the reader was interested in the identity of the author, the author conversely was engaged in interrogating and shaping the identity of the reader. The category of ephemera, however, ultimately came to describe forms of print that differed from the book in a number of key respects: it referred to texts that found the reader

---

[9] Donald F. Bond, 'The First Printing of the *Spectator*', *Modern Philology*, 47:3 (1950), 164–77. See also Stuart Sherman's discussion of *The Spectator* in *Telling Time: Clocks, Diaries, and English Diurnal Form, 1660–1785* (Chicago: University of Chicago Press, 1996), chap. 4.

[10] See Amélie Junqua, 'Unstable Shades of Grey: Cloth and Paper in Addison's Periodicals', in *The Afterlife of Used Things: Recycling in the Long Eighteenth Century*, eds. Ariane Fennetaux, Amélie Junqua, and Sophie Vasset (Abingdon: Routledge, 2015), 184–98.

'accidentally', that were not easily housed or immobilised, belonging as much to the world out of doors, and that were not necessarily commodities in their own right. These kinds of texts also existed outside the author–reader nexus, and did not require to be 'owned' by a printer or publisher: they could be truly anonymous, the reason why once they 'turned up' in libraries, they escaped categories of bibliographical control, as Alan Clinton noted in 1981.[11] If the authorship of such texts was uncertain, so too was the identity of their readers and also what reading such literature could potentially mean, if it was done accidentally, by means of a fragment, or even if not at all.

This context helps to explain why this dimension of *Spectator* no. 85 has been neglected and also why the essay is best known for the reference to the ballad of 'Two Children in the Wood'. The foundational role of the ballad in the development of English literature and literary criticism meant that it became distinguished from other forms of ephemeral print, such as jobbing print, with which (as Maxted shows in relation to the example of Exeter) it was circulated and used.[12] The valorisation of the ballad was implicated in the emergence of the popular as a cultural category and the conflation of the 'everyday' with the 'popular', a development which also ultimately entailed the idea of ephemera as a subaltern mode of textuality, giving access to the 'real' life of the masses or, in de Certeauvian terms, functioning as a potential source of tactical resistance to power. It is important, however, to consider the prehistory of this idea of ephemera, on the assumption that there was always ephemera before ephemera, that is, before ephemera was fully implicated in the emergence of the category of popular culture (and vice versa). *Spectator* no. 85 is a notable text in this respect because of how it locates the ballad as belonging to the contemporary world of 'accidental readings', reflecting the penetration of print into all aspects of social life. These modes of textuality enabled the increasing visibility of what would later be defined as the 'everyday' – mundane activities such as lighting pipes – but the 'everyday' was not yet imaginatively and ideologically associated with the category of the people. The importance of the new print media of the early eighteenth century, including *The Spectator*, was its discovery of a universal everyday and the

---

[11] Clinton, *Printed Ephemera*.
[12] Maxted, 'Single Sheets'. On the relationship between ballads and Romantic poetry see e.g. Maureen N. McLane, *Balladeering, Minstrelsy, and the Making of British Romantic Poetry* (Cambridge, UK: Cambridge University Press, 2008); Steve Newman, *Ballad Collection, Lyric, and the Canon: The Call of the Popular from the Restoration to the New Criticism* (Philadelphia: University of Pennsylvania Press, 2007).

power of particular forms of textuality to make that life more visible, and also more commodifiable. Accidental reading was potentially open to all who had the capacity to read: it was not the printed form which writing took that mattered, as much as how, where, and to whom the printed word was accessible. *Spectator* no. 85 is implicitly concerned with the potential of this inclusivity, suggesting that there was an intrinsic cultural politics to ephemerality: what constitutes 'ephemera' in the eighteenth century needs to be, at least initially, conceived in the widest possible, lateral sense, rather than according to the hierarchised model of culture implicit in the binary of elite versus popular.

Ephemerae and 'Durable Volumes'

Though Addison does not explicitly use the term, the unpredictability and anonymity implied by 'accidental readings' were associated with what was known as 'fugitive' literature, the prime example of which in *Spectator* no. 85 is the explosive projectile of the poem for victory. Samuel Johnson's *Dictionary* defines fugitive, among other things, as 'not tenable', 'not to be held or detained', 'unsteady', 'unstable', 'not durable', 'volatile', 'flying', 'wandering', 'runnagate', 'vagabond', the latter referring to fugitive in its nominative sense as meaning someone escaping the authority of the law.[13] Throughout the eighteenth century 'fugitive' was applied to 'small books' or pamphlets; periodical publications and newspapers, some of which, such as *The Spectator*, were originally published as unbound 'papers', and to collections of occasional literary pieces, originally printed in newspapers or periodicals. The author of *An Asylum for Fugitives*, a compilation of occasional poetry published in 1776, prefaces the volume by distinguishing between the domain of the single sheet and that of the book:

> He who writes on a fugitive subject, can never find so ready and proper a vehicle for his thoughts, as a fugitive publication. A leaf like the Sybil's leaves, is more precious than a volume. Books stand unmolested on our shelves, but *papers are for ever in our hands*, and on our tables; a subject of little or no importance to-morrow, may nevertheless be of great consequence to-day; and the compiler of such a diary is for the moment the author of history.[14]

---

[13] Samuel Johnson, *A Dictionary of the English Language*, 2 vols., 2nd edn (London: W. Strahan, 1755), I: entry for 'fugitive'.
[14] *An Asylum for Fugitives: Published Occasionally*, 2 vols. (London: J. Almon, 1776), I: 52 (my emphasis).

Books were, according to this writer, stand-offish, detached from the everyday world, but the single leaf was very much part of that world, its connection to the body – 'for ever in our hands' – signifying its status as digital media in the root sense of digital, as something fingered, prehensile.

In *Spectator* no. 85 the fugacity of print relates to its penetration into all aspects of life and its capacity to draw attention to the persistent sacrality of the word, but as yet print has not become too diverse or too much. By the mid-eighteenth century, however, the growth of the print trade and its role in social life was such that the scale and diversity of printed ephemera were demanding attention and analysis. This is evident in paratexts written by Samuel Johnson for *The Harleian Miscellany*, a selection of sixteenth- and seventeenth-century political and religious pamphlets from the library of Robert Harley, first Earl of Oxford, published in eight quarto volumes by Thomas Osborne between 1744 and 1746. Osborne published a six-page octavo advertisement or *Proposals* for the *Miscellany*, to which Johnson anonymously contributed 'An Account of this Undertaking' (hereafter 'An Account'). Johnson also wrote an introduction to the first volume that was later reprinted as an 'Essay on the Origin and Importance of Small Tracts and Fugitive Pieces'. 'An Account' differs from its companion introduction in that it was a fugitive text in its own right. It was distributed for free at 'all Booksellers both in Town and Country', and reprinted in the *General Advertiser*.[15] It was also printed on the blue paper that formed the cover or wrappers of unbound books such as John Smith's *Memoirs of Wool* and the *Harleian Miscellany* itself. (The only surviving copy of the latter was in the John Johnson collection but was lost in the collection's move to the Bodleian Library in the 1960s).[16]

The 'Account' exemplifies a distinctive ephemera genre, the 'fugitive' book prospectus, which Johnson uses to argue why this very mode of textuality needs to be secured in book form.[17] The bookishness of *The Harleian Miscellany* lay in how, in a Derridean sense, it brought together and immobilised its constituent texts. Johnson justified the enterprise in terms of the tendency of 'small Pamphlets' or 'single sheets' to 'take their

---

[15] *General Advertiser*, 19 March 1744.
[16] O. M. Brack and Mary Early, 'Samuel Johnson's Proposals for the "Harleian Miscellany"', *Studies in Bibliography*, 45 (1992), 127–30 who note that a 'unique copy' of the first printing of 'An Account of this Undertaking', dating from 30 December 1743 is in the Chetham's Library, Manchester (128).
[17] For book prospectuses see John Feather, *English Book Prospectuses: An Illustrated History* (Newton, PA: Bird & Bull Press, 1984).

Flight, and disappear for ever' and advocates the need to 'fix those Fugitives in some certain Residence', suggesting that the *Miscellany* is a kind of house arrest, a zone of containment and surveillance.[18] Gathered together in this way, these texts can be secured for posterity and 'Learning' because separately they are incapable of constituting Learning in their own right:

> The obvious method of preventing these losses, of preserving to every man the reputation he has merited by long assiduity, is to unite these scattered pieces into volumes, that those which are too small to preserve themselves, may be secured by their combination with others; to consolidate these atoms of learning into systems, to collect these disunited rays that their light and their fire may become perceptible.[19]

Even while promoting the value of the Harleian pamphlets, the metaphor of 'combination' has the effect of insinuating their subordinate status within the literary economy, as literary journeymen or labourers, rather than masters. By 'combining', the 'atoms' of learning represented by pamphlets and single sheets could protect themselves from the fate of absolute ephemerality, but combinations, from a paternalistic viewpoint, also needed to be managed, if the authority of the master discourse was to be maintained. Thus knowledge, Johnson claimed, was a 'lake into which all those rivulets of science have for many years been flowing; but which, unless its waters are turned into proper channels, will soon burst its banks, or be dispersed in imperceptible exhalations'.[20] The codex form of the *Miscellany*, by gathering and immobilising the tide of ephemeral print, constituted these 'proper channels'. Whereas in *Spectator* no. 85 ephemerality is defined in terms of a cycle of disaggregation and reconstitution, underpinned by a sense of the residual, curious sacrality of the word, Johnson's 'Account' is notable for introducing the idea of ephemerality as signifying an overload or flood of information and the related concept of the 'enduring ephemeral' – the idea that 'atoms' of knowledge may not in fact disappear but instead continue to haunt the 'proper channels'.[21]

In 'An Account' and the 'Introduction' to *The Harleian Miscellany*, ephemerality is defined in terms of the proliferation and potential

---

[18] Samuel Johnson, 'Proposals for the *Harleian Miscellany*. An Account of This Undertaking', in *Samuel Johnson*, ed. Donald Greene (Oxford: Oxford University Press 1984), 120.
[19] Johnson, 'An Account', 120. [20] Johnson, 'An Account', 121.
[21] For the long-standing conceptualisation of information as an overload or 'flood' see Daniel Rosenberg, 'Early Modern Information Overload', *Journal of the History of Ideas*, 64:1 (2003), 1–9; Ann M. Blair, *Too Much to Know: Managing Scholarly Information before the Modern Age* (Chicago: University of Chicago Press, 2010).

uncontrollability of fugitive texts, which are endowed with a kind of independent agency, for example in Johnson's advice that they 'combine' or unionise. (This trope of personification, as we have seen in relation to Timothy Young's insistence that there is something 'innate' and uncontrollable in printed ephemera, is thus a long-standing one). In *Rambler* no. 145 (1751), Johnson moves from a focus on fugitive texts themselves and on fugacity in general to the writers who produce such texts, introducing authorship rather than the form of the book miscellany or repository as a means of mediating ephemerality. Recognising the complexity and diversity of contemporary print culture, particularly its role in enabling and sustaining daily life through genres such as the newspaper, Johnson argues for the legitimacy of those who produce such 'papers'. They are part of a literary commonweal in which some must labour for the common good in the same way as 'the meanest artisan or manufacturer contributes ... to the accommodation of life'.[22] Like the 'husbandman, the miner or the smith', the journalist, periodical writer, abridger, or epitome writer makes a necessary and valuable contribution to the cultural economy, one that is worthy of recognition, but which is thereby naturalised as different in value and status from the works of the masters of learning.[23] Working 'to the clock' and with no concern for posterity, or that what they write will last longer than a day or a week, the 'manufacturers' of ephemeral texts are 'diurnal historiographer[s]'.[24] While in *Spectator* no. 85 poetry is implicated, in a concrete material sense in everyday things (and vice versa), being both perishable and readable in the same ways as the paper scrap, in *Rambler* no. 145 Johnson uses the idea of writing as a hierarchised natural economy to suggest that all texts are not equal, certainly are not equally 'ephemeral', and that some texts are more suited than others to the apprehension of the everyday. The everyday does not have the universalised significance it had in Addison's essay but is beginning to perform the dual work of, on the one hand, distinguishing the emergent category of the popular and, on the other, creating the possibility of an alternative to the everyday – a realm of 'durable', transcendent value.

The significance of *Rambler* no. 145 in shaping modern ideas of ephemerality is apparent in Johnson's reconfiguration of the key metaphors of light and water that he used in 'An Account'. Justifying why the 'abridger, compiler and translator' should not be 'rashly doomed to annihilation', he argues:

---

[22] Johnson, *Works*, III: 8.   [23] Johnson, *Works*, III: 10.   [24] Johnson, *Works*, III: 11.

> Every size of readers requires a genius of correspondent capacity; some delight in abstracts and epitomes because they want room in their memory for long details, and content themselves with effects, without enquiry after causes: some minds are overpowered by splendor of sentiment, as some eyes are offended by a glaring light; such will gladly contemplate an author in an humble imitation, as we look without pain upon the sun in the water.[25]

In 'An Account' Johnson had argued that pamphlets and single sheets gathered together in book form could comprise the 'fire' or light of learning, but in *Rambler* no. 145 light is identified with the sublimity of authorship, which ephemeral literature diffuses, ameliorates, and also potentially weakens. The essay identifies two classes of authorship – the real thing and its 'humble imitation'. Fugitive texts, even when 'combined', cannot constitute the light of pure knowledge; they can only mediate. Water, which in 'An Account' represents a lake of texts, forms a similar mediatory role, serving as a reflection, a medium, in which the sun of authorship can be viewed without harm. The evolution of ephemera as a category is thus a factor in the mid-eighteenth-century development of 'mediality' as, in David Welberry's terms, 'the general condition within which, under certain circumstances, something like "poetry" or "literature" can take shape'.[26] It is in this context that Johnson introduces the idea of the products of the 'diurnal historiographer' as *Ephemerae*, the first instance, according to the *Oxford English Dictionary*, of ephemera being used in this way:

> That such authors are not to be rewarded with praise is evident, since nothing can be admired when it ceases to exist; but surely though they cannot aspire to honour, they may be exempted from ignominy, and adopted into that order of men which deserves our kindness though not our reverence. These papers of the day, the *Ephemerae* of learning, have uses more adequate to the purposes of common life than more pompous and durable volumes.[27]

The rhetorical effect of Johnson's emphasis on authorship as a way of mediating cultural distinction falters as 'authors' become conflated or subsumed by 'the papers of the day': the agency of textual materiality resurfaces in a forceful way. By '*Ephemerae*' Johnson was making an analogy between these kinds of texts and insects that only lived for a

---

[25] Johnson, *Works*, III: 11–12.
[26] David E. Welberry, 'Foreword' to Friedrich A. Kittler, *Discourse Networks 1800/1900*, trans. Michael Metteer, with Chris Cullens (Stanford. CA: Stanford University Press, 1990), xiii.
[27] Johnson, *Works*, III: 11; 'ephemera, n.2.', *Oxford English Dictionary*.

day, suggesting the idea of learning as a complex ecosystem with its own evanescent life forms, part of an enduring and hierarchical natural order. '*Ephemerae*' supplemented the well-established use of 'grub', as in 'Grub Street', used to signify a class of hack-writers who, maggot-like, fed on the genius of other writers: to the idea of literary 'grubs' as the lowest form of life, '*Ephemerae*' added the idea of the transience of that life and the 'grubby' papers it was producing.[28] The use of 'ephemera' in medicine, referring to a temporary fever, may also be embedded in Johnson's *Ephemerae*: it suggests an idea of such papers as feverish emanations, purged from the body of learning.

'*Ephemerae*' is semantically contiguous with 'diurnal', the term used by Johnson to characterise the 'historiography' of journeymen writers. Describing the revolution of the earth that produced night and day, 'diurnal' was applied in the seventeenth century to the Europe-wide circulation of daily news sheets, in both handwritten and printed forms. Stuart Sherman has argued that the late seventeenth and early eighteenth centuries are characterised by a new consciousness of diurnal time, driven by technological and media change and by the daily transactions of commerce. Inventions such as the pocket watch and the minute hand, by which the individual could possess and monitor precisely a personalised sense of time, were aligned, according to Sherman, with the emergence of the 'diurnal form' of diaries, journals, newspapers, and the novel.[29] Though Sherman does not address the relationship between the diurnal and the ephemeral, I would argue that the diurnal consciousness of the early Enlightenment was the necessary condition for the later emergence of ephemera as a media category and a criterion of value. The increasingly mediatised unit of the day became a key element of modern temporality, interacting with and sometimes subsuming other daily routines such as religious observance that began and ended the day with prayer. The observance of the secular day became crucial to modern subjectivity in ways that accentuated time consciousness: if individuals could 'own' time in the form of the pocket watch, they could also be made more aware of time's passing. The concept of the diurnal assumed confidence in every day's return – the sun always sinking to rise again – a pattern exploited by new media such as the newspaper which, while only 'fresh' for a limited period, was renewed in the form of the next edition. This print mediatisation of daily life was signified by the 'times' of the newspaper, sounded by the post boy's horn or the hawker 'crying' in the street, the subject of

---

[28] See McDowell, 'Of Grubs and Other Insects', 54.   [29] Sherman, *Telling Time*.

poetry by William Cowper and George Crabbe.[30] The tendency of the newspaper to absolute ephemerality in terms of both its content and materiality was therefore always potentially in tension with the diurnal periodicity of the form: as Michael Harris notes, the 'inescapable fact about the newspaper is that it is a serial product and, in this respect, cannot be disposed of. Throw one away and the periodical flow will bring another one along behind.'[31] 'Ephemeral' differed from 'diurnal', however, in offering no consolation of the possibility of another day: a thing that was ephemeral lived for a day and then quickly died. Whereas the diurnal was cosmological in scope, associated with astronomy and the divine, the ephemeral was micrological and sublunary, deriving from the empiricism of the natural sciences and the increasing awareness of both the diversity and the evanescence of myriad forms of life.

In choosing to use '*Ephemerae*' rather than 'fugitive' or 'diurnal', Johnson attempted to fix the uncontrollability of the single sheet, the pamphlet, and implicitly the full spectrum of the loose or 'flying' paper economy in terms of a naturalised, more stable distinction between the mass of ephemeral papers and the codex-form book. While it may be more 'pompous', in line with its privileged status, and less amenable to the representation of 'common life', the codex-form book is represented as more 'durable', essentially different from the mass of paper products that surround it. In 'An Account', the concept of the fugitive text means that, theoretically, the 'atoms' of learning can be gathered up to create a powerful fire or light – the *Miscellany* itself, a form of book making. The project of *The Harleian Miscellany* is analogous to Addison's band-box in so far as the individual 'scraps' of fugitive texts, gathered together, have the capacity to constitute the whole 'book'. However, in *Rambler* no. 145 the ephemeral text can only refract the light of a pure and durable knowledge that is linked with a reification of authorship and an essentialised differentiation between the book and other forms of textual production. The Enlightenment idea of the book was therefore predicated on the construction of a particular idea of ephemerality and vice versa, a development which Johnson himself enacted in the period between writing 'An Account' (1743) and *Rambler* no. 145 (1751). He moves from a fugitive

---

[30] William Cowper, *The Task and Selected Other Poems*, ed. James Sambrook (London: Routledge, 1994), 140; George Crabbe, *The News-Paper: A Poem* (London: J. Dodsley, 1785), 4. For an important analysis of both poems see Kevis Goodman, *Georgic Modernity and British Romanticism: Poetry and the Mediation of History* (Cambridge, UK: Cambridge University Press, 2004), 67–105. For Cowper on the post boy see Chapter 7.
[31] Harris, 'Printed Ephemera', 125.

single sheet to the 'volume'; from an idea of literature as a containment or repository of the fugitive text to literature as sublimating the ephemeral through the medium of the essay genre; from writing as advertisement to writing as art; from the writer as anonymous 'manufacturer' to the writer as 'author' function ('Johnson'). In the course of making this move, Johnson importantly inaugurates the symbiosis of ephemerality and 'common' or everyday life and the incipient configuration of the latter in terms of a subaltern popular culture.

The Ephemeral 1790s

Johnson's application of *ephemerae* to contemporary print culture did not, however, significantly take off in the second half of the eighteenth century. A notable exception is George Crabbe's 'The News-Paper' (1785) which adapts Johnson's concept of *ephemerae* to stigmatise the profusion of information as an unnatural 'swarm' or plague of paper with no intrinsic, durable value:

> ... soon as Morning dawns with roseate hue,
> The HERALD of the morn arises too;
> POST after POST succeeds, and all day long,
> GAZETTES and LEDGERS swarm, a noisy throng ...
> In shoals the hours their constant numbers bring,
> Like insects waking to th'advancing spring,
> Which take their rise from grubs obscene that lie
> In shallow pools, or thence ascend the sky;
> Such are these base Ephemeras, so born
> To die before the next revolving morn.[32]

The records of Eighteenth Century Collections Online, however, suggest that the dominant meanings of 'ephemera' in the late eighteenth century continued to be those associated with zoology, medicine, and astronomy. This is in spite of the fact that there was an expansion in all kinds of ephemeral print after 1750, particularly the form that became known as the handbill, a format which, as I shall argue, is crucial to how the meaning of 'ephemera' was configured decisively in the context of the political crises of the 1790s.

The origins of the handbill date back to the beginning of moveable type, and in particular the use of print for the purposes of advertising,

---

[32] Crabbe, 'The News-Paper', 4–5. Crabbe explains 'Ephemeras' in a note as: 'The Ephemera, or May-fly, is an insect remarked by naturalists for the very short time it lives, after assuming its last and more perfect form' (5).

particularly of quack medicine, but also of exhibitions, and news of curious events and natural phenomena.[33] In *Journal of the Plague Year*, Daniel Defoe reported 'how the Posts of Houses and Corners of Streets were plaster'd over with Doctors Bills, and Papers of Ignorant Fellows', reflecting the ubiquity of the printed word out of doors that also drew the attention of Addison.[34] However, it was only after the mid-eighteenth century that a specific form of single-sheet advertising became identified as a 'handbill'. The *Oxford English Dictionary* dates the first use of the term, meaning 'a printed notice or advertisement on a single page, intended to be delivered or circulated by hand', to 1753. A dictionary published in 1759 defines handbill more narrowly to refer to a form of advertisement – a 'description of some curiosity or commodity delivered by the persons who show or sell it' – suggesting its importance to the street theatre of Georgian commercial life.[35] The handbill could serve a variety of uses: as a form of advertisement for a wide range of goods and services and a medium for both 'official' and private communication – a wanted notice for a thief, for example, or an attempt by an individual to respond publicly to an insult or injury. The importance of the handbill (and of jobbing print in general) to the eighteenth-century print trade is apparent in the material from the archive of the Tunbridge Wells printer, bookseller, and circulating library proprietor, Jasper Sprange (1746–1823). In addition to books, Sprange's output included playbills, auction notices, tavern bills, reward notices, and advertisements for events such as diversions on Tunbridge Wells commons in 1797.[36] Sprange also sold trade cards, bookplates, book prospectuses and catalogues, and tickets to plays, assemblies, and concerts.[37]

The 'hand' in handbill drew attention to this mode of communication as an embodied, prosthetic practice (the common size of a handbill, 6 inches by 3.5 inches (144 mm by 86 mm), approximating the size of the hand itself). Visible on posts, doors and walls, handbills were easily

---

[33] See Roberta Mullini, '"With Such Flourishes as These": The Visual Politics of Charlatans' Handbills in Early Modern London', *Textus: English Studies in Italy* 22:3 (2009), 553–71.
[34] Quoted in Mullini, 553.
[35] 'BILL' in William Rider, *A New Universal English Dictionary* (London: W. Griffin for I. Pottinger, 1759).
[36] *Wednesday, August 16th 1797, Diversions on Tunbridge-Wells Common* ... [Tunbridge Wells: Jasper Sprange, 1797].
[37] For Sprange's collections, now held in the Tunbridge Wells Museum, see R. C. Alston, 'A Provincial Printer at Work', *Factotum*, 10 (December 1980), 6–7; also Jude Freeman and Roger Wells, 'Jasper Sprange, Printer of Tunbridge Wells', in *A Common Tradition: Popular of Britain and America*, eds. Andy Durr and Helen Martin, exhibition catalogue, Brighton Festival, 6–24 May 1991 (Brighton: Brighton Polytechnic, 1991), 23–34; Raven, *Publishing Business*, 65–6.

carried or hidden on the body, or quickly screwed up and disposed of as rubbish: as such they were capable of quickly, even instantaneously telescoping public and private domains, ranging from the world out of doors to the somatic intimacy of a paper document held close to the body. The adaptability of the handbill as a print format made it important as a medium of political communication, extending from its customary use in elections to more 'inflammatory' applications, in Wilkite radicalism, in the Gordon riots in 1780 and, most strikingly, in the 1790s.[38] During that decade, particularly until 1795, there was a considerable investment on the part of the London Corresponding Society and other extra-parliamentary political organisations in the full range of non-book print – from job printing that enabled and sustained associational culture, such as tickets, rule books, and blank books that recorded resolutions and meetings, to newspapers and periodicals, pamphlets and tracts and single-sheet publications of all kinds (such as handbills, posters, and songs).[39] Such investments in print culture by both radicals and loyalists have long been acknowledged, but the impact of specific media formats, such as the handbill, particularly on the evolving discourse of ephemera and ephemerality in the 1790s–1800s, still remains to be properly explored.

The visibility of the handbill as a potent means of political communication in the 1790s begins with the Birmingham 'Church and King' riots of 1791. The riots commenced on the evening of Thursday 14 July with attacks on Quaker and Unitarian meeting houses and the homes of leading Dissenters, most notably Joseph Priestley, whose library, scientific apparatuses, and manuscripts were destroyed, forcing Priestley and his family to flee Birmingham and ultimately England for America in 1793.[40] In its report of the riots on Tuesday 19 July *The Times* reprinted a 'remarkable composition of intended insurrection', an 'inflammatory and treasonable hand-bill', circulated in Birmingham on Wednesday 13 July, that is two days after the commemoration dinner was advertised

---

[38] For handbills in Wilkite politics see John Brewer, *Party Ideology and Popular Politics at the Accession of George III* (Cambridge, UK: Cambridge University Press, 1976), 147.

[39] See e.g. Mary Thale (ed.), *Selections from the Papers of the London Corresponding Society 1792–1799* (Cambridge, UK: Cambridge University Press, 1983); Jon Mee, *Print, Publicity, and Popular Radicalism in the 1790s: The Laurel of Liberty* (Cambridge, UK: Cambridge University Press, 2016); Michael T. Davis, *London Corresponding Society, 1792–1799*, 6 vols. (London: Pickering & Chatto, 2002).

[40] The standard account of the riots is R. B. Rose, 'The Priestley Riots of 1791', *Past & Present*, 18 (1960), 68–88. See also Jonathan Atherton, 'Rioting, Dissent and the Church in Late Eighteenth Century Britain: The Priestley Riots of 1791', PhD thesis, University of Leicester (2012).

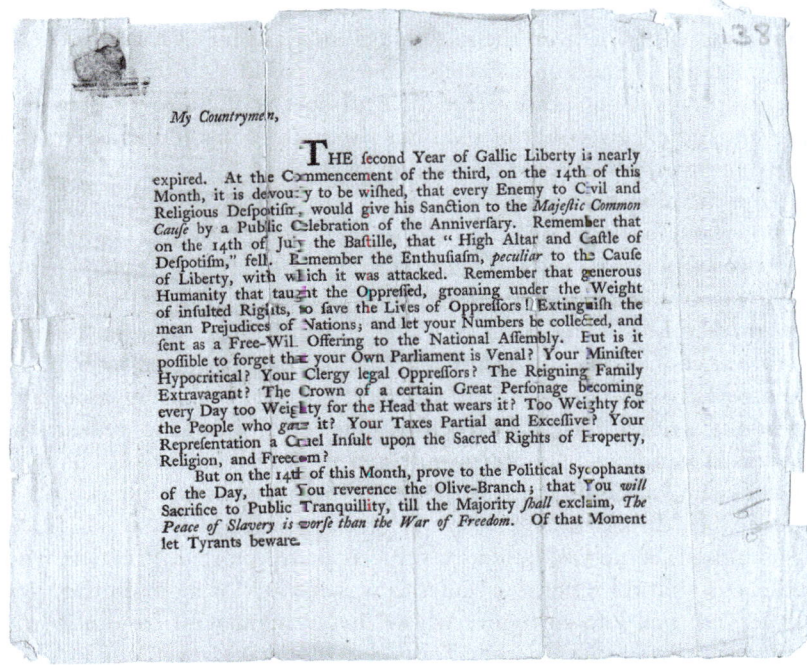

Figure 1 Anonymous handbill encouraging a public celebration of the second year of Gallic Liberty, 1791.
Permission The National Archives, HO 42/19 (138)

in the newspapers on 11 July and the day before the dinner was held.[41] One of the bills distributed as this time was sent to the Home Secretary, Henry Dundas, (at 2:20 in the afternoon on Sunday 17th) and is now in the UK National Archives (Figure 1).[42] The identity of the author or authors of the handbill as well as its printer were never conclusively established, however, and even in its report of 19 July, *The Times* conceded that it 'might be a forgery'. William Hutton, the Birmingham stationer and dissenter, claimed later that the handbills had been produced in London and planted by agents provocateurs in Birmingham: they had been, he said, 'privately scattered under the table at an inn'.[43] The sponsors of the commemoration dinner denied responsibility for the

---

[41] 'Riots at Birmingham', *The Times*, 19 July 1791.   [42] HO 42/19 (138).
[43] Llewellynn Jewitt, *The Life of William Hutton* (London: Frederick Warne, 1869), n221.

handbill in an advertisement published in newspapers on Thursday 14 July but it was too late to avert the riots that evening. As James Keir, the chemist and member of the Lunar Society who had presided at the dinner, commented: 'It was not possible for them to do any thing more effectual to prevent bad effects from this seditious paper, or to rescue themselves from the calumny of their being the authors of it'.[44]

The defining feature of the political handbill in the first part of the 1790s was anonymity, which could be used for both radical and counter-revolutionary purposes. Handbills could be insidious and unpredictable in their effects, related to how certain forms of fugitive print operated outside the marketplace, being given away free or, in the form of advertisements, acting as commodity surrogates. Though not explicitly naming handbills, George III's proclamation of 21 May 1792 against 'divers wicked and seditious writings that have been printed, published, and industriously dispersed, tending to excite tumult and disorder' was broad enough to include the handbill, which of all the print media of the period was the most easily 'dispersed'.[45]

Handbills could make fugitive subjects such as Joseph Priestley, whose exile as a political refugee to America was the first of many in the 1790s. Other less well known figures whose involvement with handbills led to exile from Britain were James Tytler and Thomas Fyshe Palmer. Tytler, a Scotsman, had a varied career as a Greenland whaler, a chemist, a journalist, and a printer and publisher.[46] In October 1784 he applied his skills in chemistry, mechanics, and print publicity to stage the first manned balloon flight in Britain, in Edinburgh, and became briefly famous as 'Balloon Tytler' (see Chapter 4). He was primarily, however, a superior literary journeyman, whose profile is more recognisable in the light of the digital literary economy of today: that is, he combined the roles of self-publishing and content provider, most notably for the second edition of the *Encyclopedia Britannica* on which he worked, writing articles for seven years between 1777–83. Tytler's politics became progressively more radical after the French Revolution. In 1791–2 he revived his profile in Edinburgh literary and political circles through his editorship

---

[44] 'Letter from James Keir, Esq.', *Lloyd's Evening Post*, 22–25 July 1791.
[45] *Parliamentary Papers: Consisting of a Complete Collection of Kings Speeches*, 3 vols. (London: J. Debrett, 1797), II: 469.
[46] The best account of Tytler's career is Stephen Brown, 'James Tytler's Misadventures in the Late Eighteenth-Century Edinburgh Book Trade', in *Printing Places: Locations of Book Production & Distribution since 1500*, eds. John Hinks and Catherine Armstrong (New Castle, DE: Oak Knoll Press, 2005), 47–63.

of the *Historical Register, or Edinburgh Monthly Intelligencer* and in late 1792 engaged with a printer, William Turnbull, to produce a handbill entitled 'To the People and their Friends'. In this he excoriated parliament as an unrepresentative 'vile junto of aristocrats' and declared: 'we must have our voice in framing our laws, or they are none of ours'.[47] The politics of the handbill were not avowedly republican however: Tytler emphasised the importance of petitioning the King as the ultimate authority who could dissolve parliament and prepare the way for its reform. It was claimed in court that 500 copies of this handbill were produced and circulated in Edinburgh in late 1792.[48] On 4 December Tytler was arrested under the Seditious Writings Act but before he could be tried in early January the following year he fled the country while on bail, travelling first to Belfast and then to America. He was tried in his absence on 7 January 1793 and convicted of being the 'guilty actor' of the handbill for which he was declared an 'outlaw and fugitive from his majesty's laws'.[49] Tytler settled in Salem, Massachusetts, where he continued his writing career for another ten years, as a newspaper editor and author of works on medicine and history. In January 1804 he was discovered drowned near Salem, having presumed to have fallen into the sea while on a drunken excursion to borrow a candle from a neighbour.[50]

Throughout his career Tytler had been what Samuel Johnson called a 'diurnal historiographer', working in journalism and other kinds of hack literary work. In 1792 Tytler chose not to seek visibility as a political author through the more conventional means of pamphlet and book publishing but instead embraced the fugitive mediality of the handbill as a way of reaching 'the people' and possibly speaking more directly to power by provoking the attention of the law. Tytler was able to elude punishment for the publication of a handbill but for his contemporary, Thomas Fyshe Palmer, the outcome was very different. Fyshe Palmer was one of the so-called Scottish Martyrs who, with Maurice Margarot, Joseph Gerrald, and Thomas Skirving, were transported for sedition to New South Wales in 1794. An Englishman who abandoned a promising career in the Church of England in the early 1780s to become a Unitarian minister in Scotland, Fyshe Palmer had an established profile as a preacher and sermon and pamphlet writer: in other words, he was much more of a

---

[47] T. J. Howell, *A Complete Collection of State Trials* (London: Longman, Hurst, Rees, Orme, and Brown, et al., 1817), XXIII: cols. 2, 3, 4.
[48] Howell, *Complete Collection of State Trials*, col. 4.
[49] Howell, *Complete Collection of State Trials*, col. 6.
[50] See Brown, 'James Tytler's Misadventures'.

'proper' literary man than Tytler.⁵¹ On 12–13 September 1793 Fyshe Palmer was tried in Perth for, in the words of his indictment, 'wickedly and feloniously WRITING or PRINTING ... seditious or inflammatory writing' in the form of a handbill that had been circulated and posted up in Dundee in July 1793.⁵² The handbill had been authorised by a General Meeting of the Society of the Friends of Liberty held at the Berean meeting house in Dundee. The text of the handbill was reproduced in full in the edition of Fyshe Palmer's trial, first printed in 1793 and later again in Howell's *State Trials*.⁵³ Much of the examination of Fyshe Palmer and other witnesses at the trial focused on the circumstances of the production of the handbill with the aim of establishing Fyshe Palmer as the author of it. As such, the trial text put on record the material and social dimensions of the production of the handbill for a much wider readership, in effect staging a discursive re-enactment of fugitive mediality under the sign of the law. The handbill 'archive' of the 1790s and of political fugitive print in general in this decade is primarily located in the publication of trials, often by radical publishers such as H. D. Symonds and James Ridgeway, that highlighted attempts by authorities to control it. Handbills, tickets, songs, mock playbills, newspapers, and pamphlets were tendered as material evidence, circulated in court and forensically analysed in a deictic way that drew attention to the handbill's presence in court and circulation in society as a whole.

The text of the Dundee handbill of July 1793 contained an appeal for universal suffrage and general reform of parliament 'founded upon the eternal basis of justice, fair, free, and equal' (8). Evidence in the trial indicated that it was primarily the work of a Dundee weaver, George Mealmaker, who produced a manuscript of the address for the General Meeting at which it was discussed and collectively approved for publication. James Ellis, a cotton-spinner and protégé of Fyshe Palmer, who voluntarily accompanied him to New South Wales, testified that he had argued that the handbill should be signed with someone's name: 'for as there was no name to it, they would say that we wished to steal into the world; and we were sorry that those in power should think that we meant any thing wicked' (98). Fyshe Palmer's role had been to edit Mealmaker's

---

⁵¹ See A. H. Millar, 'Palmer, Thomas Fyshe (1747–1802), Unitarian Minister and Radical', *Oxford Dictionary of National Biography*, Oxford University Press, 2004; online edn, January 2008 [www.oxforddnb.com/view/article/21220, accessed 2 August 2018].

⁵² *The Trial of the Rev. Thomas Fyshe Palmer, Before the Circuit Court of Justiciary, held at Perth, on the 12th and 13th September, 1793* (Edinburgh: W. Skirving, 1793), 5; subsequent page references in parentheses in text.

⁵³ Howell, *Complete Collection of State Trials*, 237–382.

text, 'softening' some of its expressions and correcting the spelling (97). He then took control of the production of the handbill, ordering its printing and organising distribution: about 1,000 copies were printed, some of which were posted on walls and others left in bookshops (100). One Dundee bookseller, David Miller, testified that Fyshe Palmer delivered copies to his shop, commending the handbill as 'a wonderful thing . . . the production of a common weaver' (104). Miller subsequently hid the handbills in his 'shaving tub' and later destroyed them (104). The evidence of the trial indicates that Fyshe Palmer used his connections with printers and booksellers and his gentlemanly standing and address to ensure the publication and dissemination of the handbill. Fyshe Palmer corrected Mealmaker's style and promoted the publication of the handbill as a thing of 'wonder', the literary invention of a 'common weaver'. Nonetheless it was Fyshe Palmer who was indicted and condemned to seven years in New South Wales, even though George Mealmaker declared his authorship of the handbill and virtually the last statement that Fyshe Palmer made at the end of the trial was that Mealmaker had written it 'independent of any one else'.[54] In this case fugitive mediality – the circumstances of who had 'authored' the handbill, and how the handbill was produced and transmitted – was as least, if not more, important as its contents. The prosecutors acknowledged the right to petition parliament but it was a different matter altogether for 'any public or private man, clergy or laity' to call meetings and 'collect together mechanics' who were unqualified to express a political opinion.[55] Nor indeed was it permissible for that 'man' to seek to disseminate the voice of the lower orders in the form of the public sphere of print, that is soliciting printers and booksellers to publish the handbill. Even though the Society of the Friends of Liberty had authorised the handbill, it was unclear whose voice it truly represented because of this literary collaboration between a gentleman and a weaver. No name could be put to the handbill as it did not have a 'name' that in 1793 could be signified. The case of Thomas Fyshe Palmer thus

---

[54] Howell, *Complete Collection of State Trials*, col. 376. George Mealmaker would himself be transported to Australia, in 1800, for organising the United Scotsmen in Scotland by means of seditious handbills and the administering of unlawful oaths: like Tytler he had gone further into rather than retreating from the hinterland of print culture where writing was indistinguishable from performative speech. He died in 1808, like Tytler, from the effects of alcohol, an exile in a foreign land. See Michael Roe, 'Mealmaker, George (1768–1808)', *Australian Dictionary of Biography*, Melbourne University Publishing, 1967; online edn published by National Centre of Biography, Australian National University [http://adb.anu.edu.au/biography/mealmaker-george-2441/text3253, accessed 3 August 2018].

[55] Howell, *Complete Collection of State Trials*, col. 292.

exemplified the danger for the authorities of expanding political literacy in the 1790s – the experiments in genres, media, audiences, and forums for speaking such as debating clubs that were producing mixed, adulterated voices and confounding the 'natural' alignment of social distinction with cultural hierarchies. The prosecution of Fyshe Palmer was designed to warn men such as him not to speak with or for 'the people' and specifically not to engage with the kind of fugitive mediality – the handbill – that made that communication possible.

While punishing men such as Fyshe Palmer for authorising the Dundee handbill, loyalists and the government also recognised the potency of fugitive print as a force of counter-revolution. The Association for Preserving Liberty and Property against Republicans and Levellers, established in November 1792 by the lawyer and civil servant John Reeves to counter the threat of popular radicalism, engaged the London Corresponding Society's methods in similar terms by producing thousands of handbills, ballads, and pamphlets that were distributed by the Association's networks across the country. In 1793 the Association published a compilation of its publications in a single volume entitled *Association Papers*, which was divided into two parts, one consisting of notices of the Association's resolutions, originally published as handbills or pamphlets, and a second part of nine numbers of 'tracts', each comprising a collection of pamphlets that were designed for the lower orders (including Hannah More's tract *Village Politics*, originally published separately). Though not using the term 'ephemera', the preface to *Association Papers* distinguishes between its contents as works of only transitory relevance as opposed to the durability of the codex-form book in which they were gathered together:

> The occasion of these little Publications is in every one's remembrance; they have had their use for the time; and they are now collected into a volume, as a library-book for such as have any curiosity to preserve the productions of the day.
> When they were sold for a penny, they were designed for a different class of readers and purchasers from those into whose hands the present volume many chance to come. Such as may condescend to turn over this Collection should remember, that the times are happily changed since the months of November and December last; and we must travel back to that period of anxiety and public alarm, in order to feel the sentiments, and to relish the style, of many of these papers.[56]

[56] *Association Papers: Part I. Publications printed by special order of the Society for Preserving Liberty and Property against Republicans and Levellers, at the Crown and Anchor, in the Strand. Part II. A Collection of tracts, printed at the expence of that society* (London: J. Sewell et al., 1793), preface.

Like *The Harleian Miscellany* the purpose of *Association Papers* was to 'fix' or immobilise the Association's own ephemeral publications. In this way, the not-so-recent past could be recognised as the past and relished as a literary experience, a matter of 'style' and 'sentiments', for which those who read these papers in fugitive form were presumably excluded because this volume could not conceivably 'come' into their hands on account of its price. The codex-form book, gathering together these fugitive leaves, was in this case an instrument of power, enabling a historicisation of the crisis of 1792–3 that had political meaning beyond the contents of the 'papers' themselves.

After Thomas Paine's trial in absentia for the seditious libel of *Rights of Man* Part II in Dec 1792, William Godwin highlighted the uses made of the handbill by Reeves and his supporters:

> We all know by what means a verdict was procured: by repeated proclamations, by all the force, and all the fears of the kingdom, being artfully turned against one man. As I came out of court, I saw hand-bills, in the most vulgar and illiberal style distributed, entitled, The Confessions of Thomas Paine. I had not walked three streets, before I was encountered by ballad singers, roaring in cadence rude, a miserable set of stanzas upon his private life. You know best, Sir, [addressing Reeves] what concern you had in these things . . . . No sooner were the cheap pamphlets of Mr Paine, and the hand-bills of his partisans suppressed, than pamphlets, printed sheets, and hand-bills without number issued from the press in answer to his reasonings.[57]

Godwin analyses the verdict against Paine in terms of a struggle for the control of fugitive mediality in the 1790s, beginning with the use of royal proclamations, printed as broadsides, and the deployment of ballads and handbills on behalf of the government. The impact of such print is immediate as Godwin is assaulted with 'vulgar and illiberal' handbills as he leaves the court, the performativity of the judge's spoken verdict being amplified and echoes by the 'roar' of the ballad singers. The bookish syntax of the phrase 'cadence rude' is a form of resistance to the intermedial noise of both print and voice that greets him. The roaring ballad singers are particularly significant because, in their peddling of rumours about 'Mr' Paine's private life, they combine politics with the commercial appeal of scurrility. Godwin is fundamentally concerned that fugitive mediality, once galvanised, cannot be controlled by anyone and that it could lead to a dangerous loss of reason and the atavism of the mob. He questions the

---

[57] William Godwin, *Political and Philosophical Writings of William Godwin, Volume II: Political Writings II*, ed. Mark Philp (London: Pickering & Chatto, 1993), 17.

hypocrisy of the Association in condemning handbills and other kinds of ephemeral print, and then using such media in its own cause, arguing the precedent of what had happened in Birmingham:

> What is there in these instruments of hand-bills, ballads, and pamphlets, that should render them, though before profane, sacred the moment they come into your hands? If Mr Paine may not inflame the vulgar against the House of Brunswick, what right do you excite them; for that is the direct tendency of your proceedings, to pull down the houses and destroy the property of dissenters?[58]

Godwin's wariness of the handbill, as deployed by both sides of the Revolution debate, anticipates later ideas of the mass media, particularly the daily news media, as unreliable and unpredictable purveyors of the truth, and of its readers or, rather, passive consumers, as easily manipulated by partisan, invisible forces.

It was in order to tackle the specific threat of the radical handbill as a medium of communication that an Act was passed in 1799 'for the more Effective Suppression of Societies established for Seditious and Treasonable Practices', otherwise known at the 'Unlawful Societies Act'.[59] An important dimension of this Act was that printers were compelled to make themselves accountable for their publications by identifying themselves on everything they produced. Debating the necessity of such measures in parliament, the government argued that the liberty of the press had been 'perverted', principally through the dissemination of:

> hand bills, tending to poison the minds of the people, to deprave their morals, to pervert their loyalty, and to undermine their religion ... Against this species of mischief some new provisions are necessary, the object of which will be, always to have responsible the author or publisher. This regulation is strictly in the spirit of the Constitution. If in its application it is new, it is because the evil is likewise new.[60]

The handbill was not a 'new' medium, but never before had it been deployed in such inventive and politically subversive ways. The Unlawful Societies Act therefore represented a response to fugitive print that targeted one of its main features – anonymity – by facilitating a system of surveillance through registration of printers and their presses.[61] The significance of this

---

[58] Godwin, *Political and Philosophical Writings*, 17–18.   [59] 39 Geo. III, c. 79 (1799).
[60] *Star*, 20 April 1799.
[61] See Raven, *Publishing Business*, 84–5. As Raven points out, the 1799 Act (ironically) created new opportunities for job printing in the form of the documents which printers had to fill in to comply with its conditions. A significant exception to the association of handbills with anonymity is one of

Act has been neglected in the context of other counter-revolutionary legislation in the 1790s. The measure meant that the authorities now had a means of registering and potentially prosecuting every printer throughout the country if they did not comply with the law. It also became more difficult in the future for the identities of the writer or writers and the printer to be blurred or confused as 'authors' of a handbill (as had been the case with Fyshe Palmer). In the long run this Act served to reinforce the idea of the handbill as primarily the product of the printer, making it, as 'mere' jobbing print, fundamentally different from the codex-form book: handbills only had printers, not authors.

By targeting the printers of radical handbills, the Unlawful Societies Act of 1799 left the field more open to loyalism's appeal to the people via fugitive print, particularly during the Invasion Crisis of 1803. A notable producer of loyalist handbills was the bookseller James Asperne (1757–1820), publisher of the *European Magazine*. In 1805 the *British Critic* noted that '*the Posting-Bills, and other cheap Papers, dispersed in the present Crisis have assisted very powerfully in exciting the Patriotic Spirit of Britons*', giving a list of such titles organised by the name of their publisher. Asperne was prominent as were John Ginger, John Stockdale, Hatchard, and others.[62] Like Reeves's *Association Papers*, this catalogue of cheap loyalist print in the *British Critic* was designed to fix the fugacity of such literature in book form, rendering it respectable, unlike its radical equivalent, by making it bibliographically visible. Asperne's own *European Magazine* expressed some concern that the 'loyal papers ... flying in long streamers from his house', though effective in penetrating 'all parts of the united kingdom' would 'soon *get out of sight*'. Using metaphors from chemistry, the writer claimed that compilations of fugitive literature, including loyalist handbills, in periodicals such as *The Spirit of the Public*

---

the most notorious of the anti-government handbills of the 1790s, Richard 'Citizen' Lee's 'King Killing' on which Lee identified himself as printer and author. Lee sold 'King Killing' and other papers, crying out 'The Rights of Man for a Penny' at the gates of the Palace of Westminster to the crowd that gathered in opposition to George III as the king progressed to parliament on 29 October 1795: *Truth and Treason! Or a Narrative of the Royal Procession to the House of Peers, October the 29th, 1795* (London: n.p., 1795), 5. Lee made himself visible as author and vendor of 'King Killing' and other similar fugitive papers in order to legitimate such documents, and the politics they were disseminating, as part of the normative economy associated with the codex-form book. For discussion of 'King Killing' see Mee, *Print, Publicity, and Popular Radicalism*, 162–4; John Barrell, *Imagining the King's Death: Figurative Treason, Fantasies of Regicide, 1793–1796* (Oxford: Oxford University Press, 2000), 607–8.

[62] 'Patriotic Papers', *British Critic*, 22 (1803), 214–17 (214). See also Stephen M. Parrish, 'A Booksellers' Campaign of 1803: Napoleonic Invasion Broadsides at Harvard', *Harvard Library Bulletin*, 8:1 (Winter 1954), 14–26.

Journals (also published by Asperne) represented a distillation or fixing of the volatile elements of print prevalent since the mid-eighteenth century, items that 'after having exhibited an ephemeral splendour, have faded upon the mental eye'.[63]

The use of 'ephemeral' to describe and categorise such literature in 1805 is indicative of how the term was gaining currency in relation to printed matter. While the association of ephemera with entomology, medicine, and astronomy prevailed, one work, purporting to represent neologisms in the French language following the Revolution, noted how *l'éphémère* had been inflected by the urgency of the times:

> Its application heretofore to fevers ... and to certain flowers, is now extended to all the accidents of human life of sudden alteration.
>
> The various and quick succession of the scenes on the great theatre of Europe during the space of a few late years has been well expressed by this newly adopted adjective; it is accordingly said, that the life of man is *ephemeral*, and that nothing is lasting round him but nature, reason, justice, and virtue.[64]

The discourse of ephemera and ephemerality after the French Revolution functioned as a means, firstly, of keeping the threat of fugitive mediality at bay and, secondly, as a way of registering a sense of accelerated temporality as a result of the crises of the 1790s. For loyalists the label of 'ephemera' brought texts such as the handbill out of the 'darkness' and into the light, defining them as evanescent in both their material form and in the durability of their politics. Thus the *Observations on the Government and Constitution of Great Britain* (1792) could assert that Britons would never embrace the 'new-born theory of "the Rights of Man"' in exchange for their time-honoured laws and customs', however much 'the political ephemera of the day may exclaim' against them.[65] In 1809, a writer for the *Morning Post* castigated the 'factious declaimers' that had 'appeared since the French Revolution', the weapons of which were 'all the light artillery of pamphlets and ephemeral publications ... employed to facilitate the course of things towards anarchy'.[66] 'Ephemera' objectified and fixed such publications in the way that 'fugitive' did not, in the process

---

[63] *European Magazine* 47 (1805), 282.
[64] William Dupré, *Lexicographica-Neologica Gallica: The Neological French Dictionary* (London: R. Philips, I. and T. Carpenter, and W. Clement, 1801), 111.
[65] Jerom Alley, *Observations on the Government and Constitution of Great Britain, including a vindication of the both from the aspersions of some late writers, particularly Dr. Price, Dr. Priestley, and Mr. Paine* (Dublin: William Sleater, 1792), 66.
[66] 'Factious Writers', *Morning Post*, 7 June 1809.

inflecting the category of ephemera itself with a distinctive 1790s temporality, the rapidity and evanescence of revolutionary change contrasted with the durability of bookish tradition and learning

Not only was the handbill being used extensively by radicals and loyalists alike in order to mobilise opinion, but the impact and character of the newspaper press as the dominant form of fugitive media was also being influenced by the pressure of events both at home and abroad. The number of newspapers sent by post from London increased from 4.6 million in 1790 to 8.6 million in 1797, in spite of attempts to control the radical press in particular by means of stamp duty and the Newspapers Regulation Act of 1798.[67] As Dallas Liddle has argued, newspapers in the 1790s began to devote more space and resources to the transcription of debates in parliament, trials (including numerous political trials), news from abroad, military dispatches, and accounts of political meetings. Such a 'discourse', according to Liddle, 'was a much harder currency than newspapers had ever previously been required to print ... [T]he value of transcripts depended on their being as complete, recent, and accurate as possible'.[68] An anxiety for news, stimulated by political crisis at home and increasingly the conditions of wartime, thus intensified a sense of the ephemerality of fugitive print information as a whole, particularly its lack of durability and possible unreliability.[69] The *Leeds Intelligencer* expressed concern in 1801 that the leading London papers of both the opposition and the government were indulging in rumour-mongering, the dangers of which were accentuated by the rapidity with which news was now getting out: 'It is not wise to weave cobwebs in the morning which the evening destroys. A falsehood that may run a week without confutation, must, *we should think*, be much preferable to these ephemeral productions of the fancy!'[70] However, for the literary journeyman, John Feltham, writing in 1804, the view of ephemeral print was somewhat different. 'There were

---

[67] Victoria E. M. Gardner, *The Business of News in England, 1760–1820* (Basingstoke: Palgrave Macmillan, 2016), 31.

[68] Dallas Liddle, 'The News Machine: Textual Form and Information Function in the London *Times*, 1785–1885', *Book History*, 19 (2016), 132–68 (154).

[69] On how the Revolutionary and Napoleonic wars intensified a sense of timeliness and an anxiety for news see Mary A. Favret, *War at a Distance: Romanticism and the Making of Modern Wartime* (Princeton, NJ: Princeton University Press, 2010). The need for 'transcription' of wartime events communicated rapidly to a reading public led to the first modern 'war-correspondent': see Neil Ramsey, 'The Grievable Life of the War-Correspondent: The Experience of War in Henry Crabb Robinson's Letters to *The Times*, 1808–1809', in *Emotions and War: Medieval to Romantic Literature*, eds. Stephanie Downes, Andrew Lynch, and Katrina O'Loughlin (Basingstoke: Palgrave Macmillan, 2015), 235–50.

[70] 'Saturday's Post', *Leeds Intelligencer*, 16 March 1801.

never so many monthly and diurnal publications as at the present period', Feltham writes in a section of his 1804 guide to the metropolis, *The Picture of London*, entitled 'Literature, and the Bookselling Trade':

> to the perpetual novelty which issues from the press in this form, may be attributed the expansion of mind which is daily exhibited among all classes of the people ... The morning and evening journals fall into the hands of all classes: they display the temper of the times, the opinions of the learned, the enlightened, and the patriotic. The Ephemeral press is the mirror where folly sees its own likeness, and vice contemplates the magnitude of its deformity. It also presents a tablet of manners; a transcript of the temper of mankind; a check on the gigantic strides of innovation; and a bulwark which reason has raised; and, it is to be hoped, time will consecrate, round the altar of Liberty![71]

Feltham's idea of the late Georgian 'Ephemeral press' as the bulwark of reason and liberty is exceptional, however. It was eclipsed by the view of ephemeral print as anarchy's shock troops or flimsy 'cobwebs of the morning' destined to dissipate into nothingness. The idea of printed ephemera as transient, disposable, and insignificant, eventually served to distinguish the more enduring life cycle of the book in terms of an order of nature, as well as enabling a boundary against which the proximity of the codex-form book to waste and fugacity could be imaginatively and discursively delimited. The consolidation of these meanings of ephemera also had a more specific social dimension in so far that it entailed the identification of cheap print with the category of the popular. The world of print out of doors, the street of roaring ballad sellers of 'rude cadence', would be associated, not with a universal public that Feltham sees as mirrored in the 'Ephemeral press', but with the anonymous, the unpredictable and sometimes intractable 'masses'. Such a development was constitutive of later ideas of the mass media and of everyday life. It is this transition, developing throughout the eighteenth century but which intensifies after 1789, that led to the privileging of the ballad as the dominant form of cheap print and an expression of the voice and literature of 'the people', at the expense of recognition of the diversity of cheap print and also of jobbing print media such as the playbill and the ticket.

A consequence of these changes was the eclipse of how individuals, from the seventeenth century onwards, had in fact been documenting the proliferation of fugitive print, including jobbing printing, entailed by the second printing revolution. Joseph Addison was not alone in savouring

---

[71] [John Feltham], *The Picture of London, for 1804* (London: Richard Phillips, 1804), 289–90.

the accidental readings to be derived from fugitive print. Others picked up such scraps and made collections or books out of them, creating an 'ephemerology', the science of such quick or fleeting documentation – 'a transcript of the temper of mankind' as Feltham put it – and of how fugitive print enabled and made visible the associational world of the Enlightenment. In the next chapter I go back to the seventeenth century to outline the origins of that ephemerology in the political crises of that period that, like the 1790s, were based on the tremendous communicative possibilities of the 'new medium' of fugitive print.

CHAPTER 2

Making Collections
Enlightenment Ephemerology

In June 1846 three sales by auction took place in London of the collections of the former sub-librarian of the London Institution, William Upcott (1779–1845). In addition to a large number of manuscripts, engravings, coins and tokens, and a vast collection of autographs, for which Upcott was well known, the sales also included numerous examples of his collectanea.[1] Collectanea (the plural of the Latin *collectaneus*, meaning gathered together) was a term of long standing meaning a compilation of passages or remarks. In this case, the term 'collectanea' was used to refer to Upcott's many volumes of printed, visual, and manuscript material, documenting his interests in British topography, particularly of Northamptonshire and Oxfordshire, in John Evelyn, Samuel Johnson, David Garrick, and the circles of his natural father, the artist Ozias Humphrey. Upcott was also interested in recording the scale and diversity of fugitive print relating to public culture in the eighteenth and nineteenth centuries, amassing material on the theatre, ballooning, lotteries, auction sale catalogues, shop bills, and tickets of admission to places of public amusement.[2] One lot in the sale catalogue, with the title 'Vulgaria', was described as 'A Portfolio containing a very extensive Collection of Popular Sheets and Broadsides of the last and present Centuries. Political Squibs, Caricatures, Parodies, Christmas Carols, Accidents, Fires, Crimes, Executions, &c. *some of them of great curiosity*'.[3] Indeed, Upcott's work of assemblage went so far as to preserve what was left behind after he had clipped, organised, and pasted down his myriad bits of paper. Offered for

---

[1] Janet Ing Freeman, 'Upcott, William (1779–1845)', *Oxford Dictionary of National Biography*, Oxford University Press, 2004 [www.oxforddnb.com/view/article/28005, accessed 28 August 2016]. See also 'The late William Upcott', *Gentleman's Magazine*, new ser. 25 (May 1846), 473–6.

[2] *Catalogue of the Library of the Late William Upcott, Esq.* ([London]: Atkins & Andrew, [1846]), 65, BL pressmark 11902.g.44.

[3] *Catalogue of the Library of William Upcott*, 64.

sale in June 1846 was lot 1159: 'Wastes to various Books, Blank Paper, Scraps, &c. a large parcel.'[4]

As sub-librarian of the London Institution Upcott represents what Jon Klancher has described as the new class of knowledge professionals in Regency London – directors of institutions, museums and exhibitions, lecturers, librarians and collectors, as well as writers and visual artists – whose collaborations were formative in the configuration of the relationship between the arts and sciences.[5] A similar subaltern figure is the antiquarian, bibliographer, and literary scholar Joseph Haslewood (1769–1833) who, like Upcott, made numerous collectanea of printed ephemera. Upcott and Haslewood exemplify what Ina Ferris describes as 'border figures in . . . "the bookish interim" of Romanticism'. Such bookmen 'produced books and launched book practices that ramified into the wider culture', Ferris says, '. . . at the same time, they themselves were finally absorbed within this wider culture to disappear from our own literary histories'.[6]

The bookishness of these bookmen, as both Klancher and Ferris have brilliantly shown, shaped the emergence of bibliography and literary history in the Romantic period. I wish to extend the insights of Klancher and Ferris to suggest that another dimension, or substrate, of this 'bookishness' was a fascination for ephemeral or fugitive print. The discourse of ephemerality that intensified around 1800 was important in a number of ways: firstly, in politicising the distinction between the book and the non-book, as I argued in the previous chapter; secondly, in creating the conditions for the identification of printed ephemera with the category of popular culture; and finally, in reifying the codex-form book as a vehicle for 'Literature', differentiating the book from other kinds of print media. So successful was that discourse that its impact, like Upcott and Haslewood themselves, has been absorbed and forgotten in literary history. These men could justifiably be described as 'printmen' as much as they were 'bookmen' because of their interest in ephemeral print that they organised, classified, and preserved in their collectanea. In this and subsequent chapters I want to explore the significance of the ephemera collection as a means whereby the diversity and scope of the print revolution of the early Enlightenment was apprehended, creating a branch of informal knowledge, ephemerology, that

---

[4] *Catalogue of the Library of William Upcott*, 64.
[5] Jon Klancher, *Transfiguring the Arts and Sciences: Knowledge and Cultural Institutions in the Romantic Age* (Cambridge, UK: Cambridge University Press, 2013), 2.
[6] Ina Ferris, *Book-Men, Book Clubs, and the Romantic Literary Sphere* (Basingstoke: Palgrave Macmillan, 2015), 13.

sustained and interacted with other areas of knowledge, such as printing history, topography, theatre history, and the history of entertainments, proto-disciplines that were formative in the modern disciplines of media studies, theatre studies, cultural studies, and sociology.

The making of collections was crucial to ephemerology. Though related to other kinds of collecting, of flora and fauna, artefacts, paintings, of books great and small, that form the infrastructure of the British Enlightenment, the meaning of 'collection' in this sense refers to a form of book making, comparable to similar enterprises such as the commonplace book, the grangerised book, and the scrapbook. The extra-illustrated or grangerised book, the development of which dates from the Rev. James Granger's *Biographical History of England* of 1769, is essentially a hybrid of the 'collection' and the printed book.[7] These practices were continuous with a history, going back to the Renaissance, of readers creating customised books by binding them with other kinds of printed material.[8] As assemblages of printed ephemera, entailing selection, the placing of items on a page, and often annotation, the collection is a work of writing and documentation. I thus interpret 'collection' in a bibliographical rather than a museological sense and in two main ways: firstly, as a variety of the book broadly conceived and, secondly, as a form of bibliography in its own right that documented the variety of non-book print, facilitating the possibility of other kinds of bibliographical inquiry.

The practice of making books out of ephemera has largely gone unrecognised because, like the category of ephemera itself, collectanea have a dubious bibliographical status. Categories of bibliographical description

---

[7] The *Oxford English Dictionary* dates the first use of 'scrap-book' to 1825. On scrapbooks see Ellen Gruber Garvey, 'Scissoring and Scrapbooks: Nineteenth-Century Reading, Remaking, and Recirculating', in *New Media, 1740–1915*, eds. Lisa Gitelman and Geoffrey B. Pingree (Cambridge MA: MIT Press, 2003), 207–27 and Garvey's *Writing with Scissors: American Scrapbooks from the Civil War to the Harlem Renaissance* (New York: Oxford University Press, 2013); on extra-illustration see Lucy Peltz, *Facing the Text: Extra-Illustration, Print Culture and Society in Britain, 1769–1840* (San Marino, CA: Huntington Library Press, 2017); also Luisa Calè, 'Extra-Illustrations: The Order of the Book and the Fantasia of the Library', in *The Material Cultures of Enlightenment Arts and Sciences*, eds. Adriana Craciun and Simon Schaffer (London: Palgrave Macmillan, 2016): 235–54. Another term sometimes used for the collection is 'guard book'. A 'guard' is a strip of paper placed between the pages of a book that allowed for extra matter to be inserted such as prints or even booklets. Guards were essential to the process of extra-illustrating which entailed the disbanding and then rebinding of a printed book with guards inserted for the placing of extra material. Blank guard books were sold by stationers and used as storage devices for e.g. letters, invoices, etc. by private individuals, groups, and institutions. Guard books were also used for library catalogues, most notably in the British Museum Library. 'Guard book' therefore refers primarily to a particular technology of archiving which some but not necessarily all collections used.

[8] See Jeffrey Todd Knight, *Bound to Read: Compilations, Collections, and the Making of Renaissance Literature* (Philadelphia: University of Pennsylvania Press, 2013).

that developed in the nineteenth century became centred on the codex-form book and in particular the title page as the key semantic unit defining a book. August Panizzi's 1841 'Rules' for the *Catalogue of Printed Books in the British Museum*, which established the author's name as the first point of identification of a book, included no provision for description of individual ephemeral items or of the collections housing them, though the 'Rules' do refer to 'periodical publications', 'almanacs, calendars [and] ephemerides' and 'anonymous catalogues'.[9] If an anonymous ballad, a playbill, or a handbill advertisement for a show at Bartholomew Fair which has no title page presents challenges to bibliographical description, a 'collection' of such material is even more problematic. Whereas in some cases the 'author' of a collection is indicated within the text itself or can be deduced from the evidence of library sale catalogues, many collections are anonymous. For both authored and anonymous collections, moreover, their bound state, the arrangement and sequence of items or what may have been lost or removed, is possibly the responsibility of dealers or the library that received them. They may also have been rebound by a library on multiple occasions (or even disbound altogether for the purposes of digitisation). It is therefore extremely difficult to ascribe definitive authorship to a collection of ephemeral texts that survives in a library, even when it is identified with a particular individual.

The 'collection' was therefore not a book as the book came to be understood in the nineteenth century and after; it was rather a mode of assemblage and a kind of repository. Early in the eighteenth century the scholar-librarian Humfrey Wanley, with reference to the collections of John Bagford, noted their value for a history of printing: 'a single Leaf of Paper, tho' not valuable in its self; yet when come to be part of a Collection, may be of good use, not only in respect of the *Matter* it Treats of, but as to the *Mark of the Paper, the Date, Printer's Name, Countrey, Title, Faculty*, &c'.[10] Through the process of aggregation and assemblage

---

[9] *Catalogue of Printed Books in the British Museum*, vol. 1 (London: British Museum, 1841), ix. 'Ephemerides' (the plural of 'ephemeris', meaning daily record) were calculations by astronomers of the movements and positions of the planets for every day of the year at a particular time. Ephemerides formed the basis of almanacs and were also used to calculate longitude. As developed by the educational reformer and 'intelligencer' in the early modern republic of letters, Samuel Hartlib (c. 1600–62), 'ephemerides' was also used to describe a compendium of memoranda and notes: see Richard Yeo, *Notebooks, English Virtuosi, and Early Modern Science* (Chicago: University of Chicago Press, 2014), 103.

[10] Humfrey Wanley, 'An Account of Mr. Bagford's Collections for His History of Printing, by Mr. Humfrey Wanley', *Philosophical Transactions*, 25 (1706–7), 2407–10 (2410), [London: B. Walford, 1708].

even a 'single leaf' scrap could be meaningful. These 'books' of ephemera are thus fundamentally contradictory: they are unique unreproducible volumes containing examples of texts which were manufactured in the thousands and which in some cases represent disposable 'trash'. The ephemera 'collection' therefore concentrates both poles of the Derridean paper spectrum – the priceless archive and the abjection of litter – within a single textual artefact, which is perhaps one reason why it has confounded bibliographical description. The 'collection' does not have the aura of the museum object or the manuscript because of the debased value of what it contains, nor can it be recognised as a conventional book on account of its singular mode of production.

The contents of these collections began to be recognised in the 1960s and 1970s as the bibliographers behind the second edition of the Short Title Catalogue (STC) and the Eighteenth-Century Short Title Catalogue attempted to record the full range of printed matter produced after 1540, the practice being to extract individual items of letterpress from collections. The status of the collection as a textual artefact, a supra-book in which a piece of ephemera had been preserved, who had made that book, as well as how that piece might relate to other texts in the same volume, tended to remain invisible, however. While the second edition of the STC, published in 1986, explicitly referred to 'all items bearing printed matter such as broadsides, small slips, and binding fragments', they were subsumed under 'the term "book"', largely because of the influence of Panizzi's 'Rules'.[11] The STC therefore managed the definitional problems of 'ephemera' by avoiding them altogether. The idea of the book in this sense also tended to exclude paper that bore visual images rather than verbal matter, meaning that an important dimension of many collections, their combination of engraved images and letterpress material, sometimes on the same sheet, was neglected.[12]

Another reason for the neglect of the phenomenon of the ephemera 'book' and what it contained was the idea of ephemerality as it developed in the nineteenth century, particularly its identification with popular culture and 'street literature'. The latter was shaped by Henry Mayhew's ethnography of street literature in *London Labour and the London Poor* (1851–2) and is also apparent in *Curiosities of Street Literature* from 1871,

---

[11] A. W. Pollard and G. R. Redgrave, *A Short-title Catalogue of Books Printed in England, Scotland, & Ireland and of English Books Printed Abroad, 1475–1640: A–H*, 2nd edn begun by W. A. Jackson and F. S. Ferguson, completed by Katharine F. Pantzer (London: The Bibliographical Society, 1986), xxi.

[12] See Sheila O'Connell, *The Popular Print in England 1550–1850* (London: British Museum, 1999).

an anthology of ballads, advertisements, and broadsides.[13] This idea of street literature, peddled by the lowest rank in the hierarchy of the print trade for the entertainment of the working class, informed concepts of 'popular' literature well into the twentieth century, reinforcing the idea of printed ephemera as the throwaway, trivial literature of the people. The category of 'cheap print', though more neutral, is nonetheless implicated in this binary model of popular versus elite culture and the idea of the 'cheap' ephemeral text as being opposed to the more durable 'expensive' book. Angela McShane has argued that there are 'problems with both "broadside," and indeed "ballad," as generic terms since they describe widely varying types of print product rather than literary types'.[14] 'The positioning of *all* broadside forms among the ranks of "popular" or even "cheap" print needs to be revised', she says. Not only did broadsides 'constitute the largest proportion of print products available on the market', challenging the primacy of the book, but they also took many diverse forms.[15] McShane makes a distinction between 'commissioned' broadsides such as proclamations or bills of mortality, government forms and petitions (coming under the category of job printing), and ballads, almanacs, poems, and also increasingly news-sheets, which were designed for the 'retail' market.

The ephemera 'books' of collectors in the seventeenth, eighteenth, and nineteenth centuries record the complexity of the category of 'cheap print' that McShane identifies. They reveal collectors to be interested not only in ephemeral texts for their own sake but also as part of a wider communication and associational network, an intrinsic and important element of the cycles of acquisition, circulation, and loss that were galvanising print and other economies in this period. Moreover, the collecting of ephemeral print was not simply analogous with book collecting. The very process of gathering together ephemeral texts, of making 'books' out of them, was to engage actively with ephemerality as a mode of knowledge-making. Bringing together such texts was to test the boundaries of 'useful' printed information and the possibility that there were indeed no limits to that information, as well as adumbrating the condition of 'absolute ephemerality', the loss or abjection of litter (as signified, for example, by Upcott's waste paper). Embedded within institutions (the British Museum) and households (Sir Joseph Banks's) that were engines and repositories of

---

[13] *Curiosities of Street Literature* (London: Reeves and Turner, 1871), i.
[14] Angela McShane, 'Ballads and Broadsides', in *The Oxford History of Popular Print Culture, Volume 1: Cheap Print in Britain and Ireland to 1660*, ed. Joad Raymond (Oxford: Oxford University Press, 2011), 341–62 (362).
[15] McShane, 'Ballads and Broadsides', 343.

Enlightenment science, ephemera collections such as those of Sir Hans Sloane and Sarah Sophia Banks were deeply implicated in Enlightenment aspirations to totalities of knowledge.[16] The rest of this chapter explores the genesis of the 'collection' in the seventeenth century, focusing on three crucial figures in the history of ephemera collecting – George Thomason, Anthony Wood, and Narcissus Luttrell. Their practices and fugitive legacies were to be of enduring significance in the development of ephemerology as the Enlightenment's 'other' science.

'The Method Is ... Tyme'

The outstanding collection of fugitive literature in British history was made by George Thomason (c. 1602–66), stationer and bookseller of St. Paul's Churchyard, who dealt mainly in prestigious and expensive folios for wealthy individuals and institutions such as the Universities of Oxford and Cambridge. Thomason was himself interested in material at the other end of the print spectrum: he used his income to acquire the pamphlets, newsbooks, and broadsides that were produced in significant quantities, particularly after the intensification of the crisis between king and parliament after 1641. Between 1640 and 1661 Thomason amassed a collection of more than 22,000 items that he had bound in 2,000 volumes.[17] His annotations, detailing the date of publication and purchase and sometimes giving information about their content, later proved invaluable to scholars in determining the chronology of the events of the Civil Wars and the Commonwealth period, vindicating Thomason's motto for the collection: 'Actions yt may be presidents to posteritie, ought to have their recordes, & merit a carefull preseruation'.[18]

Thomason's collection is now known as the 'Thomason tracts' referring to the preponderance within it of the kind of document described variously as 'tracts', 'pamphlets', 'libels' or 'small' or 'stitched books'. Joad Raymond has traced the derivation of the term 'pamphlet' to a fifteenth-century English adaptation of the *'Pamphilius seu de Amore'*, a form of Latin amatory verse: 'pamphlet' came to signify a small book or

---

[16] For Sir Hans Sloane's collections of ephemera see Giles Mandelbrote, 'Sloane and the Preservation of Printed Ephemera', in *Libraries Origins within the Library: The of the British Library's Printed Collections*, eds. Giles Mandelbrote and Barry Taylor (London: British Library, 2009), 146–68.

[17] See Michael Mendle, 'George Thomason's Intentions', in *Libraries within the Library: The Origins of the British Library's Printed Collections*, eds. Giles Mandelbrote and Barry Taylor (London: British Library, 2009): 171–86 (171).

[18] Quoted in Mendle, 'George Thomason's Intentions', 172 n. 8.

slight work which was not substantial enough to constitute a book.[19] By the sixteenth century, 'pamphlet' was linked with texts that, according to Raymond, were 'small, insignificant, ephemeral, disposable, untrustworthy, unruly, noisy, deceitful, poorly printed, addictive, a waste of time'.[20] 'Libel' had a similar, if less complex, semantic trajectory: derived from the diminutive of 'liber', 'libels' were invectives or satires on individuals and topical events. Libel had a primarily generic meaning taking a number of forms, including ballads and poetry, and ranging in format from broadsides to scribal publication.[21] Sometimes used interchangeably with 'pamphlet', 'libel' illustrates the fluidity and imprecision with which this kind of print was defined, reflecting the dynamics of a rapidly evolving print marketplace and complex intersecting literacies and reading publics. The other cognate term, tracts, deriving from treatise or tractate, meaning a working or handling of a particular subject, later came to signify a particular kind of pamphlet, used by religious or political groups to disseminate doctrine or propaganda.[22] 'Tracts' connoted a seriousness of purpose that was lacking in the etymological history of pamphlet, particularly the feminised associations of the latter with littleness, the trivial, and the inconsequential.

The label for this kind of literature eclipsed by the terms tract, libel, and pamphlet was the 'small' or 'stitched book', a book trade term that was adopted more widely in the seventeenth century. A stitched book was one that was bound by loose thread (or strips of leather): a quarto stitched book, for example, could vary in size from eight pages (one folded single sheet) to a collation of such folded sheets up to ninety-six pages (the maximum allowed by the Stamp Act of 1712).[23] Formal binding of a stitched book, either individually or as part of a collected volume, was thus the work of the binder at the behest of the purchaser. Individual numbers of periodicals and serial publications were also produced as 'stitched books', sometimes also with paper wrappers. After the 1730s these wrappers began to be used by booksellers as a form of advertising, the Proposals for *The Harleian Miscellany*, as we have seen, being published in this way. The covering of small books or pamphlets with such wrappers created layers of ephemerality, the pamphlet being enclosed in a

---

[19] Joad Raymond, *Pamphlets and Pamphleteering in Early Modern Britain* (Cambridge, UK: Cambridge University Press, 2003) 7.
[20] Raymond, *Pamphlets*, 10.   [21] Raymond, *Pamphlets*, 20.
[22] For the religious tract as a dominant form of print in the Victorian period see Leah Price, *How to Do Things with Books in Victorian Britain* (Princeton, NJ: Princeton University Press, 2012).
[23] Raymond, *Pamphlets*, 82.

paper which was an ephemeral text in its own right and more (or less) disposable than what it contained. The term 'stitched book' therefore had a different discursive value from 'pamphlet', 'libel', or 'tract': not only did it suggest that such texts were capable of constituting 'books', but in its emphasis on the labour that held these pages together – the stabbing and sewing together of paper – it drew attention to book making as a material process and to the printed sheet as the primary unit from which the book was created.[24] It thereby stressed the origins of the text in the print shop rather than the bookseller's.

Before being sent to the binder, multiple stitched books could be gathered, more or less systematically, in 'bundles', a term which came to stand for an interim state of organisation between purchase and formal binding. These clusters or piles of stitched books not only gave these texts a powerful material presence in small early modern rooms or closets: they also signified a method of organising them that was more provisional and less durable than binding. As Michael Mendle argues in relation to the Thomason tracts, binding 'froze a pamphlet's context. Bundles could be shuffled, loose tracts finding new mates like so many file cards' (and also, possibly, becoming lost or liable to destruction as rubbish).[25] By the eighteenth century, 'bundle' had become an established category in library sale catalogues. A 1735 sale catalogue of the library of Jonathan Swift, for example, devoted a section to his 'Bundle of PAMPHLETS', listing seventeen lots in folio, quarto and octavo, some representing multiple 'Bundles'.[26] The persistence of the term, and the market for such material, is apparent in the auction in November 1797 of the library of an anonymous 'country gentleman', consisting of books, prints and 'about 500 Volumes of Tracts ... in Quarto and Octavo' and 'a large Quantity of Pamphlets'. Many of the latter were in bundles and 'parcels' (an alternative term for bundle), including 'A LARGE bundle of old Newspapers', 'One Hundred Political Pamphlets, 2 bundles', and 'Eight dozen and a-half of Plays, octavos and twelves, 3 bundles'. The descriptions in this catalogue of the gentleman's collections are tantalisingly vague – 'A small Parcel, Historical, &c. ... A ditto, Theatrical' – indicating the resistance of the category of bundle to even elementary bibliographical description, which was both frustrating and appealing to the curious

---

[24] For a seminal account of the sheet see Graham Pollard, 'Notes on the Size of the Sheet', *The Library*, ser. 4, 22:2–3 (1941): 105–37.

[25] Mendle, 'George Thomason's Intentions', 177; see also Jason Peacey, *Print and Politics in the English Revolution* (Cambridge, UK: Cambridge University Press, 2013), 35–6.

[26] *A Catalogue of Books, The Library of the late Rev. Dr. Swift* (Dublin: printed for George Faulkner, 1745), 30.

buyer.[27] The bundle held out the promise of the unknown, as well as the opportunity of disaggregation, reconstitution, or even disposal of it as rubbish. The peculiar status of the bundle is highlighted in Thomas Frognall Dibdin's description in *Bibliomania* of the 1682 sale catalogue of the library of Richard Smith as containing some curious volumes 'huddled together in one list ... classed under the provoking running title of "*Bundles of Books,*" or "*Bundles of stitcht Books!*"': the bundle could be both coy and vulnerable, cowering before the depredations of the bibliophile, as well as 'provoking' his desire.[28]

George Thomason was careful that his bundles and parcels were systematised through the process of binding. He grouped his papers according to size, rather than by type or genre – though acts and ordinances were distinguished from the rest as a special category – and in the chronological sequence of internal dates in documents or when he had acquired them.[29] The bound collection, and the twelve-volume manuscript catalogue which Thomason made to accompany it, were designed to fix and objectify such print, virtually as it was appearing on the streets of London – it has been estimated that he collected 76.3 per cent of the newsbooks published in the 1640s and 1650s.[30] His 'Method', as he declared in the prefatory statement of his Catalogue was 'Tyme', meaning that within particular size categories a wide variety of kinds of single-sheet and pamphlet literature was collated, including newsbooks and pamphlets relating to political events but also other kinds of 'news', of sensational murders, for example, unusual weather events or wondrous natural occurrences, such as the appearance and killing of 'a great Whale' in the river Thames at Greenwich in 1658.[31]

In addition to single sheets and the 'stitched books' of poetry, play-books, and sermons, Thomason also accumulated and organised under the rubric of 'Tyme' the texts that promoted and sustained London's developing associational culture – particularly printed invitations that he

---

[27] *Books, Prints, Drawings, Manuscripts, &c. A Catalogue of the Genuine Library of Books, ... of a Gentleman, Deceased* (London: Thomas King, 1797).
[28] T. F. Dibdin, *Bibliomania; or Book Madness* (London: Printed for the author, 1811), 400. For Smith's collecting see Peacey, *Print and Politics*, 36–7.
[29] Mendle, 'George Thomason's Intentions', 178.   [30] Raymond, *Pamphlets*, 193.
[31] Quoted in Mendle, 'George Thomason's Intentions', 178; Anon., *Londons Wonder: Being a Most True and positive relation of the taking and killing of a great Whale neer to Greenwich* ... (London: Francis Grove, 1658), annotated by Thomason 'June' and 'June 6.' Wing (2nd edn)/ L2957, Thomason/ E.2134 [2], Early English Books Online. For the contemporary interest in 'wonders' see Lorraine Daston and Katharine Park, *Wonders and the Order of Nature, 1150–1750* (London: Zone Books, 2001).

labelled 'tickets'.[32] Jason Peacey has noted the importance of the crises of the 1640s for the emergence of ephemeral print as an 'organisation tool'. Tickets, produced in multiple copies on a single sheet 'offered a cheap and efficient means of conveying messages to multiple recipients simultaneously, and ... *this simultaneity* had profound consequences for the everyday world of politics and administration'.[33] The material collected by Thomason encompassed the full spectrum of the single-sheet and pamphlet paper economy, ranging from what McShane terms the 'retail' broadside to 'commissioned' broadsides in the form of official proclamations or tickets. As Michael Mendle suggests, the idea of the street represented by the Thomason tracts was not primarily identified with the lower orders out of doors but rather with an emerging ideology of the public sphere as a (quotidian) contact zone, the '*accidental* democracy of the public thoroughfare' where 'the great (rarely), the middling and humble go on their way, pass by each other, occasionally jostle. Next day it happens all over again'.[34] Thomason's collecting therefore identified a domain, the street, and a form of social experience – the accidental, quotidian, and often unconscious collectivity of commercial society in its multiple iterations – which would later acquire the rubric of 'everyday life'.

In collecting the fugitive literature of the 1640s–60s in its widest sense, Thomason established patterns of ephemera collecting which were to be enduring ones. His collection exemplified an ambition to comprehensiveness and a willingness to interleave a wide variety of texts and genres – newsbooks and broadsides, ballads, plays and poetry, and more utilitarian forms of print such as tickets. The kinds of material which later collectors amassed were remarkably consistent with Thomason's project, making it foundational for modern ephemerology. The collection is also notable for the concern with periodicity and synchronicity, of putting such texts in 'Tyme', and conversely how they created a sense of being in 'Tyme'. The significance of the Thomason collection is therefore threefold: firstly, in drawing attention to the existence and the content of the texts it contained; secondly, in creating an archive for the future, represented by the motto, 'Actions yt may be presidents to posteritie, ought to have their recordes, & merit a carefull preseruation'; and thirdly, by archiving an

---

[32] For an example of a ticket collected by Thomason see Anon, 'It is thought fit by divers persons of quality, who met on Friday last at *Scriveners Hall*, to advise how just debts may be secured ... to the Parliament.... This 16 of August, 1644' [London: 1644], Wing (2nd edn)/ I1088, Thomason E.6 [18], Early English Books Online.
[33] Peacey, *Print and Public Politics*, 334.
[34] Mendle, 'George Thomason's Intentions', 173 (my emphasis).

event in the history of the print media (arguably the first such event). In so far as Thomason was himself a participant, the media event of the 1640s–60s had the potential to figure new forms of subjectivity. The collecting of such material, and in particular, the practice of annotation, could function as a kind of autobiography – a putting of oneself in 'Tyme' – that rendered subjectivity diffuse and decentred, virtually invisible. The affective personal history that the collection represented was closely bound up – literally so in the sense of Thomason's interest in binding his material – with the history of the times in which it was made. He preserved many of the new 'diurnal' publications that, as Stuart Sherman argues, were reconfiguring a consciousness of time and the boundaries of the reading nation.[35] The collection contained a number of editions of a five-page weekly news-sheet entitled *The Brittish Mercury, or the Welch Diurnall* of 1643 *Communicating remarkable* Intelligences, *and true Newes to awle the whole Kingdom*.[36] As Daniel Woolf argues, the emergence of 'News' as a media and cultural phenomenon had 'definitively established the present as a zone of activity, as narratable as the past, but distinguishable from it . . . [The new present] thereby constructed a public space within which events could enjoy their ephemeral life before slipping into the maw of history'.[37]

Though he is concerned more with the idea of the 'present' than with the ephemeral, Woolf suggests that the 'new present' and what later became defined as the ephemeral came into being at the same time and that the two concepts are mutually constitutive. Ephemerality is thus in Woolf's formulation a precondition of 'history', a 'zone of activity', a 'public space', or 'life' that history needs to consume in order to exist. The efforts of men such as Thomason exemplified 'news' or the new sense

---

[35] Sherman, *Telling the Time*.
[36] *Mercurius cambro-Britannus, the Brittish Mercury, or, The Welch diurnall communicating remarkable* Intelligences *and true Newes to awle the whole kingdome* . . . no. 4 (11–20. November 1643), London: Bernard Alsop, 1643. Thomason/ 13.E.76 [14], Early English Books Online. See also Michael Mendle, 'News and the Pamphlet Culture of Mid-Seventeenth Century England', in *The Politics of Information in Early Modern Europe*, eds. Brendan Dooley and Sabrina A. Baron (London: Routledge, 2001): 57–79, in which Mendle writes that Thomason 'declared war on the ephemerality of little news pamphlets' (59).
[37] Daniel Woolf, 'News, History and the Construction of the Present in Early Modern England', in *The Politics of Information in Early Modern Europe*, eds. Brendan Dooley and Sabrina A. Baron (London: Routledge, 2001): 80–118 (98). For an influential account of time and *neue zeit* in particular as historical concepts or *Begriffsgeschichte* see Reinhart Koselleck, *Futures Past: On the Semantics of Historical Time*, trans. Keith Tribe (New York: Columbia University Press, 1985). Ideas of the ephemeral object and of ephemerality in general are crucial historical concepts of modernity, not often specifically interrogated in the work of Koselleck and others, e.g. François Hartog, *Regimes of Historicity: Presentism and Experiences of Time*, trans. Saskia Brown (New York: Columbia University Press, 2015).

of the present as one such 'zone of activity', suggesting that ephemerality was both a textual phenomenon and a 'zone' or practice, a way of performatively enunciating for seventeenth-century society this new sense of the present, its daily-ness and periodicity. This sense of presentness, of resistance to the 'maw' of history is most apparent in texts which, rather than being descriptive of the present in the manner of the news-sheet, were directly instrumental in its enactment. Such texts were tokens of sociability such as tickets, deeply embedded in the eventfulness of a particular social occasion. The presence of tickets in the Thomason collection is a sign of their emerging importance to the new 'present' which seventeenth-century print had brought so powerfully into being. It is important to note though that Woolf (and Mendle) are using 'ephemeral' anachronistically, in the senses that it acquired later in the eighteenth century and which Thomason would not necessarily have understood: rather than preserving a knowledge that was destined for or deserved to be lost, his diurnal historiography was designed for 'posteritie' and for what others would make of it. In other words, it was not supposed to die and would never, as indeed has been the case, be truly ephemeral.

'This I found': Anthony Wood as Ephemera Collector

Thomason's interest in fugitive print was not exceptional. Another Londoner, the Puritan wood-turner, Nehemiah Wallington (1598–1658) guiltily spent his hard-earned income on 'littel pamflets of weekly news', while the son of a printer, William Miller, was famous for his vast collection of 'Papers & Pamphlets of All Sorts'.[38] Unlike the Thomason tracts Miller's collection did not survive and was dispersed in a number of sales in the 1690s. None of these people had public eminence or status, as was also the case with another important collector, Anthony Wood (1632–95). Wood (or à Wood, as he styled himself after 1660) was born to a family with property interests in Oxford: after graduating from Merton College in 1655 he established himself as the chronicler of the university and the town. He produced a history of the university, *Historia et Antiquitates Universitatis Oxford*, in 1674 and a collection of biographies

---

[38] Nehemiah Wallington, *The Notebooks of Nehemiah Wallington, 1618–1654: A Selection*, ed. David Booy (Aldershot: Ashgate, 2007), 156; Mendle, 'News and the Pamphlet Culture', 79 n.79. On pamphlet collecting see also Michael Mendle, 'Preserving the Ephemeral: Reading, Collecting and the Pamphlet Culture of Seventeenth-Century England', in *Books and Readers in Early Modern England: Material Studies*, eds. Jennifer Anderson and Elizabeth Sauer (Philadelphia: University of Pennsylvania Press, 2002): 201–16; also Peacey, *Print and Politics*, 38.

of Oxford men, the *Athenae Oxoniensis* (1691–2), the first biographical dictionary and a precursor of the *Dictionary of National Biography*. Wood never held an official position in the university, funding his researches by means of his personal resources – an annual income of around forty pounds – limited patronage, and subscriptions to his publishing projects.[39] Though Wood characterised himself as an outsider, 'as 'twere dead to the world, and utterly unknown in person to the generality of scholars in Oxon.', he was also sociable, a denizen of the new coffeehouses and a patron of musical evenings in local taverns.[40]

The 'home' of Wood's collections consisted of two rooms in the upper storey of the family property overlooking Merton College that he fashioned into his own personal space, combining the functions of living area, library, and study.[41] The importance of spatiality in the nascent ephemerology of the seventeenth century is illuminated by Jacques Derrida's emphasis on archivisation as entailing a 'domiciliation' or 'house arrest' where archives 'take place' (in the dual sense of a performative event and as occupying a space).[42] (Derrida's idea of 'house arrest' recalls Samuel Johnson's promotion of the *Harleian Miscellany* as 'certain residence' for small pamphlets that might otherwise take flight.) For Derrida, the archive, related to the Greek word *arkheion*, the residence of the superior magistrates or 'archons' who were custodians of the documents of the state, has the dual purpose of the space 'where things commence – physical, historical, or ontological principle' and the space from which authority or the law is practiced or 'takes place'. As a place of nomological authority, the archive must shelter itself *from* 'the memory which it shelters: which comes down to saying that it also forgets it' (2). What it mainly 'forgets' is the 'principle' of 'commencement', the zone at which knowledge begins to

---

[39] Nicolas K. Kiessling, *The Library of Anthony Wood* (Oxford: Oxford Bibliographical Society, 2002), xv; a monumental work that records all the letterpress material acquired by Wood. Subsequent footnote references note the page number, in some cases preceded by the item number. See also [Wood], *The Life and Times of Anthony Wood, Antiquary, of Oxford 1632–1695, Described by Himself*, ed. Andrew Clark, 5 vols. (Oxford: Clarendon Press, 1891).
[40] Kiessling, *Library*, xiv.   [41] Kiessling, *Library*, xxii.
[42] Jacques Derrida, *Archive Fever: A Freudian Impression*, trans. Eric Prenowitz (Chicago: University of Chicago Press, 1996), 2; subsequent page references in parentheses in text. Commentary on and application of Derrida's arguments in *Archive Fever* are too extensive to detail but see Carolyn Steedman, *Dust: The Archive and Cultural History* (New Brunswick, NJ: Rutgers University Press, 2002) and Rebecca Schneider's *Performing Remains*, especially her reading of Derrida as suggesting that: 'archives are, first and foremost *theatres* for repertoires of preservation, leaning toward and into a promise of the coming "liveness" of encounter': *Performing Remains. Art and War in Times of Theatrical Reenactment* (Abingdon: Routledge, 2011), 109. I would argue that 'leaning toward' liveness is most apparent in the form of the archiving of ephemera.

'take place', 'the originary, the first, the principial, [*sic*] the primitive' (2). Another way of envisaging this zone might be as the space occupied by the inchoate, momentary, and quotidian experience to which knowledge is always relational: in other words, the absolute ephemeral or, in Blanchot's terms, 'the corrosive force of human anonymity' that is the everyday.[43]

This tension between the idea of the archive as where the beginning of knowledge takes place, in resistance to the absolute ephemeral, and a place from which authority is asserted, is demonstrated by the history of these early ephemerologists. As private men Anthony Wood and George Thomason were lacking in the status and public recognition of the *arkheion*. Wood's two rooms were overshadowed by other, more authoritative archive houses, namely Merton College and the Bodleian Library. (The relationship between Wood's space and these more public institutions anticipates the status of another set of rooms housing ephemeral material, John Johnson's Sanctuary of Printing, located unofficially as part of the printery of the University of Oxford in a tangential relationship to the institution that would eventually house it, the Bodleian Library.) Lacking the authority to constitute the law, because of the kind of document it gathers together, the ephemera archive thus tends to be a domicile within a domicile, a substrate of a substrate. However foundational in the development of institutions of knowledge, such as the British Museum and the British Library, such collections never become fully integrated and thus never fully visible because of their connection to the 'memory' of what has to be forgotten – that is, the place where knowledge begins.

Wood's two rooms were the centre of and repository for a wide range of projects: he combined the roles of antiquarian, urban historian, topographer, biographer, bibliographer, diarist, and autobiographer. His collection, like the Thomason tracts, reflects the diversity of seventeenth-century fugitive literature, ranging from official proclamations to penny ballads sold by hawkers in the street, and also the variety of formats, including the 'stitched book' and the single sheet (of various sizes). Wood amassed pamphlets, newsbooks, and broadsides concerning contemporary political events, parliament and government, affairs in Ireland, and philosophical and theological debate, including sermons. He also collected almanacs and a substantial number of ballads (some of which were topical, thereby constituting a variety of news). Wood's attention to ballads was part of a wider interest in literature, both elite and popular, including plays, elegies, prose romances, jest books, garlands, and riddles. In addition to what

---

[43] Blanchot and Hanson, 'Everyday Speech', 19.

would later be termed as handbills advertising quack medicine, he collected reports of murders, trials and executions, prophecies, and marvellous phenomena such as the appearance of the whale in the river Thames in 1658, as also recorded by George Thomason. Wood's library contains a copy of the pamphlet about the event, entitled *Londons Wonder*, which was also owned by Thomason.[44] Ephemeral 'wonders' sometimes intersected with Wood's interest in public amusements, such as an octavo broadside proclaiming the exhibition of 'The Tall *Indian*-KING' at Mr 'Cartors' in Oxford for the admission price of 3d (Figure 2).[45] Wood collected pamphlets on tobacco, smoking, card playing, angling, archery, and on coffee and coffeehouses. His library reveals the importance of the coffeehouse not only as a meeting place but also as a centre for the distribution of print, particularly from London: he picked up a number of items from coffeehouses, including newsbooks, single-sheet publications, and most notably, catalogues for book sales and auctions and book prospectuses, many of which were distributed for free in coffeehouses as a form of advertisement.[46]

Wood also purchased a number of such catalogues, including a parchment copy of the catalogue of the 'famous collection of papers and pamphlets' of William Miller, for which he paid '1s.' on 10 May 1695, that is, very near the end of Wood's own life, to one 'Harry Clement'.[47] Wood's possession of this catalogue suggests that he was aware that he was not alone in his interest in fugitive print. The first catalogue of the sale of a private library, that of Lazarus Seaman, (which Wood also possessed), was published in London soon after the auction itself in 1676.[48] The importance within ephemera collecting of the genre of the sale catalogue, and also of single-sheet book prospectuses, was to be an enduring one. Such

[44] Kiessling, *Library*, no. 4225, 393. [45] Kiessling, *Library*, no. 3754, 350.
[46] Kiessling, *Library*, xix n. 23. On the early Enlightenment coffeehouse as part of the information network of print see Joad Raymond, 'The Newspaper, Public Opinion, and the Public Sphere in the Seventeenth Century', in *News, Newspapers and Society in Early Modern Britain*, ed. Joad Raymond (London: Frank Cass, 1959), 109–40; Steven Pincus, '"Coffee Politicians Does Create": Coffee-Houses and Restoration Political Culture', *Journal of Modern History*, 67 (1995): 807–34; Markman Ellis, 'Coffee-House Libraries in Mid-Eighteenth-Century London', *The Library*, ser. 7, 10:1 (2009), 3–40.
[47] Kiessling, *Library*, no. 1566, 148.
[48] *Catalogus variorum & insignium librorum instructissimae bibliothecae clarissimi doctissimiq viri Lazari Seaman, S.T.D. quorum auctio habebitur Londini in aedibus defuncti in area & viculo Warwicensi Octobris ultimo / cura Gulielmi Cooper*. Londini: Apud Ed Brewster & Guil. Cooper, 1676. Wing/S2173, Early English Books Online. Wood's copy at Kiessling, *Library*, no. 1614, 153–4. See also Gillian Russell, 'The Reading Communities of Collecting: Sale Catalogues, Sociability and Ephemerality, 1676–1862', *Australian Literary Studies*, 29:3 (2014), 15–27.

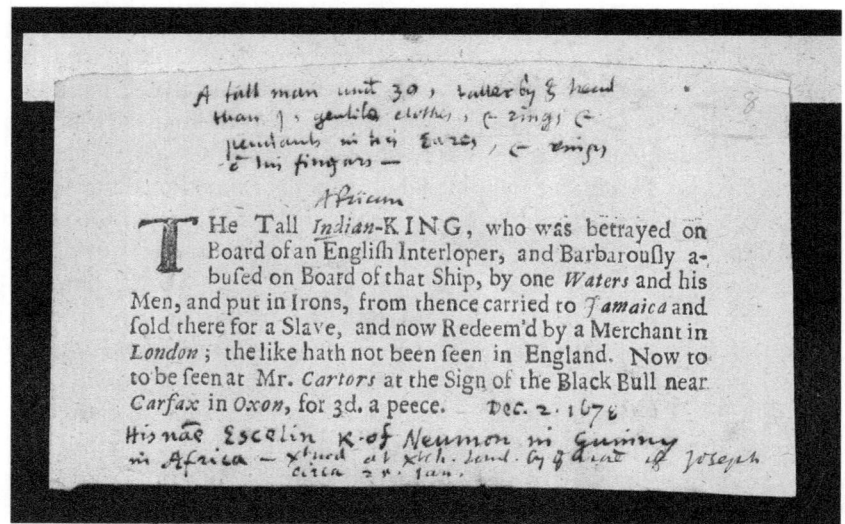

Figure 2 'The Tall *Indian*-King', handbill advertisement with annotations by Anthony Wood 1678.
The Bodleian Libraries, The University of Oxford. MS. Wood Diaries 16. Fol. 8r.

texts continue to be regarded and classified by librarians as ephemera, their main role being as sources of bibliographical information, as indeed is likely to have been their chief significance for collectors such as Wood.[49] Sale catalogues were the only means of finding out about the existence of books and fugitive literature, their possible obtainability, and their provenance in terms of the history of their previous ownership. But catalogues were also capable of being read for purposes other than the acquisition of bibliographic 'facts', purposes such as undirected curiosity and pleasure, such as becoming familiar with another person's possessions or interests, or tracking the history of an item's ownership. Sale catalogues also documented the sociability of book collecting, firstly by advertising an event in a particular place, making them analogous to tickets or playbills (hence their distribution for free in the coffeehouses of London and Oxford), and secondly as records or souvenirs of that event. Catalogues were thus a means of both real and virtual participation in the homosocial networks being created and sustained by the print trade. Anthony Wood notes that a

---

[49] See e.g. G. Thomas Tanselle, 'Some Thoughts on Catalogues', *The Papers of the Bibliographical Society of America*, 102:4 (2008), 573–80.

particular catalogue, the *Bibliotheca Oweniana* (1684) was 'Given to me by Hen. Cruttenden 1684 2 May', thereby inscribing the text with another layer of sociable (and possibly affective) meaning.[50] By collecting numerous examples of these texts, men such as Wood were able to contextualise their own practices in relation to those of others, creating a virtual community that could affirm for them that they were not alone.

The potential of the sale catalogue to be a testimony of a life's collecting was such that it later became a focus of Romantic-period bibliomaniacs, such as Thomas Frognall Dibdin. Book and ephemera collectors acquired catalogues in the knowledge that their own collecting – including those very catalogues – were likely to be publicised in the form of the catalogue after their death. An ephemeral text in its own right, such as the one for Miller's 'famous' collection of pamphlets, could be the only record that a collection had ever existed. The ephemeral status of the sale catalogue, its embeddedness and recirculation within other collections, therefore enacted, in a particularly acute way, the tension between loss and preservation, memory and forgetting, that characterised bookish knowledge as a whole.

The sale catalogue also played the important role of making printed ephemera bibliographically visible. Categories of description such as 'bundles', 'parcels', 'collectanea', or simply 'miscellaneous', recorded such collecting as a form of 'loose' book making. By grouping categories such as 'ballads', 'playbills', and 'pamphlets and tracts' together in one volume, sale catalogues also objectified the interconnections between ephemeral genres and their capacity to document associational culture as whole, a coherence subsequently lost in the stratification of 'elite' and 'popular', the distinction between literary and non-literary texts, and the failure to recognise texts such as advertisements or tickets as anything more than mere jobbing print. Sale catalogues were an important way in which, in Derridean terms, the topological dimension of the ephemera archive, the sense of it as constituting a space, both material and immaterial, could be defined: in buying William Miller's catalogue, for example, Wood was figuratively preserving the space in which Miller's 'famous papers' had been initially domiciled and authorised (conversely legitimating Wood's own two rooms in which the catalogue was housed, an acting of re-placing and re-incorporating Miller's library). The discursive housing of printed ephemera within the genre of the sale catalogue, a genre that was itself

---

[50] Kiessling, *Library*, no. 1582, 150. Henry Cruttenden was a printer in Oxford who gave Wood ten catalogues: Kiessling, *Library*, xviii n. 21.

fugitive, was crucial to the emergence of a literature of 'presentness' in the seventeenth century and afterwards. The sale catalogue helped to define a corpus of texts that resisted the 'maw' of more orthodox history to create a history of their own, a history of the performative present.

Wood had his bundles bound in relatively inexpensive pasteboard (often recording the cost of this and the name of the binder in the volume), indicating that the bound volumes were designed for practical use rather than display or pride.[51] He gave careful instructions to his binders, ensuring that the integrity of the format of his documents and especially his marginal or flyleaf annotations were retained. Wood went much further than Thomason in the practice of annotation. Above his copy of the broadside advertising the exhibition of the '*Indian*-KING' in Oxford, he added: 'A tall man, under 30, taller by the head than I, gentile clothes, & rings & pendants in his eares, & rings on his fingers –.' On the copy itself, Wood wrote 'African' over 'Indian' and below it: 'Dec. 2. 1678 [/] His name Escelin K. of Neumon in Guinny in Africa – Christned at Christ Ch. Lond. by the name of Joseph circa 25. Jan.'[52] Wood's annotations amounted to a virtual rewriting of this document. Its significance as a record of an ephemeral occasion and the existence of a particular individual is overlain by Wood's insistence on placing the Indian/African more concretely and specifically in time, as well as place. (In so far as Wood probably attended the show, had the opportunity to compare his height, and may have conversed with its subject, his annotations are also a kind of personal history). His multiple naming of the 'KING' in terms of his 'real' name and the name of 'Joseph' given to him on his christening in London, gestures towards the commanding or nomological power of a public archive, an effect which is also observable in Wood's comment on a ballad from 1660, 'The royal patient traveller. Or, the wonderful escape of ... King Charles', as 'Made by Hen. Jones an old Ballad singer of Oxon.'[53] In both cases, Wood's annotations add to the information contained in the documents, recreating the identities of figures who have been lost to history and complicating and deepening knowledge of the events to which they refer (as well as placing Wood himself as also being there). But in accentuating the sense of the presentness of this event, the annotations also intensify its ephemerality – the Indian/African King and Henry Jones remain lost, unknowable, and the nomological gesture of naming is ultimately attenuated. Some of the documents collected by Wood are

[51] Kiessling, *Library*, xxvii.   [52] Kiessling, *Library*, no. 3754, 350.
[53] Kiessling, *Library*, no. 579, 54.

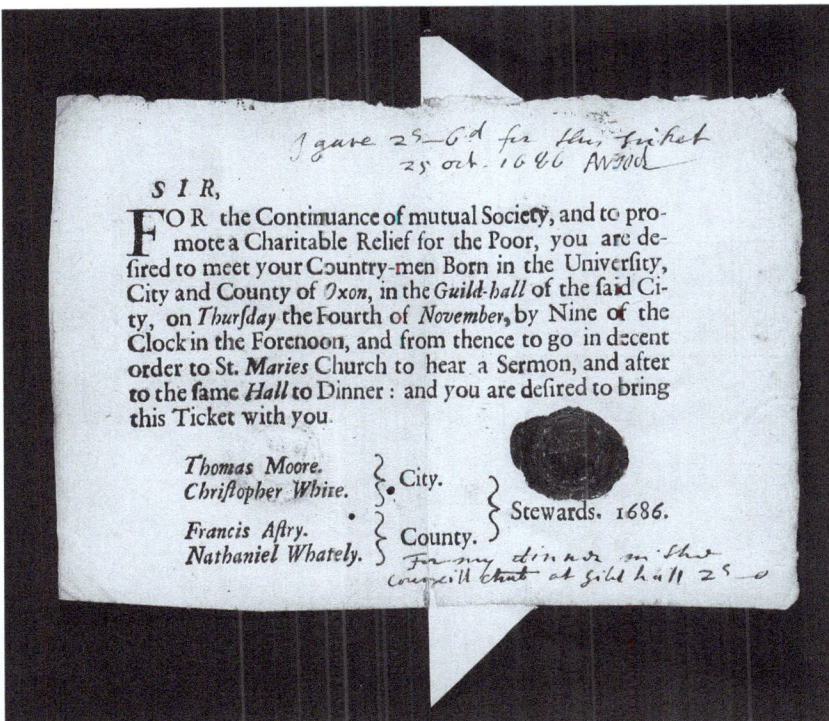

Figure 3 'Sir, FOR the Continuance of mutual Society', ticket with annotations by Anthony Wood 1686.
The Bodleian Libraries, The University of Oxford. MS. Wood Diaries 30, Item 61

therefore palimpsestically ephemeral, his annotations making them more ephemeral than they were to start with.

Like the Thomason tracts, Wood's library contained tickets for social occasions, specifically two for charitable dinners, one dating from 1662 and another from 1686. On the latter Wood wrote: 'I gave 2s-6d for this Ticket 25 Oct. 1686. AWood' and 'For my dinner in the council chamber at gild hall 2s-0' (Figures 3 and 4).[54] It is not clear if Wood attended the 1662 feast – his emphatic inscription on the 1686 ticket suggest that he probably had not. The unmarked 1662 ticket is important, however, in contextualising the later example, suggesting the history of Oxford civic sociability in which Wood asserted a socially symbolic as well

[54] Kiessling, *Library*, no. 5099, 473; no. 5100, 473–4.

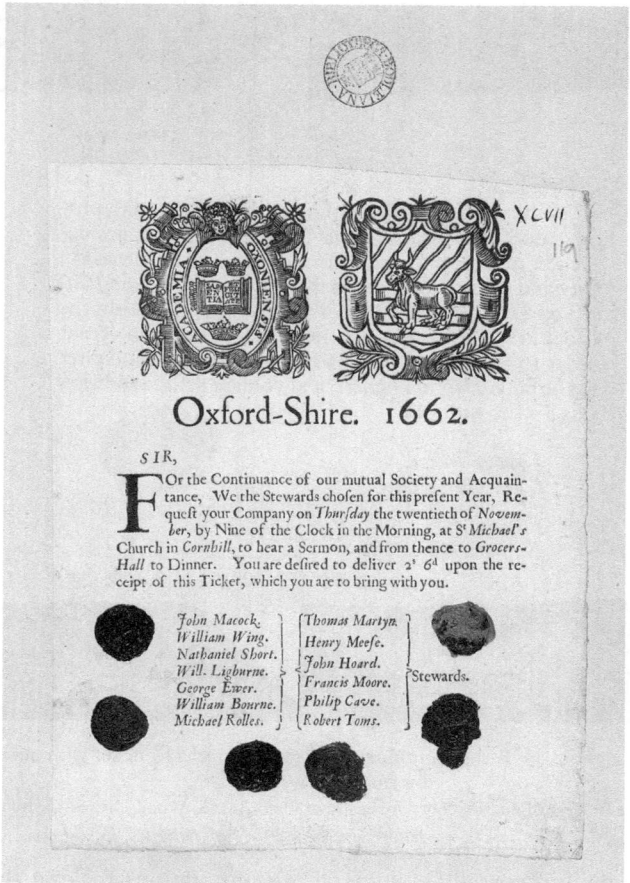

Figure 4 'Oxford-Shire. 1662.', ticket.
The Bodleian Libraries, The University of Oxford. Wood 276 B (119), Item 119

as a literal place – he had actually been at the event which the ticket both facilitated and commemorated. The ticket objectified and realised Wood's presence in Oxford society in a way that the other texts he amassed did not. Wood's collecting therefore documented the importance of printed ephemera to the developing associational culture of the early Enlightenment. In some cases his interests could take him to the very limits of the domain of the document, as in the example of a broadside petition 'To the right honourable the house of commons assembled in parliament', which was printed for James Rossington. 'This I found', Wood wrote, 'in

Dr Lowers privy house 24 May 1675 in Bow Street, Lond.'⁵⁵ A later satirical print from 1745, 'Sawney in the Boghouse' which shows the walls of a privy decorated with broadsides, suggests the privy's importance as a site of what Addison would term 'accidental reading', and the proximity of single-sheet letterpress to corporeal waste and abjection (Figure 5).⁵⁶ Cut-up newspapers and other forms of waste paper were customarily used to wipe oneself after urination or defecation, until the invention of paper specifically dedicated to the purpose in the late nineteenth century.⁵⁷ Wood's acquisition of the Rossington petition and in particular his recording of how he found it anticipate Mr. Spectator's scavenging of the printed scrap and his sensitivity to the word in any paper form. Nicolas Kiessling's description of what Wood might have done with this bit of paper – he 'took it home with him, straightened it out and set it in a bundle of political pamphlets' – is evocative of what must have been Wood's constant practice, his careful, even loving, handling of even the most apparently inconsequential and debased paper documents.⁵⁸

Plot Catalogues and Frost Fairs

The interest in printed ephemera, represented by collectors such as Thomason, Wood, and William Miller, was such that when the Popish Plot developed in the late 1670s the book trade was ready for it. Claims made in September 1678 by Titus Oates of a conspiracy to assassinate Charles II and replace him with his Catholic brother James, Duke of York, caused widespread panic in the country. In May 1679 Charles II prorogued parliament, leading to the suspension of the Licensing Act that had been in force since 1662. The relaxation of censorship triggered a boom in all kinds of print, particularly cheap print, the most significant spike in the output of such literature since the 1640s. Between 1679 and 1681, when

---

⁵⁵ Kiessling, *Library*, xix. 'To the Right Honourable the House of Commons assembled in Parliament, the humble petition of James Rossington, Clarke' [London: 1675], Wing 92nd edn)/ R1995A, Early English Books Online. The record of this broadside on EEBO does not refer to Wood's annotation.
⁵⁶ 'Sawney in the Boghouse', BM Sat 2678, 1868-8-8-12385. For a discussion of this print in relation to the 'common privy' as a 'public sphere' see Mark Jenner, 'Sawney's Seat: The Social Imaginary of the London Bog-house c.1660–c.1800', in *Bellies, Bowels and Entrails in the Eighteenth Century*, eds. Rebecca Anne Barr, Sylvie Kleiman-Lafon, and Sophie Vasset (Manchester: Manchester University Press, 2018): 101–27 (116).
⁵⁷ Another cognate term for ephemeral paper rubbish, bumf, comes from the use of paper in toilets, i.e. bum fodder.
⁵⁸ Kiessling, *Library*, xix.

Figure 5 'Sawney in the Boghouse'. Etching 1745.
© The Trustees of the British Museum

the crisis subsided, it has been estimated that there was 'anything between six and twelve million publications in circulation'.[59] In September 1680 an enterprising bookseller, whose identity has not been established, published

[59] Adam Fox, 'Cheap Political Print and its Audience in Later Seventeenth Century London: The Case of Narcissus Luttrell's "Popish Plot" Collections', in *Scripta Volant, Verba Manent: Schriftkulturen in Europa zwischen 1500 und 1900*, eds. Alfred Messerli and Roger Chartier (Basel: Schwabe, 2007), 227–42 (229).

*A Compleat Catalogue of All the Stitch'd Books and Single Sheets Printed since the first Discovery of The Popish Plot.*⁶⁰ As the title makes clear, the catalogue was primarily concerned with the pamphlet and broadside literature relating to the crisis, the kind of material perfect for 'bundles' and the pleasures of sorting and binding. The enterprise must have been successful as the catalogue was followed by two single-volume 'continuations' and a compilation of all three volumes to form *A General Catalogue*, promoted on its title page as being 'Very useful for Gent. that make Collections'.⁶¹

The Popish Plot catalogues were significant in defining the existence and value of the category of political ephemera, that is occasional literature produced to the moment of a political event such as an election or a particular crisis. The catalogues differed from those of booksellers or auctioneers in that they were a bibliographical reference work rather than an advertisement. Moreover, the phenomenon that they were referencing – a political event and an event in print culture – was in 1680 an ongoing one, as the title page suggested by signalling the possibility of a 'continuation'. The catalogues defined the temporality of the Popish Plot as it was happening and without knowledge of how it would end: like the motto of the Thomason tracts, 'Actions yt may be presidents to posteritie, ought to have their recordes, & merit a carefull preseruation', they were oriented towards futurity. When the alarms caused by the Popish Plot abated, the catalogues, either gathered loosely in bundles or more fixed in binding, served to define what had immediately occurred. In the appeal to 'Gent. that make collections' the catalogues also suggest that late seventeenth-century booksellers were aware of the interest of collectors in printed ephemera as a distinct cultural phenomenon. Harold Love claims that the Popish Plot pamphlets and broadsides were 'meant from the start for accumulation and preservation'. He makes a distinction between these 'documents of record' and 'flimsier topical pamphlets that might be purchased from a mercury-vendor, stuffed into a pocket for casual reading in a coffeehouse or during quiet times in Westminster, and finally

---

⁶⁰ *A Compleat Catalogue of All the Stitch'd Books and Single Sheets Printed since the Discovery of The Popish Plot (September 1678) to January 1679/80. To which is Added a Catalogue of all His Majesties Proclamations, Speeches, and Declarations with the Orders of the King and Council and what Acts of Parliament have been Published since the Plot. The Continuation is Intended by the Publisher* (London: 1680), Wing/ 310:12, Early English Books Online.

⁶¹ *General Catalogue of All the Stitch'd Books and Single Sheets &c. Printed the Last Two Years, Commencing from the First Discovery of the Popish Plot (September, 1678) and Continued to Michaelmas Term, 1680* (London: J. R., 1680), Wing/ 1671:02, Early English Books Online.

sacrificed to domestic uses.'[62] It is noteworthy that in order to ascribe historical value to the ephemera associated with the Popish Plot, as a moment in the development of serious journalism and part of the genealogy of realist prose fiction, Love needs to define this value in relation to more truly 'ephemeral' and vividly realised scenes of reading and applications of texts, ultimately disappearing into the vacuity of 'domestic uses'. Anthony Wood's pride in texts taken from privies or coffeehouses suggests that for him at least the distinction between throwaway 'rubbish' and the more durable record was not so clear-cut.

Wood, not surprisingly, owned copies of the three iterations of the Popish Plot catalogues, the *Compleat Catalogue* and the two sequels to it. His copy of the *Compleat Catalogue* is extensively annotated, mainly identifying authors of texts.[63] Another prominent collector of printed ephemera who also owned copies of the Popish Plot catalogues was Narcissus Luttrell (1657–1732).[64] A lawyer by training, Luttrell had two brief periods as a member of Parliament in 1679–80 and 1690–5. He spent most of his time devoted to his collections which were the basis of a chronicle of contemporary events (published in 1857 as a *Brief Historical Relation of State Affairs*) and a parliamentary diary (which appeared in print in 1972). Adam Fox has described him as 'the great chronicler of the nation in the first age of party'.[65] Luttrell's income, derived from inherited wealth, was more substantial than Wood's and he moved in more elevated social circles, but he was not a man of public eminence or fame: his collecting, and the reputation associated with it, like Wood's and Thomason's, belonged essentially to the private sphere.

Luttrell's collecting is notable for his interest in illustrated broadsides, the Exclusion Crisis marking the emergence in British culture of a market for graphic satire and increasingly sophisticated modes of visual representation in paper media.[66] He owned (at least) two copies of prints

---

[62] Harold Love, 'The Look of News: Popish Plot Narratives, 1678–1680', in *The Cambridge History of the Book in Britain, Volume 4: 1557–1695*, eds. John Barnard and D. F. McKenzie (Cambridge, UK: Cambridge University Press, 2002), 652–6 (656).

[63] Kiessling, *Library*, 151, nos. 1599, 1600, 1601.

[64] See Henry Horwitz, 'Luttrell, Narcissus (1657–1732)', *Oxford Dictionary of National Biography*, Oxford University Press, 2004; online edn, January 2008 [www.oxforddnb.com/view/article/17226, accessed 6 January 2017].

[65] Fox, 'Cheap Political Print', 233; see also James M. Osborn, 'Reflections on Narcissus Luttrell', *The Book Collector*, 6 (1957), 15–27.

[66] See M. Dorothy George, *English Political Caricature to 1792*, 2 vols. (Oxford: Clarendon Press, 1959), 52–4; Antony Griffiths, *The Print in Stuart Britain 1603–1689* (London: British Museum Press, 1998), 280–305; Joseph Monteyne, *The Printed Image in Early Modern London: Urban Space, Visual Representation, and Social Exchange* (Aldershot: Ashgate, 2007).

depicting a procession and effigy burning of the pope in 1679 and 1680, customarily performed in November on the anniversary of Elizabeth I's coronation. Luttrell's annotations of these broadsides that date his purchase to just two weeks after the processions are consistent with the practice of Thomason and Wood of placing such texts 'in time'.[67] As Joseph Monteyne notes, these images are 'remarkably modern', not only in their topicality but also in marking the emergence of politics as a media spectacle, subject to highly self-conscious and manipulative forms of textual and visual representation.[68] Luttrell's interest in such print was not unique – the British Museum has a version of a broadside depicting the 1679 Mock Procession annotated by 'Sam. Sheafe' stating 'This I saw in Cheapside'.[69]

Luttrell's interest in 'news' extended beyond political controversy to include topical ballads, poetry, and also phenomenal occurrences in nature such as an exceptionally ferocious thunderstorm in the north of Ireland, the subject of a pamphlet, listed in the *Second Continuation* of the Popish Plot catalogues, which he bought for a penny, dating it to 13 July 1680.[70] He was also interested in an event that combined a wonder of nature with the power of print to create new forms of associational identity, particularly the sense of participation in and witnessing of the new present. This event was the freezing of the river Thames in the intense winter of 1683–4 and the erection on the river of a temporary fair and marketplace. The diarist John Evelyn described the frozen Thames as being 'planted with bothes in formal streetes, as in a Citty, or Continual faire, all sorts of Trade & shops furnished'. There was 'Bull-baiting, Horse & Coach races, Pupet-plays & interludes, Cookes & Tipling, & lewder places; so as it seem'd to be a bacchanalia, Triumph or Carnoval on Water'.[71] The frost fair combined commerce, recreation, and the carnivalesque in the manner of notable metropolitan fairs such as Bartholomew Fair, except that in this case the fair as an

---

[67] 'The Solemn Mock Procession of the Pope, Cardinalls, Jesuits, Fryers, Nuns exactly taken as they marcht through the Citty of London November the 17th, 1680', BM 1849,0315.67; BM 1871,1209.6509; both annotated by Luttrell '1 Dec 1680'.
[68] Monteyne, *Printed Image*, 157.
[69] 'The Solemn Mock Procession of the Pope, Cardinalls, Jesuits, Fryers &c. through the City of London, November the 17th, 1679', BM 1849,0315.69.
[70] 'A Relation of the extraordinary Thunder and Lightning which lately happened in the North of Ireland', *Second Continuation*, in *Narcissus Luttrell's Popish Plot Catalogues*, introd. F. C. Francis (Oxford: Basil Blackwell, 1956), 6
[71] John Evelyn, *The Diary of John Evelyn*, ed. Guy de la Bédoyère (Woodbridge: Boydell & Brewer, 1995), 267.

occasion of licence was accentuated, the very foundation on which the frost fair was based having the potential to dissolve and disappear in a few hours. The frost fair was thus to other fairs as the ticket or the paper from the privy were to the pamphlet or the newspaper. In its proximity to dissolution and annihilation, the frost fair enabled the apprehension and negotiation of the condition of absolute ephemerality that was constitutive of the new sense of the present.

Appropriately, print culture was implicated in the frost fair, not only through the reporting of it, but also in the frost fair as a site in which the power of the printing press to produce and define seventeenth-century society's sense of its eventfulness, its being in time, could be theatricalised as quintessentially ephemeral. The Restoration frost fair, particularly the one of 1683–4, was a print culture event: in the wake of the explosion in print and graphic media as a result of the Exclusion Crisis there were numerous illustrated broadsides, ballads, and poems produced about the fair.[72] A number of printers also located themselves on the ice itself, selling ballads and woodcuts and souvenir slips or tickets noting the names of the recipient, the printer, and the date and place of issue. Evelyn claimed that 'the People & ladyes tooke a fansy to have their names Printed, & the day & yeare set downe when printed on the Thames', a 'humour' that was so popular that one printer 'gained five pound a day, for printing a line onely, at six-pence a Name, besides what he gott by Ballads &c'.[73] Ephemeral print commemorated both the particular occasion of the frost fair and the power of print itself to suspend or momentarily 'freeze' time in the form of these souvenir tickets recording an individual's presence on the ice. Joseph Monteyne notes that these seventeenth-century 'selfies' were 'almost certainly the first such secular souvenir objects produced in early modern England', the names printed on them representing 'middle-class Londoners who have left little or no other trace in the historical record' (Figure 6).[74] Like Wood's tickets for the Oxfordshire feast, these souvenirs highlight the capacity of a specific kind of ephemeral genre – the ticket or advertisement – to enact and realise what was at stake in print's implication in developing forms of secular associational culture. Printed souvenirs such as the frost fair ticket enabled people to be 'there', in the actual ephemeral present – a visit to a frost fair on a cold February day in 1683/4 – and to also take their place in the archive as an ephemeral substrate.

[72] For an excellent account of the relationship between the Restoration frost fair and print culture see Monteyne, *Printed Image*, 215–57.
[73] Evelyn, *Diary*, 267.   [74] Monteyne, *Printed Image*, 237–8.

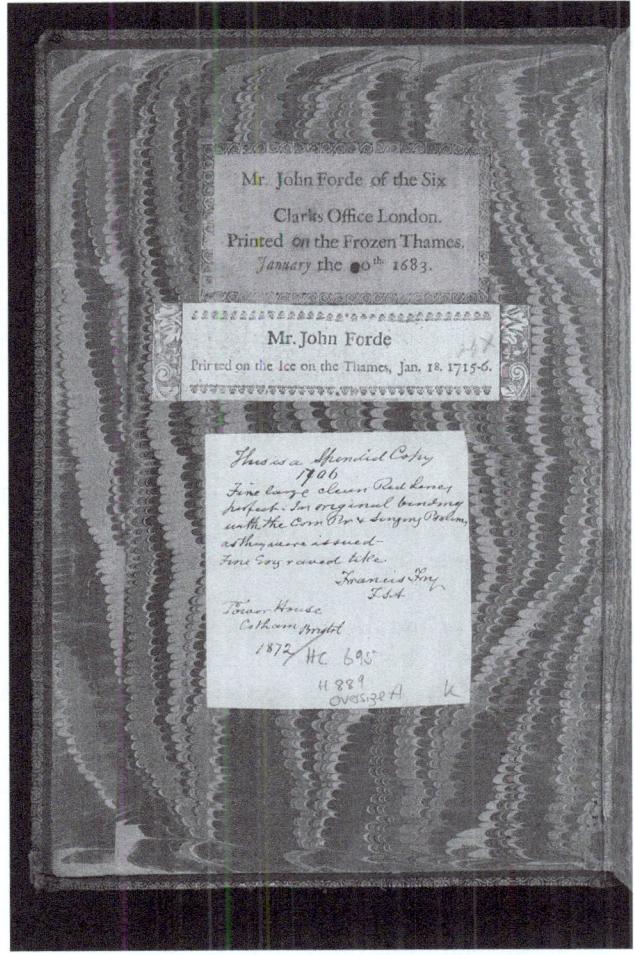

Figure 6 Frost fair tickets of John Forde which are pasted inside folio volume of 'The Holy Bible' (formerly owned by John Forde).
Permission University of Cambridge Library BSS.201 D06.2

The frost fair souvenir tickets record people like Henry Jones the Oxford ballad seller or the Indian king, who are there and also not there, shadowy and enduringly ephemeral.

Narcissus Luttrell recorded the great frost of 1683–4 in his *Brief Historical Relation of State Affairs*, noting its commencement around 15 December 1683, the freezing over of the Thames in January, and the construction of 'great many booths' upon the river.[75] In his entry for February 4th, he noted how the frozen Thames had become a virtual highway for wheeled vehicles with fifty coaches transporting people from the City to Westminster. 'I myself went in one', he comments, meaning that he witnessed and possibly bought the products of the 'three or four printing houses' which he reports as located on the frozen river.[76] On 5 February, the festivities suddenly came to an end as it 'rain'd and thaw'd much': though there was some renewal of the frost on the following few days 'there was much sunk, the tide overflowing it at high water'.[77] Luttrell's recording of the ephemerality of the Great Frost was closely related to his acquisition of the printed matter associated with it — illustrated broadsides such as 'Great BRITAINS Wonder or, LONDONS Admiration' (Figure 7) which he annotated with the price '3d.' and the date '9 Feb. 1683/84' commemorating both the date of purchase and the frost fair's demise.[78]

As mediated by print (and vice versa), the frost fair was analogous to the coffeehouse, which was included as one of the sites that this 'Citty' on ice was mimicking: a print in Luttrell's collection nominated one of the booths on the ice as the 'Royal Coffee House', the accompanying key declaring '*Coffee* and *Tea* and *Mum* doth here abound'. It also depicted the '*Printing Booth*, of wondrous Fame/ Because that each Man there did print his *Name*; / And sure, in former ages, ne're was found, / A Press to Print, where men so oft were dround.'[79] The frost fair was neither elite nor popular but openly accessible to those who could pay its price, indeed like cheap print itself. As an extreme form of the carnivalesque of the fair, subject to momentary evanescence, and fantastic, even magical, in its subversion of the order of nature, a river made solid, the frost fair signified the possibilities of the transformation of culture and knowledge which print and the new commercial spaces of sociability were effecting. Its ephemerality was intrinsic to the mixture of wonder and incomprehension with which contemporaries such as Luttrell and Evelyn tried to grasp its meaning: they did not quite know what to make of it

---

[75] Narcissus Luttrell, *A Brief Historical Relation of State Affairs from September 1678 to April 1714*, 6 vols. (Oxford: Oxford University Press, 1857), I: 294, 295.

[76] Luttrell, *Brief Historical Relation*, I: 297–8.   [77] Luttrell, *Brief Historical Relation*, I: 298.

[78] 'Great Britains Wonder or, Londons Admiration', BM no. 1880,1113.1769. Luttrell also owned the broadside, 'A True Description of Blanket Fair upon the River Thames, in the time of the great Frost', which he annotated '4d.' and '18 Feb. 1684/3': BM no. 1880,1113.1771.

[79] 'The True and Exact Representation of the Wonders upon the Water, during the Last Unparallel'd Frost', BM no. 1880, 1113.1770, annotated by Luttrell with '11 Feb. 1683/84'.

Figure 7 'Great BRITAINS Wonder: Or LONDONS Admiration' with annotations by Nicholas Luttrell (1684).
© The Trustees of the British Museum

and also what kind of society a frost fair might foreshadow, like the records which Thomason endorsed as meriting careful preservation. Luttrell's chronicling of the frost fair, both in his *Brief Relation* and through his collecting practices not only commemorated a particular event: he also made the frost fair paradigmatic of ephemerality as a condition of social transformation (and inevitable loss and forgetting) and foundational of modern ephemerology as a substrate of other, more visible, forms of historical knowledge.

Ephemeral Remains

One dimension of this ephemerology was the subsequent uses made of the collections of Thomason, Wood, and Luttrell, particularly their migration in the eighteenth century from the private sphere of the 'scene of domiciliation' to more public archives and spaces associated with the monarchy and the emerging nation state. Of the three, the fate of Wood's library is the most straightforward: in accordance with his will, his volumes and bundles were transferred to the newly established Ashmolean Museum and later went to the Bodleian Library in the 1860s.[80] George Thomason had similar ambitions for his collection of tracts: in his prefatory statement he expressed a wish that 'use may be made of them for the public' under the custodianship of Charles II. The text of this statement, including Thomason's declaration that his 'Method' was 'Tyme' was adapted for a prospectus advertising the collection published around 1685.[81] Appropriately, the first printed record of the existence of the collection, representing the beginning of its transition to the public sphere, was made in an ephemeral form and genre – the prospectus – that, like the myriad sheets it was advertising, also managed to survive. Thomason's hope that Charles II might purchase his collection was never realised and the tracts only came into royal hands when they were bought on behalf of George III by the Earl of Bute. They were deposited in the British Museum in 1762 as a gift to the nation and became known as the 'King's Pamphlets'. The tracts continued to have a powerful material presence in the Museum Library until late in the twentieth century. Michael Mendle notes how before microfilming and later, digitisation, the storage of the volumes in glass cases near the North Library enabled readers to see both the collection as a whole and the traces of Thomason's original design.[82]

One notable Romantic-period reader and handler of the Thomason tracts was William Godwin who used them for his six-volume *History of*

---

[80] See Nicolas Kiessling, 'The Library of Anthony Wood from 1681 to 1999', *Bodleian Library Record*, 16 (1999): 470–98.

[81] David Stoker, 'Disposing of George Thomason's Intractable Legacy 1664–1762, *The Library*, ser. 6, 14 (1992), 337–56 (340–1). The single sheet prospectus is: 'A Complete Collection of Books and Pamphlets Begun in the Year 1640. by the Special Command of King Charles I. of Blessed Memory' (London, 1685), Wing (CD-ROM, 1996)/ T995A, Early English Books Online.

[82] Mendle, 'George Thomason's Intentions', 185.

the Commonwealth of England (1824–8). In his advertisement to the third volume Godwin acknowledged his indebtedness to the 'collection of Commonwealth Tracts', which 'include almost every fugitive pamphlet or sheet printed during that period', ascribing it to the work of 'some industrious collector' – Thomason's role as 'author' of the collection would not be acknowledged until later in the nineteenth century.[83] Godwin compared the value of the 'Commonwealth Tracts' with the work of the Deputy Keeper of the State Paper Office, the forerunner of the Public Record Office, in organising the official records of the Long Parliament (1640–60) which, he claims, were previously in 'a state of absolute chaos'. He commended the Deputy Keeper, Robert Lemon, for 'causing to be bound up in volumes, to the amount of some hundreds, detached memoranda and single leaves of paper', to form an 'almost complete record of the pecuniary measures and financial proceedings of the Long Parliament'.[84] Lemon's practice, it is suggested, was consistent with that of his seventeenth-century precursor, the 'industrious' individual who meticulously marked on his fugitive sheets 'the day of the month on which it was bought, which is for the most part the very day of the publication'.[85] The difference between such single sheets and the barrage of noise and textuality that had so dismayed Godwin in 1792 was that the seventeenth-century equivalents of the handbill were, firstly, organised by Thomason, and then bound up in volumes and 'domiciled' in the State Paper Office: they were safely of the past rather than of the urgent, uncontrollable present. What Godwin described as the 'authenticity' of Thomason's method underpinned his own desire to produce a revisionary history of the Commonwealth, which he claims 'has uniformly furnished a theme for scurrility to the advocates of prerogative and despotism'.[86] One hundred and seventy-four years later, it was now time, Godwin argued, to make the English Civil Wars the 'province of genuine history' in recognition of the 'virtue' and disinterestedness of men who thought that they were establishing a republic 'as durable as the foundations of the world'.[87] Godwin's advertisement is thus a recognition of the importance of ephemeral print to

---

[83] William Godwin, *History of the Commonwealth of England*, 6 vols. (London: Henry Colburn, 1824–8), III: viii.
[84] Godwin, *History of the Commonwealth of England*, III: vii. For Lemon see Gordon Goodwin, 'Lemon, Robert (1779–1835)', rev. G. H. Martin, *Oxford Dictionary of National Biography*, Oxford University Press, 2004; online edn, 2004 [www.oxforddnb.com/view/article/16433, accessed 30 June 2015].
[85] Godwin, *History of the Commonwealth of England*, III: viii.
[86] Godwin, *History of the Commonwealth of England*, III: vii, v.
[87] Godwin, *History of the Commonwealth of England*, III: v, vi.

what Derrida termed the 'principle' of 'commencement' which the archive is compelled to shelter itself from or forget. In the 1820s the idea of the national archive and the emerging conceptual distinction between official or commissioned cheap print (located in government archives) and its retail equivalent in the form of news, opinion, and literature (the domain of the museum and, increasingly in the nineteenth century, the national library) was only nascent. Godwin maintains the association between 'retail' and 'commissioned' cheap print, the kind of print universe that Thomason would have recognised, in order to recover the 'authenticity' or presentness of seventeenth-century politics, bound and systematised in Thomason's collection. Writing as he was in the 1820s, Godwin's enterprise was shadowed by another revolutionary moment when men and women contemplated the possibility of a republic – the 1790s. His reference to the Thomason tracts as 'fugitive' is noteworthy in the light of the politicisation of ephemerality around 1800 that I outlined in the previous chapter (to which Godwin himself had contributed by highlighting the potency of the handbill in 1792). To insist on the material collected by Thomason as 'fugitive' rather than 'ephemeral' was to mark both the seventeenth century and Godwin's own times as not without value and not necessarily over, with the important proviso, however, that such potentially inflammatory media were properly domiciled by the *arkheion*.

While the Thomason and Wood collections remained largely intact in their new topological contexts, the fate of Luttrell's library was different. It passed through family hands until 1786 when it was sold by his descendant Edward Wynne in a famous auction which became a magnet for bibliophiles and literary scholars.[88] Among those who attended the Wynne sale was Edmund Malone, who found Luttrell material indispensable for his 1800 life of Dryden in his edition of his prose works, using Luttrell copies of *Absalom and Achitophel* and *The Medal* to date the appearance of these poems. The 'method' of Luttrell, as in the case of Godwin's response to the Thomason tracts, became the basis for an 'authentic' literary history of Dryden's poetry, Malone noting his indebtedness to Luttrell for 'the precise date of some of his political poems ... the authors of the various Answers which were made to them, as well as the time of their publication'.[89] The methodology of the earlier ephemerologists is thus an unacknowledged dimension of the development of historical bibliography in

---

[88] *A Catalogue of the Valuable Library, of Edward Wynne, Esq.* (London: Leigh and Sotheby, 1786).
[89] Edmund Malone (ed.), *The Critical and Miscellaneous Prose Works of John Dryden*, 3 vols. (London: Cadell and Davies, 1800), I: part one, 156.

the Romantic period. While Malone's interest was primarily in the literary content of Luttrell's collection, he nonetheless acknowledged its wider political and bibliographical contexts, noting Luttrell's attention to 'even the single half-sheets [which] at that period almost daily issued from the press'.[90] Malone was able to view this material in the collection of his friend, the bibliophile and antiquarian James Bindley (1739–1818), one of the most voracious customers of the 1786 Wynne sale.[91] Between 1786 and the mid-nineteenth century, Luttrell's volumes of stitched books and single sheets, including his Popish Plot catalogues, were part of the networks of information, sociability, and competition characterising the largely male homosocial world of the bibliophile. It was in this context that Walter Scott encountered Luttrell's texts. His 1808 *Life of John Dryden* made grateful acknowledgement to the 'urbanity' of Bindley and the 'liberality and kindness' of another arch-bibliophile, Richard Heber, in granting him access to these 'literary curiosities'.[92] Scott's preface to *The Life of Dryden* defines the value of the Luttrell collection in primarily literary terms. He describes Luttrell as buying nearly 'every poetical tract ... hawked through the streets in his time ... His collection contains the earliest editions of many of our most excellent poems, bound up, according to the order of time, with the lowest trash of Grub-Street'.[93] The value of Luttrell's collection and implicitly literary value in general is constructed in terms of a distinction between poetic excellence and the 'lowest trash of Grub-Street'. In contrast to Godwin's later emphasis on the Thomason tracts as enabling a 'fugitive' history, Scott's view of the Luttrell volumes is conditioned by the idea of ephemerality that emerged around 1800 – the 'trashy' worthlessness and disposability of single-sheet literature and its incapacity to qualify as a 'book'. The inevitable future of the Luttrell collection, Scott's argument implies, is disbinding and disaggregation, a winnowing out of true literary value from the chaff or trash of Grub Street.

The second major phase of the Luttrell collection's dispersal occurred with the sale of James Bindley's library between 1818 and 1820 that attracted the interest of Romantic-period bookmen such as William Upcott

---

[90] Malone, *Critical and Miscellaneous Prose Works*, I: part one, 156.
[91] Malone, *Critical and Miscellaneous Prose Works*, I: part one, v.
[92] Sir Walter Scott, *The Miscellaneous Prose Works of Sir Walter Scott*, 6 vols. (Edinburgh: Cadell, 1827), I: iv. For Heber see Arthur Sherbo, 'Heber, Richard (1774–1833)', *Oxford Dictionary of National Biography*, Oxford University Press, 2004; online edn, May 2015 [www.oxforddnb.com/view/article/12854, accessed 13 June 2015].
[93] Scott, *Miscellaneous Prose Works*, I: v.

and Joseph Haslewood whom I mentioned at the beginning of the chapter.[94] Haslewood is best known in literary history, if he is known at all, for the *Roxburghe Revels*, his account in manuscript of the extravagant excesses of the anniversary dinners and general sociability of the Roxburghe Club, the society of bibliophiles, of which he was a member. The publication, after Haslewood's death in 1834, of the *Roxburghe Revels* trashed both Haslewood's reputation and the bibliomania in general, signifying the rejection by an increasingly professionalised and middle-class literary sphere of the dilettantish excesses of a patrician elite of book collectors. As Ina Ferris points out, the Roxburghe Club was castigated not because of its exclusivity but because it 'was not "exclusive" in the right way', admitting men such as Haslewood, a London solicitor of modest means. Haslewood became a scapegoat for the aristocratic bibliophiles of the Roxburghe Club because he, like them, 'presumed to be a literary man'.[95]

Exactly what kind of 'literary man' Haslewood was has become unfamiliar to us. He combined the roles of book hunter, collector, bibliographer, editor of minor Elizabethan literature, and literary journalist. He was editor with Samuel Egerton Brydges of *The British Bibliographer* (1810) and contributed a series of anonymous articles on the history of the British theatre to the *Gentleman's Magazine* under the appropriate title of 'Fly leaf'. (Haslewood's preferred *métier* as a writer seems to have been paratexts written on the blank leaves at the end or beginning of his books and collectanea). He was also a literary archivist, amassing a collection relating to Thomas Chatterton and was closely interested in the work and life of Joseph Ritson, of whom he produced a bio-bibliography in 1824.[96] Haslewood noted how Ritson collected 'from provincial printers, historical, romantic, and legendary songs and merriments of the time, many which appeared wasted or wasting'.[97] Haslewood himself was familiar with such practices because a significant aspect of his activities as a bookman was the making of books of ephemera. His library was notable for extensive and numerous collections of playbills and other theatre ephemera, and of ballads, broadsides, proclamations, and 'curious' advertisements, often sourced from previous collectors, to which he gave idiosyncratic alliterative

---

[94] *A Catalogue of the Curious and Extensive Library of the Late James Bindley, Esq. F. S. A.* (London: Evans, 1820), 48.

[95] Ferris, *Book-Men*, 26.

[96] [A collection of extracts from periodicals and newspapers on Chatterton and his work]. BL pressmark 1870.c.20.

[97] Joseph Haslewood, *Some Account of the Life and Publications of the Late Joseph Ritson, Esq.* (London: Robert Triphook, 1824), 20.

titles such as 'Literary and Leasing Advertisements, or Puffs Predatory, Preliminary and Postliminary'.[98] In a flyleaf note to one collection, a five-volume compilation of 'Ballads and Broadsides', going back to the seventeenth century, Haslewood boasted about what a rival would need to do in order to compete with it, giving insights into the stamping grounds of the ephemerophile in Regency London:

> let him personally perform pilgrimage after pilgrimage to Grub Street; the more renowned Aldermary Churchyard, or Stonecutter Street ... or wear out morning after morning at the modern repositories of Longlane, Smithfield, Shoe-maker's Row, Blackfriars; or the huckster's grand emporium in Pitt Street, Seven Dials, &c.[99]

The 'Ballads and Broadsides' collection was listed in the catalogue of Haslewood's library as being bound by 'Lewis', a reference to Charles Lewis, the most expensive and skilled bookbinder in London. The pleasure that Haslewood took in the binding of his volumes, including his collections of ephemera, was considerable: according to Thomas Frognall Dibdin, Haslewood 'seemed to hug the volumes as his eye sparkled upon their exterior splendour; and he was sure to grumble at the charges, while he exulted and expatiated upon the skill of that renowned Bibliopegist'.[100] Haslewood's indulgence in luxury bookbinding enabled his pamphlets and broadsides to stand up in style, making his collectanea indistinguishable as books from other, more sturdy, folios.

Though later characterised as an eccentric fool, Haslewood was not alone in practising a form of universal bibliophilia, or rather typophilia, in which the printed scrap on the verge of 'wasting' was potentially as valuable as the stalwart volume. Haslewood, like his fellow bibliophiles who frequented auction rooms and pored over library sale catalogues (Haslewood's collection of catalogues amounted to ninety-eight volumes), was aware that his own practices had a history and were also capable of constituting a history.[101] In a flyleaf note, he commended Narcissus Luttrell for creating 'one of the most extraordinary and valuable collections of fugitive poetical tracts ... and also broadsides & slips, relative to his own times', expressing his regret that 'the whole of the Luttrell collections were not, unviolated, placed in [the British Museum] that truly national

---

[98] *Catalogue of the Curious and Valuable Library of the Late Joseph Haslewood, Esq. F.S.A.* (London: Evans, 1833), 2.
[99] *Catalogue of the Library of Joseph Haslewood*, 35.
[100] *Catalogue of the Library of Joseph Haslewood*, 35; Thomas Frognall Dibdin, *Reminiscences of a Literary Life* (London: John Major, 1836), 418–19.
[101] *Catalogue of the Library of Joseph Haslewood*, 65.

Repository'. Describing Luttrell's collections as exceeding 'in interest . . . the King's collection of Pamphlets', meaning the Thomason tracts, Haslewood argued for the value of the kind of aggregated, atomised collection represented by Luttrell's: 'it is by mites we form the mickle [;] the Luttrell collection was entirely formed by driblets'. Haslewood's manuscript account of Luttrell prefaced his extension of *An Historical Account of the Lives and Writings of our most Considerable English Poets, whether Epick, Lyrick, Elegiack, Epigramatists &c.*, printed by Edmund Curll in 1720.[102] Haslewood remade this book to create his own unique version of it. He inserted newspaper cuttings, scraps from texts, including the blue wrapper advertising Walter Scott's 1814 edition of Swift's *Works*, as well as his own manuscript annotations, some of which refer to Luttrell. For example, in an entry on Jabez Hughes, Haslewood annotates a reference to Hughes's *Verses occasion'd by reading Mr. Dryden's Fables* with '[March 1720/1 N. Luttrell]', indicating Luttrell's copies of Dryden's poems as the source of Hughes's work.[103] Haslewood's project is remarkable as a kind of replication of Luttrell's (and also Thomason's) 'method': rather than acknowledge Luttrell in a preface in a way that subordinates him to the role of the editor, as Malone and Scott do, Haslewood imitates Luttrell's practice, to the extent of replicating Luttrell's practices of annotation. Haslewood's mode of literary history is thus one of provisional, even accidental, book-remaking, a compilation of discrete bits and pieces, that are inescapably marked with their own precise historicity.

Haslewood's book making represents a textual materialist literary history in its broadest sense, one that made a place for the paper scrap as well as the bound black-letter treasure. The ephemerology of men such as Haslewood and Luttrell, particularly the placing of texts 'in Tyme', was foundational in the development of methods of historical bibliography, in which scholar-editors such as Malone were influential, representing what Derrida called the 'principle' of 'commencement' that institutional knowledge or 'the archive' is compelled to forget. The relationship between bibliomania and Romantic literary culture has been subject to important reassessment, as I suggested at the beginning of the chapter, but the significance of the fact that many bibliophiles were also ephemerophiles remains obscure. Jon Klancher has argued for the importance of the

---

[102] [Giles Jacob], *The Poetical Register; or, the lives and characters of the English Dramatick Poets; with an account of their writings. (An Historical Account of the lives and writings of our most considerable English Poets)* (London: E. Curll, 1720/21), copy extended by Joseph Haslewood, BL pressmark C.45.d.17–19.

[103] [Jacob], *Poetical Register*, opposite p. 85.

Romantic period as a pivotal moment when 'wild bibliography' began to be tamed: 'Take it one way, and we have new orders of book-knowledge which carve out histories and futures for the humanities that situate themselves between the "arts & sciences"; take it another way, and we have the cut-ups of the crazed bibliophiles, who tell a truth unintelligible to the same orders of emerging knowledge'.[104] Haslewood was one such 'crazed bibliophile', with predecessors in the seventeenth century such as Wood and Luttrell. Klancher's proposition would seem to suggest that Haslewood deserves to be confined to the attic of literary history but, as he also argues, the methodology of Haslewood and his fellow makers of collections can be seen as 'alternately far behind and far ahead of their modernising moment, gleefully exposing the contingent makeup and built-in hierarchies constituting the modern codex-form'.[105] Men such as Haslewood, I would suggest, did not need to knock down the castle of the codex-form book because in the landscape of print since the 1640s the book was already deconstructed, contingent. It was the emergence of the category of ephemera, in the late eighteenth and early nineteenth centuries, inter-implicated with 'tame' bibliography, which would strengthen the hierarchies buttressing the book and render the paper science of Haslewood and others invisible, a science that was potentially inclusive of everything because nothing was truly ephemeral.

[104] Klancher, *Transfiguring the Arts and Sciences*, 99.
[105] Klancher, *Transfiguring the Arts and Sciences*, 100.

CHAPTER 3

The Natural History of Sociability
Sarah Sophia Banks and Her Ephemera Collections

The interest in ephemerology, as documented in library sale catalogues and the survival of numerous collections in institutions such as the British Library, was largely associated with men. There is a remarkable consistency in the type of the ephemerophile who is often a bachelor, housing his archives in close proximity to male-dominated institutions such as universities (in the case of Anthony Wood), politics and parliament (Luttrell), or the legal profession (Haslewood). The world of the ephemerophile was also a male homosocial one, based on a network of private libraries, the auction room, the bookseller's shop, the coffeehouse, the fellowship of the outdoor bookstall, and the virtual homosociality of published sale catalogues. Could a woman possibly join this club? Certainly, there are many aspects of printed ephemera that would have been appealing to the aspiring female collector, such as its relative cheapness, the penetration of job printing into social life in general, particularly heterosocial spaces such as the theatre or the assembly room, and the fact that female occupations such as handicrafts involved the same kinds of technique and skills as the creation of an ephemera collection: that is, cutting and assemblage of paper and close-work with the eyes and hands. There is evidence that women were collectors of cheap print in the seventeenth century: the library of the Staffordshire gentlewoman Frances Wolfreston (1606–77), for example, contained a selection of chapbook romances, a 'bundle' of which is still to be found in its unbound state in the British Library, but there is no woman 'maker of collections' in that period to rival Wood or Luttrell.[1]

In the eighteenth century such a woman emerged in the form of Sarah Sophia Banks (1744–1818). (I will refer to Banks as SSB, following the abbreviated form of her signature which she used in her collections and to distinguish her more emphatically from her celebrated brother, Sir Joseph

[1] Tessa Watt, *Cheap Print and Popular Piety 1550–1640* (Cambridge, UK: Cambridge University Press, 1991), 316.

Banks). SSB's collections, like Sir Hans Sloane's ephemera and those of other collectors, were foundational in the development of the British Museum, being deposited there by Sir Joseph Banks after her death in 1818. Like the Thomason tracts they are huge in scope, representing more than 20,000 items, but unlike Thomason's archive they have remained comparatively invisible, divided as they now are between the British Library (including both its Printed Books and Manuscript sections), and two departments in the British Museum, those of Prints and Drawings, and Coins and Medals. Although they have been recognised as 'a kind of ethnography of Britain with direct parallels' to the work of her brother, SSB's collections remain under-researched.[2] One reason for the relative invisibility of her collections is the inevitable dominance in the historical record of her brother, Sir Joseph Banks. Though frequently acknowledged in Banks studies, SSB remains a marginal figure, defined as the devoted helpmeet of Sir Joseph, together with Banks's wife, Lady Dorothea, whom he referred to collectively as 'my Ladies'.[3] She is described as an 'amanuensis' or satellite, one of the many useful drones in the great 'hive' of Banks's scientific enterprise.[4] An influential account on the view of SSB as an eccentric oddity, recycled on numerous occasions in the nineteenth century and after, was J. T. Smith's remarks on her manner of dress – an '"*Old School*" Barcelona petticoat' in which she could transport books and

---

[2] Kim Sloan (with Andrew Burnett), *Enlightenment: Discovering the World in the Eighteenth Century* (Washington, DC: Smithsonian Books, 2003), 20. Research on Sarah Sophia Banks's collections, though hitherto limited, is growing: see A. G. Credland's 'Sarah and Joseph Banks and Archery in the Eighteenth Century', *Journal of the Society of Archer-Antiquaries*, 34 (1991), 42–50 and 'Sarah and Joseph Banks Contd.', *Journal of the Society of Archer-Antiquaries*, 35 (1992) 54–76; also Anthony Pincott, 'The Book Tickets of Miss Sarah Sophia Banks', *The Book Plate Journal*, 2 (2004), 3–30; Catherine Eagleton, 'Collecting African Money in Georgian London: Sarah Sophia Banks and Her Collection of Coins'. *Museum History Journal*, 6 (2013), 23–38 and Eagleton, 'Sarah Sophia Banks, Adam Afzelius and a Coin from Sierra Leone', in *The Material Cultures of Enlightenment Arts and Sciences*, eds. Adriana Craciun and Simon Schaffer (London: Palgrave Macmillan, 2016), 203–5. Arlene Leis's 2013 PhD thesis represents the first significant study of the material in the Department of Prints and Drawings: Arlene Leis, 'Sarah Sophia Banks: Femininity, Sociability and the Practice of Collecting in Late Georgian England', PhD thesis, University of York, 2013 [http://etheses.whiterose.ac.uk/5794/, accessed 2014]. Also by Leis, see 'Displaying Art and Fashion: Ladies' Pocket-Book Imagery in the Paper Collections of Sarah Sophia Banks', *Konsthistorisk tidskrift/Journal of Art History*, (2013), 1–20 and Ephemeral Histories: Social Commemoration of the Revolutionary and Napoleonic Wars in the Paper Collections of Sarah Sophia Banks', in *Visual Culture and the Revolutionary and Napoleonic Wars*, eds. Satish Padiyar, Philip Shaw, and Phillipa Simpson (London: Routledge, 2017), 183–99.

[3] Hector Charles Cameron, *Sir Joseph Banks, K. B. P.R.S.: The Autocrat of the Philosophers* (London: Batchworth Press, 1952), 273.

[4] John Gascoigne, *Joseph Banks and the English Enlightenment: Useful Knowledge and Polite Culture* (Cambridge, UK: Cambridge University Press, 1994), 25; Harold B. Carter, *Sir Joseph Banks 1743–1820* (London: British Museum (Natural History), 1988), 541.

other papers – and her reputation as an antiquated figure of the 'ton' of the previous century who had been a 'fashionable whip' in her day.[5] Smith also recounted how, on trying to buy a halfpenny ballad from a printer in Smithfield, SSB had been mistaken for one of the printer's 'chanters' or street-sellers.[6] The implied transgression by Sarah Sophia of the norms of both class and femininity was to be a persistent theme in scholarship on her brother, apparent in the inverted commas of a reference to her as '"quaint"' and '"unconventional"' in Edward Smith's 1911 biography of Sir Joseph.[7]

SSB has not been recuperated by feminist historiography, in contrast to, for example, Mary Delany, with whom she shared an interest in paper and the working method of cutting and pasting. Delany worked in the more conventionally 'feminine' pursuit of flower illustration and has been more easily assimilated by the discipline of art history.[8] As a well-connected member of the elite, Delany also achieved recognition and visibility through the publication of her correspondence in the nineteenth century. Unlike another female contemporary, Frances Burney, SSB was not a compulsive writer: though some letters and journals survive, there is no corpus of texts in which she documented her experience or articulated her subjectivity and she does not seem to have engaged in the writing of imaginative literature. Her 'life' exists elsewhere, in Sir Joseph Banks's many references to her in the margins of his correspondence and, most significantly, in the mass of material which she collected. My aim here, however, is not to piece together a biography of Sarah Sophia Banks from the single sheets and cuttings she assembled, even if such a goal was realisable. Rather, I want to focus on the more cryptic 'SSB' as a sign of the ambitious cultural project represented by her collections, as a crucial, if neglected, achievement in the history of Enlightenment ephemerology.

Her collections pose particular problems of interpretation, partly because of the invisibility of ephemerology due to its absorption and fragmentation by later disciplines and the institutional formations in which it was foundational. There is a lack of a language and a taxonomy by which the constitutive elements of the collection as an ephemera 'book', nor indeed

---

[5] J. T. Smith, *A Book for a Rainy Day: or Recollections of the Events of the Last Sixty-Six Years* (London: Richard Bentley, 1845), 211, 214.
[6] Smith, *Book for a Rainy Day*, 211–12.
[7] Edward Smith, *The Life of Sir Joseph Banks* (London: John Lane, The Bodley Head, 1911), 325 n. 1. See also Cameron's reference to her as 'something of an oddity. Tall and masculine in appearance, with her brother's deep voice ...'; Cameron, *Sir Joseph Banks*, 255.
[8] See Mark Laird and Alicia Weisberg-Roberts (eds.), *Mrs. Delany & Her Circle* (New Haven, CT: Yale University Press, 2009).

a collection of collections, such as SSB's, can be described. There is no systematic catalogue or description of their contents, for example, the best though limited account being the 1987 *User's Guide* to the Department of Prints and Drawings which gives an overview of the material held there, chiefly her tickets and trade cards.[9] A proper account of her achievement would thus have to be as encyclopedic and as thorough as the collection itself, the challenge of writing about SSB being to do justice to her attention to the particular value (social and aesthetic) of the singular ephemeral document, while at the same time recognising the architecture of her collections as a whole. In analysing SSB's collections it is easy, sometimes, to miss the wood for the (myriad) trees, but this response, I would argue, is the inevitable result of her elusive, even beguiling, methodology and the distinctiveness of her achievement as an ephemerologist.

Sarah Sophia Banks's collecting interests were diverse, ranging from coins, medals, and trade tokens, to prints (both prestige and popular), tickets (of all kinds), and books, consisting of printed books and the unique 'books' she made of her ephemera, her collectanea.[10] Even her brother was uncertain about the scope and contents of SSB's collections. In

---

[9] Antony Griffiths and Reginald Williams, *The Department of Prints and Drawings in the British Museum: User's Guide* (London: British Museum Publications, 1987), 82–4. See also A. G. Credland's descriptive list of Banks material relating to archery: Credland, 'Sarah & Joseph Banks Contd.'.

[10] There was a surge in token production of all kinds after 1787, the result of the failure of the Mint to issue a re-coinage of official regal copper and the ever-increasing demands of an industrialising economy. Tokens were used to pay workers, and also as admission tickets and advertisements for leisure enterprises such as circulating libraries, and as media of publicity, commemorating events or political causes. SSB was a major collector of tokens of all kinds, including those associated with radical politics in the 1790s. Her collection included a specimen of cheap pewter medals marking the acquittals of Thomas Hardy and Horne Tooke at the Treason Trials of 1794 and she also possessed at least seventy examples of the tokens produced by the ultra-radical Thomas Spence. For trade tokens in general see J. R. S. Whiting, *Trade Tokens: A Social and Economic History* (Newton Abbot: David & Charles, 1971); Peter Mathias, *English Trade Tokens: The Industrial Revolution Illustrated* (London: Abelard-Schuman, 1962); also W. J. Davis and A. W. Waters, *Tickets and Passes of Great Britain and Ireland: Struck or Engraved on Metal, Ivory, etc.* (Leamington Spa: Courier Press, 1922). For SSB's Hardy medal see BM Coins: registration number: SSB,227.15 catalogue number: MB3p88.377; for Spence tokens see examples listed in the British Museum Research Collection Online Database [www.britishmuseum.org/research/collection_online]. The affinity between coins and medals and print was particularly marked in the case of the relationship between 'cheap' numismatics – the trade tokens and medals sold by Spence – and ephemeral genres such as the handbill, the playbill, and the ticket, the importance of which lay in their status as circulatory media and as 'currency' that facilitated social interaction (and could be accumulated as a kind of capital). SSB's fascination for coins and medals was therefore profoundly implicated in her interest in printed ephemera (and vice versa), a connection which became lost in the division of the collection between material culture (the Department of Coins and Medals) and paper (Prints and Drawings and the British Library).

an 1818 letter to his fellow trustees in the British Museum Sir Joseph Banks donated, in what he thought were the terms of her will, her 'collection of coins and medals, and of books relating to tournaments, chivalry, orders of knighthood, ceremonials, processions, funerals etc'.[11] SSB had in fact bequeathed her collections to her sister-in-law, Lady Dorothea Banks, who later clarified the legality of Banks's deed by donating them to the British Museum in her name.[12] This incident raises the question of how SSB envisaged the destination of her collections after her death: it is possible that in bequeathing them to Lady Dorothea she wished to maintain their quasi-private status as part of the repository of the Banks establishment at No. 32 Soho Square, though she would also have been aware of her brother's long-standing connections with the British Museum and they may have informally discussed the possibility of her collections eventually being sent there. In her will SSB defined her collections in a very different way to her brother, dedicating to Lady Dorothea 'all my royal presents all my trinkets diamonds seals etc all my music my coins medal[s] books *tickets etc*' (my emphasis).[13] Whereas Banks represented his sister's interests as typical of the antiquarian (and predominantly male) virtuoso, and hence worthy of inclusion in the British Museum, SSB's will relates her collections to other kinds of property signifying her status and public recognition as a gentlewoman, such as her music and the presents given to her by royalty. The will thus asserted an association between SSB's identity as a gentlewoman and her collecting that differed from that of the male virtuoso. Her allusion to her 'tickets etc', which Banks did not mention, was crucial in highlighting that distinction. SSB's royal presents and her tickets belonged together because of their implication in the networks and sites of association, the complex patterns of gifting, exchange, debt, and obligation characterising sociable 'commerce' that enabled women in particular to assert a distinctive place in late Georgian society. SSB's tickets were a sign of her considerable investment in the fact that sociability could constitute a public life and legitimacy for women of her class; in bequeathing them to her sister-in-law she was ascribing to that life the status and transferability of a form of property, as hard and as valuable as jewels.

---

[11] P. R. Harris, *A History of the British Museum Library, 1753–1973* (London: British Library, 1998), 30.

[12] Harris, *History*, 30.

[13] Lincolnshire Archives Office, 2 Haw 2/B/64, at pp. 1–2, quoted in R. J. Eaglen, 'Sarah Sophia Banks and Her English Hammered Coins', *The British Numismatic Journal*, 78 (2008), 200–15 (207).

In what follows I wish to revise the view of SSB as an eccentric hobbyist by placing her in the tradition of ephemerology as practised by predecessors such as Thomason, Wood, and Luttrell, and by contemporaries such as Daniel Lysons, Horace Walpole, and Dawson Turner. I also want to resist the identification of Sarah Sophia Banks's interests as psychopathological, a form of 'bad' collecting as opposed to her brother's 'good' collecting, analogous to 'deviant' hoarding practices of the twentieth and twentieth-first century in which paper detritus such as stacks of newspapers often loom large. At the same time, however, there is still something 'quaint' or we might say, 'queer', about Banks's collecting which, like that of predecessors such as Anthony Wood, was assured in its objectives, as well as doggedly and passionately pursued.[14] Ultimately referring to possible frameworks for understanding Sarah Sophia Banks in the work of Walter Benjamin and Deleuzian-influenced ideas of assemblage, this chapter and the one following, compelled by SSB's own methods, combine the perspectives of systematic description with close reading of the particular ephemeral artefact, focusing in particular on SSB's fascination with the ticket. I discuss the significance of her documentation of fashionable sociability in relation to the larger projects of her brother, suggesting ways in which feminised sociability and the domains of Sir Joseph Banks were inter-implicated. Sarah Sophia Banks deserves to be recognised, in her own way, as the first historian of fashionable sociability, which she archived as it was happening in the late eighteenth century: what her brother was doing for the flora and fauna of the world she was also doing for the 'world' of polite society with important implications for our understanding of the politics of the public sphere, media history, and ephemerality.

'Id genus omne': SSB as Collector

While the scale of Sarah Sophia Banks's collecting and its orientation towards polite sociability are exceptional, she was not the lone eccentric as represented by Smith and later Banks scholars. SSB belonged to a diverse community of like-minded individuals, many of whom were aware of her reputation. Her collecting was consistent with the long-standing status of printed ephemera as part of what Marilyn Butler termed 'popular

---

[14] For 'good' and 'bad' collecting see James Clifford, *The Predicament of Culture: Twentieth-Century Ethnography, Literature, and Art* (Cambridge, MA: Harvard University Press, 1988), 219; also Scott Herring, *The Hoarders: Material Deviance in Modern American Culture* (Chicago: University of Chicago Press, 2014), 34, 47.

antiquarianism' – 'the study of British national culture: of English, Welsh, Gaelic, and Irish as vernacular languages, and of their oral as well as written traditions – not merely literary forms and art, but beliefs, customs, and festivities'.[15] An aspect of this popular antiquarianism was its orientation towards a proto-sociology or ethnography of the present, taking account in particular of the new public sphere engendered by the combination of print, the commercialisation of leisure, the growth of associational culture, and the emergence of new material spaces, such as the coffeehouse. Ephemeral print, as I suggested in the previous chapter, was at the forefront of the development of this new public sphere, which was not, strictly speaking, 'popular' in the sense of being identified with the culture of the lower orders but was a space, both literal and metaphorical, in which all classes were potentially present and mixed together. The frost fair is exemplary of both the fantasy and the ephemerality of this idea of the public sphere. While orienting herself in many ways towards both elite and popular antiquarianism – in her interest in ancient coins, heraldry, chivalry, and the history of archery – SSB combined this with a focus on contemporary phenomena such as innovations in fashionable entertainments, sociability, commerce, and the printed paraphernalia associated with such developments: visiting cards, tickets of admission, trade cards, the trade token, handbills, and newspapers. In this respect her range of interests were similar to those of Daniel Lysons (1762–1834), best known for his *Environs of London* (1792–6), a four-volume topographical history of parishes surrounding the metropolis. Lysons also produced multi-volume collections of newspaper cuttings, broadsides, and prints, dealing with remarkable contemporary events and people; exhibitions and places of amusement; advertisements, particularly relating to quack medicine; and theatrical ephemera – playbills, portraits, and caricatures of actors and actresses. As in the case of SSB's collections, there has been no systematic study or ephemerography of Lysons's collections as a whole, the best, though sketchy, description of their contents being the account of them in the sale catalogue of the library of Philip Hurd, which indicates that Lysons shared some interests with SSB. He collected cuttings related to private theatricals, part of what the Hurd catalogue promoted as 'AN INEXHAUSTIBLE SOURCE OF AMUSEMENT AND THEATRICAL INFORMATION', as well as

---

[15] Butler, 'Antiquarianism (Popular)', 328. SSB was also interested in Lincolnshire dialect, compiling a glossary of words she had come across on the Banks's estate at Revesby Abbey: British Library Add MS 32640; see also William Matthews, 'The Lincolnshire Dialect in the Eighteenth Century', *Notes and Queries*, 169 (1935): 398–404.

accounts of the funerals in 1806 of Pitt and Fox, and handbills and other advertisements relating to archery, masquerades, and ballooning.[16] Lysons also documented frosts and frost fairs from 1683, and in his two volumes devoted to 'TRADES AND PROFESSIONS, PUFFS, EMPIRICS &c. &c.' included book catalogues and advertisements for books, and ephemera relating to 'Mails, Post Chaises, Inns, Taverns, Passage-Boats, Steam Boats'.[17] These kinds of text – documenting natural wonders, book trade publicity, and transport infrastructure – are consistent with material to be found in Anthony Wood's library, illustrating the nature of late Georgian ephemera collecting as a distinctive variety of auto-ethnography going back to the previous century. SSB would also have been familiar with the investments of Horace Walpole in the ephemeral paper economy of sociability. Walpole's elaboration of his domain at Strawberry Hill entailed, as Barrett Katler notes, the production of 'a large amount of ephemera: trade cards, invitations, bookplates, even tickets for tours of Strawberry Hill'.[18] Walpole not only utilised such material to regulate and publicise his sociability, some of which was archived in SSB's collections, but collected it in scrapbooks made by his in-house printer, Thomas Kirkgate.[19]

The connection between SSB and Lysons was even closer than a shared interest in fugitive print and public culture. Daniel Lysons and his brother Samuel, also an antiquary, were part of the Banks circle, Sir Joseph Banks being a patron of Samuel.[20] SSB's archery volumes record Daniel and Samuel Lysons' presence at archery meetings at the Banks estate at Revesby Abbey in Lincolnshire; like the cuttings from the *Environs of London* which she used in her archery collections and elsewhere, these documents represent an assimilation of Lysons both as a subject and an authority within the purview of her collections.[21] Another figure in the Banks circle who was a compiler of collections was the Yarmouth banker, botanist, and

---

[16] *Catalogue of the Splendid, Curious, and Valuable Library, of the Late Philip Hurd, Esq.* (London: R. Evans, 1832), 50, 52, 54, 53. For details of Lysons's collectanea in the British Library see the entry under Lysons [www.bl.uk/reshelp/findhelprestype/prbooks/namedcolnprintedmat/named colnprintedmatl/namedcolprintedl.html, accessed 15 August 2018].
[17] *Catalogue of the Library of Philip Hurd*, 51, 54.
[18] Barrett Kalter, *Modern Antiques: The Material Past in England, 1660–1780* (Lewisburg, PA: Bucknell University Press, 2012), 162.
[19] See Stephen Clarke, *The Strawberry Hill Press & Its Printing House: An Account and an Iconography* (New Haven, CT: The Lewis Walpole Library, 2011), 23. SSB's collection included a ticket of admission to Strawberry Hill, handwritten by Walpole, permitting access to SSB herself: British Museum Department of Prints and Drawings, C,2.1079.
[20] Rosemary Sweet, *Antiquaries: The Discovery of the Past in Eighteenth-Century Britain* (London: Hambledon, 2004), 104.
[21] Credland, 'Sarah & Joseph Banks Contd.', 67.

antiquarian Dawson Turner (1775–1858).[22] A fellow of both the Linnean and Royal Societies, Turner was a correspondent and friend of Sir Joseph Banks, one of the many associates who came and went at No. 32. Turner combined his scientific interests with antiquarianism (both elite and popular) and art and book collecting.[23] As in the case of many Romantic-period bibliophiles, his interest in the book was not confined to prestigious old volumes but extended to various modes of book making. In conjunction with the women of his family, who were accomplished artists and botanists, Turner engaged in large-scale extra-illustrating projects, most notably an enlargement of Francis Blomefield's *An Essay Towards a Topographical History of the County of Norfolk* (1739–75).[24] He also made a number of collections of fugitive material – advertisements, newspaper cuttings, book and periodical prospectuses, handbills, and posters, especially relating to the social history of Yarmouth.[25] The catalogue of the sale of his library in 1859 indicates that he was interested in what other people had collected in this line: he possessed volumes of newspaper cuttings made by Joseph Haslewood as well as two volumes of Lyson's collectanea.[26] Turner's library also included seventeenth-century tracts and proclamations, indicating continuities with the interests of men such as Thomason, Wood, and Luttrell.[27]

Turner regarded his ephemera collecting as performing an important social role. In a MS note to a collection of lottery handbills he asserted its value as a 'historical document' designed to demonstrate the iniquity of lotteries. 'An idle itch of senseless miscellaneous collecting' he declared, 'had no share in inducing me to attempt to give a degree of permanence to

---

[22] For Turner see Angus Fraser, 'Turner, Dawson (1775–1858), banker, botanist, and antiquary', *Oxford Dictionary of National Biography*, Oxford University Press, 23 September 2004 [www.oxforddnb.com.rp.nla.gov.au/view/10.1093/ref:odnb/9780198614128.001.0001/odnb-9780198614128-e-27846, accessed 15 August 2018]; also the essays in Nigel Goodman (ed.), *Dawson Turner: A Norfolk Antiquary and His Remarkable Family* (Chichester: Phillimore & Co., 2007).

[23] See David McKitterick, 'Dawson Turner and Book Collecting', in *Dawson Turner: A Norfolk Antiquary and His Remarkable Family*, ed. Nigel Goodman (Chichester: Phillimore & Co., 2007), 67–110.

[24] See Jane Knowles, 'A Tasteful Occupation? The Work of Maria, Elizabeth, Mary Anne, Harriet, Hannah Sarah and Ellen Turner', in *Dawson Turner: A Norfolk Antiquary and His Remarkable Family*, ed. Nigel Goodman (Chichester: Phillimore & Co., 2007), 123–40 (131).

[25] See John Boneham, 'The Dawson Turner Collection of Printed Ephemera and Great Yarmouth', *The Electronic British Library Journal* (2014) [www.bl.uk/eblj/2014articles/pdf/ebljarticle132014.pdf, accessed 2015].

[26] *Catalogue of the Principal Part of the Library of Dawson Turner, Esq.* (London: Sotheby & Wilkinson, 1853), 119, 1.

[27] *Catalogue of the Library of Dawson Turner*, 174, 200–1.

objects naturally transitory'.[28] In another note Turner claimed that the very act of gathering together and preserving such material was of intrinsic value: 'Miscellanies of various kinds, – advertisements, handbills, lottery-puffs, cuttings from newspapers, prospectuses etc. "id genus omne" – articles which are commonly thrown away, ... acquire an interest, and sometimes a remarkable one, from juxta-position'.[29] This commitment to the gathering together and assembling of ephemeral textuality, evoking a sense of the interconnectedness of 'id genus omne', aligns Dawson Turner as a collector with the practices of SSB. Writing about Turner as a book collector, David McKitterick notes that 'it is impossible to treat [him] simply as a collector of discrete kinds of document, printed or manuscript, book or letter, drawing or etching, lithograph or engraving ... For him, each kind of document, like each part of a document, supplemented and supported others.'[30] These observations also apply to SSB for whom letterpress and engravings, newspaper cuttings, cheap and prestige single sheets, and the codex-form book, are in similar kinds of fluid interplay and conjunction, confounding distinctions between the domains in the British Museum and British Library across which they are currently distributed. Though SSB may not have been aware of Turner's interest in printed ephemera, and many of his collections were made after her death in 1818, his activities are an important context for her achievement, indicating that she was not exceptional. Indeed, it is possible that Turner learnt from her, as he did implicitly from the practices of men such as Lysons, Haslewood, and William Upcott. Dawson Turner's interest in such material highlights its importance as a distinctive and long-standing strand of popular antiquarianism which was an integral part of the scientific and broadly literary inquiry in which Turner and Sir Joseph Banks were engaged. Curiosity licensed and amplified the scope of what was accessible to knowledge, making the most transitory document an object of potential value to the future and, in SSB's case, enabling women to contribute to an informal, expansive, science of the present.

The 'Social Life' of the Ticket

Sarah Sophia Banks, like Turner, was interested in single-sheet publications of all kinds, including letterpress and historical, satirical, and

---

[28] [A collection of handbills, newspaper cuttings, etc., relating to lotteries between 1802 and 1826, formed by Dawson Turner. With a MS. note by the collector], BL pressmark 8225.bb.78.
[29] Quoted in McKitterick, 'Dawson Turner and Book Collecting', 90.
[30] McKitterick, 'Dawson Turner and Book Collecting', 73.

topographical prints. She also collected both prestige and cheap forms of print such as, for example, ballads and lottery advertisements. Her major focus, however, was the ticket, which she collected in the thousands. The status of the ticket as a form of jobbing print has meant that, until recently, its ubiquity in eighteenth-century social and cultural life has gone unnoticed by historians, though, as I have suggested, collectors such as Thomason and Wood were recording its role in associational culture as early as the seventeenth century. In the first major article on the penetration of the ticket into eighteenth-century culture, Sarah Lloyd highlighted how the medium facilitated all kinds of social interaction, from 'high' to 'low'.[31] The term 'ticket' itself encompassed mundane uses of print such as dockets or labels on goods as well as prestige souvenir objects such as tickets for coronations. As Lloyd shows, tickets were essential to the activities of, for example, charitable societies, religion, especially Methodism, the functioning of the British navy in, for example, payments to sailors, the public culture of Enlightenment science in the form of lecturing, as well as diverse modes of leisure – theatres, pleasure gardens, assembly rooms, and music concerts. The provision of tickets was a substantial part of the business of jobbing printers such as Jasper Sprange in Tunbridge Wells and William Davison of Alnwick, Northumberland. In addition to producing tickets for balls, theatres, and lectures, Davison was responsible for producing 'House of Industry "spinning tickets" (to keep track of inmates' labor), soup tickets and ... non-transferable Alnwick parish "pay" tickets', by which the poor could claim relief.[32] The scope of Davison's business highlights how, by the early nineteenth century, social life in its broadest sense was dependent on the currency of ephemeral jobbing print in all its forms, but particularly on the ticket. As Lloyd argues, 'an ability to recognize and use tickets had become an essential form of literacy' for all levels of society.[33] This 'literacy', moreover, was multivalent: 'tickets were ... experienced through the eye, touch, imagination, and memory. Circulation, form and use gave tickets "social lives," so that their specific histories disclose the processes that created

---

[31] Sarah Lloyd, 'Ticketing the British Eighteenth Century: "A thing ... never heard of before"', *Journal of Social History*, 46:4 (2013), 843–71. See also Sarah Lloyd, 'The Religious and Social Significance of Methodist Tickets, and Associated Practices of Collecting and Recollecting, 1741–2017', *The Historical Journal*, 1–28. doi:10.1017/S0018246X19000244. See also the catalogue of an exhibition held at the Museum of London, 1980: Victoria Moger, *The Favour of Your Company: Tickets and Invitations to London Events and Places of Interest c. 1750–1850* (London: Museum of London in assoc. with The Wynkyn De Worde Society, 1980).

[32] Lloyd, 'Ticketing', 854.   [33] Lloyd, 'Ticketing', 855.

substance, feeling and value'.³⁴ It was this elusive and affective dimension of ticket literacy, the 'social life' that specific tickets were capable of disclosing, that was the focus of Sarah Sophia Banks's collecting.

SSB was primarily interested in tickets produced by the process of printing from the etching and engraving of a copper plate, known as intaglio printing.³⁵ The techniques of intaglio printing allowed for more elaborate and decorative design elements than were possible in letterpress printing, often making these tickets arresting visual artefacts that integrated the arts of word and image.³⁶ Specially commissioned by individuals, for example for customised visiting cards, or by tradesmen and merchants as a form of advertisement, these tickets lacked the impact or ubiquity of forms of cheap print such as ballads or lottery advertisements, produced in the hundreds of thousands, but they were no less ephemeral. They represent a different kind of ephemerality that combined the evanescence associated with jobbing print with the art object's claims to preservation and durability. The intaglio-printed ticket could thus be described as having the potential to intensify and aestheticise ephemerality in an auratic way, in its significance as a trace of a specific social encounter between individuals, an event in time in place, or, as in the case of an invitation to a funeral, a lost life. The affect of these traces of sociability was accentuated by signatures, seals, and other kinds of handwritten inscription, or by material signs of use such as folding, torn corners, staining, frayed ribbons (used to attach tickets to bodies), or simply by the sense of pasteboard itself as a particularly absorptive medium, dense with a history of human handling.

The main kinds of 'ticket' which Banks collected included trade cards, British and foreign visiting cards, and tickets of admission. She also had a collection of bookplates, which were included in the eighteenth-century understanding of the ticket as a form of label reflexively marking the object, place, or event with which it was associated and the individual or institution performing that act of marking or tendering.³⁷ Banks, as we shall see, was particularly interested in the bodies which tickets extended prosthetically and also in how the ticket signified the corporeality of sociable life. Most of these tickets combined word and image and were thus related to Banks's collecting of prints, including the caricatures of

---

[34] Lloyd, 'Ticketing', 847.
[35] For a useful description of intaglio printing see Raven, *Publishing Business*, xi–xii.
[36] Graham Hudson, *The Design and Printing of Ephemera in Britain and America 1720–1920* (London: British Library, 2008), 14.
[37] Pincott, 'The Book Tickets of Miss Sarah Sophia Banks'.

artists such as Bunbury, Gillray, and Sayer, and representations of topical events, buildings, and places — public ceremonies such as funerals and notable trials and occasions of national celebration such as the 1789 thanksgiving for George III's recovery. Combined with her accumulation of tickets, her print collecting was consistent with the kind of sociotopography and documentation of public ceremonies and civic life to be found in the work of Luttrell and Wood.

Banks's ticket files that are now in the Department of Prints and Drawings intersect with another way in which she organised other kinds of fugitive material, as collectanea, located in the British Library. These volumes were compilations of a variety of single-sheet texts, both printed and engraved (including tickets), ranging from cheap handbills to prestige coloured engravings, interspersed with newspaper cuttings that often acted as a form of commentary and annotation. Banks's collectanea, in the British Library, pressmark L.R. 301.h.3–11, consist of nine volumes which differ from the more generic ticket or print collections now housed in the Department of Prints and Drawings in their mixing of types of ephemera and their more topical orientation. The main topics of the collectanea, very broadly defined, are as follows: ballooning and material relating to the London 'Monster'[38] (h.3); ceremonials, coins (h.4); newspaper cuttings from the Regency mainly relating to the royal family and elite sociability (h.5); 1790s politics, loyalism, and war (h.6); funerals of Nelson, Fox, and Pitt in 1806 (h.7); lotteries, archery, and medical advertisements (h.8); ballads and occasional poetry (h.9); political and miscellaneous broadsides 1720s–90s (h.10); and the Jubilee of 1814 (h.11).

Unlike contemporaries such as Haslewood and Turner, Banks did not preface her collections with flyleaf explanations or justifications of her methods. She may though have made an indirect claim for her collections by inserting a cutting from the *Gentleman's Magazine* in one of the volumes now in the British Library, L.R. 301.h.10. Dating from 1784, the cutting was a letter by 'S. Ayscough', probably Samuel Ayscough (1745–1804), the librarian and antiquary, in which he declared the value of 'original papers' as 'the best materials from which historic facts are to be deduced'. Such papers, however, were difficult to access even in public libraries where 'they remain undescribed, or buried under a general title of collections, &c. [and]

---

[38] The 'London Monster' referred to a series of sensational attacks on women in the streets of London between 1788–90. Rhynwick Williams was tried and convicted for the assaults. See Jan Bondeson, *The London Monster: A Sanguinary Tale* (Philadelphia: University of Pennsylvania Press, 2001) which acknowledges Banks's collections as a primary resource: xiv–v.

are consequently unknown ... In private collections their use must be more confined'[39] Ayscough goes on to suggest how such collections might be described, giving the example of a list of the contents of one of the manuscripts from the library of Robert Cotton in the British Museum. Banks inserted this cutting between a newspaper account from 1776 of the trial of the Duchess of Kingston and a handbill notice about damage done to trees in the Botanic Garden in Chelsea, annotated as 1817, dates that span her adult life and also, incidentally, the ascendancy of Georgian fashionable sociability.[40] This cryptic act of placing indicates that she was at least aware of the collection as a mode of history making and also its status as a form of 'buried' knowledge, even within public institutions.

In addition to these volumes, Banks made collectanea of material relating to specific interests, namely archery and private theatricals. (The latter volume, credited in the British Library catalogue to either Banks or Charles Burney Jr, is now acknowledged to be the work of the former).[41] Both volumes use a range of different kinds of ephemera – broadside engravings, newspaper and periodical cuttings, playbills, tickets – to document sociable networks, practices, and spaces in which Banks was often directly involved. In the case of archery, for example, she created an archive of the emergence of the sport in the late 1780s as a fashionable pastime, particularly for women, linking this with the history of archery as an object of antiquarian interest.[42] Banks herself was active in the sport: part of her collections that her brother donated to the British Museum contain target cards recording scores in meetings involving Sarah Sophia, Sir Joseph Banks, and Lady Banks and their guests.[43] Her archery collections are split between the manuscript and letterpress sections of the British Library. The collectanea

---

[39] *Gentleman's Magazine*, 54:2 (November 1784).   [40] At L.R.301.h.10, f. 25.

[41] [A collection of playbills, notices and press-cuttings dealing with private theatrical performances, 1750–1808] BL pressmark 937.g.96. On this volume see Gillian Russell, 'Sarah Sophia Banks's Private Theatricals: Ephemera, Sociability, and the Archiving of Fashionable Life, *Eighteenth-Century Fiction*, 27.3–4 (Spring–Summer 2015), 535–55.

[42] The fashion for archery developed after 1780, when Sir Ashton Lever established the 'Toxophilite Society', linked to his establishment in Leicester Fields. After it was favoured by the Prince of Wales, archery became the sport of *bon ton* fashionability, particularly for women. The son of Lever's secretary, Thomas Waring Jr, became the leading archery entrepreneur with a shop near Bedford Square. Banks was a customer of Waring and archived his shop-bills and trade cards, as well as collecting Waring's books on the subject. See A. G. Credland, 'Sarah and Joseph Banks' and 'Sarah and Joseph Banks Contd.' and Linda V. Troost, 'Archery in the Long Eighteenth Century', in *British Sporting Literature and Culture in the Long Eighteenth Century*, ed. Sharon Harrow (Farnham: Ashgate, 2015), 105–24.

[43] British Library ADD MSS 34721 A & B, covering the period 1793–1807. The cards, bound by ties in the corner and contained in boxes, create a record of quotidian sociability, representing another form of Banks's book making.

relating to the sport contain newspaper and periodical cuttings, handbill notices, tickets, prospectuses for books about archery, and shop-bills of the archery entrepreneur Thomas Waring. In addition Banks collected books on archery, part of her library that is now dispersed in the British Library's collection. Some of these books can be identified as belonging to her through her practice of annotation or through reference to her in subscription lists.[44] Her large collection of books on numismatics (donated by Sir Joseph Banks to the Royal Mint), on heraldry, and archery, suggest that her library served her other collecting interests rather than vice versa.

It is impossible to determine how accurately her collectanea as they now exist in the British Library reflect the organisation of her material in No. 32 Soho Square but they at least suggest that the ephemera 'book' was for her a permeable, adaptable entity. Binding her material in ways that would fix it in stable, recognisable categories was not as important as replicating the mobility of the fugitive text – its role as part of a complex traffic of constantly criss-crossing ephemeral genres. Hence to read the collectanea primarily in terms of chronology or as records of specific historical events, people, or ephemeral genres is to miss how their constituent elements – tickets, playbills, cuttings, prints – relate to each other and intersect. George Thomason's method in collecting was time, to which Luttrell added space and the visual image to create a contemporary topo-ephemeral history. SSB used these methodologies to define and make visible a particular sociality, an interconnectedness, as it was happening. She adopts an ephemeral genre that was nascent in the seventeenth century – the ticket – and defines it as the connecting tissue of polite Enlightenment culture in the late Georgian period. The most appropriate term for Banks's practice and what she achieved is 'assemblage' which was a term used well into the nineteenth century to describe collections of ephemera such as those of the Shakespeare scholar Isaac Reed – 'A Large Assemblage of Broadsides, Old Ballads, Scraps etc.' – or a collection of material relating to ballooning – 'a very large assemblage of portraits, plates, and woodcuts, with some fragments of balloons, mounted in 240 leaves'.[45] 'Assemblage' conveyed the looseness of such combinations of texts, whether in bound or unbound form, and the possibility of dis- or

---

[44] For Banks's annotation of books see H. J. Jackson, *Romantic Readers: The Evidence of Marginalia* (New Haven, CT: Yale University Press, 2005), 212–13, 239–40.

[45] *Catalogue of the Rare and Bijoux Portion ... from the Library of Mr. J. W. Southgate ... A Large Assemblage of Broadsides, Old Ballads, Scraps, &c. Collected by the late Isaac Reed* (London: Southgate, Grimston and Wells, [1833]); *Catalogue of a Collection of Miscellaneous Books, Including Many on Angling: The Property of the Late Mr. Boosey* (London: Leigh Sotheby, [1841]), 29.

re-aggregation, based on the integrity of the individual items of which they are composed. In Banks's case the other contemporary meaning of 'assemblage' – a gathering of people – is also relevant because of both her interest in sociable life and the status of her collections as documenting a virtual sociability.[46]

Fashionable Sociability and the 'Ticket System'

Sarah Sophia Banks used the science of ephemerology to document a particular phase in the history of associational culture: that is, the expansion of forms of entertainment after 1760 which enabled women to forge a distinctively feminised zone, intersecting between the domain of what Jürgen Habermas termed the 'town' or market of culture products and the male homosociality of the republic of letters.[47] This zone of fashionable sociability comprised spaces and practices such as pleasure gardens, assembly rooms, art exhibitions, theatre, concert and opera going, promenading, shopping and visiting. It stimulated and was in turn re-commodified by print and visual media such as newspapers, the novel, satirical and portrait engravings, and all the paraphernalia of printed ephemera. The headquarters of fashionable sociability were the metropolitan pleasure palaces of the 1760s and 1770s, beginning with Teresa Cornelys's Carlisle House in Soho Square, established in 1760 (and just a few steps away from Banks's home at No. 32), followed by Almack's, the Pantheon in Oxford Street, and the gambling club known as the Ladies Coterie. These winter sites of assembly had their summer counterparts in the longer established pleasure gardens at Vauxhall and Ranelagh, in many respects the template for fashionable public sociability throughout the eighteenth century and beyond. The innovation of Carlisle House and the Pantheon lay in how these venues combined the sociable freedom of the outdoor pleasure garden with the cachet of elite modes of entertaining 'at home', in which women traditionally dominated as hostesses. As the paper instrument that publicised, commodified, regulated, and ultimately commemorated fashionable sociability, the ticket was of crucial importance. Tickets made the value of sociability mobile and transferable as part of a wider cultural economy, embedded in other exchange relations – familial, sexual, political, and

---

[46] E.g. definition of 'assemblage' in Johnson's *Dictionary*: 'A collection; a number of individuals brought together': *A Dictionary of the English Language*, 10th edn (London: Rivington et al., 1792).
[47] For a more extensive discussion of fashionable sociability see Gillian Russell, *Women, Sociability and Theatre in Georgian London* (Cambridge, UK: Cambridge University Press, 2007).

financial. Tickets sustained what Sarah Lloyd defines as a 'ticket system', a complex pattern of interlocking institutions, sites, and people, a system which was itself the subject of commentary in newspapers and periodicals.[48] Part of the media event of Enlightenment culture, therefore, was the media event of the ticket – as artefact, system, and discourse – which after 1760 became more complex and far-reaching than it had ever been before. In assembling her tickets and other kinds of related printed ephemera, Banks enacted her own kind of materialisation of fashionable sociability based on the ticket and the event it both facilitated and documented.[49] In so far, then, that the ticket was performative of a particular sociable occasion, Sarah Sophia Banks's archive was performative of the event of fashionable sociability as a whole.

The history of polite sociability that the collections narrate begins roughly with the Mischianza, the fete held in 1778 in Philadelphia in honour of Sir William Howe, represented by the elaborate ticket which served to both publicise and commemorate it, followed by the 'balloon-mania' of 1783–4, the Handel commemorations in 1784, the beginning of the impeachment trial of Warren Hastings in 1788, the Richmond House theatricals of 1787–8, the thanksgiving for the recovery of George III in 1789, loyalist polite sociability in the late 1790s related to the Revolutionary and Napoleonic wars and the volunteer movement, the funerals of Pitt, Fox, and Nelson in 1806, and the Jubilee peace festivals of 1814. The archive as a whole reveals how fashionable sociability of the 1760s and 1770s, and the feminised public sphere it created, was adapted in the 1790s to counter the threat of a radical public sphere (for which, as we have seen, ephemeral genres such as the handbill were crucial).

Material relating to these events can be found across the full range of Banks's archive: that is, in the nine volumes of collections of cuttings now held in the British Library, her ticket files in the Department of Prints and Drawings, and her coins and tokens in the Department of Coins and Medals. The method of organising her material prioritised the documentary record as well as enabling the possibilities of synchronic, transmedial and fugitive readings or connections. (Hence the 'history' I have outlined is not readily apparent but only emerges through immersion in the detail of the collections as a whole). Similarly, as a history of sites and practices,

---

[48] Sarah Lloyd, *Charity and Poverty in England c. 1680–1820: Wild and Visionary Schemes* (Manchester: Manchester University Press, 2009), 236.

[49] For a comparable practice see James D. Lilley, 'Studies in Uniquity: Horace Walpole's Singular Collection', *ELH*, 80:1 (2013), 93–124.

the collections document the development of some of the key venues of fashionable sociability such as the Pantheon, from its grand opening in 1772 to its destruction by fire twenty years later. The Pantheon as a recurrent focus of Banks's collecting is contextualised in relation to less celebrated venues and occasions – for example, assemblies in Hackney, Highbury, Hampstead, and Chelsea, venues that also feature in the fiction of Frances Burney. Banks, like Burney (and later Jane Austen), was engaged in documenting how the ripples of fashionable sociability were spreading through polite culture in general, offering possibilities of social transformation for women.

The tickets in Banks's collection follow a range of formats – the vast majority consist of pasteboard cards, some take the form of handbills, and a few are made of silk. Those housed in the Department of Prints and Drawings are contained in a series of double folio sheets of paper, most of which are labelled in SSB's hand on the outside front page. The tickets within are normally annotated according to the date of acquisition, thereby recording the development of the collection, and sometimes include information about who gave SSB the ticket, or occasional contextual detail. An example is a comment added to a ticket for the King's Theatre at the Pantheon on 14 January 1792, noting that this was the day on which the Pantheon was destroyed by fire, thereby accentuating the poignancy of this record of an already ephemeral occasion.[50] Another way in which SSB annotated her tickets was through the inclusion of cuttings of newspaper paragraphs (the size and scale of which represented a miniaturised version of the ticket itself). Some of these newspaper cuttings were commentaries on the quality of the tickets themselves and therefore a kind of para-ticket, as in the case of the ticket for a gala at Brooks's Club to celebrate the King's recovery in 1789, to which SSB added a cutting from *The World*, dated 21 April 1789, describing the ticket and noting the quality of the engraving as 'very wretched' (C,2.746). Her collection included specimens of works by the most prominent engravers of the day, Francesco Bartolozzi and Giovanni Baptista Cipriani, and also tickets associated with notable events of the 1780s and 1790s, such as the impeachment trial of Warren Hastings, the tickets publicising the private theatricals at Wynnstay, and the Handel commemorations.

Some of these tickets had a wide currency (and, indeed, are still in circulation today via antique print sellers). SSB's primary interest, however, was curious or exceptional tickets with a striking pictorial design,

---

[50] C,2.1438. For the Pantheon fire see Russell, *Women, Sociability and Theatre*, 117, 232, 234.

particularly those executed by women. The collection included visiting cards designed by a number of ladies – Lady Frances Scott, Eliza B. Gulston, Lady Portarlington, and Miss Thickness – a category which also included SSB's designs for her own tickets.[51] A sequence of sheets includes an assemblage of her own cards with various addresses ranging from Chelsea where she lived with her mother before her move to Soho Square, mapping the progress of her life (C,1.716–49). The capacity of her modes of assemblage to construct meanings, however cryptic, for her tickets, is illustrated by one of the sheets of her collection of bookplates which she labelled 'Book Tickets. Ladies' (D,3.161–73).[52] It includes a ticket belonging to Anne Seymour Damer, devised and drawn by Agnes Berry (D,3.163), which Banks placed in the homosocial company of the tickets of a number of other ladies (Figure 8). Designed to be affixed to a book as a mark of ownership, rather than tendered as part of a social occasion, the bookplate was in theory not as ephemeral as other kinds of tickets. It could signify a possible lifetime of an owner's connection with a book, how it was handled, circulated, loved, and also possibly, disposed of: it could also, as in the case of Berry's plate for Damer, encode bonds of friendship. The paratextual significance of the bookplate in this latter respect was supplemented by its status as a gift, either in its own right or in possible conjunction with the exchange of books. By abstracting her bookplates from the book and arranging them in this way, Banks accentuated the work performed by such texts as prostheses of bodies and filters of social interaction.

One of the most notable examples of Banks's interest in tickets produced by women and the female homosocial contexts in which they circulated are three hand-painted tickets for a ball held at the assembly rooms in Norwich, two with ribbons attached, illustrating flowers, a butterfly, and a garland (J,9.237, J,9.238, J,9.239; Figure 9). Placed loosely within a sheet devoted to balls in suburban London (e.g. in Hackney, Kentish Town, and Hampstead) (J,9.200–43), these tickets are enclosed within a letter to Banks from a Mrs Peele within which there was another letter, to Mrs J. Wheler from Mrs Peele, giving an account of the origin of the tickets.[53] The occasion was a ball held in the Assembly rooms

---

[51] C,1.296 (Scott); C,1.471(Gulston); C,1.586 (Portarlington); C,1.2212 (Thickness).
[52] For Banks's bookplates see Pincott, 'The Book Tickets'.
[53] The following account of these documents is based on how I encountered them in the Banks collection in 2011. The image of them in the British Museum Research Collection Online Database suggests that the arrangement of them has changed.

Figure 8   Bookplate of Anne Seymour Damer. Collection of Sarah Sophia Banks D,3.162.
© The Trustees of the British Museum

in Norwich in January 1802 to celebrate the Peace of Amiens.⁵⁴ According to Mrs Peele,

> The Tickets with the numbers were to be drawn by the Ladys (who had no place by birth or marriage) to fix their set and station. The butterfly Tickets were given by the Mayoress to the Marry'd Ladys for one of [*sic*] Tables at Supper. (To prevent Confusion in setting down.) Mrs Ireby's sister (Miss Drake) & another young Lady painted the tickets. the [*sic*] Butterfly is meant to be emblematical, after having flutter'd about, it has chosen a favourite flower on which it was stationary. (J,9.240)

In this case tickets not merely facilitated access to an event but also regulated and made visible the social codes, particularly relating to class

---

⁵⁴ 'On Monday evening a Ball and Supper, in the first stile of elegance, was given at our Assembly-Rooms, [Norwich] by Jeremiah Ives, ... and Mrs. Ives, to between 5 and 400 ladies and gentlemen of this city and neighbourhood': *Bury and Norwich Post*, 20 January 1802.

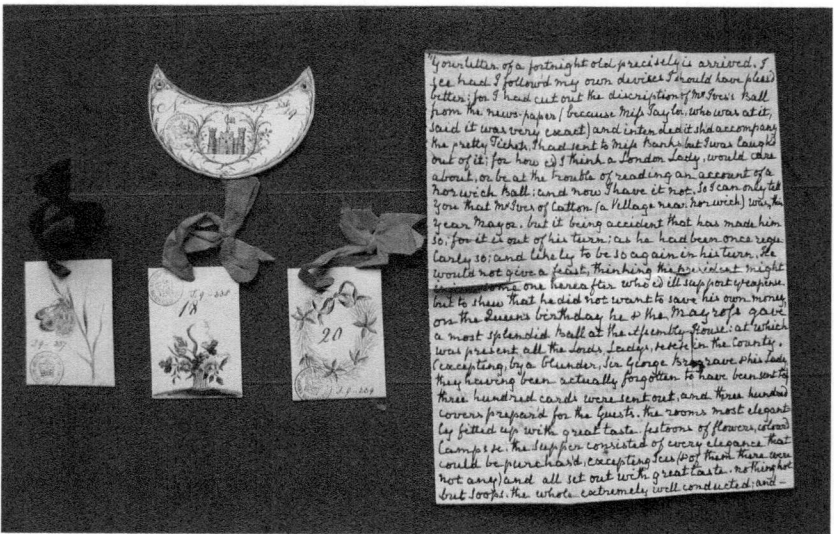

Figure 9 Lady's ticket to a ball in Norwich; with delicately drawn butterfly on blade of grass; Lady's ticket to a ball in Norwich; with hand-drawn vase of flowers, and red ribbon; Lady's ticket to a ball in Norwich; with hand drawn wreath with red flowers and blue bow. Collection of Sarah Sophia Banks J,9.237–239.
© The Trustees of the British Museum

and marital status, which underpinned such occasions. Pinned to gowns, as signified by the ribbons, the tickets were badges of progress in the life cycle of coming out, courtship, and marriage. The butterfly design possibly for some of the women concerned a poignant reminder of the ideal state of pre-marital life: previously free to flutter at will, they were now 'stationary', as pinned down as a specimen in a collector's cabinet. Richly contextualised in this way, it is not surprising that SSB preserved the tickets in the original letters in which she received them. Writing to Mrs Wheler, Mrs Peele acknowledged SSB's interest in such things, claiming that she had originally intended to send with the tickets an account of the Norwich ball but 'was laugh'd out of it; for how c'd I think a London lady, would care about, or be at the trouble of reading an account of a Norwich Ball' (J,9.240). The 'London lady' did indeed care about this communication, both for the tickets themselves and the paratextual information that illuminated them. Mrs Peele's reference to Sarah Sophia Banks not only indicates the extent to which her interest in tickets was known outside the immediate Banks circle but also involves SSB herself as part of a relay of transactions between women. Retaining the tickets as enclosures within a letter within another letter implicated Banks as part of the lost 'liveness' of an inconsequential ball, the ephemerality of which is 'emblematically' signified by the butterfly image. Her method of preserving these tickets, moreover, had a certain theatricality: they are not immediately accessible within this sheet but have to be taken out of the paper enclosures to be discovered, a pleasure which Banks was able to replicate by retaining them in this way. (Also, by not attaching them to the sheet she risked the possibility of losing them altogether). Because of this method of preservation, the Norwich tickets are as bright and vivid as when they were originally painted, another way in which the specificity of the occasion could be re-vivified. Each time she unwrapped them from their enclosures, Banks was setting something free – the ephemerality of the event itself and the butterfly lives that had inhabited it. The looseness of the Norwich ball tickets within this particular sheet also signifies the tension between the broader taxonomic principles and ambitions of the collection and the specificity of the ephemeral event or life experience to which such documentation gave access. The tickets documented a country ball, indeed the very kind of social occasion that was the focus of Jane Austen's contemporary attention in *The Watsons* and later *Pride and Prejudice* and *Emma*, indicating how the ephemeral imagination could intersect with prose fiction's investment in evoking the minutiae (and the hinterlands) of everyday social and affective experience. If Banks's ambitions as an archivist of sociability can be described in this respect as novelistic, then writers such as Austen can be similarly seen as connoisseurs of the ephemeral.

SSB's recording of how she acquired her tickets illustrates her interest in the sociable networks that tickets created and sustained and in the sociability created by a flow of paper information as well as the 'liveness' of face-to-face or group encounters. The correspondence of her brother indicates that Sir William Hamilton sent her parcels of visiting tickets of the Italian nobility on a number of occasions.[55] She sometimes directly solicited such material via her brother while his contacts, aware of 'Miss Banks's' interests, offered coins, medals, and tickets to her as part of their communication with Sir Joseph. In this way, SSB not only publicised her collecting amongst her brother's vast network of correspondents but also

[55] E.g. in 1783 Sir William Hamilton advised Banks that 'Earthquakes permitting I will bring your Sister a fine Collection of Visiting Tickets': Sir Joseph Banks, *Scientific Correspondence of Sir Joseph Banks, 1765–1820*, ed. Neil Chambers, 6 vols. (London: Pickering & Chatto, 2007), II: 53–4; and in 1785 he told him to tell his sister that 'her Collection of Tickets [in Naples] increases daily': Banks, *Scientific Correspondence*, III: 11.

integrated its focus on sociability, however tangentially, within the purview of legitimate scientific curiosity. Rather than being a 'private' enterprise, SSB's collecting was widely known in Sir Joseph Banks's circles in Britain and Europe: moreover, it functioned, not as a form of conspicuous consumption through monetary exchange, but within the economies of solicitation, gifting, obligation, and the principles of the disinterested exchange of information that underpinned associational culture, for both men and women. SSB thereby made a focus of her collecting an important dimension of ephemerality as noted by Alan Clinton – the fact that it stands outside or even resists 'normal channels' of monetary commercial exchange, circulating and making visible aspects of social life that were not easily commodifiable or which, in Addison's terms, compelled modes of reading that were not sought out but 'accidental'.

Sarah Sophia Banks's 'Sociablarium'

The primary location of Banks's collections was in her bedroom in No. 32 Soho Square, located directly above her brother's study, but as Arlene Leis has shown, the collections were also distributed throughout the domestic spaces in the Banks household.[56] In 1810 Banks wrote that his sister's room was 'so full of her Collections that I would not wish to have that usd if it Can be avoided Lest something should be displacd'.[57] No. 32 was divided between a front part facing Soho Square containing the main family residence and the 'back buildings' accessed from Dean Street that consisted of a galleried library and an herbarium and engravers' room located above a coach house and stables: as a whole the space was occupied by around twenty people, consisting of family, servants, and Sir Joseph Banks's research 'team'.[58] Harold Carter describes Banks's domain as the centre of a 'worldwide communications' network and a kind of sacred site of British science, with a 'solid claim to have foreshadowed the British Museum (Natural History) as we know it now'.[59] No. 32 was itself an important site of sociability, Sir Joseph Banks entertaining associates, friends, and clients in his weekly breakfasts and Sunday evening 'levees' or 'conversaziones' at which Sarah Sophia and Lady Banks were often

---

[56] Leis, 'Ephemeral Histories': 184–6.
[57] Sir Joseph Banks to Everard Home, 11 October 1810, in Banks, *Scientific Correspondence*, VI: 46.
[58] Carter, *Sir Joseph Banks*, 336.
[59] Harold B. Carter, *Sir Joseph Banks 1743–1820: A Guide to the Biographical and Bibliographical Sources* (London: St Paul's Bibliographies, 1987), 207, 242.

present.[60] SSB's collecting is a particularly striking example of how ephemerology has a spatial dimension, and how this archival 'domiciliation' is often contingent on, and constitutive of the larger archival 'space' in which the ephemera room is housed.

SSB's ticket collections now held in the Department of Prints and Drawings – the tickets of admission, visiting cards, book tickets (bookplates), and trade cards – represent an attempt to collate and systematise these texts in an analogous way to how her brother and his collaborators were interpreting the flora, fauna, and artefacts flowing in and out of No. 32. The major influence on Banks's classification of such material was the system of Carl von Linné (Linnaeus), whose division of the natural order into a binomial distinction of genus and species, according to John Gascoigne, 'greatly facilitated the task of *neatly docketing away* new species and thus of strengthening confidence in the belief that, like Adam and Eve of old, the human race was more and more the ruler of the natural world' (my emphasis). The Linnaean system, according to Gascoigne, 'brought to botany and zoology a degree of order; it thus helped to make accessible and comprehensible the ever-mounting number of specimens that European (and especially British) commercial and naval power was steadily augmenting throughout the century'.[61] The activities of No. 32 were indebted, like many other aspects of eighteenth-century life to jobbing print and what Raven calls 'typographic assuredness', being reliant on actual dockets – small printed labels – to systematise and make accessible knowledge of the world.

The order according to which Sarah Sophia Banks attempted to organise her tickets was that of social class: her collection of visiting cards, for example, was filed according to rank, beginning with 'English Dukes' followed, in order of precedence, by barons, then Scotch and Irish titles (Figure 10). Subsequent files in this British section of the visiting cards were organised alphabetically, ending with an appendix of miscellaneous items. Banks also made a collection of 'Foreign' visiting cards, alphabetised according to country of origin, beginning with America but mostly focusing on countries in Europe. The influence of Linnaean methodologies also extended to the specific material way in which Banks organised her tickets in folded single sheets. The custom of preserving plants by drying and then

---

[60] The artist and diarist Joseph Farington noted an encounter with 'Mrs & Miss Banks' at a breakfast in 1794. Sir Joseph Banks presented him on leaving with 'a Card of Invitation' to his Sunday evening 'conversazione': Joseph Farington, *The Diary of Joseph Farington*, eds. Kenneth Garlick and Angus MacIntyre, 16 vols. (New Haven, CT: Yale University Press, 1978), I: 188–9.
[61] Gascoigne, *Joseph Banks*, 99.

Figure 10 Second page of a folded sheet, twenty-one undecorated visiting cards, one MS note, and three newspaper cuttings 1779–1815. Collection of Sarah Sophia Banks C,1.2401–2426.
© The Trustees of the British Museum

pressing them on sheets of paper which were subsequently bound as books dates from the sixteenth century. Linnaeus introduced the practice of keeping the sheets separate and storing them horizontally, making it easier to add to or adapt the collections as well as countering possible damage to specimens caused by shelving them vertically in book form.[62] SSB would certainly have been aware of how the practice was developed by Solander and later Dryander in the Soho Square herbarium. (Solander is acknowledged as the inventor of the solander case, a levered box in which the herbarium sheets could be stored horizontally and is still widely used in archives today). In 1818 Sir Joseph Banks advised Lady Charlotte Jane Seymour to 'make an herbarium by Drying the Plants you Collect between Sheets of Paper, and keeping them Separate from Each other', advice he may also have given to his sister many years before.[63] By emulating the herbarium, Banks legitimated her labours in relation to the activities of the Banks household as a whole (also making her collections more portable and malleable).[64] The spatial dimensions of the suffix '-arium' in herbarium – meaning, according to the *Oxford English Dictionary*, a 'thing connected with or employed in, place for' suggesting the idea of knowledge as being placed or locatable – also relate to the spatial dimensions of Banks's archival practices. The domestic quarters of No. 32 Soho Square were thus a 'sociablarium', a place for ephemeral textuality in its multifarious forms.

Organised in this quasi-Linnaean way, Banks was able to document and classify the ruling elite of not only Britain and Ireland but also Europe as an order analogous to that of the natural world itself. The importance of the ticket, particularly the visiting card, was in manifesting new forms of sociability and association through networks of correspondence and the republic of letters, supplementing and reinforcing traditional ties of family and politics that had hitherto bound Europe's elite. Another category of ticket, the ticket of admission, which Banks organised alphabetically according to types of event such as balls, concerts, and exhibitions, complemented her visiting cards by documenting the wider associational world in which the people of her visiting cards were participating, creating new forms of publicity for themselves. Banks's collection of tickets therefore recognised the role of sociability, print culture, and commerce in creating transnational and cosmopolitan connections that supplemented older modes of elite association. Rather than mapping traditional lineages of national and patriarchal pedigree, the focus of contemporary

---

[62] W. T. Stearn, *An Introduction to the Species Panatarum and Cognate Botanical Works of Carl Linnaeus* (London: Ray Society, 1957); G. P. Dewolf Jr, 'Notes on Making an Herbarium', *Arnoldia*, 28:8–9 (1968), 69–111.
[63] Joseph Banks, *The Letters of Sir Joseph Banks: A Selection, 1768–1820*, ed. Neil Chambers (London: Imperial College Press, 2000), 34c.
[64] Leis, 'Ephemeral Histories', 185.

publications such as Burke's *Peerage*, Banks documented the importance of international elite sociability in creating a different, more lateral web of affiliation and also a more synchronic concept of history, focused on the ephemeral present.

Another influence on the arrangement of Banks's ticket collections is likely to have been her interest in numismatics. Coins and medals, of both ancient and modern kinds, were often illustrated in groups laid out on a horizontal plane, a practice that was adapted for botany and zoology and other branches of antiquarianism, including the representation of artificial curiosities from voyages of discovery. Artefacts such as spears, headdresses, and ornaments were depicted as abstract objects, denuded of their originating context, whose only relationship was to each other within the blank space of the engraved plate. Nicholas Thomas argues that this decontextualisation had the effect of 'licensing' the power of curiosity about such objects and the cultures they came from by situating them in 'a wholly imaginary field'.[65] As in the case of the herbarium, Banks would have been intimately familiar with this mode of illustration, as her brother was both its sponsor and producer, the engravers' room in No. 32 being the source of many of the illustrations of the Cook voyages. Banks's assemblages abstracted her tickets from associations with the mundane world of quotidian social interaction which verged on the abjection of absolute ephemerality, to make them objects of notice in their own right, thereby rendering sociability potentially admissible to the discursive field of curiosity.

This abstraction also had a powerful aesthetic element, related to design features of specific tickets and their arrangement on the page of the folded folio sheet. (Banks's modelling or mapping of her tickets on a planar dimension anticipates the application of 'assemblage' around 1960 to forms of twentieth-century art which 'stress the accumulation of found elements in such a way that they remain separately recognizable', expressive of what is 'ephemeral in modern life'.)[66] A substantial number of her visiting cards, integrated into the British section, consisted of blank designs such as what Banks termed 'figures' or squares, as well as blanks which she classified by type of imagery, such as animals, architecture, or picturesque ruins.[67] These sheets indicate her interest in the blank ticket as a formal design in its own right, thereby accentuating the visibility and power of the

---

[65] Nicholas Thomas, *In Oceania: Visions, Artifacts, Histories* (Durham, NC: Duke University Press, 1997), 105.
[66] John Elderfield (ed.), *Essays on Assemblage* (New York: Museum of Modern Art, 1992), 7, 8.
[67] C,1.2470–4996 (approx.).

medium's instrumentality (and indirectly that of paper media as a whole). This interest in graphic design also extended to the material archived in her cuttings collections now in the British Library, such as lottery advertisements with arresting typography, linking Banks with the importance of ephemerology to the history of printing. Importantly, tickets were not only something to be looked at but were also material objects to be handled. Part of Banks's aestheticisation of such ephemera entailed an accentuation of its materiality – the significance of traces such as signatures, seals, ribbons, the very indentations of letterpress or intaglio printing on paper or pasteboard that encouraged a kind of optical tactility, a caress with the eye of the form of the imprint of letter or script on paper. Banks's practices therefore endowed the ephemeral text with a uniquity, its own auratic signature, mediated in terms of her own cryptic 'presence' in the collection as its maker through the practices of selection, fixing, and annotation, and through her use of sheets, a layering of paper upon paper, to contain and display the ticket. In this respect Banks was a virtuoso of quotidian sociability, seeking to draw attention to ephemerality's aesthetics of loss – tickets being particularly powerful traces of elusive human contact – while at the same time trying to synthesise such texts to form a coherent body of knowledge on the model of her brother's enterprise. Rather than being tangential to the project of No. 32 Soho Square, Banks's activities can therefore be said to have realised its fundamental tensions – between the desire to know and acquire everything about the world and the awareness that such knowledge would always slip away into ephemerality. The following chapter outlines how those tensions were manifested with particular reference to Banks's 'ticketing' of her brother's career and the phenomenon which may have started her interest in documenting knowledge, like fashion, as airy and fleeting – the advent in the 1780s of balloonmania.

CHAPTER 4

Sarah Sophia Banks's 'Magic Encyclopedia'

The Norwich ball tickets exemplify how Sarah Sophia Banks's interest in the ticket as an object that aestheticised ephemerality was contextually dependent on use – the events and places tickets signified, the people who exchanged them, and ultimately, SSB's own handling of them. While SSB's collections were focused on elite and polite sociability, she was aware of the wider currency of tickets in Georgian society. In a sheet of tickets documenting Sir Joseph Banks's sociability as President of the Royal Society, such as invitations to his 'at homes' at No. 32, SSB included a selection of 'sticklers tickets' (D,3.501–4; Figure 11).[1] These were printed handbills authorising individuals to collect fuel from various woods on the Banks estate in Lincolnshire. Sarah Sophia contextualised these tickets by including a handbill, printed by Weir of Horncastle, notifying that such 'Tickets will be granted on application to such poor and industrious persons as deserve them'; if caught taking wood without these 'passports', individuals would be regarded as trespassing (D,3.513). The sticklers' tickets represent a glimpse of bodies largely absent in SSB's archive – those of the lower orders – showing how elite sociability intersected with other kinds of ticket economies, as detailed by Sarah Lloyd.[2] In the context of Sir Joseph Banks's reliance on tickets for the maintenance of his scientific networks, the sticklers' tickets reveal such paper filters to be also important in his role as a prominent landowner. The tickets facilitated a system of surveillance. By soliciting for them the lower orders identified themselves to Banks's steward for evaluation as deserving, while carrying them was an

---

[1] A 'stickler' was someone who was authorised to take wood from e.g. royal parks, and had a history in feudal custom. See definition in James Orchard Halliwell-Phillipps, *A Dictionary of Archaic and Provincial Words, Obsolete Phrases, Proverbs, and Ancient Customs, Volume II: J–Z* (London: John Russell Smith, 1847), 805: 'A small officer who cut wood for the priory of Inichester within the king's parks of Clarendon. *Blount.*' Banks was thus combining feudal practice with a modern medium of print publicity – the handbill.

[2] Lloyd, 'Ticketing'.

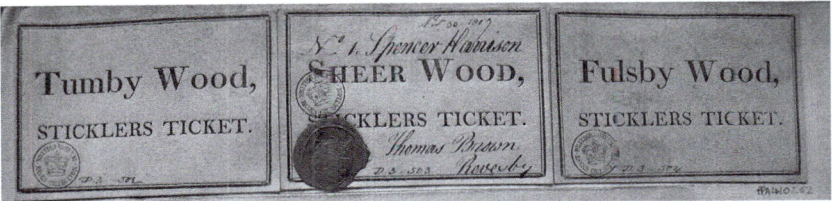

Figure 11 Sticklers tickets (c. 1807). Collection of Sarah Sophia Banks D,3.501–504.
© The Trustees of the British Museum

acknowledgement of the 'gift' of Banks's charity and a deference to his authority. Banks's resort to the local printing press to enable him to manage such relationships was a sign of his confidence in the power of print communication to objectify and facilitate an ideal of enlightened stewardship that nonetheless served to reinforce status and the security of property. Printed paper in the form of a ticket enabled this ideal to be enacted practically, as well as creating a potential public record of what was hitherto a matter of informal, private, social relations – a steward's verbal permission or a nod and a wink. Sarah Sophia's self-defined role was to commemorate her brother's commitment to paper communication in every aspect of his public life. Rather than being of trivial or 'ephemeral' value, the sticklers' tickets had the potential to reveal just how penetrating and potentially transformative of social relations and knowledge eighteenth-century print could be.

The sticklers' tickets were only part of SSB's documentation of her brother's investment in the ticket economy of late Georgian Britain. Joseph Banks's admission into circles of influence in British Enlightenment culture began at the age of twenty with his first reader's ticket to the British Museum, 'dated 3 August 1764'.[3] This particular ticket does not appear to be in his sister's collections though she did possess a later example of one of Banks's reader's tickets from 1777 (J,8.6 – Banks became an ex-officio trustee of the Museum in 1778 when he became President of the Royal Society). There were three kinds of tickets associated with the Museum: readers' tickets admitting a very select group of learned men to the use of the library; tickets for visits to the collection by the public which had to be applied for in advance and were only awarded to those deemed to be of the appropriate 'condition'; and, finally, tickets

---

[3] Carter, *Sir Joseph Banks*, 27.

for the Museum garden to the north of Montagu House.[4] Visitors to the garden, which took up seven acres, needed written permission from a trustee or officer of the Museum. Originally designed to be of botanical interest, the garden, according to Anne Goldgar, 'dwindled to a pleasant place to promenade ... [and was] abandoned to the fashionable public'.[5] The early British Museum therefore had three gendered spatial dimensions: the male homosocial space of the library, the predominantly male homosocial one of the museum as a whole to which women were occasionally admitted as members of the public; and the out of doors of the garden, a more feminised site of heterosocial promenade (which also permitted children who were expressly prohibited from Montagu House). SSB's collection of admission tickets contains a sheet devoted to the British Museum in which she placed a number of tickets to both the museum and the garden. The sheet includes a communication dated 1802 from the librarian Joseph Planta enclosing 'the Six Garden Tickets she desired to have', also giving advice about how the tickets should be validated: the name of the person using it was to be written 'above the line on the front', with the signature of the trustee or officer below (J,8.103). As in the case of the Norwich ball tickets, SSB documents her own role as part of a correspondence network, Planta's communication anticipating the distribution of these tickets to SSB's guests (though she retained two blank ones for her collection).

This correspondence entailed an acknowledgement of SSB's privileged status as sister of a trustee, social capital she was able to display in gifting the tickets to others. She was thereby able to assert a place for herself, literally and figuratively, at an institution with which No. 32 Soho Square and her brother's career were closely linked. The fact that this 'place' was the British Museum garden may initially check a feminist reading of SSB's collecting practice in this instance. In confining herself to the garden or the role of a temporary visitor she can be said to be conforming to women's roles as outsiders or satellites of the domains of male-dominated learning. However, rather than being at its periphery, the 'fashionable public' into which knowledge 'dwindled' was in fact an integral part of the Museum 'complex'. The deployment of the ticket system from the inception of the Museum located it within a more expansive idea of the public, including polite associational culture in which women were playing a transformative

---

[4] See Anne Goldgar, 'The British Museum and the Virtual Representation of Culture in the Eighteenth Century', *Albion*, 32:2 (2000), 195–231.
[5] Goldgar, 'British Museum', 206, 207.

role in the 1760s and 1770s.⁶ SSB's archival practices documented how access was regulated in the form of the ticket as well as applying to the 'humble' ticket the methods and principles of taxonomy that underpinned the work of the Museum: she was implicitly making the pleasure garden as legitimate a place of knowledge as a cabinet of curiosities.

Other examples of tickets in SSB's collection associated with her brother, in addition to the sticklers' tickets and those for his 'at homes' at No. 32, include a range of his visiting tickets (e.g. C,1.716–21). The collections show Banks to be both a giver and a receiver of tickets. In one notable example he was also a ticket designer and producer. In 1803 Sir Joseph Banks took responsibility for supervising the design and printing of the tickets for a fete at Ranelagh to commemorate the formal installation of the Knights of the Order of the Garter. Banks had been made a Knight of the Garter by the king in 1795, in recognition of his services to the Royal Society and the government, the occasion for James Gillray's print, 'The great South Sea Caterpillar, transform'd into a Bath Butterfly'. Gillray depicted Banks as a caterpillar, which had 'first crawl'd into notice from among the Weeds & Mud ... of the South Sea', now metamorphosed into its present shape due to the warmth of royal favour, represented in the print by the rays of a sun with a crown at its centre.⁷ Published at the apogee of Banks's success, the print was a reminder of his reputation in the early 1770s as a macaroni dilettante, tainted by his association with Tahiti and libertine licentiousness. As I have argued elsewhere, Banks's return to England in 1771 after the *Endeavour* voyage coincided with the expansion of fashionable sociability in venues such as Carlisle House in Soho Square and the Pantheon and the rise of heterosocial gambling clubs such as the Ladies Coterie.⁸ Banks engaged directly with fashionable culture through public socialising with elite women, self-publicity in the press, and portraits such as Benjamin West's of 1773, which depicted him accoutred in Pacific artefacts. In the 1770s Banks was the explorer as celebrity man of fashion (and vice versa), a focus of the gossip of the *Town and Country Magazine* and the target of satiric libertine verse. Fashionable sociability, the main focus of SSB's collections, was therefore formative in her brother's early career, and Gillray's print was an uncomfortable reminder of that

---

⁶ See Russell, *Women, Sociability and Theatre*.
⁷ James Gillray, 'The great South Sea Caterpillar, transform'd into a Bath Butterfly', published Hannah Humphrey, 1795. BM 1868,0808.6454.
⁸ Gillian Russell, '"An entertainment of oddities": Fashionable Sociability and the Pacific in the 1770s', in *A New Imperial History: Culture, Identity, and Modernity in Britain and the Empire, 1660–1840*, ed. Kathleen Wilson (Cambridge, UK: Cambridge University Press, 2004), 48–70.

history at the apparent height of his success and recognition. Banks, Gillray was suggesting, was an ephemeral being who had manufactured himself out of nothing and was ultimately dependent on royalty for his survival. As Alan Bewell comments: 'Banks is both the soil *and* the insect; he is his own monstrous self-product, a creature of autogenesis, having crawled out of his own mud and weeds.'[9]

Sarah Sophia Banks collected other Gillray prints but does not seem to have owned a copy of this one, though she is highly likely to have been aware of its existence. Sir Joseph Banks was not formally installed as Knight of the Order of the Bath until 1803. Such ceremonies normally took place every nine years but due to the war with France one had not been held since 1788. The Peace of Amiens represented an opportunity for the installation to be revived, part of an elaboration of royal ceremonial during the Revolutionary and Napoleonic wars. The installation took place at Westminster Abbey on May 19th and at least one newspaper reported the special attention given to Banks by Queen Charlotte who acknowledged the fact that he was unable to stand due to his gout: 'with this mark of his QUEEN'S regard SIR JOSEPH appeared much pleased'.[10] The ceremony was then followed a fortnight later by a lavish ball, staged in a specially designed temporary building next to the main rotunda at Ranelagh. The evening featured a ballet and songs by leading performers from the theatres in the presence of the royal family, followed by supper for more than two thousand people.[11] Banks took responsibility for the design and production of the ticket for this event, liaising with the engraver Abraham Raimbach and George Nicol, the king's bookseller. The design of the ticket, which featured a classical female figure wielding a banner on which is inscribed 'Ball at Ranelagh', was by George Smirke. Sir Joseph Banks's involvement was such that he had a say in the design of the lettering and even the kind of paper used by Nicol.[12] (It is possible that he consulted his sister, making her a silent partner in the ticket's

---

[9] Alan Bewell, '"On the banks of the South Sea": Botany and Sexual Controversy in the Late Eighteenth Century', in *Visions of Empire: Voyages, Botany and Representations of Nature*, eds. David Philip Miller and Peter Hanns Reill (Cambridge, UK: Cambridge University Press, 1996), 173–94 (190).

[10] *Morning Chronicle*, 20 May 1803. [11] *Morning Chronicle*, 3 June 1803.

[12] For Banks's responsibility for the design and engraving of the ticket see Carter, *Sir Joseph Banks*, 439; Banks's letter to Raimbach in which he gives directions for letter is summarised in Sir Joseph Banks, *Supplementary Letters of Sir Joseph Banks*, ed. Warren R. Dawson (London: The Trustees of the British Museum, 1962), 60; see also a letter from George Nicol on 16 May 1803 in Sir Joseph Banks, *The Banks Letters: A Calendar of the Manuscript Correspondence*, ed. Warren R. Dawson (London: The Trustees of the British Museum, 1958), 639.

conception: at the very least Banks would have been familiar with the kinds of tickets she was collecting). The success of the ticket's design was remarked upon in publicity for the event, the *Morning Post* commenting that the 'tickets, well designed, and beautifully engraved, by RAIMBACH, may serve as lasting monuments of this fete'.[13] The event was typical of some forms of late Georgian fashionable sociability which sought to project elite privilege in the terms of the commercialised public sphere – through the use of venues such as Ranelagh, mediation through newspaper and other forms of print publicity, and the involvement of professional performers – without compromising the aura of exclusivity. The ticket therefore assumed a particular significance as the token or mechanism by which the particular quasi-public/quasi-private status of the event was maintained. The ticket both effected exclusivity and served as a 'monument' or proof that this exclusivity had been achieved. Hence reporting of the event paid particular attention to the process and drama of the vetting of the tickets:

> They were sealed with two seals; the first Lord HENLEY's, the other Sir A. CLARKE'S: the first seal was torn off at the entrance, and then returned to the Lady or Gentleman who brought it, and they gave it to a person stationed in the interior, who broke off the other seal, and by that means rendered the ticket useless. This plan precluded the possibility of improper persons gaining admittance. During the time the Tickets were passing the fiery ordeal, some of the owners waited the result in a state of the most anxious suspense; and so much alarmed were many of the ladies, for fear their's should prove a forged ticket, that when it was returned to them to pass on, their hands shook with agitation. Happily for all parties, no forged tickets were presented.[14]

Such anxiety was not unwarranted: in 1800 it was widely reported that routs at the house of the Marquis of Abercorn had been compromised by forged cards of invitation.[15] The elite's engagement with the wider paper economy meant that the authenticity of its signature was liable to replication; the auratic ephemeral, in the form of the ticket as an art object or a communication endorsed by a seal, was threatened by the ephemerality of endlessly reproducible paper 'rubbish'. Such anxieties related to the controllability of the boundaries of privilege in the wake of the 1790s and the politicised meanings of ephemerality – the fact that 'improper persons' might inveigle their way inside, combined with an underlying concern that

---

[13] *Morning Post*, 2 June 1803. [14] *Morning Post*, 3 June 1803.
[15] Sarah Sophia Banks collected newspaper cuttings related to the Abercorn hoax: see sheet C1,2375–2430.

the elite bodies tendering these tickets might not be able to substantiate their value as sociable currency – hence the trembling hands of the ladies who proffered them and the uncanny metonymy of the tickets which underwent the 'fiery ordeal' of authentication on their subjects' behalf.

Sir Joseph Banks himself underwent a form of authentication on the occasion of the 1803 fete. His elevation to the Order of the Bath (and acknowledgement in such a familiar way by Queen Charlotte) represented public recognition of his place at the very centre of the British state. Banks had been metamorphosed from the transient social butterfly of the 1770s to the man of substance, no longer the creature of the ephemeral tides of fashion, but a member of a chivalric order and thus enshrined by history. Sarah Sophia Banks's collections interpret her brother's elevation in these terms by contextualising the installation ceremony and the Ranelagh ball in relation to the long-established history of the sociability associated with the Order of the Bath. Her admission tickets in the British Museum's Department of Prints and Drawings include a proof copy of the ticket for the Ranelagh ball and other copies signed and with seals, thereby validating both the efficacy of the ticket in regulating and ultimately constituting the event and its status as a form of commemoration – a textual monument (C,2.1915, C,2.1913; Figures 12 and 13). The proof version of the ticket in conjunction with other used copies enabled SSB to assemble a particular kind of ephemeral temporality: the proof version was 'pure' ticket, signifying a potentiality, an event to come, of which the torn, sealed, and signed versions are its validation, 'proofs' that the event had taken place. SSB also placed material on the installation ceremony and the Ranelagh ball in her collectanea: her volume on ceremonials (L.R.301.h.4) contained tickets for the installation itself in Westminster Abbey, broadsides listing the order of the ceremonial, a proposal for a coloured engraving by Ackermann depicting the ceremony, and a page of newspaper cuttings, including references to Sir Joseph.[16] In this respect the collectanea complemented her collection of admission tickets, the former focusing on the installation, the latter on the fashionable sociability that amplified it.

While the newspaper cuttings drew attention to Sir Joseph Banks's presence at the installation, thereby personalising his sister's archive, she did not highlight his role in the design of the Ranelagh ball ticket. Banks's supervision of the design and manufacture of the ticket shows him not only to have been a participant in the installation – the object of a Queen's care and attention – but also its impresario, engaging in the

---

[16] L.R.301.h.4, ff. 1–8.

Sarah Sophia Banks's 'Magic Encyclopedia'   133

Figure 12   Ticket to a Ball at Ranelagh on 1 June 1803. Collection of Sarah Sophia Banks C,2.1915.
© The Trustees of the British Museum

manufacture of the kinds of paper media by which fashionable sociability was conducted and publicised. Banks was thus not simply 'made' but also the maker of the installation as a socio-political event, a theatricalisation of elite power in terms of a feminised fashionable sociability. This 'making' entailed a fabrication of himself, consistent with his long-standing capacity for auto-genesis. Sarah Sophia's inclusion of the Ranelagh ticket in her archive as just another example of a ticket is an acknowledgement of how successful that self-fabrication had been, in so far as it enabled a

Figure 13   Ticket to a Ball at Ranelagh on 1 June 1803. Collection of Sarah Sophia Banks C, 2.1913.
© The Trustees of the British Museum

transcendence of the vestiges of her brother's association with a more pejoratively ephemeral fashionability and a more thorough-going and invisible identification with the enduring theatricality of state power. The Ranelagh ticket is thus a counter-apotheosis to Gillray's 'Bath Butterfly'. Sir Joseph Banks was now an acknowledged member of the greater royal 'family', even though he was still required to ensure, behind the scenes, that the show of power could be effectively orchestrated. The installation and the Ranelagh ball warrant little more than a footnote in Banks scholarship, his role in designing a mere ball ticket meriting even less attention, but for Sarah Sophia Banks they are likely to have been very significant. The ball ticket can be regarded as the brother and sister's gift to each other: in creating it, Sir Joseph Banks was acknowledging the importance of the sphere of fashionable sociability to print culture, politics, and elite authority, implicitly recognising that sphere as an object of legitimate inquiry. In turn, Sarah Sophia's archiving of the Ranelagh tickets was a confirmation of what Sir Joseph had designed, both specifically and ideologically. It recognised what the cultivation of a public role had entailed for her brother, its costs as well as its triumphs.

Ballooning as Media History

The contiguity between Sarah Sophia's collecting and the projects of her brother is also apparent in their shared interests in the craze for ballooning which took off in Britain in late 1783. Harold Carter describes the year 1783 as being 'pregnant with a full litter of embryonic ideas' for Sir Joseph (including the genesis of the idea of a colony in New South Wales).[17] Chief among these thought 'bubbles' was the possibility of man-powered flight, inspired by news from France of the launching of a hot-air balloon by the Montgolfier brothers in Paris in June 1783, followed by a balloon flight powered by hydrogen by Jacques Charles and the Robert brothers on 27 August. (The first manned balloon flights in France occurred a few months later in November). Banks's chief informant about these innovations was Benjamin Franklin to whom he wrote that he was beset with questions from 'all sorts of people Concerning the Aerostatique Experiment'.[18] Though Banks was wary of the 'balloonmania', he was nonetheless intrigued and excited by the possibilities of ballooning, particularly in relation to flight, writing to Franklin: 'I consider the present day, which has opend a road in the Air as an epoche from whence a rapid increase of the stock of real knowledge with which the human species is furnishd must take its date'.[19] In the late summer and autumn of 1783, when Banks and the ladies were on their annual migration to the Banks's country seat at Revesby Abbey in Lincolnshire, there was a flow of paper information concerning ballooning in and out of No. 32, not only letters from Franklin and other correspondents, but also visual images, periodical publications, and pamphlets. In October 1783, for example, Charles Blagden reported

---

[17] Carter, *Sir Joseph Banks*, 190.
[18] Sir Joseph Banks to Benjamin Franklin, 13 September 1783, in Banks, *Letters, 1768–1820*, 62.
[19] Sir Joseph Banks to Benjamin Franklin, 13 September 1783, in Banks, *Letters, 1768–1820*, 62.

to Banks the arrival at No. 32 of a 'parcel of pamphlet[s] & Journals ... on the subject of the balloons'.[20]

Inevitably the experiments with ballooning in France spread to Britain. On 4 November 1783 two Italians, Count Francesco Zambecarri and Michael Biaggi, launched a small balloon from Highgate to Waltham Abbey, followed by a flight three weeks later at the Artillery Ground at Moorfields. Banks described the latter to Franklin as a 'miserable Taffeta Balloon', noting how the Italians had capitalised on the novelty by exhibiting it 'for several days floating about in a public room at a shilling for the sight & half a crown for the Admission when it should be let loose'.[21] From the outset, ballooning in Britain was appropriated by the showmen of the Enlightenment working in conjunction with the print media. The phenomenon also quickly spread beyond the metropolis: experiments similar to those of Zambecarri and Biaggi were made in towns such as Bath, Bristol, Manchester, Colchester and Derby, as well as in Scotland and Ireland.[22] It was in Edinburgh that the first manned flights in a Montgolfier hot-air balloon were made in Britain by the chemist, journalist, and printer James Tytler, on 25 August and 1 September 1784. They were followed by the more celebrated ascension of Vincent Lunardi from the Artillery Ground at Moorfields in London on 15 September. Banks was a major sponsor of Lunardi's enterprise as one of its public subscribers, a role which Franklin acknowledged in a letter congratulating him on the fact that 'Experiments with the Balloons' were beginning in England.[23] Banks himself did not witness Lunardi's flight as he was ensconced with the ladies at Revesby. SSB's curiosity about ballooning is suggested by a letter from Charles Blagden to Banks, dated 16 September 1784, in which he states that the naturalist John Lloyd 'has written so full an account of Lunardi's balloon to Miss Banks, that I can add nothing to it, having not been myself at the Artillery ground'.[24] Lloyd's letter indicates SSB's involvement in Banks's correspondence networks concerning balloons, including the possibility that she read Franklin's letters to her brother.

---

[20] Blagden to Sir Joseph Banks, 14 October 1783, in Banks, *Scientific Correspondence*, II: 173.
[21] Banks, *Scientific Correspondence*, II: 217.
[22] Michael Lynn, *The Sublime Invention: Ballooning in Europe, 1783–1820* (London: Pickering & Chatto, 2010), 18.
[23] Banks, *Scientific Correspondence*, II: 299.
[24] Charles Blagden to Sir Joseph Banks, 16 September 1874, in Banks, *Scientific Correspondence*, II: 304.

The balloonmania is possibly the first major contemporary phenomenon that SSB documented by means of printed and visual ephemera and it may well have been the catalyst for her interest in such textuality. Material relating to ballooning is contained in the first volume of her 'Collectanea' in the British Library (L.R.301.h.3), entitled 'Balloons, Sights, Exhibitions, Remarkable Characters, Katterfelto, the Monster'. In addition to balloons, the volume documents curious exhibitions at Astley's circus, the activities of the scientific showman and quack doctor Gustavus Katterfelto, the most famous person in London in 1782–3, various sensational shows such as the Wonderful Pig in 1785, and finally material relating to the London 'Monster'.[25] While it is possible that SSB was not the author of this arrangement, and indeed the sequence of the nine volumes of the collection as a whole, the material in this first volume is coherent in its focus on sensations of the 1780s that attracted considerable, and particularly ephemeral, print publicity. The themes of the volume – 'wondrous' inventions, quackery, curious exhibitions, strange events – are also consistent with the focus of previous ephemera collectors going back to Anthony Wood. SSB was therefore contextualising the balloon craze as another, albeit highly significant phase, in the history of the nexus of the print media and the ephemerality of exhibition culture of all kinds, both 'elite' and 'popular', that underpinned Enlightenment modernity. As I shall argue later this context is important in determining how ballooning and the ephemeral archive can be interpreted in terms of the evolution of disciplinarity.

SSB's balloon material, which crosses both the collectanea in the British Library and the collections in the British Museum (including her coins and medals – she possessed a medal commemorating Lunardi's flight on 14 September 1784),[26] consists of prints, handbill advertisements, pamphlets, slip poetry, newspaper and periodical cuttings, and tickets. It is predominantly a visual record of ballooning. Print sellers produced numerous illustrations of balloon launches which functioned as both records and souvenirs of these events, as well as aesthetic objects in their own right, evoking the awe and pleasure of the 'aerostatic' spectacle. Examples of such prints by sellers such as Carington Bowles, who catered to the middling and fashionable classes, and cheaper woodcuts by Marshall & Co. of Aldermary Church Yard in Bow Lane indicate SSB's interest in the broad

---

[25] For Katterfelto and the Wonderful Pig see Richard D. Altick, *The Shows of London* (London: Belknap, 1978), 40–2, 84–5; see also Deirdre Coleman, 'Entertaining Entomology: Insects and Insect Performers in the Eighteenth Century', *Eighteenth-Century Life*, 30:3 (2006), 107–34.
[26] BM Coins SSB,245.141.

appeal of such images and how they defined a cross-class balloon-viewing 'public'. She also documented the marketing of access to ballooning by means of ephemeral print. From the very beginning of the craze in Britain, balloon entrepreneurs adapted the ticket system associated with fashionable sociability in order to commodify their 'product', define their public, publicise balloon events through networks of ticket-related publicity, and ultimately commemorate what had occurred. 'Subscription packages' were devised, whereby the viewer could pay to view the balloon before launch, hear a lecture on aeronautics, or even experience for themselves what it felt like to sit in a gondola.[27] Those interested in prolonging the experience could also view the balloon after it had made its voyage. Jonas Dryander reported to Banks (and the ladies) in October 1784 that it was 'quite the fun now to go to/the/Pantheon to see Lunardi's dog and cat [which he had taken up with him in his balloon] ... It is said that he takes about 100 pounds a day for admissions'.[28] While Banks was wary of such commercialisation, as in his complaint about Lunardi's 'miserable taffeta' balloon floating about in a public room, his comment, like that of Dryander about Lunardi's milking of his fame, was a recognition of fashion as a context and indeed an analogy for the work of No. 32 and the Royal Society.

Sarah Sophia Banks's archive of ballooning documented how fashion, visual culture (in the form of the print), and the ephemerality of sociable life – the idea of the 'public' connoted by Banks's reference to a 'public' room – were capable of forming 'a stock of real knowledge' in their own right. While Sir Joseph Banks was writing, reading about, and disseminating information about balloons in No. 32 Soho Square, SSB was involved in her own flow of ephemeral balloon information and undoubtedly the two streams overlapped. The contingency of 'mainstream' and 'ephemeral' knowledges therefore had a specific material and spatial meaning, a daily enactment. Michael Lynn claims that '[a]s balloons came to symbolize the age of reason, especially with their focus on the conquest of nature and the potential utility of the invention, aeronauts implicitly carved out a new manner in which individuals, *for the price of a ticket*, could become active members of the Enlightenment'.[29] Rather than being of marginal significance, the ticket was therefore potentially the most important textual record of the ballooning phenomenon because it enabled and signified

---

[27] Lynn, *Sublime Invention*, 122.
[28] Jonas Dryander to Sir Joseph Banks, 19 October 1784, in Banks, *Scientific Correspondence*, II: 317.
[29] Lynn, *Sublime Invention*, 123 (my emphasis).

an active participation in a more open configuration of Enlightenment culture. SSB's collecting was both a recognition of the value of the ephemeral record in this respect and her own implicit claim to membership in the public it created.

Thus the material relating to ballooning in the first volume of the collectanea begins, appropriately, with a ticket, a 'billet d'entrée pour l'experience de la machine Aérostatique'.[30] It was followed by a number of illustrations, both French and British, of the experiments of the Mongolfiers and of Charles and the Robert brothers. (It is possible that some of these represent prints sent by Franklin to Banks). SSB was thus framing her collection in the same terms as her brother – as an international phenomenon, underpinned by correspondence networks and, as she was highlighting here, the wider paper economy of the republic of letters. The French prints are then followed by a number of illustrations of the ascent of Blanchard's 'Grand Aerostatic Balloon' from Lochee's Academy in Chelsea which took place on 16 October 1784. The power of late Georgian ephemeral print, such as the ticket for the Parisian balloon which she definitely could not have seen, was its capacity to suggest a virtual witnessing, apparent in Banks's inclusion of balloon tickets as a category in her collection of tickets of admission. They occupy two sheets and include another French ticket, for Charles and Robert, dated 27 August 1783, two tickets for Lunardi flights, from the Artillery Ground and the Chelsea Hospital Garden, a ticket for Tytler's balloon in Edinburgh, one for Birmingham, and two examples of tickets for the 'British Balloon' launched at Tottenham Court Road in March and May 1785 (Figure 14).[31] Covering a range of material from 1783 (Charles and Robert) to a ticket for the 'Aerial Machine' (1796; C,2.15), this file contextualises the phenomenon not in terms of a history of wonders or news sensations of the 1780s, as the collectanea does, but as a type of sociability, filed between sheets concerning archery and 'balls at court'. SSB orients ballooning, both literally and figuratively, in relationship to sociability and fashionable life. Moreover, these tickets represent a highly selective sample, an assemblage of specimens or curiosities that combine historical information with visual aesthetic appeal. The ticket for Tytler's 'Edinburgh fire balloon', for example, features an engraved image of the balloon (the only visual record that exists of it) (C, 2.23; Figure 15).

---

[30] L.R.301.h.1, f. 1. The ticket was for the ascension of Charles and Robert on the Champ de Mars, 27 August 1783.
[31] The sheets are C,2.11–28 and C,2.29–26.

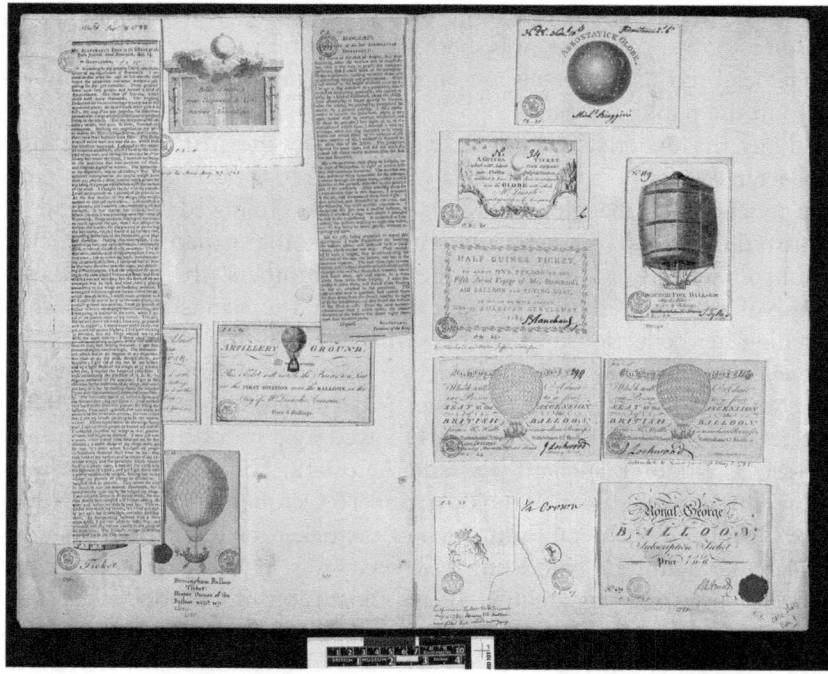

Figure 14 Fourteen admission tickets and two newspaper cuttings relating to ballooning events; dated 1783–96. Collection of Sarah Sophia Banks C,2.11–28.
© The Trustees of the British Museum

Ballooning enabled Tytler to achieve astonishing, if ephemeral, fame: as the *General Evening Post* noted, he was 'the first person in Great-Britain who has navigated the air'.[32] The Tytler ticket illustrates how ballooning could enable, in Lynn's terms, 'active' membership in the Enlightenment, for Tytler himself, the people who bought the ticket, and ultimately for Banks herself as its archivist. As we have seen, less than ten years later, in January 1793, Tytler was indicted for circulating a seditious handbill and fled Scotland for America to avoid imprisonment.[33] The audacity of his balloon flight in 1784 and the 1792 handbill that would exile him from Scotland are similar because they were exercises in the untethering of knowledge, highlighting the links between experiments of ballooning in the 1780s and more politically radical 'flights' of knowledge in the decade that followed.

[32] *General Evening Post*, 31 August–2 September 1784.   [33] See Chapter 1.

Figure 15 Edinburgh Fire Balloon. Collection of Sarah Sophia Banks C,2.23.
© The Trustees of the British Museum

SSB was also fascinated by occasions when the romance of ballooning was not realised, when balloons did not leave the earth. She included a ticket for the British Balloon which she annotated as 'intended to have gone up May 3 1785', and also two torn tickets for the attempt at Chelsea

'M. de Monet' [*sic*] on 11 August 1784 to which she added, 'The Balloon was filled but would not go up' (C,2.25, C,2.26).³⁴ These tickets are comparable to others in the collection such as the ticket for the Pantheon on the day it was destroyed by fire. SSB's annotations supplemented the information of the tickets by making them records of the failure of an advertised event properly to take place. They were thus exceptionally 'curious'. Tickets such as those for the British Balloon and de Moret's show at Chelsea represented the capacity of jobbing print to advertise the future and, in some cases, even to document the failure of that future to arrive. These tickets do not represent momentous events in the history of ballooning; like the Norwich ball tickets, they are historically obscure, warranting, at best, tiny (ticket-like) paragraphs in the London papers. But SSB thought they were important enough, like Tytler's ticket, to place them in the context of the more famous ascents of Lunardi and Blanchard. Floating in the blank space of the 'sociablarium' sheet, the balloons depicted here rise again as signs of an exoticised ephemerality which does not simply record transient or fleeting events but also the condition of being aware of the distinctive historicity of ephemeral time itself.

Sarah Sophia Banks was not the only individual to document the balloonmania in this manner. Her contemporary Daniel Lysons included ephemeral material on the topic in the third volume of his collection on 'public exhibitions and places of amusement', contextualising balloons in relation to, among other sensations, debating societies of the 1780s, the activities of the quack showman James Graham, and the Handel commemorations of 1784.³⁵ Another collector, the shadowy 'G. S.' of Peckham, was also compiling an ephemeral history of aerostation at this time. Advertised in a sale catalogue of 1841 as part of a vast collection of 'exhibition bills' of the Georgian period, ranging from exotic animal shows to 'WORKS OF HUMAN INGENUITY', this collection consisted of '[u]pwards of 500 Bills, Admission Tickets, Particular Accounts of, Songs, and other Poetic Effusions on the various Ærial Voyages, from Montgolfer's [*sic*] Ascent in 1783 to Mr. Green's 278th Ascent in 1840'. A '*very large assemblage*', the collection even included '*some fragments*' of actual

---

[34] For the British Balloon at Tottenham Court Road, see *Public Advertiser*, 2 May 1785; on de Moret see *Morning Post*, 12 August 1784: 'the balloon having burst, either by accident of otherwise, nothing but the gas mounted into the air: the rest of the balloon ... was consigned by the irritated and disappointed mob to a still more inflammatory element'. See also Lynn, *Sublime Invention*, 134.

[35] *Catalogue of a Portion of the Very Valuable Library of the Rev. Daniel Lysons* ... (London: Evans, 1828), 34.

balloons.[36] While the fate of this collection is uncertain – it was most likely disaggregated and ultimately lost – the 'balloon book' of another notable ephemerist is much better documented. It was made by William Upcott, the 1846 *Catalogue* of Upcott's library describing his balloon material as a 'most extensive Collection of Tracts, Advertisements, Newspaper-cuttings, Prints, &c. relating to Balloons, comprising many hundred Articles'.[37] Listed as 'unbound', Upcott's balloon sheets found an institutional 'home' in the 1950s, when they were donated, as a 455-page folio book, to the Smithsonian Institute. In preparation for an exhibition on early aeronautics at the Smithsonian in the 1990s, conservators decided to reconstitute the Upcott scrapbook in three volumes, a process which revealed the volume's 'harsh history', specifically the fact that it had been 'rebound at least twice'.[38] The Upcott scrapbook was accorded this treatment not because of its contents but on account of its relevance to the early history of aeronautics – the 'roads in the Air' that Banks had so eagerly anticipated. It is for this reason that we have one of the rare documentations of the material history of an ephemera 'book'.

No longer viewed through the lens of the history of science, in which it has tended to be identified as a technological 'failure', ballooning is now recognised as a complex imbrication of late Georgian trends in scientific inquiry, entrepreneurialism, fashion, gender, and in the evolution of public spheres and print publicity.[39] The multivalence of ballooning is such that it tends to resist tethering to a particular disciplinary framework or frameworks; Clare Brant describes it as 'predisciplinary' in the dual sense of anticipating the development of the physical sciences and also as an 'unruly defiance of disciplinarity'.[40] Ballooning was above all a phenomenon of the print media and related communication networks: it was pressure of news from France in the London papers that caused Sir Joseph Banks to contact

---

[36] *Catalogue of a Collection of Mr. Boosey*, 29.   [37] *Catalogue of the Library of William Upcott*, 65.

[38] Janice Stagnitto Ellis, 'Aloft in a Balloon: Treatment of a Scrapbook of Early Aeronautica Collected by William Upcott, 1783–1840', *The Book and Paper Group Annual*, 16 (1997) [http://cool.conservation-us.org/coolaic/sg/bpg/annual/v16/bp16-02.html, accessed 27 September 2016].

[39] In addition to Lynn, *Sublime Invention*, see also Barbara M. Benedict, *Curiosity: A Cultural History of Early Modern Inquiry* (Chicago: University of Chicago Press, 2002), 202–44; Paul Keen, *Literature, Commerce, and the Spectacle of Modernity, 1750–1800* (Cambridge, UK: Cambridge University Press, 2012), chap. 2; Clare Brant, '"I Will Carry You with Me on the Wings of Imagination": Aerial Letters and Eighteenth-Century Ballooning', *Eighteenth-Century Life*, 35:1 (2011), 168–87; Clare Brant, 'The Progress of Knowledge in the Regions of Air?: Divisions and Disciplines in Early Ballooning', *Eighteenth-Century Studies*, 45:1 (2011), 71–86; Siobhan Carroll, *An Empire of Air and Water: Uncolonizable Space in the British Imagination, 1750–1850* (Philadelphia: University of Pennsylvania Press, 2015).

[40] Brant, 'Progress of Knowledge', 75–6.

Franklin. Banks's subsequent engagement with ballooning was partly an exercise in information monitoring and management (to which SSB both implicitly and explicitly contributed). The balloonmania can therefore be seen as a distinctive moment in the history of disciplines and disciplinarity in the eighteenth century, relevant to Clifford Siskin and William Warner's idea of the Enlightenment as an 'event *in* the history of mediation'.[41] Aerostation can be seen as a 'hot' period in the longue durée of Enlightenment mediation that began in the seventeenth century, its lineage being apparent in similar ephemerally mediatised phenomena such as the frost fair. Texts such as the ticket were capable of interpellating the bodies that bore them as part of the balloon public; as Lynn suggests, the ticket enabled its bearer to become 'an active member of the Enlightenment'. This reconfiguration of cultural 'citizenship' also included women who participated in ballooning as aeronauts, spectators, consumers of balloon entertainment and fashion products, and, as in SSB's case, balloon archivists. The Pantheon, as I have discussed elsewhere, was associated with long-standing ideas of fashion as a form of dilation and magnification, associated with libidinised femininity: the temporary housing of Lunardi's balloon in this space, the dome mimicking the dome of the sky, manifested the links between fashion and experimental science in the 1780s.[42] Sociability and natural philosophy could be complementary kinds of knowledge, a connection which SSB's archive, by interleaving balloon tickets with those for balls, made manifest.

The Pantheon was also the site of one of the most intriguing balloon experiments – the flying sculptures of the German showman and illusionist Johann Karl Enslen who visited London in 1786. Enslen was responsible for the launch of the first Montgolfier in Germany two years previously and subsequently toured Europe with his 'Cabinet of Aerial Transparent Figures'.[43] The latter were sculptured and decorated balloons made out of gold-beater's skin, the outer membrane of ox intestine used in the manufacture of sheets of gold leaf. Gold-beater's skin was notable for its strength, transparency, and lightness: Enslen made much of how he could easily transport his deflated figures in a hand satchel. Banks's collection includes a handbill advertisement for the showman's debut

---

[41] Siskin and Warner, 'If This Is Enlightenment', 285.
[42] Russell, *Women, Sociability and Theatre*, 105–6.
[43] Deac Rossell, 'Enslen, Johann Carl (1759–1848)', in *Encyclopedia of Nineteenth-Century Photography*, ed. John Hannavy (London: Routledge, 2013), 491–3; Stephan Oettermann 'Die fliegenden Plastiken des Johann Karl Enslen/Johann Karl Enslen's Flying Sculptures', *Daidalos*, 37 (15 September 1990), 44–53; *General Advertiser*, 6 January 1786.

appearance in London on 9 January 1786, subtitled 'Thin Glitt'ring Textures of the Filmy Dew', quoting from the description of the sylphs in Pope's *The Rape of the Lock*. Enslen's sculptures were a baroque theatricalisation of ballooning's wondrous promise of the possibility of being able to leave the earth. The centrepiece of the show was a winged horse and warrior representing Pegasus and Perseus which, according to the handbill, could 'ascend by its own specific lightness, float with grace through the aerial fluid, and always preserve its lovely form ... every thing impresses the spectator's mind with the idea that he really sees a supernatural being'.[44] Enslen's figures, floating in the half-light of the Pantheon dome, hazy with the smoke of candles, also included '[a]n elegant and lovely Nymph, with a balloon head-dress, eight feet high, weighing 10 ounces'.[45] A French print illustrating the nymph is in SSB's collection (Figure 16).[46] Enslen remained in London for most of 1786, exhibiting his 'air-figures' in the open air at Bermondsey Spa in July and later at the Lyceum in the Strand for which he charged 'only SIX-PENCE', suggesting that the London public, satiated with sensation in the 1780s, were beginning to tire of this particular novelty.[47] He later returned to the continent, where he continued to experiment with and display mechanic works of ingenuity such as automata, the camera obscura, the phantasmagoria, and the mobile panorama. He was also a pioneer in early photography.[48] The material which Enslen used for his flying sculptures – gold-beater's skin – was later adapted for experiments in telephony and the manufacture of zeppelin airships in the twentieth century.[49]

Enslen's shows in the Pantheon, which Banks may have witnessed, are among the most extravagant manifestations of the importance of that venue as fashion's pleasure dome, a site in which the utopian possibilities of corporeal and ideological transformation, particularly for women, could be both performed and imagined. The 'air-figures' were signs of how women could use fashion and sociability to effect a kind of dematerialisation, floating free to become fugitive beings, like the sylphs of Pope's poem, a foundational text for the imagination of both the possibilities and the dangers of elite female sociability. Appropriately it was the ephemeral text – the handbill and the souvenir French engraving – in which the phantasmic possibilities of women floating free of materiality and

---

[44] L. R. 301.h.3, f.58 : 'Pantheon. Thin glitt'ring textures of the filmy dew'.
[45] *General Advertiser*, 6 January 1786.   [46] L. R. 301.h.3 f. 45r, 'L'experience de cette Figure ...'
[47] *General Advertiser*, 19 August 1786.   [48] Rossell, 'Enslen'.
[49] 'Goldbeater's skin': https://en.wikipedia.org/w/index.php?title=Goldbeater%27s_skin&oldid=678468780, accessed 27 September 2016.

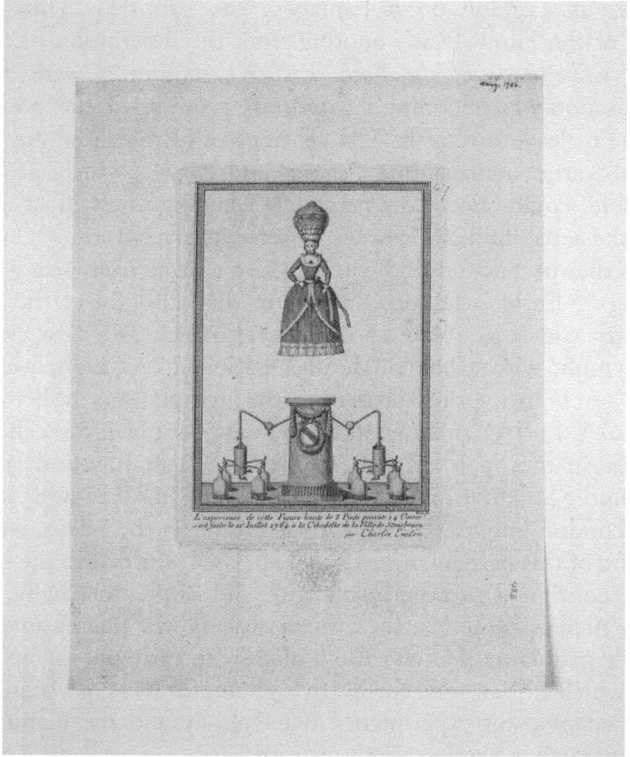

Figure 16 'L'experience de cette Figure ...'. A collection of broadsides, cuttings from newspapers, engravings, etc., of various dates, formed by Miss S. S. Banks. Bound in nine volumes.
© The British Library Board. L. R. 301.h.3 f. 45r

contingency are represented, an ephemerality which also extends to SSB herself as a possible witness of Enslen's show. Her presence as a spectator and ultimately the subjectivity that this presence might inscribe are as indeterminable as the hazy outlines of Enslen's figures: Sarah Sophia Banks cannot be easily pinned down. This evanescence even applies to Enslen himself: he came and went from London in less than a year, leaving the traces of a few advertisements in the newspapers and the loose handbills and images that Banks retained. However, though Enslen is a marginal figure in the history of balloonmania in Britain in the 1780s, his later career and the applications of the technology which he used to create his spectacles make him central to the importance of ballooning as an event in the history of media. The conjunctions of experimental science, entrepreneurship, multi-media publicity, and the creation of a mass public sociability represented by balloonmania anticipated later innovations in media and visual culture. Enslen's shows in the Pantheon in 1786 enacted these conjunctions by combining the evanescence of fashion, emblematised by the Pantheon, with the future-oriented temporality of experimental science – its faith in known unknowns (and hence the possible ephemerality of what it knows now). The floating nymph thus prefigures telephony, cinema, and the technologies of war, such as the zeppelin, making SSB herself, whether or not she was there in the Pantheon, a similar kind of witness and fabricator of a world to come. In that sense, the 'supernatural' dimension of what was exhibited at the Pantheon referred not only to Enslen's balloons, but also to the wonder and beauty of ephemeral historicity itself.

In 2002 Enslen's floating nymph figuratively rose again in the form of the frontispiece to Barbara Benedict's *Curiosity: A Cultural History of Early Modern Inquiry*, the source of the print being SSB's collections in the British Library. The volume from which the image derives, L.R.301.h.3, is also a major source for a chapter in Benedict's book entitled 'Performing Curiosity' which links the phenomena covered by SSB – Astley's circus, Katterfelto, the London Monster, and ballooning – with the Gothic novels *Caleb Williams* and *Frankenstein*. The eponymous protagonists of these fictions are inheritors, Benedict argues, of both the heroism and the vainglory of the balloonists and showmen of the 1780s: 'such men made reason itself ridiculous even as they trotted it out as mankind's defining power'.[50] Benedict's cultural history elides the originating cultural history of Banks's work as a collector of ephemeral texts relating to these phenomena. Indeed, SSB barely figures in the apparatus of *Curiosity*: she is mentioned once in a footnote and does not have an entry in the index. The virtual invisibility of Banks's archive of the balloonmania partly relates to the dubious status of the collection as a textual artefact. As we have seen previously, the protocols of library cataloguing as they developed in the nineteenth century privileged the author-title as the semantic unit defining the book, rendering collectanea and their contents comparatively invisible or 'buried', as Samuel Ayscough feared they would be. Following bibliographical protocol, Barbara Benedict correctly refers to the volume by its pressmark, L.R.301.h.3, not its author. While this form of description downplays SSB's agency in producing this ephemeral book, the

---

[50] Benedict, *Curiosity*, 243.

classification of the volume in this way actually serves to highlight its relational meaning, both internally, as a conglomeration of texts, and as part of the wider archive of No. 32 Soho Square, and subsequently the British Museum library. Classification by pressmark thus denotes the ephemeral book's embeddedness within a potential infinitude of texts and also allows works of ephemera such as the image of the nymph to be extracted, re-contextualised and re-authored, as Benedict does in *Curiosity*. Later library practice, then, affirmed the fugitive status and ephemeral integrity of such texts and the fundamental provisionality of SSB's act of gathering them together: neither she nor the limits of the ephemeral 'book' could authorise or contain them.

The invisibility of Banks's balloon archive within *Curiosity* also reflects how ephemerology as an aspect of popular antiquarianism was later eclipsed by the emergence of now dominant disciplines in the humanities, social, and physical sciences. Ephemerology was the body of knowledge about quotidian life, associational culture, customs and amusements, the mundane and the marvellous, as documented in fugitive print and visual culture. The 'discipline' of ephemerology was manifested in the mutual awareness and informal associations of individuals interested in 'making collections'. Its informal 'ephemerography', as I suggested in Chapter 2, was based in the genre of the sale catalogue. Considered in terms of the longue durée of this kind of collecting, the balloon 'books' of SSB, Lysons, and others were not radically new in their methodologies, which would have been recognised by predecessors such as Luttrell. Balloonmania differed from the documentation of the seventeenth-century frost fair only in its scale and scope as a multi-media event. Ballooning was therefore as indebted to the news revolution of the seventeenth century as much as it anticipates the mediatised culture of the twenty-first. Its documentation by SSB and others suggested that the 'discipline' of ephemerology was fundamentally concerned with how, where, and by whom knowledge, in its widest possible sense, is first laid down, as a substratum or a 'principle' of 'commencement', in Derrida's terms. The work of these ephemerists represented a science of the inchoate, of the immediate, transient event or trace, or even, as in the case of Banks's balloons that failed to go up, a science of failure, of what did not happen. The balloon collections of SSB, Lysons, and others do not represent a pre-discipline in a teleological sense or a defiance of disciplinarity, as Clare Brant suggests, but rather are para-disciplinary in the topological sense of surrounding or constituting a threshold or entry point. The para-disciplinarity of ephemerology surrounds or conditions modern disciplinary formations and, in so far as it continues to perform this para-disciplinary role, the ephemerology of Banks, Lysons, Upcott, and many others remains invisible in contemporary scholarship such as Benedict's and recent work on ballooning in general.

In the context of contemporary queer theory and performance studies, José Esteban Muñoz has influentially located ephemera with

> alternate modes of textuality and narrativity like memory and performance; it is all of those things that remain after a performance, a kind of evidence of what has transpired but certainly not the thing itself... [It is] interested in following traces, glimmers, residues and specks of things... Ephemera, and especially the ephemeral work of structures of feeling, is firmly anchored *within* the social.[51]

Banks's archive as a whole can be said to be the first significant articulation of ephemera's anchoring '*within* the social', building on the work of Wood and others in the previous century.[52] Her discovery of how ephemera can constitute an 'archive of feelings' *avant la lettre* is also similar to how her practice and ethos of assemblage anticipate assemblage in modern art of the twentieth century and the Deleuzian-influenced applications of assemblage in contemporary political theory and materialist philosophy. As we have seen, the idea of assemblage underpins Banks's project both in terms of its subject – the sociable gatherings or assemblages of people – and the method of documenting such behaviour through the practice at both a micro and macro level of gathering texts together in an ephemeral 'book'. The Deleuzian idea of assemblage as, in Manuel DeLanda's terms, a 'theoretical alternative to organic totalities' is also applicable to the Banks archive, as a means of conceptualising the relationship between the ephemeral text and the systems in which Banks was placing it – both her own collections and the larger flows of knowledge represented by No. 32 Soho Square.[53] As DeLanda explains, in an assemblage 'being part of a whole involves the exercise of the part's capacities but is not a constitutive part of it', an observation which can be applied to how the parts of Banks's archive such as, for example, the Norwich ball tickets, Tytler's balloon ticket, or Enslen's flying nymph retain a striking

---

[51] José Esteban Muñoz, 'Ephemera as Evidence: Introductory Notes to Queer Acts', *Women & Performance: A Journal of Feminist Theory*, 8:2 (1996), 5–16 (10).

[52] For a discussion of SSB and another important collector at the British Museum, Augustus Wollaston Franks, in relation to the importance of ephemera and ephemerality in queer studies see Gillian Russell, 'Ephemeraphilia: A Queer History', *Angelaki: Journal of the Theoretical Humanities*, 23:1 (2018), 174–86.

[53] Manuel DeLanda, *A New Philosophy of Society: Assemblage Theory and Social Complexity* (London: Continuum, 2006), 10.

singularity, related to but not dependent on or subsumed by the contexts in which they have been placed.[54] As in the case of applications of ephemerality in queer theory, eighteenth-century ephemerology thus 'queerly' anticipates themes in twentieth-century sociology and philosophy. DeLanda, for example, nominates 'conversations between two persons' as the most elemental form of social assemblage, related to larger, more complex, assemblages between networks and persons. He describes such encounters, based on co-presence, non-linguistic forms of expression, and the territorialising of behaviour by the 'borders of space and time' as 'ephemeral assemblages'.[55] The ambition of SSB's project was such that she sought to create a record of social encounter as a mode of 'ephemeral assemblage', evoking the co-presence of people together, talking or not talking, within the borders of space and time, such as a Norwich ballroom in 1802, or the Edinburgh park where Tytler first fired his balloon in 1784.

The other notable figure whose work Banks's archive prefigures is Walter Benjamin. In his profile of Benjamin, Theodor Adorno noted his fascination in the *Arcades Project* for 'small and shabby objects' and how he was drawn to 'everything that slipped through the conceptual net'.[56] 'The subjectivity of [Benjamin's] thought', Adorno observed, was of a distinctively singular cast, deeply invested in the 'contingent, ephemeral, [the] utterly worthless'.[57] Benjamin, he claimed, 'overexpos[ed]' the object in his 'micrological and fragmentary method', 'for the sake of the hidden contours which one day, in the state of reconciliation, will become evident'.[58] Sarah Sophia Banks lacked Benjamin's mysticism or the conceptual models (Hegelian, Marxian, or Freudian) with or against which to 'think' and make her collections. However, her work and that of the *Arcades Project* share a kind of historical materialism that is concerned, not with progress, but with what Benjamin termed 'actualization', historical '"understanding"' being 'the afterlife of that which is understood'.[59] Both SSB and Benjamin are drawn to understanding, as it happens, is present, and is alive, before it becomes the 'afterlife' of understanding as it is understood by history. Benjamin defined the 'method' by which this understanding was to be realised as: 'literary montage. I needn't *say*

---

[54] DeLanda, *A New Philosophy*, 10. [55] DeLanda, *A New Philosophy*, 52.
[56] Theodor W. Adorno, *Prisms*, trans. Samuel Weber and Shierry Weber (Cambridge, MA: MIT Press, 1983), 240.
[57] Adorno, *Prisms*, 229. [58] Adorno, *Prisms*, 236, 241.
[59] Walter Benjamin, *The Arcades Project*, trans. Howard Eiland and Kevin McLaughlin (Cambridge, MA: Harvard University Press, 1991), 460.

anything. Merely show ... the rags, the refuse – these I will not inventory but allow, in the only way possible, to come into their own: by making use of them.'[60] SSB's project is similarly 'literary' or aesthetic – in allowing her tickets to 'come into their own', by a process of assemblage that is barely an inventory, and by 'saying' even less in terms of commentary than Benjamin or SSB's contemporaries such as Turner and Haslewood. Adorno's idea of Benjamin's project as practising an 'overexposure' is also relevant to SSB in that her practices of assemblage encourage an intense form of looking at or exposure to the light of an inchoate knowledge of the otherwise 'small shabby object', practices that can draw in or beguile the twenty-first-century historian.[61] This looking, as I have argued, also entailed a form of optical tactility that fused perception of the verbal or visual signs carried by an ephemeral text with attentiveness to materiality – paper, script, the imprint of letterpress, traces of use. It is this mode of intense attention or exposure to history which endows the Norwich ball tickets, the Tytler ticket or, as we shall see in Chapter 6, the visiting card of Omai, with their communicative power. Sarah Sophia Banks was a connoisseur of how, as Sarah Lloyd observes, 'tickets lived in, through and *beyond* print'.[62]

Walter Benjamin also argued that 'for the collector, the world is present, and indeed ordered, in each of his objects', the history of each object, its 'entire past' coming together to 'form a whole magic encyclopedia, a world order, whose outline is the *fate* of his object'. In handling such objects the collector is able to 'look through them into their distance, like an augur'. Benjamin qualifies this observation, however, by parenthetically noting that the bibliophile is different, being the only type of collector 'who has not completely withdrawn his treasures from their functional context'.[63] If the bibliophile is an imperfect collector who is not able to reify or detach his objects from their original contexts, then the ephemerophile is arguably even more embedded in the contextual materiality of the scraps she or he accumulates. In other words, the ephemerist is so fully immersed in context and materiality that she is able to create the impression of realising the 'thing' itself – the ephemeral life of sociability – at the cost (or profit) of her own absorption into the 'maw' of history. If Banks acted as an 'augur' it was of Benjamin's *Arcades Project* itself: indeed, the ephemerology of the long eighteenth century deserves to be recognised as a genealogy of his own

---

[60] Benjamin, *Arcades Project*, 460.
[61] For the queerness of this 'literary method' see Russell, 'Ephemeraphilia'.
[62] Lloyd, 'Ticketing', 861 (my emphasis).   [63] Benjamin, *Arcades Project*, 207.

ephemeral 'book'. In her attention to documenting the theatricality of the ephemeral event as a condition of modern social life, Banks assured the conditions of her own disappearance from the archive, but also her own enduring haunting of it as an ephemeral trace or remain. It is only with the technological transformation of the twenty-first-century archive, and sea changes in the disciplines, that we are beginning to recognise that she was and is there.

CHAPTER 5

'Announcing Each Day the Performances'
Playbills as Theatre/Media History

In 1803 the governor of New South Wales, Philip Gidley King, wrote to Sir Joseph Banks, enclosing some specimens of printing from the colony. 'I hear one of the Ladys [i.e. Sarah Sophia Banks] wants ... our Printed Notes &c.', King stated, adding, 'we no longer have plays or play bills.'[1] In line with her modus operandi, Banks had made the most of her brother's correspondence networks to extend her interest in printed ephemera to the very edge of the known world. Her particular desire to acquire a playbill from New South Wales may have been piqued by newspaper and journal reporting in the 1790s, often by means of reprinted playbills, of 'Botany Bay theatricals'. By informing Banks that he 'no longer' had playbills, King did not only mean that they had been lost or destroyed (though many of them undoubtedly had). At least one Sydney playbill, documenting a performance of the tragedy *Jane Shore* at Sydney in July 1796, had already been acquired from him, probably also in 1796, by an associate of Sir Joseph Banks, William Chalmers, chief clerk to the Privy Council, antiquarian, and Shakespeare scholar. Sarah Sophia Banks had in this case been outdone by a competitor: she was seven years too late.

Of the range of printed ephemera in late Georgian Britain, the playbill, with the significant exception of the lottery ticket, was the most ubiquitous. Its presence as part of a late Georgian media ecology is apparent in a comment made by Samuel Taylor Coleridge in a letter to Sara Hutchinson in 1802. Designing himself as a stage manager of the deity's theatre of nature in the Lake District, Coleridge writes:

---

[1] Philip Gidley King to Sir Joseph Banks, 5 March 1803, quoted in Elaine Hoag, 'The Earliest Extant Australian Imprint, with Distinguished Provenance', *Script & Print*, 31:1 (2007), 5–19 (11).

153

Blessings on the mountains! to the Eye & Ear they are always faithful. I have often thought of writing a Set of *Play-bills* for the vale of Keswick – for every day in the Year – announcing each Day the Performances by his Supreme Majesty's Servants, Clouds, Waters, Sun, Moon, Stars, &c.[2]

Coleridge imagines himself as a kind of diurnal historiographer, the playbill representing the possibility of inscribing and retaining traces of the constantly changing beauty of the natural 'scene'. As stage manager of God's theatre of the world Coleridge not only exemplifies a Romantic poetics of ephemerality – which in its epistolary instantiation is itself to the moment – but also the embeddedness of such a poetics in the symbiosis of ephemeral textuality and sociability which Sarah Sophia Banks had sought to archive. The relationship of such a poetics to textual materiality is highlighted by the fact that a file of playbills for Keswick does in fact survive, in the playbill collections of the British Library.[3] These playbills serve as a correlative of and also, we might say in their status as printed ephemera, an enabling condition of Coleridge's theatre historiography of the everyday. The playbill, which is of central significance to the history of Georgian ephemerology, thus deserves to be recognised as having a place in a cultural history of Romantic textuality as a whole. This chapter will outline a history of Romantic-period culture's investments in the playbill, exploring how it was used, read, and collected, before returning to the particular case of the 1796 Sydney playbill that escaped Banks's acquisitive zeal.

Holding the Playbill to the Light

The importance of the playbill in theatrical and urban culture dates from the early modern period, the records of the Stationers' Company showing that a succession of printers were authorised to produce playbills from 1587 onwards. As well as being distributed within and around playhouses, these bills would have been posted on walls and doorways, amplifying the impact of the theatre, as Tiffany Stern has argued, within the cityscape as a whole.[4] No playbills survive from this period. It was in the eighteenth century, with the expansion of both the print trade and the theatre, that

---

[2] Samuel Taylor Coleridge, *Collected Letters of Samuel Taylor Coleridge*, ed. E. L. Griggs, vol. I: *1801–1806* (Oxford: Clarendon Press, 1956), 825.
[3] British Library pressmark Playbills 291.
[4] Tiffany Stern, *Documents of Performance in Early Modern England* (Cambridge, UK: Cambridge University Press, 2009); see also David Gowen, 'Studies in the History and Function of the British Theatre Playbill and Programme 1654–1914', DPhil, University of Oxford, 1998.

the playbill became widely used and also archived. The production of playbills was a significant dimension of the jobbing trade for printers, both in London and the provinces. Some of the major metropolitan theatres had their own in-house printing shops, while there was a close association between local print trades and theatre in the provinces, particularly after the boom in theatre building caused by changes in the regulation of the theatre in 1788.[5] In many cases these booksellers, who printed and disseminated playbills and related textual paraphernalia such as tickets, were also publishers of local newspapers in which performances were advertised, reinforcing the association between theatre and local print. We know of the value of this trade to the booksellers Jasper Sprange in Tunbridge Wells and the Soulbys in Bridgnorth because they included their playbills as part of a documentation of their output, kept in guard books, which functioned as both an advertisement to potential customers and a personal archive. Such collections are important for contextualising playbills as part of the diversity of jobbing print as a whole.[6]

One of the ways in which the Georgian playgoer encountered the playbill was as a large or 'great' bill stuck on walls, doorways, and shop windows in the vicinity of the playhouse and often printed in vivid red and black to attract the attention of patrons. In Thomas Holcroft's *Hugh Trevor* (1794–7), for example, the eponymous hero sees a crowd gathered outside Drury Lane theatre: 'The play bills were pasted in large letters, red and black, against the walls. I read them, and their contents told me it was one of my most favourite tragedies, Rowe's Fair Penitent, and that Mrs. Siddons was to act'.[7] But by far the most widespread and enduring form of theatre publicity until the early nineteenth century was the smaller handbill advertisement, sold both outside and inside the playhouse. The bill-seller, often a woman, was the first point of contact with the theatre, informing the audience of what they were about to see and contributing to the sense of anticipation and excitement that defined the occasion.[8] In 1830 Leigh Hunt claimed that 'without a play-bill, no true play-goer can

---

[5] Valerie Fairbrass, '"What Printers Ink Does Each Week for the Theatres": Printing for the Theatre in the Eighteenth and Early Nineteenth Centuries', *Publishing History*, 67 (2010), 39–63.
[6] For Sprange's collections see Alston, 'A Provincial Printer at Work', *Factotum* no. 10 (Dec. 1980); also Freeman and Wells, 'Jasper Sprange, Printer, of Tunbridge Wells'. For the Soulbys see Michael Twyman, *John Soulby, Printer, Ulverston: A Study of the Work Printed by John Soulby, Father and Son, between 1796 and 1827* (Reading: Museum of English Rural Life, 1966).
[7] Thomas Holcroft, *The Adventures of Hugh Trevor*, ed. Seamus Deane (Oxford: Oxford University Press, 1978), 105.
[8] For a later account of playbill selling in Victorian London see Henry Mayhew, 'Of the Street Sellers of Play-Bills', *London Labour and the London Poor* (London: George Woodfall, 1851), 287–9.

be comfortable', declaring his 'respect for the common "house-bill," associated with the cry of "bill o' the play".⁹ There was thus an aural dimension to playbill publicity, as was also the case in the country where strolling players would announce their arrival by sounding a drum and proclaiming the playbill, as illustrated in Richard Newton's 1793 print, 'Progress of a Player'.¹⁰

The information conveyed by the playbill remained standard until the early nineteenth century. It told the reader where and when a performance was taking place, the sequence of the entertainments in the evening's 'whole show', and listed the performers. Ticket prices for particular sections of the house would be indicated and there were also directions as to where the tickets could be obtained, such as the theatre itself, the lodgings of the performers, or the printer of the bill, thereby facilitating and documenting varieties of parasociability surrounding the main sociability of the performance event itself. The conventional phrases of the playbill such as 'By permission of', 'Theatre –', 'tickets to be had of', or 'vivant rex and regina' were expressions of both the uniqueness of the performance advertised and simultaneously its embeddedness in what was already known, while the titles of the plays functioned as micro-performance texts in their own right.¹¹ The communicative power and attraction of letters on playbills as visual graphic signs were a print culture correlative of the theatre's emphasis on seeing. This transmedial tendency extended to the status of the playbill as a performance text in its own right, one that was 'cried up' outside the theatre or proclaimed. The playbill thus reliably appealed, as Coleridge thought the show of nature did, to both 'Eye & Ear'. Moreover, as a text that had the potential to survive the event it was advertising the playbill enabled the recovery of the immediacy of a particular performance, the sense of it as being yet to come, as not yet having become history.

The playbill was not only important to the operations of the theatre but was also paradigmatic of the fugitive tendencies of printed ephemera in general. In the form of the poster affixed to walls it was static, but as the 'house-bill' it was portable, picked up from the bill-seller on the way into the theatre or from the orange-girl inside. Its fugitive tendencies meant that the playbill was a familiar sight beyond the immediate environs of the

---

⁹ Leigh Hunt, 'The Play-Bills', *The Tatler* no. 12 (17 September 1830), 45.
¹⁰ BM Prints and Drawings, 1948,0214.339.
¹¹ Michael Issacharoff describes play titles as 'the shortest theatrical text': see *Discourse as Performance* (Stanford, CA: Stanford University Press, 1989), 28.

theatre. In the 1790s, while on a walking tour, the Cambridge clergyman James Plumptre 'espied' a playbill advertising Shakespeare's *Richard III* and *The Agreeable Surprise* by John O'Keeffe on an 'inn window shutter' in the small Leicestershire village of Kibworth, deep in the English midlands.[12] The ubiquity and relative cheapness of the playbill – bought for a penny at the theatre, viewed on walls or on doorways, or retrieved from rubbish in the streets – meant that it and other similar texts could be the instruments in an informal, democratic education, potentially open to everyone. In his autobiography Robert Southey recounted how as a small boy in the late 1770s and 1780s he spent a number of years in the care of his theatre-mad aunt Elizabeth Tyler, who lived independently in Bath and had connections with the Bath theatre. She 'preserved the playbills' which formed the materials by which the later poet laureate learnt to read and form his letters:

> I was encouraged to prick them with a pin, letter by letter ... I learnt to do it with great precision, pricking the larger types by their outlines, so that when they were held up to the window they were bordered with spots of light ... I have done it to hundreds; and yet I can well remember the sort of dissatisfied and damping feeling, which the sight of one of those bills would give me, a day or two after it had been finished and laid by. It was like an illumination when half the lamps are gone out.[13]

Southey was practising on the playbill a particular form of close reading, a re-inscription of the power of this kind of text to evoke the ephemerality of the event it was advertising. His tracing of the letters with a pin and then holding it up to light created a new thing of beauty, his own private theatre. (The National Library of Australia has a copy of a playbill for a performance of Nicholas Rowe's *Jane Shore* at the Theatre Royal Liverpool in 1830 which has evidence of pinpricks outlining the letters; Figure 17).[14]

The educative value of the playbill was later alluded to by Charles Dickens. In *Bleak House* the rag-and-bottle dealer Mr. Krook learns to read and write by means of a bundle of 'dirty playbills'.[15] Other more

---

[12] James Plumptre, *James Plumptre's Britain: The Journals of a Tourist in the 1790s*, ed. Ian Ousby (London: Hutchinson, 1992), 25.
[13] Robert Southey, *Life and Correspondence*, ed. C. C. Southey, 6 vols. (London: Longman, Brown, Green & Longmans, 1849), I: 72–3.
[14] Theatre-Royal Liverpool ... This present SATURDAY will be performed August 21, 1830, Rowe's celebrated Tragedy of Jane Shore, [Liverpool: Melling and Co., 1830]. Ashford collection of theatre playbills from English theatres from English theatres between 1796 and 1905. National Library of Australia. I am grateful to Kate Horgan for drawing my attention to this playbill and to the staff of the National Library of Australia for facilitating its reproduction.
[15] Charles Dickens, *Bleak House*, ed. Norman Page (Harmondsworth: Penguin, 1971), 254.

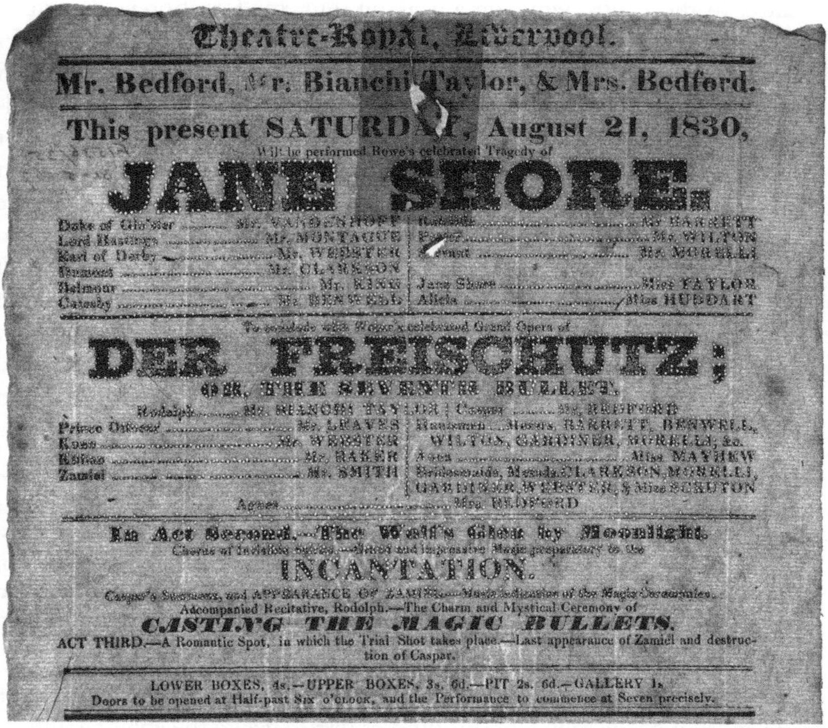
Theatre-Royal, Liverpool.

Mr. Bedford, Mr. Bianchi Taylor, & Mrs. Bedford.

This present SATURDAY, August 21, 1830,

Will be performed Rowe's celebrated Tragedy of

JANE SHORE.

Jane Shore .... Miss TAYLOR

Alicia .... Miss HUDDART

To conclude with Weber's celebrated Grand Opera of

DER FREISCHUTZ;

OR, THE SEVENTH BULLET.

Agnes .... Mrs. BEDFORD

In Act Second.—The Wolf's Glen by Moonlight.

INCANTATION.

Accompanied Recitative, Rodolph.—The Charm and Mystical Ceremony of

CASTING THE MAGIC BULLETS.

ACT THIRD.—A Romantic Spot, in which the Trial Shot takes place.—Last appearance of Zamiel and destruction of Caspar.

LOWER BOXES, 4s.—UPPER BOXES, 3s. 6d.—PIT 2s. 6d.—GALLERY 1s.

Doors to be opened at Half-past Six o'clock, and the Performance to commence at Seven precisely.

Figure 17 Theatre-Royal Liverpool . . . This present SATURDAY will be performed August 21, 1830, Rowe's celebrated Tragedy of Jane Shore. [Liverpool: Melling and Co., 1830]. Ashford collection of theatre playbills from English theatres between 1796 and 1905. National Library of Australia.
Permission National Library of Australia

mundane uses of the playbill in Dickens's work, indicating the playbill's proximity to the abjection of rubbish, include Martin Chuzzlewit's consumption of a takeaway meal of 'cold beef' that comes 'wrapped in a playbill'. Chuzzlewit prepares for his meal by 'spreading that document on the little round table with the print downwards . . . arranging the collation upon it'.[16] This is a playbill that has become detached from the time and place of the theatrical event and is in process of being absorbed into the vacuity of absolute ephemerality. The fact that the print of the playbill is turned 'downwards', not to contaminate the meal with ink, is a sign of the printed scrap's loss of connection with what inspired it: nonetheless in this

[16] Charles Dickens, *Martin Chuzzlewit*, ed. Margaret Cardwell (Oxford: Clarendon Press, 1982), 228.

recycled form it tenuously survives. Dickens suggests an essential continuity between the playbill as a record of an ephemeral theatrical event and the trivial rituals that constitute everyday life. The playbill is similarly represented elsewhere in his fiction as having a perverse life beyond the domain of the theatre, being thoroughly assimilated into domestic life and ultimately the bodies of individuals. Using playbills to curl her hair, Miss Blimber in *Dombey and Son* appears as a grotesque walking advertisement: '"Theatre Royal" over one of her sparkling spectacles, and "Brighton" over the other'.[17] The playbills in this case can be said to 'perform' Miss Blimber – she is their prosthesis rather than the other way round. Miss Blimber is a walking one-woman archive, as is also the case with the two Edinburgh attorneys who feature in the introductory chapter of Walter Scott's *Heart of Midlothian*. Scott describes the typical contents of their pockets as consisting of 'old play-bills, letters requesting a meeting of the Faculty, rules of the Speculative Society, syllabus' of lectures ... everything but brieves and bank-notes'.[18] The attorneys carry with them the kind of jobbing print that sustained associational culture, indicating a life of underemployed conviviality. The presence of 'old play-bills' and other similar scraps in their pockets signifies both the ephemerality of sociability and the power of such texts to create an archive of that sociability. These papers are portable, malleable, always prone to loss and decay, like the bodies of the attorneys themselves to which they were held close and which theoretically warmed them.

The fiction of both Dickens and Scott registers how the playbill, particularly the handbill form of the playbill, the 'common house-bill' as Leigh Hunt termed it, could be an intimate, even somatic, textual thing, adaptable to a range of uses. The playbill exemplified the accessibility of the handbill in general to close reading and handling. One read the handbill form of the playbill in a similar way to how one accessed the page of a book or a newspaper, holding it at arm's length or closer. Throughout the eighteenth century the handbill therefore represented the point at which the print of the world indoors intersected with that of the street and the out of doors in general, the political dimensions of such a distinction having particular resonance in periods of crisis such as the 1790s. As I argued in Chapter 1, the handbill became important in the 1790s as a medium of radical political communication and organisation – it could be produced in large quantities relatively cheaply and quickly and

---

[17] Charles Dickens, *Dombey and Son*, ed. Alan Horsman (Oxford: Clarendon Press, 1974), 195.
[18] Walter Scott, *Heart of Midlothian*, ed. Tony Inglis (Harmondsworth: Penguin, 1994), 23.

could be easily and, if necessary, clandestinely disseminated in both indoor and outdoor space. Some of the handbill communications of the London Corresponding Society, for example, are recorded as being 'thrown' into public meetings and doorways, suggesting the incendiary, missile-like, quality of the medium.[19] Found accidentally, in all kinds of spaces, the radical handbill of the 1790s exemplified the potency of printed ephemera as a medium that escaped the mechanisms of control, including those of the market.

The sophistication of radical print culture's use of printed ephemera is illustrated by how it adapted the familiar form of the playbill. There are examples of mock playbills from earlier in the century but the decade of the 1790s is particularly significant for the frequency and ingenuity by which the playbill was exploited. As John Barrell has argued, 'By its sheer ubiquitousness, the language of theatre advertising could function as a language that addressed the polite and the vulgar much more effectively than the language ... of formal political debate'.[20] In other words these playbills appealed to the same idea of the universal public, or in Michael Mendle's terms the 'accidental democracy of the public thoroughfare', that is evident in the kind of broadsides collected by Thomason and Luttrell in the seventeenth century.[21] A notorious example of such a bill was one advertising 'a new and entertaining Farce' entitled 'La Guillotine! or George's Head in the Basket!' which dates from mid-1793, after the execution of Louis XVI in January of that year.[22] The title of this 'performance' suggested that the British public would soon witness George III receiving the same fate as the French king. (John Barrell suggests that it is possible that the playbill was in fact 'loyalist black propaganda', designed as a weapon to counter the growing influence of the London Corresponding Society).[23] This bill later became a prize exhibit for the government when it tried a number of leading radicals for high treason in 1794; it was handled and displayed in evidence in court and later reprinted in the *State Trials*, prolonging its fugitive 'life'. The authors of these mock playbills wanted the people who read them to imagine that the great show of the

---

[19] Mary Thale (ed.), *Selections from the Papers of the London Corresponding Society 1792–1799* (Cambridge, UK: Cambridge University Press, 1983), 108.
[20] John Barrell, 'Radicalism, Visual Culture, and Spectacle in the 1790s,' *Romanticism on the Net*, 46 (2007), 1–30 (24).
[21] Mendle, 'George Thomason's Intentions', 173.
[22] No original copies of this playbill survive: for a useful commentary see John Barrell, *'Exhibition Extraordinary!!' Radical Broadsides of the mid 1790s* (Nottingham: Trent Editions, 2001), 2–5.
[23] Barrell, *'Exhibition Extraordinary!!'*, 3.

British Revolution was just about to, and indeed, must happen: the fact that the British government took them seriously indicates that it appreciated the playbill's communicative effectiveness. Exploiting the conventions of the playbill for the purposes of political satire, the mock playbill demanded forms of close reading that integrated knowledge of how to read the typographic and linguistic conventions of the ordinary playbill with the kind of reading practices associated with the appreciation of irony and parody. The very fact, moreover, that it is possible to conceive of such texts as having 'authors', as being more than the product of the typesetter's manual labour, suggests that by the 1790s printed ephemera could be adapted as a form of literary art. Indeed, as Barrell suggests, it is possible that the mock playbills may have been primarily designed to appeal to collectors such as Sarah Sophia Banks as 'curiosities', or as entertainment for educated radical gentlemen.[24] The aestheticisation of the playbill as a semantically complex text indicates both how reliant radical culture was on ephemeral 'information' and how it was able to amplify its meanings: elaborating the conventions of the playbill in this way communicated the necessity of momentous change in the theatre of the world – an 'entire change of performances' – that could make monarchy itself ephemeral.

Dead Walls

In the early nineteenth century the playbill and indeed jobbing print as a whole underwent a significant technological change due to the introduction of new forms of typeface: fat face, developed by Robert Thorne in 1803, Egyptians (1815), and then sans serif in 1816. These typefaces were bigger and bolder, making them more visible from a distance than the neoclassical and old face types which had been the norm: according to John Lewis, 'The appearance of bills and posters, labels, letterheads, tickets and other kinds of ephemeral printing changed completely'.[25] Maurice Rickards notes the suddenness of the change: 'not only was this the biggest thing to hit printing for some three hundred years, it was also the quickest. Printers who had been sedately chugging along with their book-style layouts suddenly found a whole new typographic world'.[26] After 1803 playbills became more elaborate, making a verbal and visual assault upon the

---

[24] Barrell, 'Radicalism', 25.
[25] John Lewis, *Typography: Design and Practice* (London: Barrie and Jenkins, 1978), 13.
[26] Maurice Rickards, *The Public Notice: An Illustrated History* (Melbourne: Wren Publishing, 1973), 10.

attention of the playgoer: twenty years later the *Theatrical Examiner* was noting 'how the large type staggers under the weight of so much gorgeous announcement, which naturally enough requires the aid of letters an inch long.'[27] A writer for *Tait's Edinburgh Magazine* recalled in 1851 the posters for entertainments at Vauxhall as 'colossal words of fire ... oracular announcements' that 'flamed from a background of the blackest wood'. Like Southey, these flaming letters seared the writer's childhood imagination:

> the Vauxhall alphabet of fire struck us as the effect of enchantment. By this excellent mode of inculcating the first rudiments of education we learned our earliest lessons in orthography ... The play-bills of Astley's are also inscribed upon the tablet of our memory. They are so many sheets of heraldry; the vignettes of pageantry.[28]

The typographic revolution, of which the magnification of the playbill was the epitome, is important for Romantic media history in a number of ways that have gone unnoticed by literary and book historians. Until the early 1800s handbills and posters had been similar to the page and ultimately the printed book in the scale and layout of their typography and size of paper, but the emergence of the poster represented a challenge to both the traditional broadside and the codex.[29] As early as 1805 William Wordsworth had identified the impact of this change on the cityscape of London. In Book 7 of *The Prelude* he writes:

> Here files of ballads dangle from dead walls,
> Advertisements of giant-size from high
> Press forward in all colours on the sight:
> These, bold in conscious merit, lower down,
> That, fronted with a most imposing word,
> Is peradventure one in masquerade.[30]

A 'dead' wall was one unbroken by a door or a window: it could mark the boundary between a road or pathway and adjacent ground such as a park or a back yard. In the rapidly transforming London of the early nineteenth century there were many such 'dead walls' in all parts of Westminster and the city, including at Hyde Park and Buckingham House. Outside the

---

[27] 'Theatrical Examiner', *The Examiner*, 6 April 1823, 232–4 (232).
[28] 'Play-Bill Reminiscences', *Tait's Edinburgh Magazine*, 18 (1851), 761–2 (761).
[29] The *Oxford English Dictionary* dates the earliest example of 'poster', meaning a 'printed or written notice posted or displayed in a public place as an announcement or advertisement', to 1818.
[30] William Wordsworth, *The Prelude: The Four Texts (1798, 1799, 1805, 1850)*, ed. Jonathan Wordsworth (Harmondsworth: Penguin, 1995), 1805: ll. 209–14 (262).

surveillance of a property owner or householder and in the absence of a police force, the dead wall was a recognised as 'no-man's land', a site of anonymous inscription, transient commerce (including prostitution), and of cheap and jobbing print. Sign-writers would advertise goods and services on dead walls which were also used for political sloganeering, particularly in the 1790s when both seditious and loyalist 'Lucubrations' were scrawled across them.[31] Dead walls were the venue for the publication of political handbills; the *Morning Chronicle* ironically recommended in 1793 that bills could be consulted on the dead wall of the British Museum which was a 'fund of public information'.[32] They were also places where retail cheap print was traded. A mid-nineteenth-century account of 'low life' in London described how the ballad seller would 'take his stand against a dead wall ... first festooning it liberally with twine' and pinning up 'two thousand ballads for public perusal and selection'. This writer claimed that the heyday for this practice was the early nineteenth century before 'dead-walls gave place to shop-fronts' about twenty years before (i.e. the 1830s): 'we are old enough to remember the day when a good half-mile of wall fluttered with the minstrelsy of war and love ... along the south side of Oxford Street alone'.[33] In addition to cheap print the dead wall was also the site of improvised, transient commerce, bric-a-brac, fruit, and flowers displayed one day and gone the next, leaving 'not a vestige of all this life and traffic – nothing but a void area and a veritable Dead Wall'.[34]

The dead wall was therefore a paradigmatic site of ephemerality and inscription in the late Georgian and Victorian city, the place at which the tide of commerce, including print culture and writing itself, washed up against obsolescence and loss. Moreover, the dead wall was to be found throughout London rather than just at its suburban margins: it was a reminder that everywhere the metropolis was constantly dying and reinventing itself. In relation to print, the 'dead walls' of *The Prelude* suggest how the typographic revolution of the early nineteenth century had made ephemeral print pressing, 'bold', and visually overwhelming, particularly out of doors. Retail cheap print in the form of ballads dangling in files (like hanged men and women) is associated or 'filed' in Wordsworth's poem with lurid advertisements and the latter's literary prostitution – the bill in

---

[31] *Morning Post*, 16 December 1794. [32] *Morning Chronicle*, 18 January 1793.
[33] Charles Manby Smith, *The Little World of London: or, Pictures in Little of London Life* (London: Hall & Virtue, 1857), 256–7.
[34] 'A Dead Wall', *The Leisure Hour* (18 August 1859), 526–8 (528).

'masquerade' possibly referring, as Barrell suggests, to the political mock playbills of the 1790s.[35]

Wordsworth's acknowledgment of the 'dead wall' of ephemerality and in particular the typographic revolution that transformed jobbing print relates to how Book 7 of *The Prelude* as a whole is concerned with innovations in media in general around 1800 – visual entertainments such as the panorama and the rise of intermedial genres such as melodrama – changes which implicitly included the status of poetry itself as a 'medium'. John Guillory has observed that what a medium does is to make something 'visible that before could not be seen', primarily through remediation, 'the first major practice of remediation' being 'the invention of printing, which reproduced the content of manuscript writing at the same time that it opened up new possibilities for writing in the print medium'.[36] As a form of mimesis, poetry (like story-making and drama) belonged to both before and after print, meaning writing and speech before print, and writing, speech, *and* print after the advent of print. Celeste Langan and Maureen N. McLane have argued that the Romantic period is crucial in the evolution of poetry from a literary kind to a medium that would be able to compete with and exceed the power of both the printed word and the visual media: the origins of poetry 'in the far, oral past ensured that poetry, unlike, for example, the novel, had a stronger claim to be considered a supermedial, transhistorical venture: it had preceded writing, preceded print, and could indeed outlast them'.[37] The success of Romantic poetry lay in how it defined itself as a middle or medium between orality (meaning an idea of pure mimesis, often associated with the ballad) and the artificiality or alienating tendencies of print. It did so by producing what Langan terms, adapting Friedrich Kittler, an 'audio-visual hallucination' whereby the techniques of print communication – the reading of printed lines of poetry on a page or in a book – became so deeply naturalised that experiences could be imaginatively 'heard' and 'seen', the artefactuality of poetry as print becoming an invisible blank screen. Such reading practices – silent and internalised – enabled 'the production through reading of an interior, of (literate) subjectivity as a virtual space

---

[35] Barrell, 'Radicalism', 56: as he notes, 'Wordsworth was living in Lincoln's Inn in early 1795, in the months when almost all of these bills were produced'.
[36] John Guillory, 'Genesis of the Media Concept', *Critical Inquiry* 36:2 (2010): 321–62 (324).
[37] Celeste Langan and Maureen N. McLane, 'The Medium of Romantic Poetry', in *The Cambridge Companion to British Romantic Poetry*, eds. James Chandler and Maureen N. McLane (Cambridge, UK: Cambridge University Press, 2008), 239–62 (255).

modeled on the page'.[38] Romantic poetry was thus able to refashion or modernise itself as a supermedium, not merely a genre, that could surpass other art forms (e.g. the drama) in its capacity to render an idea of an experience that was unmediated. This process thus exploited the materiality of print as well as being dependent on the very suppression of that materiality.

Book 7 of *The Prelude* is remarkable for acknowledging printed ephemera as a cultural phenomenon occupying a literal and imaginative space and having a communicative or medial function – though ephemera collectors had been recognising this medial function for years. However, what is being remediated to make visible Wordsworth's poem as a 'supermedium' is not the ballad as a trace of 'before print' (the ur-literacy of modern literary culture based on poiesis) but the ballad as the product of retail cheap print, contextualised in relation to jobbing print as a whole, such as 'advertisements of giant size'. The orality to which the ballad and ephemeral print as a whole gave access was not the 'truth' of unmediated poiesis but the orality of the everyday, the hubbub of myriad speech acts and communicative exchanges that ephemeral print had made visible since the seventeenth century. Wordsworth's remediation of the materiality of ephemera and ephemerality in *The Prelude* was therefore designed to assimilate to the medium of poetry the poetics of everyday sociality represented by forms of printed ephemera and spaces such as the dead wall (part of the project of Romantic poetry as a whole to make lyric capital out of mundane, transient, ordinary things).[39] At the same time, however, Wordsworth was demarcating the dead wall as a space that poetry could never properly inhabit. The danger of the dead wall is expressed in the specific terms of the change in ephemeral print whereby innovations in type had transformed the letter and the word into flaming, 'giant' visual artefacts. In terms of media history, this change represented an echo (or remediation) of the pre-print status of the word as a predominantly vertical inscription on walls, monuments, and gravestones, the dead wall, as we have seen, also being a site for graffiti and signwriting.[40] The positioning of

---

[38] Celeste Langan, 'Understanding Media in 1805: Audiovisual Hallucination in *The Lay of the Last Minstrel, Studies in Romanticism*, 40 (Spring 2001): 49–70 (58).

[39] See Mary Jacobus, *Romantic Things: A Tree, a Rock, a Cloud* (Chicago: University of Chicago Press, 2012); Daniel Tiffany, *Toy Medium: Materialism and Modern Lyric* (Berkeley: University of California Press, 2000).

[40] Cf. Walter Benjamin in 'Painting and the Graphic Arts' (1917): 'is it only when *we* read that we place the page horizontally before us? And is there such a thing as an original vertical position for writing – say, for engraving in stone?': Benjamin, *Selected Writings: 1913–1926*, eds. Marcus Bullock and Michael W. Jennings (Cambridge, MA: Harvard University Press, 1996), 82. See also Roger

the word in this sense relates to Nancy's distinction between the kind of print that faces out and is militant and the book as an entity that has 'no end outside of itself'.[41] Wordsworth can be said to have recognised, whether consciously or not, changes in the typography of ephemeral print as signifying a possible dissociation of the power of the word from the printed paper artefact, including his own poetry 'book'. Just when poetry was sublimating the materiality of printed ephemera in order to remediate the orality of the everyday, ephemeral print itself was escaping a dependence on both the page and the book to perform its own form of remediation of the power of the letter 'before print'.

These changes represented an intra-medial shift that had implications for the history of printed ephemera as a whole. Though the handbill endured as an important ephemeral format well into the nineteenth century, the association between printed ephemera and the book represented by the handbill's size, its typeface, and its somatic connection with hands and bodies gradually diminished. The poster and advertising signage in general came to characterise the landscape of urban modernity. In an essay for *Household Words* published in 1851, Charles Dickens described London as a virtual paper city, its fabric of bricks and mortar having been absorbed by the posters and paste of the bill-sticker. He describes 'an old warehouse':

> so thickly encrusted with fragments of bills, that no ship's keel after a long voyage could be half so foul. All traces of the broken windows were billed out, the doors were billed across, the water-spout was billed over ... The forlorn dregs of old posters so encumbered this wreck, that there was no hold for old posters, and the stickers had abandoned the place in despair, except one enterprising man who had hoisted the last masquerade to a clear spot near the level of the stack of chimnies, where it waved and drooped like a shattered flag.[42]

The rise of the poster represented a shift in the cultural politics of ephemerality as it reinforced a distinction between textuality out of doors and that within, a boundary which the handbill could always easily cross,

---

Chartier, *Inscription and Erasure: Literature and Written Culture from the Eleventh to the Eighteenth Century*, trans. Arthur Goldhammer (Philadelphia: University of Pennsylvania Press, 2007); Armando Petrucci, *Public Lettering: Script, Power, and Culture*, trans. Linda Lappin (Chicago: University of Chicago Press, 1993); Sara Thornton, *Advertising, Subjectivity and the Nineteenth-Century Novel: Dickens, Balzac and the Language of the Walls* (Basingstoke: Palgrave Macmillan, 2009).

[41] Nancy, *On the Commerce of Thinking*, 6.

[42] Charles Dickens, 'Bill-sticking', *Household Words*, 52 (22 March 1851), 601–6 (601). The 'last masquerade' is a reference to the last masquerade of the season at Vauxhall Gardens.

carried as it was by people across thresholds for both inside and outside reading. A poster on a wall was more immediately striking as a visual artefact but was less mobile and malleable than a handbill. The poster could never be spread out for private reading or as support for an improvised meal: it was thus more limited in its fugacity and ultimately more ephemeral, as posters on walls were quickly pasted over or decayed and could not be retrieved and reworked. Many posters were displayed on placards, that is, broadsides stiffened with cardboard for ease of transportation and display. Placards remain important in political demonstrations, functioning as extensions or prostheses of the bodies that hold or wave them. The word placard derives from an old French term for armour so there is a sense, like broadside, that this method of displaying print was an expression of militancy, a means of making the printed word emphatically stand up.

Technological change to typefaces therefore reinforced the tendency towards the estrangement of printed ephemera from the codex-form book in the early 1800s, even though throughout the nineteenth century collectors continued to make the connection between the book and ephemera by integrating the poster with other ephemeral formats. The very act of rendering the poster horizontal, taking it away from the domain of the dead wall, was an interpretative gesture that countered the poster's apparent alienation of the printed word from the book, the page or even the handbill. Wordsworth himself can be said to be doing something similar in remediating ephemerality through the medium of poetry, by making the files of a ballad singer and giant advertisements a 'book' to be read and handled within leaves of the 'book' of *The Prelude*.

Garnering the Playbill

The importance of the playbill in late Georgian politics and culture was also signified by the mediatory practice of collecting. Robert Southey's playbill education was made possible through his aunt's preservation of the playbills of the Bath theatre while Thomas Noon Talfourd noted the importance of a collection of playbills 'as the most precious of literary curiosities – as forming a series of golden links in a chain of delight'.[43] James Plumptre's encounter with the playbill 'espied' on the inn window shutter at Kibworth in the 1790s is an example of playbill collecting as a record of 'accidental reading'. It was partly for such experiences that

---

[43] *New Monthly Magazine* 3 (1821), 163.

Plumptre was making his tour, which combined visits to churches and country houses with playgoing and the pursuit of traces of theatrical performances in the form of playbills. Unable to stay in Kibworth for the advertised performance of *Richard III*, Plumptre collected two playbills as souvenirs (leaving the one on the inn window shutter to flutter in the wind and decay) and subsequently went to the nearby town of Market Harborough to buy some 'old bills' from the printer that worked for the company that was performing at Kibworth (the kind of jobbing printer who like Jasper Sprange may have been keeping his own scrapbook of playbills). When he later visited Shakespeare's birthplace, Stratford-upon-Avon, he went to the printers to get 'as many Playbills as I could' and after a personal tour of the theatre in Worcester 'obtain'd a few playbills from the man who shew'd me the House'.[44] Plumptre's journal shows that his theatric tourism was combined with a form of media tourism (comparable indeed to Wordsworth's imaginative 'collecting' of the ballads and advertisements on the walls of London as recalled in *The Prelude*).

As an enthusiast for the theatre, Plumptre is likely to have been aware that he was not alone as a playbill collector.[45] An archival resource for playbills, as I have suggested previously, was the printing trade, which Plumptre turned to in his travels. Another repository was the acting profession itself. Many performers retained their playbills as a means of self-advertisement and self-preservation, a way of holding on to the evanescent nature of a career. Such auto-archiving was also practised at an institutional level. Theatres of all kinds, ranging from the huge metropolitan establishments of Covent Garden and Drury Lane to playhouses in the provinces, kept files of playbills as a form of corporate memory. Playbills were the means of keeping a formal printed record of a theatre's repertory, enabling managers and performers to track what had been performed, when, and by whom (and to compare this record with other forms of institutional memory – a playbill is no guarantee that a performance actually occurred or particular actor appeared in the role advertised). It is to this practice that Coleridge was referring when he imagined himself writing and archiving the diurnal record of the natural theatre of Keswick. For provincial companies the playbill record also served as a history of survival, often in difficult circumstances. Notable playbill collectors included the actor John Philip Kemble, who in 1820 sold his collection of old plays and bills to the Duke of Devonshire for the

---

[44] Plumptre, *James Plumptre's Britain*, 25, 26, 27, 29.
[45] Plumptre was a playwright, most notably of *The Lakers* (1798).

enormous sum of £2,000. The comedian Charles Mathews not only amassed his own collection of playbills but also bought up those made by other performers, including a fifty-five-volume collection of Covent Garden and Drury Lane bills from 1774 to 1830, compiled by the actor John Fawcett and his father.[46] Playbill collecting and transmission linked with realia such as costumes, could thus serve as a medium for intergenerational memory and genealogy formation for actors. Mathews was reputed to have given five pounds to an impoverished fellow actor who had found 'two or three letters' of Richard Brinsley Sheridan in a 'heap of MS., sold to a cheesemonger as waste-paper', accidental reading being the occasion for both the honouring of Sheridan's memory and an act of charity to a fellow performer.[47] Mathews's home in Islington, where his collection was housed in a special room, became well known as an informal museum and portrait gallery of the theatre.[48] Another informal 'theatre museum' was the Garrick Club, founded in 1831, which became a repository for paintings collected by Mathews and the archive of James Winston, perhaps the most significant collector of playbills from within the theatrical profession. After achieving modest success as an actor Winston moved into theatre management, mainly in charge of day-to-day business, making him responsible for the production and distribution of playbills. He was also an entrepreneur in theatre journalism, producing the *Theatric Tourist*, and was the secretary and driving force in the development of the Garrick Club. When he died in 1843, the *Gentleman's Magazine* noted that he had:

> enjoyed opportunities for making a vast collection of dramatic information and curiosities, and sedulously availed himself of the power. His masses of playbills, correspondence, rare pieces, pictures, anecdotes, biographies, and other matters, from the merest odds and ends to the most curious and interesting documents, form an extraordinary accumulation.[49]

Playbill collecting was not confined to the theatre profession but after 1750 was an intrinsic part of the broader phenomenon of the documentation of contemporary social life and customs by means of ephemeral

---

[46] James Boaden, *Memoirs of the Life of John Philip Kemble*, 2 vols. in 1 (London: Colburn, 1825), II: 578; 'John Fawcett, Esq.', *Gentleman's Magazine*, new series 7 (1837), 550–2 (552).
[47] 'Charles Mathews, Esq.,' *The Mirror of Literature, Amusement, and Instruction*, 26 (1835), 44–7 (47).
[48] Ifan Kyrle Fletcher, 'The Theatre for Collectors', in *Talks on Book Collecting* (London: Cassell and Co., 1952), 85–99 (87). For Mathews's portrait collecting see Jim Davis, *Comic Acting and Portraiture in Late-Georgian and Regency England* (Cambridge, UK: Cambridge University Press, 2015), 195–229.
[49] 'JAMES WINSTON, Esq.', *Gentleman's Magazine*, 174 (September 1843), 325–6 (326).

textuality that this book as a whole has been exploring. Sarah Sophia Banks was particularly interested in elite private theatricals while her fellow collector Daniel Lysons compiled a five-volume collection of materials relating to the theatre as part of his collecting project as a whole. His 'Collectanea Dramatica', described as 'MATCHLESS' by the 1828 *Catalogue* for the sale of his library, consisted of 'a Selection from the Newspapers, Play Bills, (many of them very rare,) &c. &c. Chronologically arranged, with Manuscript Notes ... a complete Index to each volume, and the sources from which every article is taken pointed out'.[50] The earliest record of theatrical activity that Lysons included in the collection was from a news-sheet, the *Perfect Diurnal of Proceedings* of 11 October 1647, highlighting the conjunction between theatre and the rise of the newspaper press since the seventeenth century. Such forms of print and the modern theatre were mutually constitutive. The author of the 1828 *Catalogue* of Lysons's library enthused that his theatre volumes would be 'a most important acquisition to a Dramatic Collector', the 1820s being a particularly fertile decade for such interests as some notable collections, beginning with those of Kemble, came on the market.[51] One such collection was that of the antiquarian John Field, whose library of Shakespeare first folios and other rarities such as a copy of Ben Jonson's *Sejanus* signed by the author, also contained numerous playbills: the 1827 sale catalogue advertised it as 'the largest Collection of PLAY BILLS ever submitted to Public Notice'. The first item in the section of the catalogue devoted to playbills was a compilation of single-sheet *Spectators*, 'the original Edition as it appeared in Daily Papers'.[52] As in the placing of the *Perfect Diurnal of Proceedings* at the head of Lysons' collection, the volume of collected *Spectators* in the Field sale catalogue implicitly aligned theatre history with the history of print media. In addition to its assemblage of playbills the Field sale was also notable for a collection of 'Checks and Tickets of Admission to various Theatres, and other Places of Public Amusement', ranging from a token for the Swan Theatre from 1668, 'very ancient and curious', to checks for the Pantheon (from 1791) and a selection for the London pleasure gardens.[53]

A notable example of such a playbill collector was Joseph Haslewood who, as we have seen previously, acquired material from the sale of

---

[50] *Catalogue of the Library of Daniel Lysons*, 31.   [51] *Catalogue of the Library of Daniel Lysons*, 31.
[52] *Bibliotheca Histrionica. A Catalogue of the Theatrical and Miscellaneous Library of Mr. John Field* (London: Sotheby, 1827), title page, 68. (The copy of the catalogue in the Bodleian Library indicates that this file was bought by Charles Mathews).
[53] *Bibliotheca Histrionica*, 70.

Narcissus Luttrell's library and was a maker of idiosyncratic ephemera books. One of Haslewood's many interests was the history of the theatre. His library included a twenty-eight-volume collection of dramatic tracts, described in the catalogue as a 'most curious and extensive assemblage', and multiple volumes of playbills, including one set devoted to 'Private Performances [and] Provincial Theatres', and a nine-volume collection entitled 'Plays, Players, and Play-Houses'.[54] Haslewood's MS preface to the collection claimed that it was designed as material for an unrealised 'History of the English Theatre in London' and that it was drawn from 'very promiscuous, very extensive, and very uncommon' sources such as 'rare old publications' and 'things fallen into desuetude'.[55]

As Kristian Jensen has brilliantly explored, bibliography and literary culture in general were transformed by the effects of first the French Revolution and later the Revolutionary and Napoleonic wars which emptied the libraries of aristocrats and religious foundations across Europe of incunabula. The traffic in such material across Europe represented a decontextualisation and desacralisation of incunabula and their transformation into luxury goods or art objects. In other words, old books had become fugitive, no longer fixed in the contexts that had defined them as stable and enduring for centuries, with implications for the status of the codex-form book as a whole. The traffic in incunabula and the commodity fetishism of bibliomania entailed the supplanting of the book's association with religion and rank by the ideology of the market and the necessity for more inclusive criteria of value that would enable these books to function properly as commodities: according to Jensen, 'for things to gain value in the market they must be identifiable as belonging to a class of objects, but they must also be distinguishable within the class. There is no market for an unidentifiable mass of material'.[56] Jensen argues that in order to make such distinctions a new 'object-based discipline' emerged after 1789, influenced by philology, antiquarianism, and historiography, particularly printing history, and conducted outside the established centres of learning. It is at this point that the earliest forms of ephemera begin to be sought after by collectors, the most prominent bibliophile of the period, Earl Spencer, buying three 'scraps of vellum' in 1800–1, 'indulgences, items for

---

[54] *Catalogue of the Library of Joseph Haslewood*, 77, 83, 84.
[55] [Joseph Haslewood], "Of Plays, Players, and Play-Houses, with other incidental matter," 8 vols., British Library pressmark 11791 dd 18, vol. 1 f. 3.
[56] Kristian Jensen, *Revolution and the Antiquarian Book: Reshaping the Past, 1780–1815* (Cambridge, UK: Cambridge University Press, 2011), 86.

which there had been no market until then'.⁵⁷ This development illustrates how revolution and war after 1789 had profoundly relativising effects on the spectrum of print, producing the 'wild' bibliography identified by Jon Klancher.⁵⁸ On the one hand these events granted a new visibility to the ephemeral text as a potential object of value because the most prestigious sacral books had become displaced, fugitive, subject to appropriation and in some cases purgative recontextualisation – all books were in a sense now 'ephemeral'. On the other hand they reinforced ephemerality as a way of defining the limits of value in the market economy of print, particularly the boundary of the 'unidentifiable mass of material' which is not commodifiable. Thus the bibliomaniac and the ephemerophile were not necessarily antithetical but were important to each other and in the case of Haslewood and numerous other book collectors of the period were embodied in a single individual. Haslewood's career in particular illustrates the synthesis of philology, antiquarianism, and historiography underpinning the 'object-based discipline' of Romantic textual materialism that Jensen identifies, to which I would also add the constitutive importance of ephemerology.

The late Georgian period was therefore one of tremendous archival energy in relation to ephemerality, in which the playbill was central. 'Extraordinary accumulations' of playbills were made, preserved, circulated, and deposited, not only in the metropolis but also throughout Britain. In 1946, *Notes and Queries* published 'a census of extant collections of English provincial playbills' of the eighteenth century, noting that while some had been destroyed in the Second World War 'very little' had actually 'perished as a result of air-raids'.⁵⁹ Perhaps the most striking example of the material richness of the late Georgian playbill archive, apart from Winston's 'extraordinary accumulation' now disseminated across the globe, is the playbill collections of the British Library. At the centre of those collections are the files made by Charles Burney Jr, the brother of the novelist Frances Burney. Like Haslewood, Burney combined the identities of book lover and ephemerophile. He gained notoriety and caused enduring damage to his career when he was expelled from Cambridge in 1777 after stealing books from the University Library. He was also a lifelong

---

⁵⁷ Jensen, *Revolution and the Antiquarian Book*, 49.
⁵⁸ Klancher, 'Wild Bibliography: The Rise and Fall of Book History I Nineteenth-Century Britain', in *Bookish Histories: Books, Literature, and Commercial Modernity 1700–1900*, eds. Ina Ferris and Paul Keen (New York: Palgrave Macmillan, 2009), 19–41.
⁵⁹ Frederick T. Wood, 'Census of Extant Collections of English Provincial Playbills of the Eighteenth Century', *Notes and Queries*, 190:11 (1946), 222–6 (222).

collector of newspapers and playbills, the latter as a basis for an unrealised history of the British theatre and in particular of the actor-manager David Garrick.[60] The file of Keswick playbills was part of this collection. Burney's library, including a collection of theatrical portraits, now in the Department of Prints and Drawings, was bought by the British Museum in 1821, three years after it acquired Sarah Sophia Banks's collections. Together Burney's newspapers and playbills and Banks's collections, foundational in the development of the British Museum and Library, constitute the most comprehensive documentation of polite life and associational culture that had hitherto been made in world history.[61] The Burney collection of newspapers was digitised in the 2000s and is now one of the British Library's most valuable resources, sold by the e-research and educational publisher Gale Cengage to libraries across the world, and his playbill collections are also beginning to appear in digital form. Considered in its totality, Burney's collecting can be seen as an attempt to capture, as it was happening, the immediacy and complexity of the daily traffic of Georgian society's information networks, the precedent for which was the practices of seventeenth-century collectors such as Thomason and Wood. It is not accidental that first-level playbill collectors were printers and booksellers such as Sprange, postmasters such as Rodgers in Whitby, coffeehouse owners and theatre managers, men and women who were themselves nodes in such networks, who handled and facilitated the flows of paper of which the playbill was only one stream. While important in the documentation of contemporary theatre, the playbill was therefore also an important part of a wider archiving of the print media and its relationship to quotidian, associational life. Men such as Burney and women such as Southey's aunt Tyler were thus as much media, as they were theatre, historians.

In her discussion of James Winston's archive of the late Georgian theatre, Jacky Bratton notes how he seemed to collect 'everything – the death of a long-serving dresser alongside Sheridan's receipts for his fire-insurance premium and a newspaper biography of Thomas Holcroft; ephemera like bills for goods and services and tickets are pasted in, or sometimes described and copied'. (It is noteworthy that Bratton used the term 'ephemera' to make distinctions within the mass of material collected

---

[60] Lars Troide, 'Burney, Charles (1757–1817)', *Oxford Dictionary of National Biography*, ed. H. C. G. Matthew and Brian Harrison, Oxford University Press, 2004; online ed. Lawrence Goldman, January 2008 [www.oxforddnb.com.virtual.anu.edu.au/view/article/4079, accessed 18 June 2014].

[61] For similar practices in Edo Japan, suggesting a 'new understanding of the quotidian as an object of historical inquiry', see Jonathan Zwicker, 'Playbills, Ephemera, and the Historical Imagination in Nineteenth-Century Japan,' *The Journal of Japanese Studies*, 35:1 (2009), 37–59 (39).

by Winston, whose practices appear similar in this respect to those of Sarah Sophia Banks). Bratton adds that Winston 'seems to have been the kind of man for whom the computer database would have been a perfect tool, or rather, perhaps, an end in itself'.[62] The activities of men such as Winston were regarded, Bratton argues, as a primitive antiquarianism, superseded after the 1830s by more 'scientific' and literary models of theatre historiography that rejected the gathering together of mere fact and anecdote in favour of a synthesising analysis based on rigorous principles of textual criticism. This development led ultimately to a theatre historiography dominated by the idea of the decline of the dramatic genius represented by Shakespeare, the superiority of the closet over the stage, and the stigmatisation of spectacle as popular mass (or ephemeral) entertainment. It resulted in what Bratton terms the 'discrediting' or 'defeat' of histories of theatre such as John Genest's ten-volume *Some Account of the English Stage, from the Restoration in 1660 to 1830*, published in Bath in 1832.[63] Genest was a retired clergyman who, like James Plumptre, had an avid interest in the theatre. His book is an annual register of theatrical performances in London, Bath, and Dublin, ranging from the patent theatres to fairground booths, combined with opinion and analysis. Genest's history would not have been possible without the playbill and the history of playbill collecting after the mid-eighteenth century. Indeed, his reliance on the playbill was so transparent that a later commentary, published in the *New Monthly Magazine* in 1851, was able to envisage Genest at work as a diurnal historiographer: 'Doubtless his playbills came down by the post to Bath (where the book was published), every morning, and he looked, and he extracted, and he filed'.[64]

Genest acknowledged his indebtedness to the playbill by giving an account of the Field sale in 1827, revealing himself to be a buyer, via the bookseller Thomas Rodd, of many of its volumes. Distinguishing between what he calls 'real playbills' and those cut out of newspapers, Genest notes the price he paid and the value of collections such as that for Drury Lane, Goodman's Fields, and the Haymarket for 1733–4 – 'the Hay. Bills proved of great importance to me'.[65] Genest also noted various lots of playbills that had been sold to other people, including Charles Mathews,

---

[62] Jacky Bratton, *New Readings in Theatre History* (Cambridge, UK: Cambridge University Press, 2003), 31, 33.
[63] Bratton, *New Readings*, 35, 90.
[64] 'The "Keans"', *New Monthly Magazine*, 91 (1851), 515–16 (515).
[65] John Genest, *Some Account of the English Stage, from the Restoration in 1660 to 1830*, 10 vols. (Bath: H. E. Carrington, 1832), XI: 406.

suggesting that he owned an annotated copy of the catalogue of the Field sale.⁶⁶ In its permeability to the materiality of the playbill and the playbill as a mode of archivisation, as well as to the ephemeral genre of the sale catalogue, Genest's theatre history showed its affinities with the loose, expansive book making of collectors such as Haslewood or Winston, practices that could accommodate tickets or insurance receipts. His account of 'Mr. Field's Sale', included in his chronicle of events of 1827 rather than as an appendix, acknowledged the materiality of his own history and its open transparency to archival sources. It grants the playbill collection a topological status within his own text as a form of accreted, bundled knowledge that had moved between many hands before it reached him and would presumably move again.

Digitisation, as Bratton suggests in her comparison of Winston's archive with a computer database, enables us to see the playbill and other similar kinds of texts such as the ticket as a form of data storage and the practice of collecting as, in Benjamin's terms, a mode of 'actualization'.⁶⁷ Rather than viewing projects such as Winston's (and also Burney's and Haslewood's) as failed or 'defeated' histories, why not consider them as indeed ends in themselves? Genest's model of a capacious or fugitive theatre history was later stigmatised as 'bill-sticking history' that was too invested in the ephemeral.⁶⁸ Bratton claims that 'anecdote, inherited wisdom, professional interest in the box office – *all the material and emotional heritage of the stage* – was viewed merely as the context which helped (or more often hindered) the realisation of the written dramatic text' (my emphasis). In other words, 'all the material and emotional heritage of the stage' was increasingly rendered as ephemeral in contradistinction to the enduring qualities of the literary dramatic text or 'playbook'.⁶⁹ The perishability of the playbill (and the kind of knowledge associated with it) was thus necessary to defining how theatre, for all its reliance on the ephemeral, could possibly transcend time, through its importance to national literary heritage, embodied above all in the genius of Shakespeare.

One consequence of the eventual disciplinisation of 'theatre science' as a branch of the study of the arts, crossing the domains of literary studies and history, was that its original status as a form of media history that implicitly situated theatre in relation to the development of associational culture as a

---

⁶⁶ Genest, *Some Account*, 407.   ⁶⁷ Benjamin, *Arcades Project*, 460.
⁶⁸ *Fraser's Magazine* 2 (January 1831), 736, as part of a commentary on James Boaden's biography of Dorothy Jordan.
⁶⁹ Bratton, *New Readings*, 90.

whole was eventually forgotten. Theatre history in Britain, as Bratton suggests, is an early Enlightenment phenomenon: it began with James Wright's *Historia Histrionica* (1699) and John Downes's *Roscius Anglicanus* (1708) and was thus linked with the wider documentation of contemporary public culture as a result of the expansion of the print media, practised by men such as Luttrell. Considered within the context of ephemera collecting, the history of the Georgian theatre looks very different, that is, as primarily driven by media change, the theatre's own investments in the evanescence of the performance event being translatable to ephemeral print's capacity to mark time and vice versa. Collectors of ephemera were able to document such investments, situating theatre as part of a wider media ecology and traffic in sociability, constructing histories that, because they tended towards the encyclopedic, could accommodate theatre in all its diversity, including unrespectable or illegitimate forms. In a preface to his collection 'Of Plays, Players, and Play-Houses', Joseph Haslewood claimed that if the public patronised entertainments such as rope-dancers and performing monkeys, 'it may be expected the readers of a future day will be eager to have some information of such inconsequential diversions ... as well as the slip slop of times past'.[70] It was thus the duty of the collector-historian to record such performances, a catholicity that is also reflected in the scope of other collections that placed together or consigned the theatre of Garrick with the fairground (and also the frost fair). Part of the process of cultural distinction underpinning the development of theatre history as a discipline in the nineteenth century was the exclusion or ephemeralisation of the 'slip slop' of the theatre as a worthy object of inquiry. This process entailed the estrangement of theatre itself, now reified as an art form, from its relationship with other forms of entertainment and sociability, such as pleasure and tea gardens, assembly rooms, exhibitions, ballooning, and so on.

Ephemerality was not only deployed as a criterion of distinction whereby the field of theatre knowledge was reconfigured in a Bourdieuvian sense but, as was the case with Johnson's conceptualisation of ephemera a hundred years before, was also used to define the rhythms of media shift – particularly the sense of print as becoming too much. The commentary on Genest's *Some Account of the English Stage* published in the *New Monthly Magazine* in 1851 claimed that his kind of history was no longer possible due to the proliferation of playhouses after the relaxation in 1843 of the licensing laws that regulated the theatre. In the 1850s there were now simply too many theatres and too many playbills:

[70] Haslewood, 'Of Plays, Players, and Play-Houses', f.3.

[H]ow could [Genest] possibly have taken in every bill of every establishment? What room in his house, what house in his row, would have held them all . . .? Had he attempted to publish them or their contents, however condensed, how many volumes would he have filled, even at this short march from 1830? If endowed with the spirit of an ancient philosopher, he would have burned himself on a blazing pyre of playbills, just as Empedocles sought death in the crater of Etna.[71]

The acquisition of ephemeral knowledge, in the form of an excess of paper information, conceived topologically as a room crammed with stuff, was by 1851 a shameful, embarrassing practice: it was the abyss against which history had to define itself. Theatre history would have to bury its origins in such practices and in the history of associational culture as a whole, disavowing its continuing reliance on the ephemeral archive. However, if the nexus between theatrical culture and ephemeral print was increasingly untenable by the 1850s, such a development enables us to recognise what had been possible before that date. Between the seventeenth century and the mid-nineteenth century the full spectrum of the paper economy, particularly forms such as the newspaper, the handbill, and the ticket, were recognised as being capable of mediating the fleetingness of social experience, thereby making ephemera visible as a medium and the collecting of that medium a mode of history making. The Romantic period is notable as the period when the mediality of printed ephemera is recognised as being capable of constituting or, in Wordsworth's case, of being remediated, as a poetics. In envisaging himself as a writer of playbills and God's theatre manager, Coleridge was expressing the power of ephemerality as a way of apprehending or actualising the passage of time: as the *New Monthly Magazine* writer said of John Genest, one could 'look', 'file', and 'extract', and the momentariness of experience might still be there.

'THEATRE, SYDNEY'

The archival energy focused on the playbill in the Romantic period forms a context for the playbills with which I began this chapter – those sought by Sarah Sophia Banks from the new colony of New South Wales. The Sydney playbill for the performance by convicts of *Jane Shore* on 30 July 1796 is a particular example of the paradox of the ephemeral text's durability and its tendency to escape, in this case into an unimaginable future[72] (Figure 18).

---

[71] 'The "Keans"', 515.
[72] For the benefit of J. Butler and W. Bryant: at the Theatre, Sydney on July 30, 1796, will be performed Jane Shore ... National Library of Australia F692 RBRS N 686.2099441.

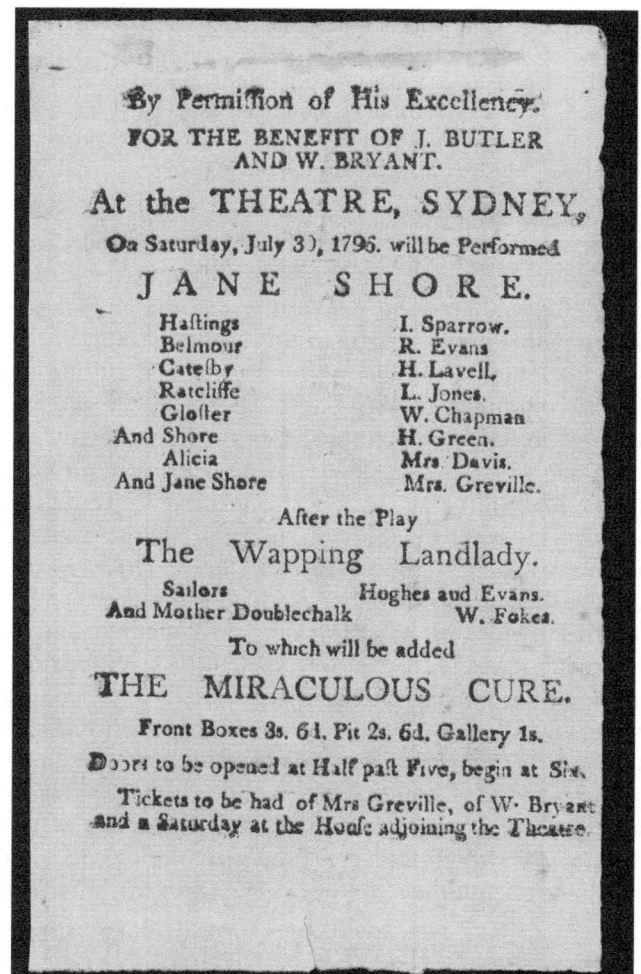

Figure 18 For the benefit of J. Butler and W. Bryant: at the Theatre, Sydney on July 30, 1796, will be performed Jane Shore ... [Sydney: George Hughes, Govt. Printer for Theatre, Sydney, 1796]. National Library of Australia F692 RBRS N 686.2099441.
Permission National Library of Australia

This playbill was created many thousands of miles away from Britain in a starkly different environment but it was nonetheless shaped by the circumstances of the 1790s, particularly the importance of handbills in the propaganda wars of this decade. In the light of what was happening in

Britain in the 1790s and the history of government sensitivity in relation to the theatre, it is remarkable that Governor John Hunter allowed a playhouse to be established in the colony of New South Wales in the first place. Hunter's authority is signalled by the first line of the playbill, 'By Permission of His Excellency', placing him in a position equivalent to that of the king when he attended command performances. From the outset, the playbill made it clear that this was a government-sanctioned event.

Not only did Hunter permit the performances that evening, he also authorised the printing of the playbill itself. There was only one printing press in the colony, a small wooden screw press that was in the cargo of the First Fleet in 1788. The purpose of this press was to print general orders, rules, and regulations, necessary for the administration of the colony. There was, however, no one with the necessary printing skills to use the press until the arrival in 1795 of the convict George Hughes, described by David Collins as 'a very decent young man ... of some abilities in the printing line'.[73] Printing was also constrained by limitations on the basic resources of type, paper, and ink. A paper-making mill was not established until 1818 and until that time the colony was reliant on supplies of paper from England.[74] In these circumstances – the scarcity of resources for printing and the need to meet the demands of governing the colony – the fact that any playbills at all were produced in these years is remarkable, even miraculous. Hughes's playbill, though a less polished production, is essentially similar to the 'common house-bill' used in Britain, the plainer, more austere eighteenth-century handbill on the cusp of the typographic revolution of the early 1800s. This playbill, moreover, is not the only example of playbills from the Sydney Theatre to survive. Two others, advertising George Farquhar's *The Recruiting Officer* and Shakespeare's *Henry IV* in the March and April of 1800 respectively, were discovered by chance in the 1930s, interleaved in a volume of the *Sydney Gazette*, the first Australian newspaper. An account of this discovery described how these playbills, like butterflies, 'fluttered forth' from the pages of the newspaper.[75] Playbills were thus not only allowed to be printed in these exceptionally difficult circumstances, but they also formed a numerically

---

[73] David Collins, *An Account of the English Colony in New South Wales* (London: Cadell & Davies, 1798), 435.

[74] Jane Waslin, 'Paper Industry', in *Australian Encyclopaedia*, ed. Tony Macdougall, 6th edn, 6 vols. (Terrey Hills, New South Wales: Australian Geographic, 1996), VI: 2343–4 (2343).

[75] John Alexander Ferguson, *Bibliography of Australia, Volume 1: 1784–1830* (Canberra: National Library of Australia, 1975), item nos. 319, 320: J. A. Ferguson, A. G. Foster, and H. M. Green, *The Howes and Their Press* (1936), quoted in Ferguson, *Bibliography of Australia*, 121.

significant and prominent aspect of print production in the colony in its earliest days. The first book to be printed in Australia, *New South Wales General Standing Orders*, appeared in 1802, followed by the first newspaper, the *Sydney Gazette*, in 1803. Between 1795, when Hughes commenced work, and 1802, the printed material being produced by the colony was thus exclusively broadside in nature.[76]

We do not know how many playbills were printed for the Sydney Theatre or how exactly they would have been distributed. It is unlikely that playgoers on that July evening would have encountered bill-sellers outside the theatre, nor would they have seen large bills in red and black blazoning the performance. These absences would have accentuated the importance of the handbill as the only form of publicity for *Jane Shore*, stuck on posts or doorways, possibly next to official government notices, or most likely distributed personally by the actors themselves. Declaring the existence of the 'THEATRE, SYDNEY', the playbill was thus a performative act that announced the universality and durability of the values underpinning the venture in New South Wales. In this respect, the capitalisation, even the comma, between 'THEATRE' and 'SYDNEY' were significant. Following the boy Southey's practice of close reading, if we were to hold this phrase up to the light, as it were, the comma between Theatre and Sydney shines out as signifying both the curiosity and the possibility of the conjunction of 'theatre' and the new colony: it performatively enacts the anticipation of what is not yet known, as well as, in its following of playbill conventions, creating the temporary impression, the fantastic consolation, that life in a new land could still be recognizable as continuous with 'home'.

Another possible reason why Hunter allowed Hughes to print playbills for the Sydney Theatre was the prospect of them reaching a wider audience in Britain, through newspaper publicity. In July 1797 the *Oracle* in London reprinted a playbill advertising the entertainments at the Sydney Theatre for 23 July 1796, that is, a week before *Jane Shore* was performed on 30 July. This 'Copy of a *Botany Bay Play Bill*' was described as demonstrating the 'degree of refinement that settlement has already attained'.[77] The plays performed on that occasion were Susannah Centlivre's comedy *The Busy Body* and *The Poor Soldier* by John O'Keeffe, and the report also gave an account of some of the performers, most notably Robert Sidaway. Described as 'an *old offender*', Sidaway was said to be

---

[76] Ferguson, *Bibliography of Australia*, 358.
[77] *Oracle and Public Advertiser*, 13 July 1797; also reported in the *Morning Post*, 13 July 1797.

making a fortune as a baker and had no desire to return to Britain.[78] Clearly the playbill had been sent to London with some kind of written explanation of it. This playbill was published in the *Oracle* nearly a year after the performance had taken place. The *Oracle*'s report was picked up by other newspapers and Sidaway became a minor celebrity, the focus of often joking references to this '*Remarkable Instance of the versatility of Fortune*'.[79] 'Botany Bay Theatricals', the headline echoing the reporting of elite amateur theatricals, became a recognisable topic in the newspapers and magazines of the late 1790s and early 1800s. We do not know how the playbill for the 23 July performance reached the *Oracle* offices, nor what happened to it subsequently. The account of the 'Botany Bay' playbill in the *Oracle* was printed, not in the main body of the newspaper as might have been expected because it was a news item, but on the front page next to playbills for performances at the Theatre Royal in the Haymarket and at Astley's Circus, giving it similar status as an advertisement. Appearing just a few years after the mock playbills satirising the British government had been reprinted as part of the reporting of the 1794 Treason Trials, there was always the chance, however, that the Sydney playbills might be faked. The latent literariness of the playbill genre in the 1790s, apparent in the radical mock playbills, expressed the British response to news from Sydney Cove as a sense of wonder at the strangeness or unreality of the real, like an encounter with a whale in the Thames or a frost fair on the same solid river. This page of the *Oracle* therefore suggests that before it was anything else the history of Australia was a theatre/media history. Sydney Cove was apprehended in terms of the conventions and poetics of fugitive media which, like the comma between THEATRE and SYDNEY, manifested the cusp between the familiarity of a living tradition and what was unknown or yet to be.

The playbill for the performance on 23 July 1796 of *The Busy Body* (or a copy of it) made its way to England within a year of the production to be reprinted in the *Oracle* in 1797 before it disappeared from the historical record. The playbill for the performance of *Jane Shore* on the following Saturday, 30 July 1796, had a more chequered but also more enduring history. We know from annotations on the back that it was owned by the then lieutenant-governor, Philip Gidley King: it may have been a souvenir of his attendance at the Sydney Theatre on 30 July or something he picked up as a curious product of Hughes's press (Figure 19). The notes that he

---

[78] *Oracle and Public Advertiser*, 13 July 1797. [79] *London Chronicle*, 31 August 1797.

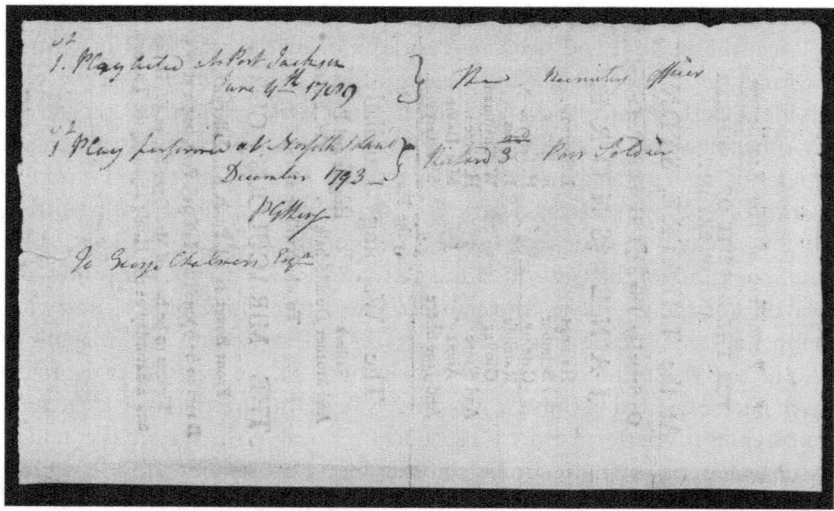

Figure 19 For the benefit of J. Butler and W. Bryant: at the Theatre, Sydney on July 30, 1796, will be performed Jane Shore ... [Sydney: George Hughes, Govt. Printer for Theatre, Sydney, 1796]. National Library of Australia F692 RBRS N 686.2099441, recto. Permission National Library of Australia

made on the back gave the playbill and theatrical activity in the colony as a whole a history by listing the first play to be performed at Port Jackson, *The Recruiting Officer*, on 4 June 1789, and on Norfolk Island, including Shakespeare's *Richard III* (Figure 18). King was therefore acting as a kind of theatre historian, in a comparable way to the actors and managers for whom playbills were the material of institutional memory. The playbill was a means of recording the history of the colony virtually as it was happening. As a colonial bureaucrat, King was also accounting for his and Hunter's proper administration: his notes on the back of the playbill proved that the authorities were keeping a close eye on theatrical activity in the colony from the very beginning. The playbill was thus both a personal and an official record, King's notes on the back reinforcing the declaration on the front that the theatre was 'by permission' of the authorities.

As an educated military gentleman, King possibly knew too of the interest that the playbill was likely to create in Britain among collectors such as Sarah Sophia Banks. It is likely that King, who was visiting London for health reasons, gave the playbill to George Chalmers, in 1796, meaning that the bill was being circulated in Britain very soon after the performance in Sydney.[80] Chalmers, who was an associate of Sir Joseph Banks, combined scholarly pursuits as an antiquary and historian with the position of chief clerk to the Committee of the Privy Council.[81] His collection of books, manuscripts, and broadsides was eventually sold by his descendants in 1841. The playbill which King had gifted to him was one of a number of what the catalogue described as 'fugitive pieces, chiefly single leaves', amounting to 1,100 items.[82] The Sydney playbill was therefore part of the trade in playbills and playbill collections between private individuals that occurred in the nineteenth century. Chalmers's three volumes of 'fugitive pieces' were bought by Dawson Turner who, as we have seen, was also a member of the Banks circle and an avid collector of scraps and compiler of ephemeral books. Turner made new scrapbooks in which to house the 'fugitive pieces' he acquired from Chalmers and after his death the scrapbook was acquired by the Library of the Parliament of Canada and subsequently the National Archives of Canada. It was only in the 2000s, when archives had to be removed from a vault in which they were stored that the playbill came to light once more. The miracle of its survival is underscored by the fact that it had not been secured in Turner's scrapbook but was loosely inserted, meaning that it could easily have been lost.[83] The archivist Elaine Hoag recognised the value of the playbill as an early example of Australian printing and in 2007, with much fanfare, the playbill was returned to Canberra as a gift of the Canadian people to Australia. The then prime minister of Canada, Stephen Harper, used the opportunity of the Asia-Pacific Economic Cooperation meeting in Sydney in that year to present the playbill to his Australian counterpart, John Howard.[84]

Because of its status as the earliest existing printed document in Australia's history (and only secondarily as an archive of the theatre), the playbill has run the gamut from print 'rubbish' to the 'condition of the priceless archive'. The 1796 playbill is currently accessible in two ways: as

---

[80] Hoag, 'The Earliest Extant Australian Imprint', 10–11.
[81] Alexander Du Toit, 'Chalmers, George (*bap.* 1742, *d.* 1825), *Oxford Dictionary of National Biography*, Oxford University Press, 2004; online edn, May 2011 [www.oxforddnb.com/view/article/5028, accessed 11 January 2017].
[82] Hoag, 'The Earliest Extant Australian Imprint', 12.
[83] Hoag, 'The Earliest Extant Australian Imprint', 12–16.
[84] 'Australians Delight in Canada's Gift of Historic Document', 2 February 2006 [www.collectionscanada.gc.ca/whats-new/013-301.1-e.html, accessed 1 December 2008]; 'Harper Returns Archival Document to Australia', Canadian Broadcasting Corporation, 11 September 2007 [www.cbc.ca/news/entertainment/harper-returns-archival-document-to-australia-1.686084, accessed 1 December 2008].

the original document in a rare books collection and as a digitised image, part of the National Library of Australia's digital collection of books and serials. The digitisation of the playbill, making it globally accessible at the touch of a button, is consistent with its career as a fugitive text, beginning with when it was taken to England in 1796. It is tempting to regard the differences between the 'real' playbill and its digital image as a sign of the tendency of digitisation to dematerialise the printed document. The digital image of the playbill lacks the palimpsestic materiality of the 'original' document – the 'before' of the texture of the paper from which the playbill was made, the imprint of the type on this paper, and the history of its subsequent handling, the folds being like lines on a body. Much more than would be the case in lighting conditions of a rare books room, the digitised playbill appears cleaner, less battered, and shining with a distinctive electronic brightness. However, it must be emphasised that the digitised playbill is not an analogue image, like a photograph, that maintains the primacy of the paper original, but is a reconstitution or translation into the language of computing. The playbill has entered the realm of the enduring ephemeral in the technical sense of needing to be refreshed and renewed in order to be read, thereby existing in a state of permanent impermanence (or impermanent permanence). It is now part of the 'undead' of digital information that can never be truly lost or eradicated.

The 1796 playbill was included in the Australian UNESCO Memory of the World Register in 2011 and was installed in the Treasures Gallery of the National Library of Australia, an exhibition of the Library's (and the nation's) most valuable documents, on the opening of the Gallery in 2012. The playbill was located behind the centrepiece of the Treasures Gallery, Captain James Cook's *Endeavour Journal*, a substantial folio book, which is on permanent exhibition in the Library. At time of writing, the playbill is no longer on display, having been withdrawn into rare books sequestration. It has been apparently deemed as less 'permanent' than Cook's *Endeavour Journal*, in spite of its status as the earliest printed document in Australia to be discovered to date. Its temporary instantiation in the Treasures Gallery represents an (unrealised) desire for the priceless, original paper object, a foundational document of the white settlement of Australia, the dream of which the playbill as an ephemeral document inevitably ironizes. The playbill cannot be foregrounded or rendered 'permanent' in the same way as the *Endeavour Journal*, not only because of its association with the ephemeral arts of the theatre, but also because it simply is not 'book enough'. Rather than being a debased simulacrum of the playbill's authenticity as a paper object, the digital image's enduring ephemerality,

I would suggest, is consistent with the recalcitrant ephemerality of the paper original: both are documents that cannot be fixed in time and place. Both keep moving.

Jacques Derrida claimed that changes in the technologies of writing, specifically word processing, had the potential to render '*other* our old sorting out ... our family scene, if I may call it that, when the written thing first appeared'.[85] A similar process can be said to be taking place in relation to the digital and print media, digitisation compelling a re-vision of 'our old sorting out' of the history of print. A consequence of this is the new visibility of ephemera, or the increasing recognition of ephemera's role in enabling the idea of the durability of the book. Thus the historical moment of the Sydney playbill after its return to Australia in 2007 suggests how digitisation and digital cultures, rather than superseding print and paper, are expanding or dilating the boundaries of the spectrum of textuality, as well as challenging ideas of what constitutes an archive and the kinds of knowledge that archives can make. The discursive phenomenon of 'Botany Bay theatricals' was a minor event in the vast output of print in the 1790s, but the fugitive playbills from Sydney that found their way into London newspapers represented an important historical development that resonates in the context of digitised information today. The remediation of these playbills in the newspaper press in the 1790s made the newspaper visible as a medium that confounded the distances of time and space, creating an idea of synchronous media time and media time as a kind of theatricality. Everywhere could be assimilated to the 'new present' and vice versa, the Botany Bay playbills representing the globalising potential of print in a strikingly curious way because Botany Bay was so far away and strange but now, through the medium of the playbill, apparently close and familiar, happening in a mediatised 'real time'. It is not surprising, therefore, that Sarah Sophia Banks wanted to possess a Botany Bay playbill as it would have been the ultimate confirmation of the reach of ephemeral knowledge and the capacity of that knowledge not only to shape history but also to define how history felt like, as it was happening, in the global, ephemeral, here and now.

---

[85] Derrida, *Paper Machine*, 25.

CHAPTER 6

Transacting Hospitality
The Novel Networks of the Visiting Card

The playbill exemplifies the democratic, global, and intermedial reach of jobbing print in the eighteenth century. An even more distinctively Georgian innovation was the visiting card or ticket, a small piece of stiff paper or pasteboard, approximately the size of the palm of a hand, on which messages, names, and sometimes designs could be written, printed, or engraved. A subgenre of the ticket, the visiting card, as we have seen, was a major focus of Sarah Sophia Banks, who collected them in the thousands. These cards were developed in the early eighteenth century in order to facilitate, regulate, commodify, and ultimately archive the sociability of the personal visit. The implications of this innovation would be far-reaching, scholars of twenty-first-century media acknowledging the visiting card as part of the genealogy of text messaging. Esther Milne describes visiting cards as 'avatars of presence and identity, a complex language system which allowed the discursive agents to mediate social relations according to various degrees of intimacy that were desired', anticipating 'a range of contemporary technologies of propinquity'.[1] The old 'new media' of the eighteenth century thus becomes belatedly visible through the development of (old) 'new media' of the twenty-first. Until work such as Milne's, the visiting card had barely featured as a textual artefact in its own right in eighteenth-century social and cultural history, interest in it being confined to the non-academic study of related collectibles, such as visiting card cases.[2] This invisibility belies the ubiquity of the visiting card in Georgian polite culture and its effectiveness as a medium of sociability. As Sarah Sophia Banks recognised in her collecting, the visiting card was a particularly powerful example of the capacity of paper as a bearer of writing to act as a prosthesis of individual identities

---

[1] Esther Milne, '"Magic Bits of Paste-board": Texting in the Nineteenth Century', *M/C: A Journal of Media and Culture*, 7:1 (2004) [www.media-culture.org.au/0401/02-milne.php, accessed 2014].

[2] E.g. Noël Riley, *Visiting Card Cases* (Guilford: Lutterworth Press, 1983).

and a filter of relationships between people. The visiting card represented the currency of an economy of social relations at its most fundamental level, that is, the tendering of oneself to the possibility of welcome or rejection by another, a micro-sociability that was constitutive of the theatre of sociality as a whole. The elaboration of polite sociability and the ideologies and ethics associated with it, relating to fellowship, commercial exchange, cosmopolitan hospitality, the free flow of information, communication, and conversation, were all ultimately dependent on the initial gesture of proffering the ticket of oneself on the threshold of the other, and of individuals or groups allowing admission to the stranger or alternatively keeping the stranger out. Rather than being of trivial or marginal significance, the visiting card was thus a key building block of the edifice of polite associational culture in the eighteenth century: it made social relations happen, occupying and making visible the hyphenation, the 'with-one-another' or 'pure essence of association' that Georg Simmel saw as intrinsic to sociability.[3]

The fact that eighteenth-century men and women entrusted themselves to the power of a tiny piece of pasteboard to effect, police, and commemorate such threshold moments indicates an important historical change, an investment in the mediatisation or systematisation through paper instruments of all aspects of social life. What was formerly an oral and thus more profoundly ephemeral exchange was now allowed to be 'spoken' through the medium of paper. These performative dimensions of the visiting card, allied with its capacity to encode the affective meanings of the transient social encounter, makes it, like the playbill, a textual artefact that combines the irreducibility of the 'thing' – social life itself – with the transparency of the object. As object/thing, the visiting card was particularly relevant to other aspects of print culture that had an investment in sociable life such as periodical literature, particularly that engaged with the arbitration of manners and taste, and prose fiction. In the late 1980s J. P. Hunter argued that the novel emerged from the 'moment-centred consciousness' of the late seventeenth century, the interest in novelty, strange events, and discovery that underpinned the collecting interests of men such as Wood, Pepys, and Luttrell (all of whom possessed bundles of romances and 'penny histories'). 'Distasteful as it may be to traditional literary history', Hunter also commented, 'the relationship between ephemera and serious literature in the mid-eighteenth century was a very close one, not always clear even to the

[3] Simmel, 'Sociology of Sociability', 120.

writers who were producing one or the other'.[4] In this chapter I explore one particular aspect of the contiguity of 'serious literature' and ephemera in the form of how Horace Walpole and Samuel Johnson responded to the new medium of the visiting card, and the political, social, and affective dimensions of sociability that the card made visible. I argue that 'serious literature' effected various forms of remediation not only of the textual materialism of the card and the threshold moments of hospitality that the card realised, but also of the practices of aggregation or assemblage exemplified by the ephemera 'books' of the collectors. The latter is illustrated by the importance of the visiting card and other kinds of jobbing print in Maria Edgeworth's *The Absentee* (1812), a novel that analogises the principles and practices of ephemeral knowledge-making as a mode of Enlightenment inquiry, exemplified by the collections of Sarah Sophia Banks. *The Absentee* functions here as a case study of how one writer was attentive to the relationship between printed ephemera and the form, both generic and material, of the Romantic-period novel. Edgeworth was not alone in this interest, a notable precedent for the representation in prose fiction of printed ephemera, particularly the ticket, being the novels of Frances Burney.[5] The full extent of the engagement of prose fiction with ephemeral textuality is beyond the scope of this book, but I want ultimately to develop Hunter's insights into the relationship between 'serious literature' and ephemera by signalling the importance of the early nineteenth century as the period when the novel consolidated its significance through an aestheticisation of the fleeting and ordinary social exchanges that textual ephemera such as the card brought to notice. Firstly, however, I want to outline a (brief) cultural history of the emergence of the visiting card as one of the most important new paper media of the eighteenth century.

The Paper Economy of the Visiting Card

Paying and receiving visits in the eighteenth century was an entrenched social practice, associated with gift-giving and other forms of status

---

[4] J. P. Hunter, '"News, and New Things": Contemporaneity and the Early English Novel', *Critical Inquiry* 14:3 (1988), 493–515 (495, 514).

[5] There are references to tickets and other kinds of printed ephemera such as the playbill in all four of Burney's novels as well as in her correspondence and journals. She attended the Hastings trial in 1788, the tickets for which formed a major part of Sarah Sophia Banks's collection in the Department of Prints and Drawings, and discusses the tickets to the trial extensively in her *Court Journals*: see Frances Burney, *The Court Journals and Letters of Frances Burney*, Vols. III and IV, ed. Lorna J. Clark (Oxford: Oxford University Press, 2014). Burney's fiction and writing as a whole is a notable example of literary engagement with what Lloyd describes as the 'social life' of tickets.

recognition that maintained and reinforced ties within and between families.[6] It was one of the duties that elite and middling-order women were expected to perform and in the course of the century increasingly became a source of pleasure and diversion for them. It was important for men too, calling on friends, acquaintances, and prospective clients or patrons, as William Godwin's diary shows, being part of the repertoire of daily life, essential to the development and maintenance of the networks that sustained careers and relationships.[7] By the 1740s visiting by both men and women was increasingly dependent on the card. Visiting cards, or tickets as they were also known, took a variety of forms. These included calling cards inscribed with the name only to indicate that a visit had taken place; cards acknowledging a visit, often using the phrase 'thank you for your obliging inquiries'; cards inviting guests to particular social occasions in the household such as private masquerades; and cards announcing an individual's arrival in town for the season and availability to be visited or, conversely, cards announcing departure – the latter were known as 'ppc' cards, from the abbreviation of the French phrase, 'pour prendre congé'. Related to these forms of visiting cards were more elaborate forms of the calling card, on which the correspondent would write a message, and the message card itself, not directly linked with a specific visit or invitation, but making a form of third-person address to the recipient, as in, for example, 'Lady — presents her compliments to Lady — and hopes that her health has improved.'

The origins of the visiting card were ascribed later in the nineteenth century to an adaptation of the playing card, the antiquarian E. Walford reporting that he had a collection of Georgian visiting cards belonging to George Selwyn, many of which 'were written on the backs of [playing] cards which have been used or handled at gaming clubs or houses'.[8] It is possible that gamblers unwilling to leave the table may have resorted to

---

[6] On visiting, hospitality, and gender see e.g. Naomi Tadmor, *Family and Friends in Eighteenth Century England: Household, Kinship and Patronage* (Cambridge, UK: Cambridge University Press, 2001); Amanda Vickery, *Behind Closed Doors: At Home in Georgian England* (New Haven, CT: Yale University Press, 2009); Felicity Heal, *Hospitality in Early Modern England* (Oxford: Oxford University Press, 1990); Tracy McNulty, *The Hostess: Hospitality, Femininity, and the Expropriation of Identity* (Minneapolis: University of Minnesota Press, 2007); Anna Bryson, *From Courtesy to Civility: Changing Codes of Conduct in Early Modern England* (Oxford: Oxford University Press, 1998); Susan E. Whyman, *Sociability and Power in Late-Stuart England: The Cultural Worlds of the Verneys 1660–1720* (Oxford: Oxford University Press, 1999); on charitable visiting see Sarah Lloyd, *Charity and Poverty in England c. 1680–1820: Wild and Visionary Schemes* (Manchester: Manchester University Press, 2009).
[7] For the Godwin diary see http://godwindiary.bodleian.ox.ac.uk/.
[8] E. Walford, 'Visiting Cards', *Notes and Queries*, ser. 8, 6 (11 August 1894), 117.

cards to send messages, leading ultimately to the more widespread adoption of cards as a convenient mode of communication. The card became a useful means of soliciting contact, of making or unmaking appointments and visits, and generally oiling the wheels of all kinds of 'business' in eighteenth-century life. A parallel and in many cases intersecting phenomenon is the rise of the trade card by which men and women of commerce promoted their goods and services.[9] The convergence of the playing card with the visiting and trade card was more than just a matter of function: it signals the affinity between gambling, sociability, and trade as forms of sociable 'commerce', an affinity that Sarah Sophia Banks made visible in her collecting practices. Sociability entailed a form of risk-taking, like both gambling and more conventional capitalist enterprises: like the name of a popular card game of the period, it could be a 'speculation'.

The basic form of the visiting card was the simple blank card, upon which a name or short message could be written. Reflecting the traditional privileging of manuscript over print and the status of the communication as 'private', it was customary for cards sent between members of the elite to be handwritten.[10] By the mid-eighteenth century, the visiting card was becoming commercialised. In 1760 John Gretton of Old Bond Street advertised that 'the great Demand he [had] been for some Time honoured with, for VISITING TICKETS and MESSAGE CARDS', had led him to establish a separate printing office in Albemarle Row in order to dispense them.[11] A trade directory published three years later described Gretton as 'Remarkable for selling elegant Message Cards, and fine Dutch Sealing Wax'.[12] Message and visiting cards also feature prominently among the goods sold by the bookseller and stationer George Kearsly in Ludgate Street: a newspaper advertisement from 1764 promoted his 'STATIONARY [sic] WARES, consisting of a great Variety of WRITING-PAPER, MESSAGE-PAPER and CARDS; SHOP-BOOKS, POCKET-BOOKS; LETTER, INSTRUMENT, and TRAVELLING CASES; PENCILS, best

---

[9] On the trade card see Rickards and Twyman, *Encyclopedia of Ephemera*, 334–5; Maxine Berg and Helen Clifford, 'Selling Consumption in the Eighteenth Century: Advertising and the Trade Card in Britain and France', *Cultural and Social History*, 4:2 (2007), 145–70; also Chloe Wigston Smith, 'Clothes without Bodies: Objects, Humans, and the Marketplace in Eighteenth-Century It-Narratives and Trade Cards', *Eighteenth-Century Fiction*, 23:2 (2010–11), 347–80.

[10] For visits to Strawberry Hill and Walpole's use of tickets see Stephen Clarke, '"Lord God! Jesus! What a House!": Describing and Visiting Strawberry Hill', *Journal for Eighteenth-Century Studies*, 33:3 (2010), 357–80 (365).

[11] *Public Ledger*, 22 December 1760.

[12] Thomas Mortimer, *The Universal Director: Or, the Nobleman and Gentleman's True Guide to the Masters and Professors of the Liberal and Polite Arts and Sciences* (London: J. Coote, 1763), 167.

DUTCH SEALING-WAX, PENS, QUILLS, INK, INK-POWDER, VISITING-TICKETS, PLAYING CARDS, &c. &c'. Kearsly's 'NEW BOOKS, PAMPHLETS, PLAYS and FARCES' take second billing to his stationery wares, indicating how books were marketed and experienced by consumers in the context of paper goods and the related paraphernalia of writing.[13] The expansion of literacy and of commerce of all kinds created a demand for the tools and materials of writing: hence the growth of the stationery trade, based on commodities from all corners of the globe. As Konstantin Dierks notes, 'Ink combined oak galls from Syria, gum arabic from Sudan, and alum and copperas from England', while pounce, a powder used to prevent ink from spreading, 'was derived from gum sandarac, from Morocco'. The bulk of paper production was British-based although the finest quality writing papers were still imported from Holland and France and even further afield. Dierks describes these raw materials of the stationery trade as 'stealth commodities', in so far as 'an extraordinary network of extraction, trade, production, and retailing' that was associated with them had become 'routinized and normalized by the 1750s'.[14]

This 'extraordinary' network sustained a highly sophisticated stationery trade, capable of meeting the demands of the mundane work-a-day world, as well as the highest standards of elegance and luxury. The range of stationery goods and their sensory appeal to the connoisseur of pen and paper is apparent in the 1785 catalogue of the bookseller Anthony Edwards of Cork in Ireland. On offer were multiple grades of paper from 'Superfine London parliament-paper' to 'Tissue paper for balloons' as well as the various accoutrements of writing, ranging from 'Fine white marble dust' to 'Asses-skin memorandum books'.[15] Anthony Edwards's message cards and visiting tickets take precedence to books, his 'many thousand tragedies, comedies, operas and farces' being easy to miss in the plethora of waxes, wafers, and 'Ward's essence for a head-ache'.[16] The focus of literary history on the selling and lending of books, especially the novel, has obscured the extent to which books actually jostled for attention among a range of other paper and paper-related products. Thomas

---

[13] *Gazetteer*, 26 January 1764.
[14] Konstantin Dierks, 'Letter Writing, Stationery Supplies, and Consumer Modernity in the Eighteenth-Century Atlantic World', *Early American Literature*, 41:3 (2006), 473–94 (480, 481, 482).
[15] Anthony Edwards, *Catalogue of Books, in Most Branches of Literature* (Cork: Anthony Edwards, 1785), 2.
[16] Edwards, *Catalogue*, 3.

Hookham's bookshop in Old Bond Street was notable for its trade in 'Visiting Tickets, and Complimentary Cards' that it advertised prominently in conjunction with its stock of bibles and dictionaries and its facilities for bookbinding.[17]

The form of card sold by bookshops catering to a more polite metropolitan clientele such as Hookham's included printed designs framing either a blank space or a text with blanks in which names could be written. These formulae, as in, for example, 'Lady — desires the company of —', encoded the imaginative potential of sociability: there was something pleasurable in contemplating whose names might be inscribed there, and what doors the cards might open. Though 'private' in the sense that their circulation, unlike the post, was outside the control of the state, cards were often more public and visible than letters within the space of the household. Letters were circulated openly and read aloud but they could also be concealed in closets, in the drawers, secret or otherwise of writing desks, or conceivably on an individual's body, Richardson's *Pamela* being the most celebrated literary example of how letters could be hidden in clothing. Cards, on the contrary, were meant to be in public view: hence they were to be found in hallways, stuck in the frames of mirrors, or, in the latter part of the period, displayed in card racks, which enabled the individual to organise and review their sociable commitments.[18]

The most prestigious form of the 'display' card was that produced by intaglio processes. Letterpress printing could not compete with the sophistication and beauty of the engraver's art. Customers bought either the engravers' standard stock of cards or would commission personalised designs. Notable engravers, ranging from Francesco Bartolozzi and Giovanni Battista Cipriani to even William Blake, produced such cards to commission for individual clients.[19] These cards were works of art designed to enhance both the status of the card itself as a commodity of sociability and the prestige of its bearer: we have already seen how Sarah Sophia Banks was a connoisseur of the ticket as auratic art object, especially prizing its proof or 'pure' form. A striking or attractive image enabled a card to stand

---

[17] *The Maid of Kent*, 3 vols. (London: T. Hookham, 1790), I: unpaginated end matter. Jan Fergus notes that Hookham's bookshop sold more tickets than books: *Provincial Readers in Eighteenth-Century England* (Oxford: Oxford University Press, 2006), 17; see also Raven, *Publishing Business*, 80.

[18] For images of Regency card racks see nttreasurehunt.wordpress.com/2011/03/09/how-were-they-used, accessed 7 February 2014.

[19] Blake produced cards for George Cumberland that were among his last work before his death in 1827: see e.g. British Museum Department of Prints and Drawings 1918,0413.45.

out among the many passing through the doors of elite households or displayed in drawing rooms or boudoirs: it might even ensure that the card survived the occasion it represented to be archived in a personal scrapbook or a family's papers. In some cases, instead of resorting to professional engravers, eighteenth-century men and women designed and engraved their own cards. As we have seen, the Banks collection contains a number of visiting cards created by women, suggesting that the design of cards was a legitimate, if unrecognised, form of female artistic and craft practice. A series of Sarah Sophia Banks's own visiting cards, with a variety of addresses reflecting the households in which she lived, and comparable examples designed by her brother, also suggest the importance of the medium to the rites of passage structuring a young person's entrance into the 'world': creating one's own visiting card was a performative gesture and utterance, a crafting of social status, place, and 'name'.

One of the most striking examples of an engraved card from this period is one in the Banks collection addressed from 'Mr. Omai' to 'Miss Banks', which is dated by Banks to 1776 (C,1.2225; Figure 20). Brought to England in 1774 from Raiatea in the Society Islands as part of Cook's second voyage, Omai became a metropolitan celebrity when 1770s fashionable sociability was at its apex.[20] He was introduced at court, made appearances at public places, and socialised in the circles of his patrons Joseph Banks and the Earl of Sandwich. His activities were chronicled in the newspapers and journals and he was the subject of a number of portraits and later, in 1785, a spectacular Covent Garden pantomime. Omai's visiting card suggests the importance of the medium to 1770s polite sociability – he could not participate in London society without one – and also its performative meanings. Engraved by 'Hughes', it is not clear if the card was specially designed for Omai or chosen from the engravers' stock. It takes the form of a framing Chinoiserie design which encloses engraved text with inserted handwriting. The frame has the effect of combining two codes of exoticism and fashionable commodification – the Pacific in the form of Omai himself and East Asia signified by the card's design. The card was a formulaic reply in acknowledgement of one from Sarah Sophia Banks, thanking her for her 'Obliging Enquiry's'. Though Omai had been instructed in reading and writing English, the extent of his proficiency in both is uncertain. Only three examples of writing associated with him survive: this card, a manuscript account of

---

[20] The best account of Omai remains E. H. McCormick, *Omai: Pacific Envoy* (Auckland: University of Auckland Press, 1977).

Figure 20   Mr. Omai Presents his Compliments to Miss Banks. Visiting card 1776.
Collection of Sarah Sophia Banks, C,1.2225.
© The Trustees of the British Museum

his expenses, and a note making an appointment to visit a Mr. Pigott.[21] All three texts are written in the confident hand of someone practised in penmanship. The signature in this card is therefore no guarantee of an authentic subject behind it. The card is part of a relay of texts – an acknowledgement of Sarah Sophia Banks's card, possibly delivered on her behalf by a servant – which does not necessarily mean that a personal meeting between the two took place. It merely returns the favour of Sarah Sophia Banks's 'Obliging Enquiry's'; it contains no promise of future contact, nor indeed does it seek it. It is possible that this virtual sociability was in fact what Sarah Sophia Banks wanted, and that she was more interested in obtaining Omai's card to add to her collection than in actually meeting him. Dating from 1776, when Banks herself was at the beginning of her collecting career, the Omai card was a curiosity, but not prestigious enough to trump the hierarchy of rank by which Banks organised her

[21] 'Account of the bills for Omai', National Library of Australia MS 9-Papers of Sir Joseph Banks, 1745–1923 (bulk 1745–1820) [manuscript]./ Series 1/ Item 6, digitized at http://nla.gov.au/nla.obj-222963611/view. The note to Mr. Pigott was sold at auction in 2011 [see a description of it at www.bonhams.com/eur/auction/19386/lot/391, accessed 7 March 2014].

'visitors'. She filed it in an 'Appendix' with cards relating to the fashion for rural breakfasts in the 1790s and cards for metropolitan hotels.[22]

As traces of Omai, this card and the message presenting his 'Compliments to Mr. Pigott' indicate the importance of sociable visiting in late Georgian culture and, conversely, the value of the card as a means of sustaining and mediating this kind of interaction. In April 1777 the *Daily Advertiser* and other newspapers carried news of Omai's death after he returned to Tahiti with Captain Cook in July 1776. The newspaper recalled how before he left London,

> being in Company with some Gentlemen at a Tavern, in Fleet-Street, he dictated in his own simple, honest Manner, the following farewel [*sic*] Card, copies of which he sent next Day to several of his noble Friends. 'Omai take Leave. Thank you for ever. Omai never forget England. God bless King George. Good by! Good by!'
> OMAI.[23]

The style of this 'card' is very different from the confident signature of 'Mr. Omai' in the card to Sarah Sophia Banks. The reference to it being 'dictated' suggests that Omai indeed could not write: what is 'written' for him here is not the politeness encoded by his name on the Banks card but the pleasurable entertainment to be derived from the exotic 'other' performing politeness, hence the violation of the linguistic conventions of grammar and spelling which does not occur in the Banks card where his name, including the very 'r' in 'Mr.', is politely and insistently correct. Omai's leave-taking of his London circle is also a leave-taking of Britain as a whole and, in so far that news of his death is the occasion of this report, it is also his epitaph. As in the Banks card this farewell card is about meetings not taking place: it announces the withdrawal of Omai's presence, proleptic of his disappearance into death and also, one might say, fully into textuality. Not only is Omai's farewell card 'dictated' for him by his tavern friends but in the form of the card's reproduction in the newspaper it is mediated again by print, reflecting how much Omai had been a creation of print publicity in the mid-1770s. The signature in the *Daily Advertiser* – 'OMAI' – and the handwritten 'Mr. Omai' of Banks's card are therefore essentially similar – they are both equally opaque.

As the exotic other, the barbarian stranger, Omai's presence in London had the potential to disrupt the refined and complex codes by which that society governed and evaluated itself. In his account of hospitality, Jacques

---

[22] C, 1.2222–91. [23] *Daily Advertiser*, 11 April 1777.

Derrida distinguishes between a 'conditional' hospitality in 'the ordinary sense' that 'presupposes the social and familial status of the contracting parties' and 'absolute hospitality' which 'requires that I open up my home ... to the absolute, unknown, anonymous other, and that I *give place* to them, that I let them come, that I let them arrive, and take place in the place I offer them, without asking of them either reciprocity ... or even their names'.[24] Elsewhere, Derrida claimed that hospitality 'is a self-contradictory concept and experience which can only self-destruct ... or protect itself from itself, auto-immunize itself in some way, which is to say, deconstruct itself – precisely – in being put into practice'.[25] The 'conditional' hospitality of the eighteenth century was predicated upon and even haunted by the possibility of an 'absolute hospitality', particularly the possibility of the irruption of an absolute hospitality into the conditional, when the seemingly familiar visitor at the door turns stranger, or when the visitor cannot be identified by 'name'. The visiting card was therefore a textual manifestation or trace of not only the ludic sociability celebrated by Simmel but also a sign of sociability's other, the possibility of sociability's failure or of an anti-sociability. In Derridean terms Omai challenged 'conditional hospitality' with having to entertain the needs and demands of 'the absolute, unknown, anonymous other'. The incorporation of Omai into London society and the multiple mediations of his name can therefore be seen as a means of keeping the necessity of an 'absolute hospitality' at bay. Omai's observation of the protocols of visiting in the form of his farewell card broadcast in the *Daily Advertiser* is an acknowledgement of his hospitable reception – that his hosts had behaved with civility towards him – as well as confirming that as a barbarian stranger he was always only a guest, never truly 'at home'.

Card Dramas

Omai's visiting cards suggest how the medium could resonate in political, moral, and philosophical, as well as strictly social, ways. Throughout the British Isles and the empire, virtually every day, the possibilities and the

---

[24] Jacques Derrida, *Of Hospitality: Anne Dufourmantelle Invites Jacques Derrida to Respond*, trans. Rachel Bowlby (Stanford, CA: Stanford University Press, 2000), 25, 23, 25.

[25] Jacques Derrida, 'Hostipitality', *Angelaki: Journal of the Theoretical Humanities*, 5:3 (2000), 3–18 (5). David Simpson notes, in reference to Derrida, that 'reckoning with the stranger "in theory" very soon produces a sense that one cannot be either welcoming or rejecting without risking some degree of self-harm': Simpson, *Romanticism and the Question of the Stranger* (Chicago: University of Chicago Press, 2013), 9; see also Peter Melville, *Romantic Hospitality, and the Resistance to Accommodation* (Waterloo: Wilfrid Laurier University Press, 2007).

limits of eighteenth-century hospitality were being explored and tested. What kind of risk was the visitor taking in approaching someone else's door; would they be admitted; if so, would the visit be pleasurable for either or both parties or would it be something to be endured for 'form's' sake? Conversely, in what position did the visit place the visitee? Could visiting be a form of harassment, an unwelcome invasion of space and time belonging to others? Could the hostess possibly become a hostage in her own home? The contact zone that defined the visit – the material space of door and hallway, the words exchanged between visitor and servant, the cusp between 'at home' and 'not at home' – was the point at which the visiting card was most potent. (As Derrida notes, 'for there to be hospitality, there must be a door').[26] The visiting card concretised social desire and the anxieties, dismay, and vulnerability contingent on social failure: it could be a shield, a talisman, and a weapon.

These dimensions of the apparently simple act of tendering one's card are present in Jane Austen's *Northanger Abbey* which has two scenes involving visiting cards, the first occurring when Catherine Morland, distracted by John Thorpe, misses a visit by Henry Tilney and his sister Eleanor:

> As she entered the house, the footman told her, that a gentleman and lady had called and inquired for her a few minutes after her setting off; that, when he had told them she had gone out with Mr Thorpe, the lady had asked whether any message had been left for her; and on his saying no, had felt for a card, but said she had none about her, and went away.[27]

As this was a prearranged visit, Eleanor Tilney had no reason to bring a card with her; Austen also suggests that the kind of formal visiting for which a card was necessary was not normally Eleanor's style. We see Catherine's reaction to this news from the perspective of the footman, the important conduit of paper and verbal communication, as 'pondering over these heart-rending tidings', she walks 'slowly up stairs' and into the house (88). The next day Catherine tries to remedy her omission by paying a visit to the Tilneys' lodgings:

> She reached the house without any impediment, looked at the number, knocked at the door, and inquired for Miss Tilney. The man believed Miss Tilney to be at home, but was not quite certain. Would she be pleased to send up her name? She gave her card. In a few minutes the servant returned,

---

[26] Derrida, 'Hostipitality', 14.
[27] Jane Austen, *Northanger Abbey*, eds. Barbara M. Benedict and Deirdre le Faye (Cambridge, UK: Cambridge University Press, 2006), 88; subsequent page references in parentheses in text.

and with a look which did not quite confirm his words, said he had been mistaken, for that Miss Tilney was walked out. Catherine, with a blush of mortification, left the house. She felt almost persuaded that Miss Tilney *was* at home, and too much offended to admit her. (90–1)

As Catherine's visit to the Tilneys' lodgings is not prearranged, a card is essential to effect entrance. Catherine's card could have been blank with a handwritten inscription or one with an engraved or letterpress printed message, possibly purchased from Taylor's Circulating Library in Bath which, since at least the 1770s, was advertising 'gilt and plain Message Cards [and] Visiting Tickets'.[28] Of all places in eighteenth-century Britain, Bath exemplified the culture of visiting in its most concentrated form. Visiting was part of the daily ritual of sociable life there and for a population of transient strangers the card was an essential means of introducing oneself to others. For a young woman such as Catherine Morland it was part of the accessories, in addition to a dress made of sprigged muslin or the latest novel, that would enable her to 'figure' in the world. As Sarah Sophia Banks had done in engraving her own cards, Catherine Morland was writing a public, sociable identity for herself in inscribing her name and Austen's finely calibrated account of her visit makes clear the stakes at play in this performative act. 'She gave her card' – the emphasis of this sentence conveys the momentousness and even bravery of Morland's act and the fact that it entails a kind of giving of herself.

Approaching a door, card in hand, thus went to the core of deep-seated meanings of polite hospitality and sociality in eighteenth-century culture. On the visitor's side of the door, these meanings related to the need, both individual and collective, for companionship and communality, and the fear of alienation and even abandonment. Hence in *Northanger Abbey* Catherine Morland must make the journey to the Tilneys' lodgings by herself. '[T]ripping lightly through the church-yard' (90), she is the ingénue engaged in a kind of fairy-tale ordeal, while 'the man' at the Tilneys' door is a gatekeeper, his information that Miss Tilney is not 'at home' being a wounding and humiliating rejection of Catherine who is ignorant of such conventions: 'She knew not how such an offence as her's might be classed by the laws of worldly politeness, to what a degree of unforgiveness it might with propriety lead, nor to what rigours of rudeness

---

[28] W. Taylor's Circulating Library. *This book belongs to W. Taylor's Circulating Library, In Church-street, Kingston Buildings, Bath, where books are to be lent to read at 10s. 6d. at year, 4s. a Quarter, and 2s. a Month, sells all sorts of Bibles, Common-Prayers, &c. [. . .] gilt and plain Message Cards; Visiting Tickets; and every other Article in the Bookselling or Stationary Branches, at the lowest Prices* [Bath], [1770?].

in return it might justly make her amenable' (91). For the host inside, the arrival of the visitor was also possibly an occasion of apprehension. Every opening up of one's home to an outsider, even if the visitor was known, contained the possibility in a Derridean sense of an unconditional hospitality – subjection to the other – that in order for mastery of the home to be maintained, Derrida argues, could not happen. The language of 'letting in' was therefore expressive of the profound ambiguity of visiting as both a sign of assertiveness – a demand for attention – and a commensurate vulnerability of both parties on either side of the door.

The speech acts of 'at home'/'not at home' had the effect of calibrating the degree to which a household was open to visitors. 'At home' allowed people in, creating a semi-public space of areas such as the drawing room, while 'not at home' defined a kind of invisible barrier that the visitor could not cross. If applying in person rather than through the intermediary of a servant, the genteel visitor would receive partial admission, it being impolite to conduct such business in the public view of the street, but if 'not at home' was the answer to an inquiry she or he could go no further. This is what happens in the case of Catherine Morland; after receiving Eleanor Tilney's rebuff 'with a blush of mortification' she 'left the house', meaning that she had actually entered the building (90). The hallway in an eighteenth-century house therefore had a distinctive and powerful liminality; it was a space in which the dramas of threshold hospitality were enacted. The hallway was, above all, the domain of the card. It was where cards were tendered by visitors or their servants, accepted or denied, or where they were displayed and accumulated as a kind of message bank for the householder. In giving her or his card to the servant at the door the visitor was engaged in a process of transmission, in the root sense of the term – the card was 'handed' over. Sending 'in' or 'up' also suggest the space which the card had to traverse and the fact that it was out of control of the visitor. His or her name and reputation were literally and figuratively born by a lower-class servant, whom they had to trust to deliver the message properly and to be a reliable conduit of the host or hostess's response. As the intermediary between the visitor and the host, the servant played a potentially complex double role – standing for the visitor in handing over his or her card, or speaking for his master and mistress on his return to the expectant visitor in the hall, a performance that could add another dimension to the experience of visiting. Austen highlights the mediating role of the servant in *Northanger Abbey*, in her reference to his 'look which did not quite confirm his words' when he tells Catherine that 'he had been mistaken' in thinking Miss Tilney to be 'at home' (90). The servant's 'look' is a non-verbal communication, the meaning of which is enigmatic. It suggests that Catherine should read more into his message but its exact import and 'tone' is unclear: whether or not it is kind to Catherine, or if it represents embarrassment on his own, Catherine's, or his mistress's behalf.

Archiving a 'Whole Life'

The new medium of visiting and message cards and the sociable protocols they regulated or made visible is the theme of Horace Walpole's 'A Scheme for Raising a Large Sum of Money for the Use of the Government, by laying a Tax on Message-Cards and Notes', an essay first published in Robert Dodsley's periodical *The Museum* in 1746 and later reprinted in Walpole's *Fugitive Pieces in Verse and Prose* (1758). Walpole's 'Scheme' indicates the extent to which the use of message cards had become widespread in polite circles by the 1740s. He describes them as 'one of the latest and most accepted fashions ... No business, that is no business, is now carried on in this great city, but by this expedient'.[29] The use of such texts is represented ironically as 'great progress in litterature', the reliance on oral communication in the time of Congreve and Farquhar being superseded by the modern system of cards (52). Walpole attempts to evaluate how many cards one fine lady would be expected to need, based on a calculation that she would hold an assembly once a month to which she invited 400 people. In addition to this four hundred, she would send 'twenty private messages every morning, in howd'ye's, appointments, disappointments, &c. and ... ten visits every *night* before she settles for the *evening*, at each of which she must leave her name on a card' (55), her visiting 'account' ultimately amounting to:

Messages to 4000 people --- --- ---   400
20 Messages a day, will be *per* month --- 560
10 Visits a night, will be *per* month   --- 280

                         Total 1240 (55)

Walpole's calculation is an attempt to give shape and meaning to the new phenomenon of female fashionable sociability. He does this by applying a particular discourse – the nascent one of political economy – to experiences and practices that rarely came within the scope of rational

---

[29] Horace Walpole, *Fugitive Pieces in Verse and Prose* (London: Strawberry Hill, 1758), 51; subsequent page references in parentheses in text.

calculation. The essay ironises both this discourse and the phenomenon of messaging itself, but there is also a sense in which the 'Scheme' wants to be able to make fashionable sociability accountable in all senses of the term, because visiting had become visible as a feminised 'no business' impinging everywhere on 'real' commerce. The centrepiece of the essay is the proposal that cards be taxed at a penny each. Based on 'a lady's sending 1240 *cards per* month, or 16120 *per annum* ... multiplied by 20,000, and reduced to pounds *sterling*', Walpole calculates that the massive sum of '£.1343333 6s. 8d.' a year would accrue to the 'cities of London and Westminster alone' (58). These spiralling numbers fantasise the realisation of what is currently incalculable but felt everywhere in social and cultural life – London's sociable economy. The point of such a scheme is not only to make money for the state – it would also be the basis for an archive:

> A friend of mine, to whom I communicated my scheme, was of opinion, that where-ever the duty was collected, the office would be a court of record, because as I propose that all engagements should be registered, it would be an easy matter to compile a diary of a Lady of Quality's whole life. (59)

This aspect of the scheme suggests the challenge which visiting and its texts represented to more conventional forms of knowledge and how they were archived. By the 1740s, the 'whole life' of the Lady of Quality no longer belonged to the private sphere of the old regime in the Habermasian sense but had taken on public representativeness, due to cultural practices such as the masquerade and forms of print such as the card and the mediating role of the periodical itself.[30] Walpole's essay asks: what is to be done with this 'whole life' now that it has become so visible? How does knowledge of sociability (and vice versa, sociability as a mode of knowledge) relate to other kinds of knowledge? In this respect Walpole's essay anticipates the ambition of Sarah Sophia Banks's attempt a few years later to document the 'whole life' of not just a particular Lady of Quality but of British fashionable society as a whole.

The ramifications of these questions are apparent in how Walpole's essay is framed in terms of the rationale of the title of the periodical *The Museum* in which it was first published. Walpole distinguishes between the different kinds of curiosity that might be housed in a 'museum' including mundane objects such as an 'old Roman shoe' made rare by antiquity, natural oddities such as 'monstrous births, hermaphrodites', or things that have become rare because they were insignificant in the first place and

---

[30] See Russell, *Women, Sociability and Theatre*.

have fallen out of use as a consequence (49). This latter kind of curiosity is epitomised by 'that noble collection of foolish tracts in the Harleian library, puritanical sermons, party-pamphlets, voyages, &c. which being too stupid to be ever re-printed, grew valuable, as they grew scarce' (49). Though Walpole does not use the term 'ephemera', his reference to the Harleian tracts nominates the reappearance of these apparently obsolete ephemeral texts, their undeadness, as exerting pressure on what counted as proper knowledge and legitimate history making, implicitly casting the destiny of his own occasional essay, itself a 'fugitive' piece, into question. At the beginning of the essay Walpole claims that the idea of a museum 'is an hospital for every thing that is *singular*', 'hospital' having the root sense of a place of reception or entertainment (47). This meaning of hospitality resonates with the theme of the essay as a whole – the hospitality represented by visiting, as mediated by the fashion for cards and notes. The subject of ephemeral visiting is therefore framed as a question of whether or not this practice and its texts, like the 'whole life' of the Lady of Quality, should be admitted as a category of knowledge into the 'Museum' of literature. The emergence mid-century of the message card, in conjunction with the publication of the fugitive papers of the *Harleian Miscellany*, was symptomatic of how print had problematised literary hospitality – to what extent should the doors of the literary museum be open? Walpole's 'Scheme' exhibits a tension between the desire to, as he states, 'give posterity some light into the customs of the present age', and uncertainty over what constitutes enduring and substantive cultural value (50). Hence literature, in the form of this essay in *The Museum*, is a 'hospital' for the fragments of the everyday, represented by cards and notes, only if it can imagine them in terms of a regulatory system, as if they were a 'real' economy. The 'whole life' of the Lady of Quality is only conceivable if it is regulated by a public office, as an archive of the state.

Essay no. 191 in Samuel Johnson's *The Rambler*, published in January 1752, is similarly concerned with sociability as a form of 'no business'. The essay takes the form of a letter to Mr. Rambler from a young lady, Bellaria, complaining about how her aunts are preventing her from engaging in the fashionable round of diversion. Confinement to her chamber means that Bellaria will be 'seventeen visits behind'; it has been three months since she has been 'suffered to pay and receive visits, to dance at publick assemblies, to have a place kept for me in the boxes, and to play at Lady *Racket*'s rout'.[31]

---

[31] [Samuel Johnson], *The Rambler. Volume the Sixth* (London: J. Payne, 1752), 144, 148; subsequent page references in parentheses in text.

The essay suggests how visiting had become part of quotidian polite life and even a repetitive, compulsive form of work. The domain of fashion had acquired the status of an unquestionable universal phenomenon, the immutable laws of which had to be observed:

> This is the round of my day; [Bellaria states] and when shall I either stop my course, or so change it as to want a book? I suppose it cannot be imagined that any of these diversions will be soon at an end, [sic] There will always be gardens, and a park, and auctions, and shows, and playhouses, and cards; visits will always be paid, and cloaths always be worn; and how can I have time unemployed upon my hands. (150)

The time that this routinised economy of sociability takes up is the time for books. *Rambler* no. 191 not only addresses fashionable sociability as an increasingly visible cultural practice but also explores sociability's textual apparatus in the form of tickets, visiting cards, and playbills and how they relate to the periodical essay and ultimately belles-lettres itself. Bellaria's friend Melissa, for example, whose freedom she envies, is imagined as getting 'a ticket for the play' (145) while ladies whom Bellaria encounters at an assembly and tries to impress, as her aunts have instructed her, with conversation 'about principles and ideas', are described as never pretending 'to read any thing but the play-bill' (149). It is the visiting card, however, that takes up the bulk of Bellaria's time: 'If, at any time, I can gain an hour by not being at home [meaning availability to be visited], I have so many things to do, so many orders to give to the milliner, so many alterations to make in my cloaths, so many visitants names to read over, so many invitations to accept or refuse, so many cards to write, and so many fashions to consider, that I am lost in confusion...' (150). In this way Johnson acknowledges how the new textual apparatus of the visiting card enabled a form of virtual sociability as well as a kind of literacy in its own right. This literacy, moreover, was intimately connected with the dominant form of materiality in women's lives – clothes and fashion – and with the lower orders who facilitated this in the form of milliners and maids, symptomatic of the proximity of ephemeral print to other forms of decorative materiality such as textiles. Altering a dress and looking at fashion plates was synonymous with checking one's visiting cards, while the business of such a life meant that the woman of fashion was perpetually in a state of agitated suspension, either admitting company to her 'at homes' or stepping out to find it.

The significance of this sociable and material literacy as competition for more orthodox and privileged forms of literacy is highlighted by how Bellaria manages to avoid the scrutiny of her aunt. She tells Mr. Rambler how for her 'amusement' and to teach her to 'moderate her desires' her aunt gave her a 'bundle of your papers' (145). On receiving a letter from her admirer Mr. Trip, Bellaria conceals it 'within the leaves' of *The Rambler* and 'with your paper before my face' fools her aunt into believing that she is reading moral philosophy when she is actually reading a love letter (145). The emphasis on *The Rambler* as it was originally published, that is, as a series of paper 'leaves', aggregated as a 'bundle', the term associated with how ephemeral texts were loosely gathered together and circulated, aligns it with other kinds of sociable texts referred to in the essay – the playbill, the ticket, and the visiting card. In this unbound state, *The Rambler* is vulnerable to being used as a mere front for other, potentially pernicious and uncontrollable forms of useless, superficial reading, such as looking 'over' the names of visitants or the fashion plates, reading that threatens not merely to take up time but to render time itself meaningless. The meta-significance of *The Rambler* in this essay as a material textual artefact reflects an uncertainty as to the role of literary culture and periodical literature in particular in relation to fashionable sociability and its associated textual currency in the form of the visiting ticket. In terms of content and materiality, especially in its unbound form, *Rambler* no. 191 was uncomfortably close to the world it presumes to scrutinise: it is itself invested in the circulatory energies of modern life and manners; it is read and handled in the same contexts as tickets, playbills, and visiting cards. Bellaria's gesture of concealing her letter by interleaving it within Mr. Rambler's 'paper' and putting it before her face, like a masquerade mask, neatly encapsulates what was at stake in mediating the conjugal private sphere, in making it constitutive of a literary public. It suggests an anxiety that proliferating and feminised forms of sociable textuality could not be so easily subsumed or controlled within the covers of the book and, conversely, that literary culture was itself profoundly invested in the material world and libidinous, ephemeral forms of value.

'Withinside': Binding Ephemera with the Novel

Maria Edgeworth's *The Absentee*, published in 1812, shares with Walpole and Johnson a fascination with the ingenious, fantasising projections of female fashionable sociability and its textual apparatus in the form of the visiting card. While writers such as Burney and Austen address aspects of the 'ticket system' in their fiction it is Maria Edgeworth who is most fascinated with situating the novel in relation to ephemeral print as part of her preoccupation with the fragility of documentary transactions in general – the liability of written records to loss, corruption, and destruction, accentuating the ephemerality of all texts, including the codex-form of the novel itself.³² Edgeworth was herself reliant on the card in all aspects of her sociable career: in London in 1813 when she went with Frances Edgeworth to 'pay visits', Mrs Edgeworth ticking off their successes (and failures) on a card as they went; in France in 1820, when the Edgeworth name inscribed on her card 'instant[ly]' gained her access to Madame de Montolieu; and in Ireland in 1834 when she had the presence of mind to write 'with ink on a visiting-ticket with "Miss Edgeworth," on it, my compliments [and] a petition for a night's hospitality' after her travelling party got bogged down on the way to Ballinahinch Castle in Connemara.³³ The latter refers to the kind of card that could be bought in bulk from an engraver with the name inscribed on it, such as those collected in the thousands by Sarah Sophia Banks. Among Banks's files of visiting cards are some originally owned by the members of the Irish aristocracy, including curious examples designed by women, such as one made by Caroline Stuart, Countess of Portarlington.³⁴ Banks also possessed a set of three visiting cards owned by the Countess Charleville, depicting the then newly constructed Charleville Castle in County Offaly: the cards were advertising both the countess's person, and her family's ambitious building venture after the Act of Union of 1801.³⁵

The value of the visiting card in eighteenth-century culture, as I have suggested, related to its capacity to objectify, commodify, and even mystify the threshold moment when hospitality was either allowed or was refused. In *The Absentee*, Edgeworth explores hospitality – the entertainment or openness to others – as a metaphor for relations between Britain and Ireland, and between the Protestant landlord class and the Catholic Irish, in the wake of the trauma of the 1798 rebellion and the Act of Union. This theme is explored primarily in terms of the attempts of Lady Clonbrony, the mother of the hero, Lord Colambre, to penetrate the inner sanctums of metropolitan high society. As 'absentee matriarch and colonial fashion victim', in Clara Tuite's memorable phrase, Lady Clonbrony is central to Edgeworth's exploration of the particular condition of the post-union

---

³² See Claire Connolly on the 'frangibility of written documents' in the work of Edgeworth and other Irish novelists: *A Cultural History of the Irish Novel, 1790–1829* (Cambridge, UK: Cambridge University Press, 2012), 113.
³³ Maria Edgeworth, *The Life and Letters of Maria Edgeworth*, ed. Augustus Hare, 2 vols. (Boston, MA: Houghton, Mifflin & Co., 1895), I: 223; Edgeworth, *Life and Letters*, II: 351, 570.
³⁴ BM Department of Prints and Drawings, Banks Collection, C,1.573–91.
³⁵ BM Department of Prints and Drawings, Banks Collection, C,1.631–3.

ascendancy class, alienated by the 1798 rebellion, and displaced in London.[36] Lady Clonbrony's hopeless, displaced hybridity and the ineffectuality of her attempts to assimilate are exemplified in her failure to sound properly English, her accent being cruelly mimicked by the ladies whose favour she is assiduously courting. The instrument on which she depends to get access to 'society' is the visiting card, its importance as an 'avatar' of identity being indicated by advice she gives early in the novel to the heroine Grace Nugent. Lady Clonbrony declares that Nugent should write 'herself on her card miss de Nogent, which would have taken off the prejudice against the Iricism of Nugent'.[37] Like Bellaria in Johnson's essay, Lady Clonbrony is obsessed with the card as a form of 'no business' in Johnson's terms, a surrogate or virtual sociability. Edgeworth comments that she 'told over her visiting tickets regularly twice a day, and gave to every card of invitation a heart felt sigh' (54). 'Visiting tickets' referred to those that Lady Clonbrony would leave at households to indicate that a visit had been paid – the code of politeness required that such a card would be acknowledged, if only by another card – while her 'cards of invitation' were direct requests to people that they visit her for one of her galas or evening parties. These cards represent a latent sociable capital that Lady Clonbrony is desperate to realise. Her particular target is Lady St James, whom she assaults with the full gamut of the 'visiting system', including 'refreshing tickets' with their corners turned up, to remind Lady St James of her failure to respond to Lady Clonbrony's initial card (55). She also sends cards to each member of the family of Lady St James and when it occurs to her that she forgot to include a 'miss somebody', a lady's companion, dispatches one to her too (56). Eventually she goes in person to the house of Lady St James, exposing herself to the elements as she negotiates in the open air with the lady's servants whom she bribes to make sure that the 'talismanic cards' reach their destination (56). With no reciprocal card forthcoming, Lady Clonbrony eventually offers Lady St James a gift of a piece of dried salmon from Ireland which the latter accepts, but while Lady Clonbrony is eventually admitted to Lady St James's soiree she is still excluded from the coveted inner circle: 'in return for great entertainments she was invited to great entertainments, to large parties; but farther she could never penetrate' (58).

---

[36] Clara Tuite, 'Maria Edgeworth's Déjà-Voodoo: Interior Decoration, Retroactivity, and Colonial Allegory in *The Absentee*', *Eighteenth-Century Fiction*, 20:3 (2008), 385–413 (390).

[37] Maria Edgeworth, *The Absentee*, ed. W. J. McCormack and Kim Walker (Oxford: Oxford University Press, 1988), 16. Subsequent page references in parentheses in text.

The 'talismanic' card and its complex protocols are central to Edgeworth's exploration of the tragicomedy of Lady Clonbrony's willingness to abase herself at the altar of metropolitan high fashion. The social comedy of the failure of her pretensions is complicated by its framing in terms of Anglo-Irish relations, alluded to by Edgeworth by means of the strategic dried salmon. Like the card, the salmon is a kind of surrogate Lady Clonbrony: its success, where she and her card are ignored, indicates the persistence of Ireland's status as a subjugated nation, whose gifts are a form of tribute, or commodities to be expropriated. The gala and the related transactions surrounding the card are therefore central to the novel's articulation of the need for the Anglo-Irish gentry to cultivate a more independent identity, a more self-sufficient sociability. Lady Clonbrony's mania for fashionable sociability is contextualised in terms of other kinds of sociability in *The Absentee*, the novel representing a graduated comparative ethnography of sociability in Britain and Ireland. The experience of Lady Clonbrony in London is contrasted, for example, with the hospitality offered to her son by a peasant family, the O'Neils, when he is travelling incognito in Ireland. In contrast to Lady Clonbrony's sociability, dominated by the arcane rituals of the card, Lord Colambre does not need to solicit hospitality: his coach driver Larry declares that the candle in the light of the O'Neil's cottage signals that there is no need to ask for admission, the inhabitants being open to the possibility of a visit from a stranger (149–50). Lord Colambre's reception by the O'Neils is a romance of cross-class and cross-cultural sociability, an unconditional hospitality, which Edgeworth suggests necessary to the reformation or 'refit' of the Anglo-Irish ruling order (84).

James Chandler has linked Edgeworth's narrative method to the distinctive culture of experimentation' associated with Enlightenment knowledge and associational networks, particularly the Lunar Society, to which her father Richard Lovell Edgeworth belonged. The 'Lunar-like interdisciplinary commitment to experiment and practical observation' which Chandler identifies in Edgeworth's *Belinda* (1801) is apparent in how she stages and implicitly compares scenes of sociability in *The Absentee*. It is also apparent in the novel's relationship to another important dimension of Enlightenment culture, its reliance on and fascination with the circulation of information through all kinds of paper and the possibility of systematising the knowledge that paper created.[38] The

---

[38] James Chandler, 'Edgeworth and the Lunar Enlightenment', *Eighteenth-Century Studies*, 45:1 (2011), 87–104 (88, 94).

Edgeworth home at Edgeworthstown in County Longford was comparable to the Bankses' 'home-cum-research institute' at No. 32 Soho Square in so far that it was a communications hub through which all kinds of documents – letters, books (including novels), newspapers, pamphlets – circulated as part of a European-wide network. The library at Edgeworthstown was the centre of the intellectual enterprise of the house, a place of reading, writing, education, and sociability, and was also the focus of the family's affective life, memorialised through the accumulation and repeated handling of its paper archive.[39] In their representation of the diversity of the paper economy, especially the materiality and performativity of mundane or ephemeral texts, Edgeworth's novels reflect a long-standing Enlightenment curiosity about the scope and potential of print as a medium of information and of sociability. Her fictional project is analogous to that of Sarah Sophia Banks in how it takes account of the diversity of the paper economy, in particular foregrounding texts such as the visiting card as a means of making sociability visible as a mode of knowledge in late Georgian culture. It is also, I wish to suggest, similar to Banks's collections as a mode of assemblage that, while assimilating and remediating other kinds of print within the form of the novel, preserves some of the material integrity or object status of such texts, thereby approximating the looseness intrinsic to the idea and practice of ephemeral book making.

Edgeworth's representation of the visiting card is thus part of an exploration in *The Absentee* of Regency communication networks in their wider sense. The novel alludes to a multiplicity of paper instruments, making it a compendium or archive of the Regency paper economy. Lady Clonbrony's cards feature in conjunction with other similar texts such as message notes and the playbill. The latter forms the prop for a performance of modesty by Lady Isabel Dashfort who is aware of the attention she is receiving from Lord Colambre in the Dublin theatre. While her mother shows off in the box, talking with 'masculine boldness' to her fellow playgoers, her daughter's attention is demurely fixed on her playbill. 'If this be acting', Colambre comments, 'it is the best acting I ever saw. It this be art, it deserves to be nature' (98). The currency of sociability in the novel circulates in the same contexts as paper relating to money such as stocks, scrip, and financial accounts, as well as legal documents such as executions for debt, a marriage certificate, genealogies, and the lease of the Clonbronys' tenants, the O'Neils, to their cottage and land. The latter is

---

[39] See Marilyn Butler, *Maria Edgeworth: A Literary Biography* (Oxford: Oxford University Press, 1972), 82, 155, 291–2.

the subject of a disputed memorandum guaranteeing them security that is rubbed out by the oppressive agents, the Garraghties. There are other, more mundane, but no less significant kinds of texts such as an address label on a cheese, one of the most common and also most ephemeral uses of jobbing print. This paper is discovered by chance by Lord Colambre and leads him to the location of Grace Nugent's grandfather and ultimately the confirmation of her legitimacy:

> The covering of the waggon caught in the hedge as the waggon turned in; and as the sacking was drawn back, some of the packages were disturbed – a cheese was just rolling off the side next lord Colambre; he stopped it from falling: the direction caught his quick eye – 'To Ralph Reynolds, esq.' – '*Toddrington*' scratched out; 'Red Lion Square, London,' written in another hand below.
> 'Now I have found him!' (233)

Edgeworth represents this discovery as a protracted moment of accidental reading, which is melodramatic in both its slow-motion theatricality and in its staging of the arbitrariness of knowledge in a world of proliferating textuality, the crucial cheese being as unconscious of the reader as the advertisements on Wordsworth's dead walls.

The insistent materiality of fugitive or ephemeral literature such as the card or the label, exemplifying an idea of knowledge as contingent, accidental, prone to loss or disappearance, but also potentially accessible to anyone who can read, also extends to books and pamphlets in *The Absentee*. There are explicit intertextual references to the *Arabian Nights*, Charles Pasley's *Essay on the Military Policy and Institutions of the British Empire* (1810), and a satirical pamphlet on post-union Dublin manners, *An Intercepted Letter from China* (1804). These texts are situated in their sociable, material contexts; conversation on 'literary subjects' at an evening party at Lady Clonbrony's, for example, focusing on the *Arabian Nights* which leads Lord Colambre to take down 'a beautiful edition' in order to find a particular story to which Grace Nugent had alluded, showing it to Miss Broadhurst, 'who was also searching for it in another volume' (46, 47). This exchange of books is contextualised in relation to Lady Clonbrony's card playing, which is taking place in the same room, situating literary sociability as a similar if superior mode of conversation and fashion to that facilitated by cards and notes: '"books and all that are so fashionable now, that it's very natural," said lady Clonbrony' (47). Pasley's *Essay* is similarly materially defined, Lord Colambre encountering it on the table at Count O'Halloran's. The book is described as having the count's pencil in it, and as being 'marked with many notes of admiration, and with hands pointing to remarkable passages', a deictic effect which is reinforced by the count's remark to his guest "'That is a book that leaves a strong impression on the mind'" (117). The material status of Pasley's *Essay* as a medium of social contact between Colambre and O'Halloran, a kind of 'card', relates to Edgeworth's linking of contemporary literary culture (Lady Clonbrony's 'books and all that') with the military and how both were capable of producing refinements of sociability. When Colambre later seeks advice from the count about whether or not he should go to the Peninsula to fight against Napoleon, the count responds that an officer's life is no longer dedicated to effeminised gallantry and idle 'lounging', officers now being 'men of education and information' (224). Count O'Halloran also declares to Colambre:

> All the descriptions which we see in ancient history of a soldier's life, descriptions which in times of peace appeared like romance, are now realized; military exploits fill every day's newspapers, every day's conversation. (224)

Edgeworth's own novel represents a similar 'realisation' of military heroism, which she achieves by on the one hand incorporating into her fiction Pasley's *Essay* as both a material, (hetero)-sociable object, and on the other by situating books such as Pasley's in the context of ephemeral print culture as a whole, the diurnal historiography that could make a 'romance' of the 'every day' and vice versa.

Another important context for Edgeworth's interest in ephemeral textuality is the intense paper 'war of ideas' contested in 1790s Ireland via newspapers, songs, and handbills, as well as in pamphlet literature and books.[40] The Society of United Irishmen, like its radical counterparts in Britain, made full use of the penetrative reach of fugitive print. As Marianne Elliott writes,

> The United Irishmen whipped up discontent with squibs, handbills, popular ballads, broadsheets ... [They were] left in bundles on the table of the United Irish Society, circulated far afield, particularly by the legal men on circuit, used as wrappers for commercial goods, distributed by pedlars and hawkers and pushed gratis through people's doors.[41]

---

[40] Marilyn Butler, 'Edgeworth, the United Irishmen, and "More Intelligent Treason"', in *An Uncomfortable Authority: Maria Edgeworth and Her Contexts*, eds. Heidi Kaufman and Christopher J. Fauske (Newark: University of Delaware Press, 2004), 33–61.

[41] Marianne Elliott, *Wolfe Tone*, 2nd edn (Liverpool: Liverpool University Press, 2012; first pub. Yale University Press, 1989), 209. A comprehensive account of fugitive print propaganda, both revolutionary and counter-revolutionary, in 1790s Ireland remains to be written: see Kevin Whelan, '"The Republic in the Village": The Dissemination and Reception of Popular Political

Edgeworth's interest in the materiality of the handbill is illustrated by one of the *Popular Tales*, 'Lame Jervas', in which the protagonist encounters news of an enemy when 'a hawker by accident flapped a bundle of wet hand-bills in my eyes, at the same instant [screaming] in my ears "The last dying speech and confession of Jonathan Clarke"'.[42] These handbills epitomise fugitive mediality as literally in your face, a fusion of print publication with 'screaming' verbal utterance. 'Wet' from the printing press, the handbills in 'Lame Jervas' also recall Edmund Burke's condemnation of the Declaration of the Rights of Man in *Reflections on the Revolution in France* as 'paltry blurred shreds of paper', used to stuff the French polity as if it were 'birds in a museum'.[43] These shreds of paper, the most abject form of paper rubbish, are blurred because they are disseminated before the ink could dry properly and also because the meaning of the French Revolution, Burke suggests, is literally illegible. Burke, like Edgeworth, reveals a sensitivity to the materiality of print, fresh from the press, sheets that flap in your face and mark you with their wet writing, a materiality that, in the context of the French Revolution and the 1798 rebellion, made reference to such print inevitably and inescapably political.

The ephemerology of *The Absentee* is most apparent in the resolution of the novel's marriage plot. The viability of the novel as colonial allegory relies on the verification of the legitimacy of the heroine Grace Nugent's birth, enabling her to marry Lord Colambre and effect the return of the absentee family to Ireland. The proof of her legitimacy is a piece of paper, the certification of the marriage of her mother to Captain Reynolds, entrusted by the latter on his deathbed to the British ambassador in Vienna. After the ambassador's own death the marriage certificate is forgotten until Colambre gains knowledge of it by chance through a conversation with Count O'Halloran. Colambre undertakes a search of the ambassador's papers and is confronted with the materiality and also ephemeral tendencies of the archive as a repository into which knowledge can disappear. He spends 'two whole days in looking over portfolios of letters, and memorials, and manifestoes, and bundles of paper of the most heterogeneous sorts; some of them without any dockets or direction to lead to a knowledge of their contents' (229). The ambassador's papers represent

---

Literature in the 1790s', in *Books Beyond the Pale: Aspects of the Provincial Book Trade in Ireland before 1850*, ed. Gerard Long (Dublin: Rare Books Group of the Library Association of Ireland, 1996), 101–40.

[42] Maria Edgeworth, *Popular Tales*, 3 vols., 4th edn (London: Joseph Johnson, 1811), I: 64.

[43] Edmund Burke, *The Writings and Speeches of Edmund Burke: The French Revolution, 1790–1794*, ed. Paul Langford (Oxford: Clarendon Press, 1989), 137.

the nightmare of the uncontrollability of paper information in the eighteenth century, its contents unsystematised and inaccessible because of the absence of dockets, that is, labels or written directions explaining the contents of a particular text or what was in a 'bundle'. Edgeworth's use of the latter term which, as we have seen, also applies to the gathering of issues of *The Rambler* in Johnson's essay, indicates the affinity between printed ephemeral textuality and other forms of loose written records: the bundle signified the point at which principles of systematisation and classification encountered the archive's latent tendencies to entropy. A bundle was close to the 'heaps' and incoherence of ephemeral rubbish. The docket as a form of ticketing which identified or labelled the bundle was an essential element of the infrastructure of the Enlightenment archive, as John Gascoigne noted in his reference to the Linnean system 'docketing' the natural world.[44] An ephemeral text in its own right, invisible in histories of print, and with no status separate from the document to which it referred, the docket ensured that other documents could be preserved from irredeemable loss.

Colambre is on the point of giving up his search when he notices 'a bundle of old newspapers at the bottom of a trunk ... old Vienna gazettes'. 'Withinside' one of these newspapers he discovers the ambassador's journal containing the Reynolds marriage certificate. Edgeworth's emphasis on the count's papers as not being docketed make the recovery of the marriage certificate even more accidental or miraculous, comparable to the melodrama of the discovery of the cheese label. 'Withinside' which means, according to the *Oxford English Dictionary*, 'the inner side of' implies a specific kind of textual materiality, the contiguity of paper surfaces entailed by the practices of folding, interleaving, and enclosure, associated with bundles, letters, and single sheets. Bellaria in Johnson's essay similarly conceals her love letters 'withinside' the unbound leaves of *The Rambler*. 'Withinside' implied a way of using, collating, and valuing the knowledge represented by unbound texts, different from what it meant to place something inside the space of a book or the range of books together on a shelf or in a library. The scrap of paper, whether a receipt or a love letter, disappears when interleaved within the codex-form book, hence the affective power of rediscovery when it drops out or escapes. Folding or interleaving a sheet of paper within other unbound sheets is different because they are similar media: one does not completely subsume the other. It is significant that the document with which the marriage

---

[44] Gascoigne, *Joseph Banks*, 99.

certificate interfaces is the newspaper, the survival of which in the ambassador's archive, related to the newspaper as a medium of military information and conversation, testifies to the value and persistent durability of the kind of knowledge that such media communicated.

Part of Edgeworth's considerable ambition in *The Absentee* was her attempt to realise, in novelistic form, the scope of the Regency paper economy in ways that diverged from the prevailing view after 1800 of the relative status of ephemera and the book. The codex-form book is not central to *The Absentee* but is located as part of a wider spectrum of forms of paper communication: some of these texts are scribal, some are letterpress, while some are strictly functional, such as address labels on cheese; all of them are potentially meaningful. The form of the novel acts as a kind of hospital for this diverse and multifarious textuality, not in the regulatory sense suggested by Walpole, but in the spirit of an open sociability, analogous to the ludic 'all with-one-another' celebrated by Simmel. Ephemeral textuality also functions as a vehicle for other kinds of political imagining in the novel: the restoration of the memorandum securing a home for the O'Neils, a memorandum written in pencil and erased by the Garraghties, suggests that some rights cannot be written out or effaced by history. An important dimension of the novel's fantasy of restitution and renewal in post-union Ireland is the idea that what seems ephemeral is never truly lost. Even the traces of pencil marks can be deciphered again and blurred, shredded words pieced together to make declarations of rights.

'Withinside' her fiction Edgeworth, like collectors such as Sarah Sophia Banks, gathered together the full spectrum of paper in a way that sociably associates the polite visiting card with the address label, in turn promoting the novel itself as the repository of knowledge of the everyday enabled by the second printing revolution. However, the novel's affinity with the scraps and detritus of the paper economy, particularly in the context of the politicised meanings of ephemera after 1800, risked the novel itself being labelled or docketed as ephemera, a development that I explore in the final chapter.

CHAPTER 7

England in 1814
Frost Fairs, Peace, *and* Persuasion

In his 1815 review of Jane Austen's *Emma*, Walter Scott commended the work as a new kind of fiction. The novel was

> far superior to that what is granted to the ephemeral productions that supply the regular demand of watering-places and circulating libraries. [It belongs] to a class of fictions which has arisen almost in our own times, and which draws the characters and incidents introduced more immediately from the current of ordinary life that was permitted by the former rules of the novel.[1]

Scott reiterated the contemporaneity of this development later in the review by tracing it to 'the last fifteen or twenty years', characterising Austen's achievement as

> the art of copying from nature as she really exists in the common walks of life, and presenting to the reader, instead of the splendid scenes of an imaginary world, a correct and striking representation of that which is daily taking place around him.[2]

Scott's review is notable for the application of 'ephemeral' as a criterion of literary value, a term which had been used to distinguish his own achievement in *Waverley*, published a year before in 1814, when a reviewer wrote: 'This novel stands much higher in the scale of merit, than most of the ephemeral productions of the same kind.'[3] The frequency with which 'ephemeral' was applied to literature in the nineteenth century was a sign of how the term had eclipsed 'fugitive' after 1800: 'ephemeral' increasingly meant what was disposable rather than durable in culture, destined to be lost to time rather than being timeless or worth preservation. As a genre

---

[1] [Walter Scott], 'ART. IX. *Emma; a Novel. By the Author of Sense and Sensibility, Pride and Prejudice, &c.*', *The Quarterly Review* (October 1815), 188–201 (189).
[2] [Scott], 'ART. IX. *Emma*',
[3] [Anon.], 'Waverley; or 'Tis Sixty Years Since', *Monthly Museum: or, Dublin Literary Repertory of Arts, Science, Literature and Miscellaneous Information*, 2 (September 1814), 225–30 (225).

that had its genealogy in the penny romances and what Hunter describes as 'the moment-centred consciousness' of the seventeenth century, the novel, more than poetry or even the drama, had long been associated with less durable kinds of literature while at the same time deriving aesthetic capital from the 'common' or 'ordinary' life that printed ephemera after the late seventeenth century had made visible. After 1800, it would seem, the very future of the novel was at stake as writers negotiated the increasing awareness of the distinction between ephemeral trash and durable literature in the rapidly changing contexts of what Scott described as 'our own times'.

One of the ways in which this negotiation took place was through the category of 'everyday life'. In Chapter 2 I noted the association of ephemerality and the everyday exemplified by Maurice Rickards's influential definition of ephemera as 'the minor transient documents of everyday life'. Noting that the relationship between ephemerality and the everyday has rarely been theorised and/or historicised, I asked: 'can you have an "everyday life" without ephemerality?' The Romantic 'everyday', or what Scott termed the 'current of ordinary life', was a means of distinguishing between different kinds of everydayness – between ephemeral 'trash' that was disposable and forgettable and the ordinary, repetitive ephemerality of 'common' life. As Deidre Lynch has argued, the evocation of the latter made the novel central to the affective rhythms and routines of human activity, establishing the everyday as that which was intimate, familiar, and sustaining rather than as something always already irredeemably lost. The recurrence of the everyday underpinned the comfort or reassurance of 'ordinary' life evoked by some kinds of Romantic fiction, making the novel an affective, durable object to which the reader could repeatedly return and affirm the novel and novel-reading as both habit-forming and immersed in the everyday 'habitus'.[4] The ephemeral, on the other hand, increasingly came to stand for what could not be easily assimilated to comforting, ordinary, daily routine – the exceptionalism of accidental readings such as Addison's scrap or the Kibworth playbill encountered by Plumptre, which made ordinary experience strange and were unrepeatable, or the evanescence of papers which fluttered for a time and disappeared from the street or the dead wall. In other words, ephemerality can be seen as everyday life's everyday: it is the zone of dissolution, banality,

---

[4] Deidre Shauna Lynch, 'Canons' Clockwork: Novels for Everyday Use', in *Bookish Histories: Books, Literature, and Commercial Modernity, 1700–1900*, eds. Ina Ferris and Paul Keen (Basingstoke: Palgrave Macmillan, 2009), 87–110; also her *Loving Literature: A Cultural History* (Chicago: University of Chicago Press, 2015), esp. chap. 4.

rubbish, and insignificance that both defines the everyday and which the discursive category of the everyday, in Maurice Blanchot's terms, 'transcribes' as the 'everyday'.[5]

This chapter explores the idea of ephemerology as everyday life's buried science with reference to a particular year, 1814, which was notable for two ephemeral events – a frost fair on the river Thames and the celebrations of the ending of the war with France, a 'peace' that, with Napoleon's return from exile in 1815, was soon over. The year 1814 is also significant in literary history as the year in which the term 'bibliography' begins to be used, as well as marking the introduction of steam press printing for the production of *The Times* newspaper. James Raven argues that this development represented the beginning of the large-scale industrialisation of print in the nineteenth century and the end of the artisanal practices that had changed little from the time of Caxton.[6] It is also the year in which Jane Austen set her posthumously published novel *Persuasion*, which displays a particularly acute sensitivity to the evanescence or 'quickness' of time, apparent in the concluding observation that the heroine Anne Elliot was compelled, as the wife of a sailor, to 'pay the tax of quick alarm'.[7] 'Quick' denotes speed of movement and time and also being alive, as in the biblical sense of the 'quick and the dead'. I want to argue that, placed in the context of shifts in book and printing history, as well as the ephemeral events of that year and the archiving of them by collectors such as Sarah Sophia Banks and Francis Place, *Persuasion* can be seen as a kind of ephemerography. The title of this chapter, 'England in 1814', with its echo of P. B. Shelley's 'England in 1819' and James Chandler's magisterial study of the same name, proposes ephemeral historicity as an important, though neglected, strand of Romantic historicism: the 'quickness' of 1814 exemplifies how ephemerality and ephemerology were constitutive of the Romantic everyday and also remediated by it.[8]

---

[5] Blanchot, 'Everyday Speech', 18. For other discussions of the everyday with specific reference to the Romantic period see Mary A. Favret, *War at a Distance: Romanticism and the Making of Modern Wartime* (Princeton, NJ: Princeton University Press, 2010), Carolyn Steedman, *An Everyday Life of the English Working Class: Work, Self and Sociability in the Early Nineteenth Century* (Cambridge, UK: Cambridge University Press, 2013), and William Galperin, *The History of Missed Opportunities: British Romanticism and the Emergence of the Everyday* (Stanford, CA: Stanford University Press, 2017).

[6] James Raven, *The Business of Books: Booksellers and the English Book Trade 1450–1850* (New Haven, CT: Yale University Press, 2007), 320.

[7] Jane Austen, *Persuasion*, eds. Janet Todd and Antje Blank (Cambridge, UK: Cambridge University Press, 2006), 275; subsequent page references in parentheses in text.

[8] James Chandler, *England in 1819: The Politics of Literary Culture and the Case of Romantic Historicism* (Chicago: University of Chicago Press, 1998).

Frost Fair 1814

The early Enlightenment frost fair on the Thames, as I argued in Chapter 2, was a theatricalised simulacrum of the associational public sphere which identified, particularly through print, the importance to that sphere of ephemeral historicity – a sense of the immediacy of the present and its inevitable, quick, transience. The fair of 1683–4 commemorated by Luttrell and Evelyn was followed by other notable fairs in 1715–16, 1739–40, and 1789 which, like their Restoration-period precedent, were predominantly associated with the products of cheap print, such as the souvenir ticket produced in situ on the ice.[9] For many people the frost fair was the opportunity to see their names in print for the first (and possibly only) time, thereby affirming the power of print to define subjectivity and sociality: 'Your Names are Printed, tho' you cannot Write', states a line of verse attached to a ticket in the name of Mrs Mary Coates, produced on the ice on 14 January 1715–16[10] (Figure 21). A similar ticket was produced for and possibly by the book-runner and collector John Bagford on the frozen Thames in January 1715–16. It combines Bagford's name with references to the invention of printing by Gutenberg and concludes with the following lines:

> All you that walk upon the Thames,
> Step in this booth, and print your names,
> And lay it by, that ages yet to come,
> May see what things upon the Thames were done.
> Printed upon the frozen River Thames,
> Jan. 18, 1715–16.[11]

Bagford did indeed obey the instruction to 'lay by' this ticket which, like the one for Mary Coates, found its way into the archive of the British Museum in a confirmation of the printer's prophecy of its value for the 'ages'.[12] Bagford's frost fair ticket also exemplifies the capacity of ephemeral print to render a particular kind of fleeting and elusive subjectivity.

---

[9] See Nicholas Reed, *Frost Fairs on the Frozen Thames* (London: Liliburne Press, 2002).
[10] *Where little wherries once did use to ride* .. [London: Printed at Holme's and Broad's Booth, at the sign of the Ship, against Old Swan-Stairs, where is the only real Printing-Press on the frozen Thames. January the 14th, 1715/6], Eighteenth Century Collections Online, Gale Cengage, ESTC no. T052370. British Library 840.m.271, facing p. 20.
[11] John Nichol, *Literary Anecdotes of the Eighteenth Century*, 6 vols. (London: John Nichols, 1812), II: 465.
[12] The ticket was included in the Harleian manuscripts, Harleian MSS 5936: Nichols, *Literary Anecdotes*, II: 465.

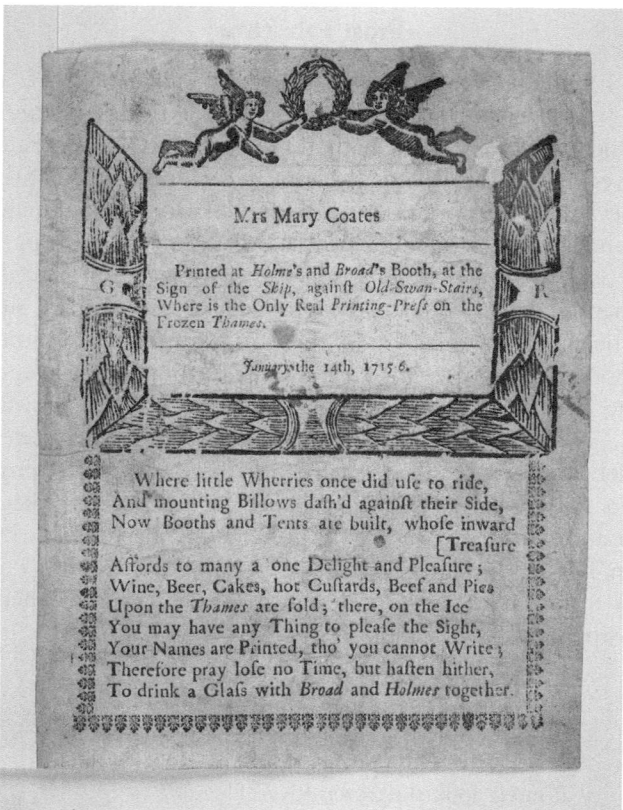

Figure 21   Where little wherries once did use to ride . . . [London: Printed at Holme's and Broad's Booth, at the sign of the Ship, against Old Swan-Stairs, where is the only real Printing-Press on the frozen Thames. January the 14th, 1715/6].
© The British Library Board. 840.m.271, facing p. 20

This ticket commemorates his presence on the frozen Thames on a particular day as well as his wider investments in ephemera as evidence of the ingenuity of the print trade and the 'science' of typography. Frost fair print was appealing to ephemerology in its synthesis of topography (especially the history of London), printing history, and the idea of a media event, and the chronicling of strange occurrences or public meteors. Other people who laid by the print products of the frost fairs included Daniel Lysons, who possessed material relating to the frost fairs of 1683–4, 1715–16, and 1740, and the anonymous individual who extended the ephemeral collections of Isaac Reed – his/her collection included a 'Wood

Cut of Frost Fair, Watch Papers, Views, Poetry, etc printed on the Ice, 5th Feb. 1814'.[13] Compilers of frost fair archives also included a 'Mrs. George' who bequeathed her precious 'Frost Fairs in folio with lock & key' to John Gregory Crace (1809–89), scion of the Crace family of interior decorators for the royal family and aristocracy.[14] Mrs. George's gift, representing fairs from 1683–4 to 1814, was donated by Crace in the 1880s to the British Museum as part of his father Frederick Crace's vast collection of maps, drawings, and prints documenting the topography of London.

The 1814 frost fair occurred towards the end of a particularly severe period of winter weather that had begun in late December of the previous year and afflicted the whole of the country: communications to the west of England and Wales were impossible and the Mersey and Severn rivers also froze over.[15] Restrictions on the flow of the river Thames through the arches of the old London Bridge (which was replaced in 1831) led to a build-up of ice between the bridge and Blackfriars and by the end of January 1814 a fair was established, the first since 1789. According to the *Gentleman's Magazine*, 'above 30 booths were erected for the sale of porter, spirits, gingerbread, &c. Skittles were played by several parties, and the drinking tents filled by females and their companions, dancing reels, while several sat around large fires drinking rum, grog, and other spirits. Several tradesmen also attended, selling books, toys, and trinkets of every description'.[16] As was customary, a number of these booths housed printing presses, selling souvenir tickets, woodcut illustrations, ballads, and watch-papers, some of the latter being collected and circulated, as we have seen, in the Isaac Reed sale. Watch-papers were small discs of paper (or sometimes of silk) that were placed in the outer case of a watch to protect the mechanism. They functioned as a form of labelling and advertising for watchmakers but could also take the form of personal tokens or souvenirs. Sarah Sophia Banks collected a number of them, often intricately designed intaglio prints, as a variety of the trade card. Some of the watch-papers in Banks's collection are proofs, that is they take the form of a square sheet of paper on a similar scale to the trade card out

---

[13] *Catalogue of the Library of Philip Hurd*, 51; *Catalogue of the Rare and Bijoux Portion . . . A Large Assemblage of the Broadsides, Old Ballads, Scraps, &c. Collected by the late Isaac Reed, Esq.* (London: Southgate, Grimston and Wells, 1833), 92.
[14] 'Crace Frost Fair', 172* h. 3, BM Department of Prints and Drawings.
[15] See *The Times*, 20 January 1814; *Lancaster Gazette and General Advertiser*, 29 January 1814.
[16] *Gentleman's Magazine*, 84 (February 1814), 192. An example of the frost fair gingerbread survives in the Museum of London [www.independent.co.uk/news/uk/home-news/when-winter-really-was-winter-the-last-of-the-london-frost-fairs-9100338.html, accessed 1 April 2014].

of which a disc would be cut to fit the watch.[17] In its proximity to a device that recorded the passage of time and as a tiny slip of paper carried on the body, the watch-paper was thus especially ephemeral.

The 1814 frost fair is also notable for the production of a book, *Frostiana*, the title page of which claimed that it was 'Printed and published on the ICE on the River *Thames*, February 5, 1814 by *G. DAVIS*' (Figure 22). A prefatory advertisement states that a 'large impression of the Title page ... was actually printed on the ICE on the RIVER THAMES!!' suggesting that the book as a whole was not in fact produced there.[18] The title page would have acted as a kind of prospectus for *Frostiana* which, as the review for the *British Critic* noted, was a compilation of frosty facts forming a 'natural history of winter' or 'Memoirs of Cold and Cold Weather'.[19] *Frostiana* combined an account of the 1814 frost fair, reproducing some its notable ephemeral literature, with a miscellany of information about notable frosts in history, the science of freezing, cold weather sports such as ice-skating, and even advice on 'How to make ICE CREAM'.[20] Proclaiming itself a product of a specific time and place – the frozen Thames on 5 February 1814 – *Frostiana* combined the ephemeral science of the local and the fugitive and of knowledge as ludic, contingent, and hyper-textual, with an evocation of frost's historicity and potentially global import.

Frostiana reproduced a number of notable print souvenirs from the 1814 fair, including one celebrating the art of printing:

> Amidst the Arts which on the THAMES appear,
> To tell the wonders of this icy year,
> PRINTING claims prior place, which at one view
> Erects a monument of THAT and YOU.[21]

The products of the fair's printing press, particularly the ticket, exemplified what Jon Mee terms 'print magic' in its elementary form: the performative capacity of a piece of print paper to create a conjunction between the 'THAT' of the material text, and the 'YOU' of the ticket's consumer or subject.[22] Another handbill took the form of an address from the Thames itself to 'Madam Tabitha Thaw', pleading for release from 'FATHER

---

[17] The British Museum Collection Online Database lists eighty watch-papers as originally owned by Sarah Sophia Banks. See Rickards and Twyman, *Encyclopedia of Ephemera*, 354–5.
[18] *Frostiana: or a History of the River Thames, in a Frozen State, with an Account of the Late Severe Frost* (London: G. Davis, 1814), iv.
[19] *British Critic*, new series 1 (1814), 221.   [20] *Frostiana*, 70.   [21] *Frostiana*, 19
[22] Mee, *Print, Publicity, and Radicalism*, 8–9.

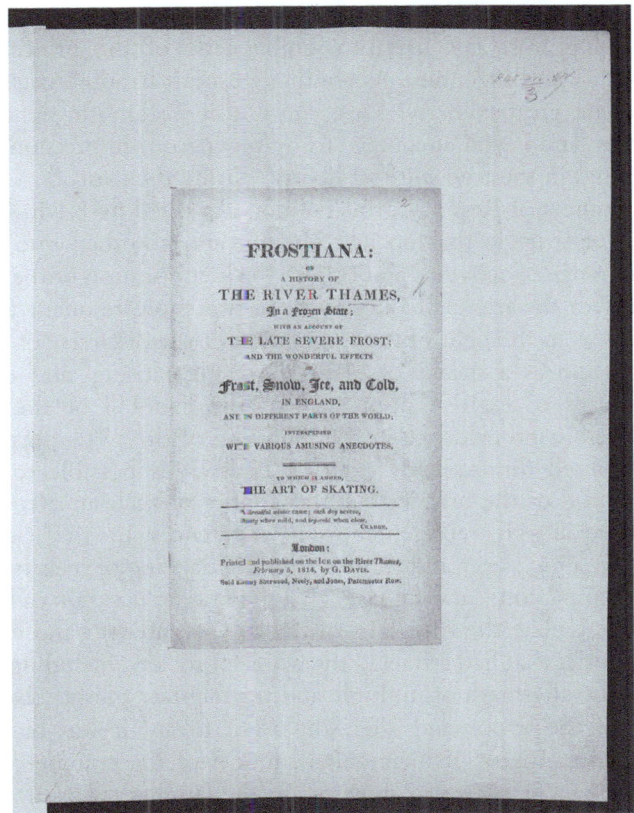

Figure 22 *Frostiana: or a History of the River Thames, in a Frozen State, with an Account of the Late Severe Frost* (London: G. Davis, 1814).
© The British Library Board. 840.m.27(3) title page

FROST and SISTER SNOW who have '*boneyed* my borders'.[23] *Kirby's Wonderful and Eccentric Museum* reported that on Sunday 6 February, 'a dreadful explosion', like a 'sudden blast of gunpowder', occurred, causing many of the fairgoers to fall into the now flowing water.[24] *Frostiana* chronicled the progress of the fair's disintegration, its authors declaring: 'while we are now writing, (half past 2 p. m.) [on 7 February] a printing press has been again set up on a large ICE-ISLAND, between Blackfriars and Westminster-bridges' where the title page of the book was 'now

---

[23] *Frostiana*, 23.   [24] *Kirby's Wonderful and Eccentric Museum*, 5 (1820), 257.

actually being printed'.²⁵ Print's heroic apotheosis was thus an icy 'real time', making frost fair literature emblematic of the printing press's indomitability and ingenuity. As another frost fair handbill declared, 'can the press have greater liberty? Here you find it working in the middle of the Thames; and if you encourage us by buying our impressions, we will keep it going, in the true spirit of liberty, during the frost'.²⁶

In the context of Regency print politics, described by Kevin Gilmartin as 'a field of struggle that opened out on, and absorbed into itself, an impressive range of activities and issues', the identification of the liberty of the press with the frost fair public sphere was more resonant than ever, particularly so in the light of the elaboration of the discourse of ephemerality post-1800 as a means of identifying, stigmatising, and ultimately policing forms of fugitive print such as the handbill or the poster.²⁷ Though there is no evidence in the reporting of the 1814 frost fair of it being mobilised for explicitly political ends, it is possible to detect a reconfiguration of the broader cultural politics of such an event and the kind of sociality it represented. The references in the *Gentleman's Magazine* to 'grog', beer and skittles, and the dancing of reels by 'females and their companions' made it clear that this was an occasion of low, loose conviviality. Unlike the frost fairs of the late seventeenth and early eighteenth centuries that had attracted the whole of society, including the royal family, in the aftermath of multiple and fragmentary publics that defined the crisis of the 1790s and after, the 1814 frost fair was incapable of standing for a unitary, if hierarchised, model of the commercial public sphere. The fair of 1814 was thus cast in the familiar terms of a low city fair, rather than, as it had been in the Restoration, a wondrous simulacrum of the synthesis of modern sociality and the 'new present' that was London as a whole. In other words, frost fairs were beginning to be rendered in polite literary discourse as popular and 'ephemeral'.

The importance of 1814 as a crucial year in the reconfiguration of ephemeral textuality is apparent in a debate that occurred in the *Gentleman's Magazine* a few weeks before the February frost fair. It was begun by 'J.K.' who, in late 1813, critiqued the bibliomaniacs for neglecting the true criterion of timeless and transcendent literary value:

---

[25] *Frostiana*, 24.
[26] Edward F. Rimbault, *Old Ballads Illustrating the Great Frost of 1683–4 and the Fair on the River Thames* (London: Percy Society, 1844), xxix.
[27] Kevin Gilmartin, *Print Politics: The Press and Radical Opposition in Early Nineteenth-Century England* (Cambridge, UK: Cambridge University Press, 1996), 68.

> If an old work be truly valuable, it will not be necessary to search Monasteries, dive into Vaults, pore over Bookstalls, or grub up all the trash which has been consigned to the silence of centuries, and which, but for their officious zeal, would have been of much more service in the shops of cheesemongers, than on the gilded shelves to which they only operate as a foil.[28]

In January 1814 'A.C.' responded by arguing for the inextricable relationship between the content and meaning of a book and its material form, the outstanding example being the Bible. 'A.C.' cited Erasmus's difficulty in locating the New Testament in Greek and Luther's discovery of the Old and New Testaments '*covered with dust* in the Monastery in Wittemburg' as evidence that even the Bible was subject to the vagaries of its material incarnation and transmission.[29] 'A.C.' went on to argue that the durability of a text was influenced by a variety of factors, such as the conditions of political and religious censorship, the perishability of paper, commercial decisions by the bookseller as to the number of copies produced, and finally, fashions in taste and opinion. As an example of the latter, 'A.C.' cited the changing fortunes of Robert Burton's *Anatomy of Melancholy* which had for many years been considered 'a waste-paper book' until Samuel Johnson revived interest in it.[30] The arguments of both 'J.K.' and 'A.C.' suggest how questions of both the material and immaterial durability of the printed word had become more pressing in the context of the radical relativisation of what constituted the book after 1789, manifested in the inter-implication of bibliomania and ephemerology in the career of, for example, Joseph Haslewood. Both 'A.C.' and 'J.K.' are haunted by the spectre of 'waste' or 'trash', the condition of absolute ephemerality into which all books, even the holy scriptures, can disappear.

It is in this context that 'A.C.' invokes another category of 'rarity', that is, '*the ephemeral nature and flimsy quality of some publications*, chiefly relating to current transactions'. Of this class of publication, 'A.C.' included 'thin pamphlets, or single sheets or half sheets of paper; such as printed notices about sales of property, papers respecting local events, and even hand-bills and ballads'. 'A.C.' also refers to having by him, as he writes, a 'thin folio volume of hand-bills, and other small papers' relating to the Glorious Revolution (the kind of material collected by Luttrell) and

---

[28] *Gentleman's Magazine*, 83 (December 1813), 544. See Ina Ferris's discussion of this debate as a response to the Roxburghe Club: *Book-Men*, 24–5.
[29] *Gentleman's Magazine*, 84 (January 1814), 33.
[30] *Gentleman's Magazine*, 84 (January 1814), 34.

'[a]nother folio volume, of the original Spectators, with the advertisements', a similar if not the actual collection later advertised in the Field sale of 1827.[31] Whether consciously or not, 'A.C.' was acknowledging the genesis of ephemera collecting in the tumults of the seventeenth century and the importance of the *Spectator* as a key text for ephemerology, both conceptually and bibliographically. As part of the spectrum of such literature 'A.C.' also included 'volumes of electioneering placards' relating to 'local disputes and temporary occurrences' which, though now 'rare' are 'not uninteresting – even those who have wasted them would afterwards be glad to recall them. As memoranda, they may be very useful to the Topographer and Historian'.[32]

The spectrum of print that 'A.C.' describes, ranging from the jobbing print of advertising to the newspaper and journal, from ballads to electioneering 'squibs', is consistent with the focus of collectors since the seventeenth century. 'A.C.' situates the documentation of contemporary life in all its diversity – what he or she terms 'current transactions' – as integral to antiquarianism as a whole and specifically the bibliomania. However, 'A.C.'s use of the term 'ephemeral' effectively demarcates these publications as different in kind or 'nature' from the codex-form book, however vulnerable the latter might also be to decay and waste. Words such as 'thin' and 'flimsy' anticipate the language used to describe printed ephemera by librarians in the twentieth century, such as Timothy Young's characterisation of ephemera as 'limp' and 'unprotected' with a tendency to 'just show up'.[33] In the debate between 'J.K.' and 'A.C.' in 1814, it is possible to discern the genealogy of the idea of printed ephemera as being rare because it was essentially different from the codex-form book and closer to the idea of an absolute ephemerality. In his *Introduction to the Study of Bibliography*, published in 1814 and widely credited as the first book to define bibliography as a field of study, the biblical scholar and librarian Thomas Hartwell Horne similarly made a distinction between books '*whose Rarity is absolute*', such as those of which very few copies were printed or books suppressed by legal authority, and '*Books whose Rarity is relative*'.[34] Hartwell Horne included 'Fugitive Pieces' in the latter category, such as 'old Newspapers, detached tracts relative to the civil wars, electioneering placards, and similar ephemeral publications'. He cited the

---

[31] *Gentleman's Magazine*, 84 (January 1814), 35.
[32] *Gentleman's Magazine*, 84 (January 1814), 35.   [33] Young, 'Evidence', 18.
[34] Thomas Hartwell Horne, *An Introduction to the Study of Bibliography*, 2 vols. (London: Cadell and Davies, 1814), I: 320

'KINGS PAMPHLETS' – that is, the Thomason tracts – as a notable collection of such material. The value of the Thomason collection was likely an influence on his view, shared by Joseph Haslewood, that 'public Libraries' should serve as repositories for such material 'to prevent their destruction'.[35] The first work to treat fugitive literature in bibliographical terms, Hartwell Horne's *Introduction* exemplifies the discursive slippage between 'fugitive' and 'ephemeral' that took place after 1800, as well as the problematic legacy of collections such as the Thomason tracts, the survival and 'matchless' value of which confounded the assumption that ephemera was of only 'relative' value, only significant for a day.[35]

The consolidation of the category of printed ephemera post-1800 and particularly in the year 1814 was a response to the stigmatisation of fugitive literature as a potent form of political communication after 1790 as well as the impact of the 'wild' relativism of the bibliomaniacs. The idea of printed ephemera as transient, like insects that lived for a day, served to contextualise the life cycle of the book in terms of an order of nature, as well as enabling a boundary against which the proximity of the codex-form book to waste and fugacity could be imaginatively and discursively delimited. Such a delimitation also had a more specific social dimension in so far as it entailed the identification of cheap print with the category of the popular and a reconfiguration of the meaning of the street, as represented in collections such as the Thomason tracts, from a space in which high and low could meet and jostle (like at a frost fair) to the street as the domain of the disenfranchised, anonymous 'other'. It is this transition, developing throughout the eighteenth century but which intensifies after 1789, that led to the privileging of the ballad as the dominant form of cheap print and an expression of the voice and literature of 'the people', at the expense of recognition of the diversity of cheap print (both retail and commissioned) and also of the importance of forms such as the playbill and the ticket. The identification of printed ephemera with the category of the popular even extended to the social status of the collectors themselves. 'A.C.' argued that for those just above the 'trading and labouring classes' the collecting of ephemeral print was preferable to 'such recreations as fighting cocks, baiting bulls, running blood-horses, or betting upon boxing-matches'.[37] This comment suggests that by the early nineteenth century the accessibility of ephemera to the lowest classes of society, enabling a cheap or poor antiquarianism, was being used to define ephemera collecting as a whole.

[35] Hartwell Horne, *Introduction*, I: 329.   [36] Hartwell Horne, *Introduction*, I: 329 n. 1.
[37] *Gentleman's Magazine*, 84 (January 1814), 36.

As handbills, playbills, tickets, and newspapers became less visible in relation to the book and defined as ephemeral 'trash', so the collectors of such material also became more shadowy. Ephemera collecting began to lose its status within antiquarianism and the related field of bibliography, and the idea of a public sphere as a jostling encounter between high and low was increasingly occluded.

Ephemeral War and Peace

On 14 April 1814, a few weeks after the frost fair, Napoleon Bonaparte surrendered to the Sixth Coalition. (In the interim period Jane Austen had visited London in early March to deliver the proofs of *Mansfield Park*, shop, and see Edmund Kean at Drury Lane theatre. She also told Cassandra Austen then that 'Peace was generally expected').[38] The grip of war, and especially of Napoleon, on the British imagination is apparent in the frost fair handbill quoted previously which complained that the cold had 'boneyed [the] borders' of Father Thames; prints of the fair also represented it as a mock military encampment, its booths festooned with signs such as 'The City of Moscow' and 'Wellington for Ever'.[39] Even before peace was declared, war's capacity to occupy and reconfigure time and place, followed by evacuation, as if it had never been there, had been anticipated by the evanescent camp on the ice. The frost fair thus gained additional meaning in retrospect for foreshadowing, in its ephemerality, the brief peace of 1814.

After more than twenty years of war the cessation of conflict with France was greeted in Britain by a series of public rejoicings and commemorations of various kinds that took up much of the summer of 1814 but which, as ephemeral occasions recording a peace that did not last, have received comparatively little attention from historians. The peace of 1814 began with the signing of the Treaty of Paris on 30 May and was followed by Lord Castlereagh's delivery of the treaty to parliament on 6 June, the proclamation of peace by the king's sheriffs on 20 June, and thanksgiving services up and down the country on 7 July. These events were marked by a period of intense 'peace sociability' between June and August, such as the lavish, well-publicised dinners held in honour of Wellington, illuminations

---

[38] Jane Austen, *Jane Austen's Letters*, ed. Deirdre le Faye, 4th edn (Oxford: Oxford University Press, 2011), 265–8.

[39] 'A View of the Frost Fair as it Appeared on the Ice on the River Thames Fby 3d 1814', BM 1880,1113.1760.

and transparencies in towns and cities across the country, and numerous peace festivals, often held in conjunction with the thanksgiving services of 7 July. Peace festivals were staged not only in major towns and cities but also in the smallest of villages and settlements: the *Bury and Norwich Post* of 20 July 1814, for example, noted events at Chedburgh and Ickworth, and that 'similar fetes have been given at Stradishall, Rede, Bacton, Shapiston, Thorston, Shimpling, Clare, Needham, Coddenham, Eye, Mendlesham, Cookley, Melton, Adleton, Sutton and Hemley'. Such reporting created contours of peace in both space and time, defining peace as both happening contemporaneously, in 'real time', and as something in the process of being normalised, made part of the everyday, like the periodicity of the newspaper itself. The mediatisation of peace in this way also worked to strengthen the political significance of the festivals as exercises in paternalism by local elites, entertainments for the people that projected the post-war future as a stable continuation of the eighteenth-century social order. In the case of one fete in the village of Ensham in Oxfordshire, the lower orders were given labels to wear on which was printed the words 'Peace and Plenty'.[40] Though popular loyalism was strong and often heartfelt, as Linda Colley has argued, this gesture nonetheless says more about the givers of the feast than those who were entertained, suggesting a desire to label or ticket the opinions as well as the bodies of the people.[41] At the same time as these festivals of national unanimity were being enacted, other forms of more exclusive peace sociability were taking place such as a ball and supper at Abingdon in Oxfordshire on 21 July 1814 for which gentlemen's and ladies tickets cost an expensive 15 shillings and 10s. 6d. respectively; tellingly, no servants were allowed to wait on table except for those approved by the stewards.[42] Local elites were on the one hand sponsoring communal celebrations of peace and on the other declaring their own capacity to withdraw from and exclude the kind of public that such entertainments embodied, a contradiction that was to be played out, on an even more phenomenal scale, by the Prince Regent's own party for the people in August 1814.

This festival, known as the Jubilee, was staged in the royal parks of Westminster on 1 August 1814. It was initially designed to complement the entertainments organised for the restored European monarchs visiting

---

[40] *Jackson's Oxford Journal*, 16 July 1814.
[41] Linda Colley, *Britons: Forging the Nation, 1707–1837* (New Haven, CT: Yale University Press, 1992).
[42] *Jackson's Oxford Journal*, 16 July 1814.

London in July, but when they left before arrangements could be finalised the event was reconfigured as a general commemoration of the peace, open to the populace of London as a whole. After further delay, the festival was rebranded as a celebration of the centenary of the accession to the throne of the House of Brunswick and, belatedly, the naval victories of Nelson. Such uncertainties over the purpose of the Jubilee – *The Times* described it as a '*sort of* general celebration . . . of War, of Peace, and of the Accession of the House of Brunswick' – contributed to the sense of the attenuation or evanescence of peace in 1814, foreshadowing the eventual resumption of hostilities in 1815.[43] The Jubilee began on the morning of 1 August as vast crowds began to enter the royal parks from all over the metropolis. Early that day a public notice had been posted declaring that Hyde Park and Green Park would be 'entirely open to the People' and that the Mall, Constitution Hill, and the lawn at St James's Park would be accessible by gates at Spring Gardens and New Street.[44] A section of the lawn at St James's Park and Birdcage Walk, where the accommodation for the royal family in the 'Royal Booth' was located, was fenced off and accessible only to those who had bought tickets. This measure was designed to ensure that the 'middle classes' of society would be secured from '*promiscuous intermixture* with the immense crowd'.[45] The tickets were purchasable from lottery-office keepers and proceeds from them were donated for the relief of war orphans.[46] Hyde Park became the main site for a people's 'fair' as the booths and puppet shows of Bartholomew and other suburban fairs set up shop there.

The entertainments began towards the evening of 1 August with a mock sea battle or naumachia on the Serpentine in Hyde Park. *The Times*, which gave extensive coverage to the Jubilee, commented that 'the immense multitude that crowded the shore, in rank upon rank, and thousand upon thousand, gleaming in that deep and coloured light, might pass for an army waiting to see the contest of the fleets decided'.[47] There then followed around 6 o'clock a hot-air balloon flight by the aeronaut James Sadler, who threw from his basket printed programmes of the day's entertainment: the balloon could be seen by the whole crowd drifting towards the east for about half an hour. It was at this point that some of the crowd attempted an incursion of the fenced-off area in St James's Park

---

[43] *The Times*, 2 August 1814.   [44] *The Times*, 2 August 1814.
[45] *An Historical Memento, Representing the Different Scenes of Public Rejoicing, which took place the first of August, in St James's and Hyde Parks, London, in Celebration of The Glorious Peace of 1814* (London: Edward Orme, 1814), 45.
[46] *Courier*, July 1814; *An Historical Memento*, 45.   [47] *The Times*, 2 August 1814.

and Birdcage Walk. The *Morning Chronicle*, which was generally lukewarm about the event, reported that 'several lads' who jumped the fence of 'this supposed seat of bliss' were repelled by some artillerymen who were guarding the enclosure.[48] About 10 p.m. the day culminated with firework displays centred on two structures, a Chinese pagoda designed by John Nash on a bridge over the Serpentine in Green Park, and the Temple of Concord, also in Green Park. The latter represented a military fortification that mutated into a temple of peace in a 'Grand Metamorphosis', which many compared to a transformation scene in a pantomime.[49] The *Morning Post*, an enthusiastic supporter of the occasion, described the firework display on the pagoda as 'a rich mass of living brilliant fire ... the water appeared to have assumed the character of the element most opposed to it, and the boats seen on it, gliding as it were on a vast sheet of liquid fire, had all the effect of magic'.[50] Towards midnight the pagoda structure unfortunately went on fire, exhibiting a spectacle that exceeded what had gone before: two people incurred injuries that led ultimately to their deaths.

The destruction of the pagoda made the Jubilee a truly ephemeral event, literally the work of a day. Using the language applied by the bibliographers to ephemeral papers, the *Morning Chronicle* commented that:

> the destruction of the flimsy building ... if it had not been accompanied by the loss of human life, would have been universally hailed as the brightest part of the shew, but the fatal accident ... made it a matter of universal regret.[51]

The smoking ruins of the pagoda on the morning of 2 August served as a reminder of the waste and suffering of war that the theatrical ephemerality of the sham-fight and the fireworks had mediated as spectacular entertainment. As a 'sort of' celebration of the peace, as *The Times* put it, the Jubilee was a multi-media hybrid event: it combined long-standing practices commemorating the temporality of war, such as the fireworks celebrating the Peace of Aix-la-Chapelle in 1749, with the scope of more recent patriotic festivals such as volunteer reviews, royal anniversaries, and even funerals, such as those of Nelson, Fox, and Pitt, documented by Sarah Sophia Banks in her collections.

The public that flocked to the Jubilee was also that which frequented London's exhibition culture, its shows, lectures, and entertainments – that is, the popular enlightenment that was the focus of Sarah Sophia

---

[48] *Morning Chronicle*, 2 August 1814.   [49] *Morning Chronicle*, 2 August 1814.
[50] *Morning Post*, 2 August 1814.   [51] *Morning Chronicle*, 3 August 1814.

Banks's collecting. This dimension of the Jubilee was exemplified by Sadler's balloon and the novelty of the Temple of Concord, which was able to revolve fully, giving spectators a complete 360-degree view. The inventor of this device, Henry Maudsley, would later found a firm that built the first steamship to cross the Atlantic.[52] Under the general supervision of Sir William Congreve (1772–1828), the inventor of the modern rocket, the Jubilee entertainments were the product of combined talents in engineering, design and fabrication, architecture, logistics, and pyrotechnics that showcased the synthesis of military science and Britain's growing power as an industrial nation. Most importantly, this show was designed for the public as a whole, even though its sponsors tried to differentiate it by distinguishing, through the demarcation of space and the use of tickets, the privilege of access through the capacity to pay. Though cordoned off, these patrons of the Jubilee saw the same thing as their fellow citizens in Hyde Park – Sadler's balloon sailing towards Kent or the fireworks exploding above them – with the sky being accessible to the vision of all. At what was supposed to be the end of the Napoleonic Wars, the Jubilee thus dramatised the idea of the mass public that had been first expressed in the balloonmania of the 1780s, and which the French Revolution and war had politicised and ultimately fragmented. As *The Times* put it, the fireworks shone a light on the 'motley groups of *universal* London' making them 'interesting as an assembly in a romance'.[53] This 'universal London' out of doors brought together, under the patronage of royalty, the publics of Vauxhall Gardens and Bartholomew Fair, the Pantheon and the pantomime; as such it represented the apotheosis of the long eighteenth-century public sphere that ephemeral print had both facilitated and documented.

Papering Peace

Fugitive print was a constitutive part of the experience of the Jubilee on the day of 1 August. Its role ranged from posters notifying the populace that the event would actually be taking place, to the tickets for the enclosed area in St James's Park and the programmes thrown to the people by Sadler in his balloon. On the model of the frost fair, a number of printing presses were set up in the fair at Hyde Park, selling souvenir handbills, tickets, and

---

[52] Melanie Doderer-Winkler, *Magnificent Entertainments: Temporary Architecture for Georgian Festivals* (New Haven, CT: Yale University Press, 2013), 198–9.
[53] *The Times*, 2 August 1814 (my emphasis).

watch-papers at the cost of a few halfpence: one of the printers was the enterprising G. Davis, the publisher of *Frostiana*. When, in the days that followed 1 August, the fair in Hyde Park was allowed to continue, the *Morning Chronicle* reported that there were plans to publish a special 'JUBILEE FAIR JOURNAL' in the park to mark the 'daily existence of the festival'.[54] Two important contemporary collections of such ephemera and related visual images of the Jubilee were made by Sarah Sophia Banks and by the radical organiser and archivist, Francis Place.[55] The material they put together to document the event configures it, not surprisingly, from different political perspectives.

Banks's archive of the Jubilee, like other aspects of her collecting, spans her visiting cards now in the Department of Prints and Drawings and the collections in the British Library. Her visiting cards in particular contextualise the Jubilee not simply in terms of a national triumph but as a celebration of the restoration of the European ruling order as a whole. Thus she includes a number of cards for the 'Great People' who visited London in July 1814 and a collection of the cards of nobles involved in the Congress of Vienna that began after the Jubilee in the autumn of 1814.[56] The material specifically relating to the Jubilee in this sequence of files includes her own ticket for the Royal Booth in Green Park, and another sent to her brother with the compliments of Sir William Congreve (J,10.416–17; J,10.414–15). The Bankses thus had direct access to the very centre of what the *Morning Chronicle* described as the 'sacred enclosure', and the fact that it was Congreve who invited Sir Joseph is indicative of the indebtedness of the Jubilee to the showmanship of Enlightenment science and innovation.[57] Banks's collection relating to the Jubilee that is now in the British Library (L.R. 301.h.11) amplifies the emphases in the visiting card files. It is primarily a visual record of the events of 1 August documented by means of both cheap and prestige prints, illustrating the mock sea battle on the Serpentine, the Chinese pagoda (including two views of the pagoda in flames), and the Temple of Concord.[58] Her visiting card collection also includes images of the Jubilee, such as the popular print 'The Grand Jubilee' (J,10.8; Figure 23). Banks collected multiple

---

[54] *Morning Chronicle*, 5 August 1814.
[55] On Banks's collecting in relation to the Jubilee see Leis, 'Ephemeral Histories', 183–99.
[56] BM, J,10.56 to J,10.400. Banks's collection of visiting cards relating to the 1814 peace and the Congress of Vienna amounts to eleven files. The Congress began formally in November 1814 and lasted until June 1815.
[57] *Morning Chronicle*, 2 August 1814.
[58] The prints depicting the pagoda on fire are at L.R. 301.h.11, f. 14.

232 England in 1814: Frost Fairs, Peace, and *Persuasion*

Figure 23   The Grand Jubilee. Hand-coloured etching. [Southwark: G. Smith, 1814].
Collection of Sarah Sophia Banks. J, 10.8.
© The Trustees of the British Museum

images of the Jubilee celebrations, twelve in all, from publishers such as Whittle and Laurie of Fleet Street, Rudolph Ackermann of the Strand, Edward Orme of Bond Street, Burkitt and Hudson of 85 Cheapside, Thomas Palser of Lambeth, and Thomas Greenwood of Holborn.[59] The

[59] L.R. 301.h.11, f. 17–25.

extent of her collection indicates the market for such images as well as Banks's diligence in visiting print shops across London to acquire them in the days following the Jubilee. Through multiple images of each of the various shows of the Jubilee, Banks was able to create an effect that is proto-photographic in the sense of anticipating how a camera could record a succession of 'shots'. Her documentation of the Jubilee in this way is thus evocative of the micro-temporality of a day and of the Jubilee as a predominantly visual experience.

Banks's collection includes not only prestige and expensive prints of the Jubilee, such as those by Orme and Ackermann, but also the kind of cheap print that was produced in the course of 1 August, such as souvenir handbills printed by G. Davis in the 'Royal Jubilee Printing Office in Hyde Park'.[60] She also supplemented the precious tickets to the Royal Booth kept in her visiting card collection with those others relating to the regulation of access and the prevention of 'promiscuous intermixture' with the Jubilee crowd. A 'Grand Jubilee Pass Ticket', for example, enabled the holder to 'pass and repass through any Friend's House Communicating with this Park': as elsewhere in her collections, Banks's attention to detail highlights the ticket system as a material and discursive practice that structured the micro-politics of sociality.[61] It is therefore possible to envisage Sarah Sophia Banks moving through the Jubilee fair in Hyde Park, as she may also have done amongst the print sellers in the days afterwards, picking up samples of cheap print before entering, by means of her own ticket, the Royal Booth, the 'sacred enclosure' from which the mass of the people at the Jubilee were excluded. Banks could thus access all areas, her collections defining a post-war, counter-revolutionary public sphere that was prepared to acknowledge the 'people' while at the same time sequestering the elite from dangerous 'intermixture' with it. This sequestering went so far as to entail a form of political invisibility. *The Times* reported that the 'chief disappointment' of the Jubilee was the failure of any 'person of distinction in rank or politics' to appear.[62] The theatricality of old regime power in a Habermasian sense, embodied in the person of the ruler, and to which the Jubilee as the Prince Regent's 'show' seemed to be alluding, was thus attenuated. There was literally no one there at the centre of the day's performances; the Royal Booth was virtually empty. As in the case of the peace festivals in the provinces, instead of enacting a unanimous social order under the Regency the Jubilee exposed an unwillingness or incapacity on the part of the elite to

---

[60] L.R. 301.h.11, f. 38.   [61] L.R. 301.h.11, f. 42.   [62] *The Times*, 2 August 1814.

engage with the people whom it had mobilised to defeat revolution and the power of Napoleon.

Taking Apart the Royal Booth

In her visit (or visits) to the booths housing printing presses in Hyde Park, Banks could possibly have bumped into Francis Place, who also made a collection of printed ephemera relating to the Jubilee. It is to be found in a two-volume collection or 'set' from the multi-volume Place Collection now in the British Library, an extensive archive of material, consisting mostly of newspaper cuttings. The Place Collection has long been used as a resource by historians of early nineteenth-century social history but it has rarely been analysed as a collection in its own right. Place created and housed this archive in his tailor's shop at No. 16 Charing Cross which he described as 'a sort of gassing shop' or 'a common coffee-house room'.[63] No. 16 was a political rendezvous, a site of sociability as well as an information resource, functioning as a radical version of No. 32 Soho Square, just a few minutes' walk away from Charing Cross. Place compiled his volumes of cuttings on a wide range of topics – elections, the history of the London Corresponding Society, economics and trade, manners and morals, the London theatres, Chartism, and North America. Representing what he thought 'might be useful at some future time, in relation to the working-classes most especially', his collecting practices and interests can be seen as continuous with those of George Thomason, particularly in their orientation towards 'posteritie'.[64]

Place was representative of the class of man, the autodidact artisan above the ranks of the labouring classes, whom 'A.C.' identified as the typical collector of ephemera in 1814. His library in Charing Cross was yet another site of archival domiciliation of printed ephemera in Regency London, in addition to the Banks household at No. 32 Soho Square, the collections of the actor Charles Mathews and William Upcott in Islington, James Winston's 'extraordinary accumulation' in Covent Garden, and Charles Burney Jr's collections of newspapers and playbills in Deptford. Though privately held, many of these collections would have been known to the circle of those who made them and beyond, as well as indicating shared interests, particularly in the theatre. Most of these collections would

---

[63] Quoted in Graham Wallas, *The Life of Francis Place 1771–1854*, rev. ed., (London: George Allen & Unwin, 1925; first pub. 1898), 177.
[64] Quoted in Wallas, *Life*, ix.

eventually be deposited in the British Museum library. *Notes and Queries* in 1866 described Place's 'pamphlets, broadsides, and scraps of all kinds' as 'the most extraordinary and curious collection of modern times ... His more particular object [being] to collect what appeared to be of an ephemeral or perishable character'.[65] In 1866 the collections were acquired by the British Museum which, in a pattern similar to the treatment of Banks's collections, made a distinction between seventy volumes of manuscript material (including newspaper cuttings and other letterpress items) and 180 volumes of newspaper cuttings, the latter being consigned to the newspaper department at Hendon.[66]

Place documented the Jubilee as one of a series of politico-cultural events between 1809 and 1814, beginning with the Old Price riots at Covent Garden theatre in 1809. The most significant theatre disturbance of the nineteenth century, the Old Price riots, which lasted for nearly two months, were a struggle between the rights of management to increase prices and the customary rights of the cross-class theatre-going public, as British subjects, to access entertainment at a price they could afford.[67] Francis Place's role in the Old Price riots was twofold: as a member of the radical Westminster Committee established in 1807 he had a direct interest in the political dimensions of the struggle between customary rights and privilege that the Old Price riots represented. His secondary role was as the chronicler of Old Price riots through collecting of media commentary on it (and later the writing of an MS memoir). In the first volume of 'set 59' Place made a MS note to the effect that his papers on the Old Price riots were 'collected *at the time* and are a tolerably perfect set', again suggesting a parallel with previous collectors such as Thomason whose amassing of ephemera was a record of both a contemporary media event and indirectly testimony that 'I was there'.[68]

The second volume of 'Set 59' contextualises the Old Price riots of 1809 in relation to other ephemeral and spectacular manifestations of Regency public culture such as panoramas, exhibitions, and the phenomenal events of 1814. Place documented the frost fair via the souvenir ticket

---

[65] T. B., 'Francis Place', *Notes and Queries*, ser. 3, 9 (March 1866), 191–2 (191).
[66] For the history of the distribution of Place's collections across the departments of the British Museum see Wallas, *Life*, viii–x.
[67] For Place's role in the Old Price riots see Marc Baer, *Theatre and Disorder in Late Georgian London* (Oxford: Clarendon Press, 1992).
[68] O. P. Riots. Exhibitions. – Panoramas. – Peace Jubilee and Sundries. 1307–1809. MS Radical Politics and the Working Man in England Set 59; Vol. I. British Library, Nineteenth Century Collections Online, Gale Cengage. Page Image 1.

printed on the ice of which he possessed a sheet of six imprints of the same ticket dated 3 February 1814 and another tiny example, possibly a watch-paper, including the text of the Lord's Prayer.[69] His more extensive record of the Jubilee consists largely of newspaper cuttings, handbills, and cheap woodcut illustrations of the pagoda and the Temple of Peace. He frames the Jubilee in terms of sceptical reporting about it in cuttings from radical newspapers such as the *Examiner* of 3 July 1814, announcing the forthcoming 'REGAL RAREE SHOW'.[70] Place also collected a seventeen-page pamphlet, entitled *Account of the National Jubilee* and published for sixpence by J. Briscoe, that satirised the orientalism of the Temple of Peace and the pagoda as a pagan 'fiction' and a 'place devoted to idolatry' respectively.[71] Congreve's rocket is described in this pamphlet as exemplifying 'the shortness of human life, and the transitory nature of all sublunary things' with reference to lines from a song entitled 'Plato's Advice':

> So flies the meteor through the skies,
> And sheds along a gilded train:
> When shot – 'tis gone – the meteor dies –
> Dissolved to common air again.[72]

A popular song in theatres, pleasure gardens, and taverns that dated from the 1760s and was reprinted in numerous songsters (that is, songbooks) until at least the 1820s, 'Plato's Advice' was here given a doubly radical inflection by citation in this pamphlet and Place's assemblage of it in his collection. Meteoric ephemerality exemplified the evanescence of 'gilded' pomp and show, the 'entire change of performances' that mock playbills such as 'The Guillotine' had announced in 1793. Place's emphasis on both the insubstantiality and the inevitable passing of the royal 'show' is also apparent in his documentation of the aftermath of the Jubilee. He includes a newspaper account of how on 12 August a crowd broke down the fence used to create the special enclosure, making two 'immense' bonfires. The crowd would have destroyed what remained of the Temple of Concord but for the arrival of the military. The Temple was in any case already in the process of dissolution, its transparent paintings having been removed, while the ruins of the pagoda were presumably also gone. Place's narrative of the Jubilee culminates with three items: a newspaper report from

---

[69] O. P. Riots. Exhibitions. – Panoramas. – Peace Jubilee and Sundries. 1809–1814. MS Radical Politics and the Working Man in England Set 59; Vol. II. British Library, Nineteenth Century Collections Online, Gale Cengage. Page Image 237.
[70] Set 59; Vol. II. Page Image 162.   [71] Set 59; Vol. II. Page Image 166–73 (172).
[72] Set 59; Vol. II. Page Image 173: *Plato's Advice, a new Song* [London? 1760?], Eighteenth Century Collections Online, ESTC no. 12150.

12 October 1814; a handbill advertisement; and an auction sale catalogue, advertising the sale of the wood, fixtures, and fittings of the Temple of Concord and the Royal Booth. The newspaper report from the *Morning Advertiser* described how a group of 'itinerant dealers in wood ... from the purlieus of Seven Dials [also a hub of cheap print production] had descended on the remains of the Temple to compete for pickings: '"Peace Returning," was purchased for 7s.; but the parapet, with "Europe Rescued," fetched the sum of 8s.'.[73] The Royal Booth, to which Sarah Sophia Banks was granted privileged access, was also literally broken up into pieces, the sale catalogue performatively confirming this dissolution by itemising the Booth's structure in lots, including one item described as 'the plume and feathers and star, boards of inscription'. The insignia of the Prince Regent, diminished in lower-case type and described as mere 'boards of inscription' were denuded of aura and dignity, to be carted away by itinerant dealers or burnt as firewood.

By linking the Old Price riots of 1809 with the frost fair and Jubilee in 1814, Francis Place identified this five-year period as crucial for the theatre and counter-theatre of late Georgian politics and society. In 1814, in the aftermath of a long, transformative war and in a dubious peacetime, what did the 'great' owe the mean of society and vice versa? Could the actual theatre, for example, be sustained as a version of the polity as a whole in which the people had a right to a place, rather than being mere consumers of culture? Was the 'universal London' brought together under the auspices of the Prince Regent, a vision or 'romance' of a viable post-war public sphere, or the beginning of the end of a distinctive phase of modernity that had its origins in the 'accidental democracy' that George Thomason had preserved for the future? Sarah Sophia Banks and Francis Place thus had very different interpretations of the condition of England in 1814. Their collections demonstrate that fugitive print was still a capacious category, that it could appeal to both high and low, the expensive and cheap, the common and rare, and that it could play a variety of political roles. As Sarah Sophia Banks was fully aware, tickets were instruments of exclusion as well as inclusion. Her collections as a whole, especially the nine-volume collection in the British Library, explore how the British elite was able to meld the innovations of fashionable sociability and ephemeral print publicity, in a way that supplemented the ancient aura of monarchical and aristocratic power with the aura of mass and multi-media celebrity. Banks documented how this alignment created a new relation between ruler and

---

[73] *Morning Advertiser*, 12 October 1814: Set 59; Vol. II Page Image 185.

ruled in which the former, via the print media, was able to project an authority that combined mystique with the fiction of accessible familiarity, creating a virtual rather than a real presence, like the Royal Booth itself.

Place's response to 1814 differs from Banks's in being committed to the long-standing view of the printing press as an instrument of enlightenment and of political change. In the form of the auction sale catalogue, ephemeral print penetrates the Royal Booth and performatively effects a demolition of it, revealing the essential emptiness of the show, in contrast to Banks's tickets that protect and enhance the Booth's exclusivity and mystique. Place's commitment to the instrumentality of the printing press is most apparent in his inclusion of a poster for G. Davis's 'Grand Jubilee PRINTING OFFICE', advertising 'Verses Printed in Memory of Peace, &c. &c.'.[74] Printed in bold fat face type, the poster was too large for a single folio page and is folded in two. Two small handbills are affixed to the recto of the poster: one depicts the Duke of Wellington, 'printed in Hyde Park' on 1 August, and another, on the folio following the poster itself, advertises the 'Grand Jubilee Fair' and 'A New Song' with a woodcut illustration at the top representing a printing press. These handbills form the 'cover' of the 'booklet' created by folding the sheet of the poster, the ink of which is visible through the paper of the poster itself. This reverse mirror image of the words of the poster, enhancing the abstract dimensions of the typography, are what the first-time reader encounters in turning the folio of 'Set 59', rendering the poster itself strange, even uncanny. The poster for the 'Grand Jubilee PRINTING OFFICE' represents the most ephemeral form of jobbing print, the kind of 'thing' that would normally occupy a dead wall or, in this case, would be pasted on a placard or fluttering on the entrance to a booth. In contrast to the handbills it is not clear that the poster was a commodity: Place may have asked for it as a souvenir or even purloined it from the printer in Hyde Park. His preservation and later assemblage of the poster has the effect of integrating the poles of the Derridean paper spectrum, making the trashiest of documents, belonging to the world out of doors, a part of his own 'priceless archive'. Place achieves this by adapting the technology of the codex, folding the sheet of the poster to create pages from it, while still maintaining the poster's radical alterity to the book. His 'bookwork' enables us to see the poster from the back as well as the front, and to see through it as well, in ways that make not only the uniqueness of this poster visible but

---

[74] Set 59; Vol. II Page Images 182–4. The British Library was unable to supply me with a reproduction of these images due to conservation reasons.

through it, the potency of print in general.[75] If Banks's 1814 collection has at its centre the mystique of the Royal Booth, to which she had privileged ticketed access, Place's destination is the alternative booth of radical print that, in the form of the poster, is identified both politically and materially with the people out of doors and transparent to the world.

Jane Austen's Newsmen

The coda to Place's documentation of the Jubilee is a small, unidentified newspaper cutting, isolated on the folio page following the auction catalogue. It is dated 27 November 1815 and notes that peace was once more to be celebrated in London, following the Treaty of Paris of 20 November that marked the final defeat of Napoleon:

> It is little more than a twelve months ago, that we had Temples of Concord that turned round on a Wheel, Pagodas that were burnt, Chinese Bridges, Roman Candles, and a British Fleet on the Serpentine River, all for a Peace that was to last forever. A very few months showed us the wisdom of our joy; and what confidence can we have in this new pacification? ...
> In the notes to the Tale of Castle Rackrent, Miss EDGEWORTH observes, that the hired mourners in Ireland, will sometimes pause in the middle of their vociferations, while they are following a funeral, and ask one another 'Arrah Honey, who are we howling for?'[76]

When these paragraphs were published, Jane Austen was progressing in the writing of *Persuasion*, which she began on 8 August 1815 and finished approximately one year later on 6 August 1816. This year coincided with the peace of November 1815 and the beginning of the experience of being 'post-war'. The newspaper paragraphs extracted by Francis Place define this experience in terms of uncertainty about how to determine the relationship between war and peace – what new pacification is this? – as well as bafflement about whom or what the public should be mourning. Set explicitly during the year before its writing and specifically during the peace of 1814, *Persuasion* shares this sense of weariness with the ontology of wartime. Its texture manifests the particular circumstances of when it was written: that is, the beginning of the loss of the immediacy of the very recent past when the eventfulness of a particular time is still palpably 'real' but nonetheless receding in both historical and communal memory.

---

[75] The term 'bookwork' is adapted from Garrett Stewart's *Bookwork: Medium to Object to Concept to Art* (Chicago: University of Chicago Press, 2011).
[76] Set 59; Vol. II. Page Image 194.

Considering *Persuasion* within the framework of the years of its dating and composition – the (just) pastness of the ephemeral peace, the unease of a short period of renewed war between March and June 1815, and the novelty (once more) of peace on the verge of the uncertainty of 'postwar' – thus accentuates the effect of its unstable manifold temporalities. While the protagonists of *Persuasion* do not know that peace will not endure, the novel itself 'knows' this, as Austen herself did, but only just, writing as she was in the immediacy of the 'new pacification'. This dimension of the novel is accentuated in the light of what Jane Austen also knew but which has been lost to history – the distinctive 'atmospheres' of 1814, firstly in the meteorological sense of the intense cold celebrated by the frost fair and secondly the uncertainty associated with the on-off peace festivities of July and August, leading to the question articulated in Place's newspaper cutting – what was all this for?

Austen's family was directly involved in the peace celebrations: her brother Henry attended the Prince Regent's ball for the emperor of Russia and the king of Prussia at Burlington House on 21 June, while her brother Edward Knight and niece Fanny, together with Henry and Cassandra Austen, were in the crowd in London to witness the procession proclaiming the peace.[77] The closest town to Austen's home at Chawton, Alton, commemorated the peace with illuminations and a dinner for the poor, in line with similar exercises in paternalism throughout the country.[78] Finally, as a reader of newspapers, Austen would have been a virtual witness of the Prince Regent's Jubilee in August 1814. A few months later in November she was invited to visit Carlton House, the scene of lavish private festivities in June, and may well have seen the temporary edifice of the Rotunda tent in the gardens of Carlton House that was later dismantled and re-erected at Woolwich to form the first public military museum.[79]

To a greater extent than Austen's other novels of this two-year period, *Persuasion* is acutely sensitive to the passing and evanescence of time. Mary Favret describes it as the 'most dated' of her books, a punning allusion to the novel's evocation of wartime as well as to specific dates such as the cryptic 'Nov. 5, 1789' that Sir Walter Elliot inserts in his copy of the *Baronetage* to mark the birth and death of his stillborn son.[80] The *Baronetage*, probably Debrett's *Baronetage of England* (1808), is the first of many

---

[77] Deirdre le Faye, *Jane Austen: A Family Record*, 2nd edn (Cambridge, UK: Cambridge University Press, 2004), 213.
[78] le Faye, *Jane Austen*, 213.   [79] For the Rotunda see Russell, 'Romantic Militarisation'.
[80] Favret, *War at a Distance*, 161. Austen, *Persuasion*, 3; subsequent page references in parenthesis in text.

books to feature in *Persuasion*, and Sir Walter's practices of annotation indicate his aspiration to be included within it as well as his alignment of his family history with other forms of dating in the print media, such as the diurnal historiography of the newspaper, for which 'Nov. 5, 1789' is just another day (334). Calendrical time, as mediated by print, is synchronised in *Persuasion* with other temporal rhythms, most notably of the seasons. The events of the novel are dated as beginning in the summer while the main part of the story takes place in the autumn, or more specifically November, when autumn is succumbing to winter, a time of year paralleled by February, on the cusp between winter and the fragility of spring, which is when Anne Elliot and Wentworth renew their engagement. The calendar of seasons in *Persuasion* is framed by the unique season of the peace that began in June 1814 and ended in March 1815, that is, just after Anne Elliot and Wentworth are reconciled. There is a number of references to 'this peace' or 'the peace' (e.g. 'this comes of the peace') that deictically foreground the agency of the 1814 settlement, making it the lens through which other kinds of temporality are mediated (19, 184, 90). The ways in which 'this' peace recalibrates the rhythms of life, including the seasons, is a sign, paradoxically, of how deeply British society and culture were imbued with the atmosphere of wartime, as Mary Favret has brilliantly argued. 'Romantic writers', she says, 'found it nearly impossible to imagine any space free from the pains – Austen's "tax" of warfare'.[81] An effect of *Persuasion*'s anachronism is the recognition of wartime as a permanent condition of modern life even when war is nominally 'over', meaning that peacetime is exceptional and can never endure: in other words, like the combustible pagoda, peace is ephemeral.[82]

Ephemeral peacetime, as well as seasonal, calendrical, and diurnal time, is linked with significant dates in Anne Elliot's familial and personal history – the death of her mother in 1801, the 'quick' few months of her love affair with Wentworth in 1806, and then, on 'the 29th September' 1814, the loss of her home at Kellynch, the direct result of the financial crisis for the Elliots caused by the end of the war (51).[83] As many commentators on *Persuasion* have noted, the novel's affective 'atmosphere' is pervaded by injury and loss – emotional, physical, and, in the sense of the war from which Britain has just emerged, the national death toll, in

---

[81] Favret, *War at a Distance*, 149–50.
[82] On Austen's uses of anachronism see Clara Tuite, '*Sanditon*: Austen's pre-post Waterloo', *Textual Practice*, 26:2 (2012), 609–29.
[83] The 29th of September represents another kind of season in *Persuasion*, the legal year, as it marks the beginning of Michaelmas term 'when the Crofts were to have possession' (35).

which Wentworth's death might have been chronicled, a possibility renewed at the end of the novel in the form of the 'tax of quick alarm' (275). In Anne Elliot's presence, Wentworth (deliberately testing his capacity to inflict a wound on her), narrates how he luckily escaped sinking with his ship, the *Asp*:

> Four-and-twenty hours later, and I should only have been a gallant Captain Wentworth, in a small paragraph at one corner of the newspapers; and being lost in only a sloop, nobody would have thought about me.'
> Anne's shudderings were to herself, alone . . . (71)

His emphasis on the speed with which his death would have been reported highlights the literally ephemeral quality of newspaper intelligence as the news of a day, quickly produced and forgotten. This episode represents another way in which *Persuasion* is 'dated': Anne's inner 'shudderings' give the day of Wentworth's death an imaginative reality that is revived at the end of the novel in the form of the 'tax of quick alarm'. Moreover, whether in war or in peace, such a day will inevitably occur. For Walter Scott, the achievement of *Emma* that distinguished it from other 'ephemeral productions' was the novelist's attention to the 'common walks of life' and to that which is 'daily taking place around' the reader. The 'dailiness' of *Persuasion* is, however, closer at times to the apprehension of an absolute ephemerality: the novel elaborates a wartime-suffused and mediatised sense of the evanescence of time that, in the form of Anne Elliot's 'shuddering' response to Wentworth's imagining of the day of his death, approaches the experience of the sublime.

The sense of ephemerality as an affect, an atmosphere, or medium, which, I would argue, is conditioned by the uncanny timeliness of 1814, is also apparent in the account of William Elliot's evening visit to the Elliot lodgings in Camden Place:

> He staid an hour with them. The elegant little clock on the mantel-piece had struck 'eleven with its silver sounds,' and the watchman was beginning to be heard at a distance telling the same tale, before Mr. Elliot or any of them seemed to feel that he had been there long. (156)[84]

This passage is concerned with time as a medium of sociability (and vice versa) and how time itself can be narrated or 'told'. The clock-time of the 'elegant' instrument on the mantelpiece chimes with the civic timekeeping of the Bath watchman whose voice, audible 'at a distance', signals the necessity for locking-up and night-time vigilance. This traditional

---

[84] The passage cites Pope's *Rape of the Lock*.

method of 'crying' the hour, often accompanied by bell-ringing, resonates with the fashionable technology of the clock in a way that synchronises indoor and outdoor worlds – the 'elegant' sociability of the Elliots and the darkening streets beyond. Both watchman and clock are reminders of the inexorable passing of time; both tell essentially the 'same tale'.

A less obvious mode of civic time-keeping is to be found in the description of Lady Russell's arrival in Bath, the noise and bustle of the town being more to her taste than the screaming children of Uppercross:

> When Lady Russell ... was entering Bath on a wet afternoon, and driving through the long course of streets from the Old Bridge to Camden-place, amidst the dash of other carriages, the heavy rumble of carts and drays, the bawling of newsmen, muffin-men and milk-men, and the ceaseless clink of pattens, she made no complaint. No, these were noises what belonged to the winter pleasures; her spirits rose under their influence; and, like Mrs. Musgrove, she was feeling though not saying, that, after being long in the country, nothing could be so good for her as a little quiet cheerfulness. (146–7)

The 'winter pleasures' that Lady Russell, as a widow of means, is free to enjoy, are the sociable activities and venues of Bath, including keeping up to date with the 'new publications' (233). She immerses herself in the traffic of the service industries of Bath that catered for visitors such as her: the delivery of both people and goods, as signified by the lumbering 'carts and drays'; the provision of perishable food-to-go (the muffins) and drink; the women 'clinking' in their pattens on the way to work as servants, laundry women, or milliners; and finally, the 'bawling newsmen', whose sound and significance I want to highlight.[85] Newsmen were an important element in what Robert Darnton described as the 'communications circuit' by which the print media, in this case mainly newspapers, connected producers and readers.[86] An essay in *The Metropolitan Magazine* of 1838 described newsmen as the 'class of persons through whom all the newspapers published in the metropolis are put, in the first instance, into circulation'.[87] The primary role of newsmen (whose ranks also included newsboys and sometimes newswomen) was to deliver newspapers as quickly as possible to subscribers. (The newsman differed from the hawker who sold newspapers to the public at large, 'crying' the title of a paper or a

---

[85] For a contemporary depiction of a muffin man see David Hansen, *Dempsey's People: A Folio of British Street Portraits 1824–1844* (Canberra: National Portrait Gallery, 2017), 188–9.
[86] Robert Darnton, 'What Is the History of Books?', in *The Book History Reader*, eds. David Finkelstein and Alistair McCleery (London: Routledge, 2002): 9–26 (11).
[87] 'The London Newsmen', *The Metropolitan Magazine*, 21 (1838), 41–8 (41).

headline, a practice that was a familiar sight and sound on British streets well into the twentieth century).[88] Newsmen would gather early in the morning outside the offices of newspapers and wholesale newsagents and run off with their bundles, a pattern repeated for the London evening editions, meaning that the work was arduous, consisting of up to fifteen hours on the move, seven days a week, for the payment of a penny per paper. Another account of the newsman described his work as 'an out-of-doors business at all seasons': 'he may be said to have been divorced, and to live "separate and apart" from society in general; for, though he mixes with every body, it is only for a few hurried moments, and as strangers do in a crowd'.[89] A rare insight into the life of a newsman was documented in the form of a broadside print, soliciting support for John Bexley (Figure 24).[90] Born in 1703, Bexley came from a poor family and worked firstly as a pedlar and then for forty-two years as a newsman for James Abree, the printer of the *Kentish Post* in Canterbury. The purpose of the print, published in 1788, was to raise funds for Bexley in the infirmity of his old age – he is described as 'bending in his Walk almost to the Earth'. It is likely that the print itself was advertised by handbills inserted in newspapers, meaning that Bexley's successors would have been instrumental in organising support for their elderly brother.

Newsmen could also deliver broadsheets, pamphlets, and books and, in some cases, independently operated a newspaper-lending service for those who could not afford the price of subscription. The newsman would wait while someone read the paper before he rushed to pass it to someone else, a practice that newspapers opposed as encroaching on their business. The newsman was thus always working to the clock, a standard complaint being the lateness of a delivery. The writer of the article for the *Gentleman's Pocket Magazine* reported how the death of a newsman occasioned the following punning response: '"We always said he *was*, and now we have proof that he *is* the *late* newsman"'.

The provision of a newspaper, like muffins and milk, was an essential part of the daily round of the consumer society of Bath. Scholars have recently drawn attention to the relevance of *Persuasion* to Romantic-period mediation and the history of the 'media concept'; with the 'bawling newsmen' Austen goes so far as to represent a certain kind of print

---

[88] C. Y. Ferdinand, *Benjamin Collins and the Provincial Newspaper Trade in the Eighteenth Century* (Oxford: Clarendon Press, 1997), 93.
[89] 'The Newsman', *Gentleman's Pocket Magazine and Album of Literature and Fine Arts*, 1 (1829), 347–52 (349).
[90] BM Prints and Drawings 1851,0308.80.

Figure 24 John Bexley, Fifty-Four Years the Canterbury News-Carrier. Engraving. [Rochester and Chatham: Gillman, 1788].
© The Trustees of the British Museum

communication – fugitive literature – as embodied and vocal, the newsman being, literally speaking, mediation on the run.[91] Moreover, the presence of the bawling newsman on the streets of Bath adumbrates other

[91] Guillory, 'Genesis of the Media Concept', 357 n. 60; Margaret Russett, 'Persuasion, Mediation', Studies in Romanticism, 53:3 (2014), 417–33.

hand-to-hand exchanges taking place daily in the city via jobbing and ephemeral print: tickets, bills of lading, playbills, receipts, and so on – and also, indirectly, more polite literary culture, such as the 'new publications' that Lady Russell is eager to pick up in town. The dating of *Persuasion* to around 1814 is important in another sense as that year, with the application of steam printing to the production of *The Times*, marks the beginning of the end of printing as predominantly a manual process, the work of many hands such as those of papermakers, compositors, and printers-devils, as well as distributors such as newsmen. In this respect it is noteworthy that Austen records the entry on the Elliots in the *Baronetage* which she 'reproduces' in her text as 'precisely' how the 'paragraph originally stood from the printer's hands' (rather than, for example, the bookseller's). This reference to the 'printer's hands' suggests a consciousness of book production and printing in general as a mechanical 'art' and the concomitant Enlightenment ideology of print as an engine of knowledge, the kind of 'wonder' that was celebrated in the 1814 frost fair and the Peace Jubilee and which Banks and Place were documenting.

It is also possible that the bawling newsmen were not, strictly speaking, newsmen on the run to subscribers but hawkers 'crying' the arrival of morning newspapers from London, as Austen 'times' Lady Russell's entry into Bath to the 'late afternoon' when the London papers would have arrived by express coach. Like the watchman calling eleven o'clock, the sounds of these newsmen were part of the diurnal pattern of urban life in Bath in which older forms of temporal observance were being overlaid by the rhythms of commerce. The genealogy of Austen's newsmen can be traced to the arrival of William Cowper's post boy in Book IV of *The Task*:

> ... the herald of a noisy world,
> With spatter'd boots, strapped waist, and frozen locks;
> News from all nations lumbr'ing at his back.
> True to his charge, the close pack'd load behind,
> Yet careless what he brings, his one concern
> Is to conduct it to the destin'd inn;
> And having dropped th'expected bag, pass on.[92]

Newsmen were primarily an urban phenomenon; the post boy (who also carried letters, bundling together the printed and the written word) was mainly responsible for delivering newspapers to the country. (Cowper omits the intermediary of the person who retrieves the newspapers from

---

[92] Cowper, *The Task*, 140–1.

the inn, presumably one of his servants). Like the newsman, the post boy is forever on the move, 'careless' of what news he brings, thereby embodying, more than the actual newspaper, a 'pure' form of mediation, a perpetual circulation that is 'careless' both of what it carries and even of time itself.

Another way in which newsmen could tell the time in the eighteenth century was through the ephemeral genre of 'newsmen's verses', broadsides, consisting of verses and often an accompanying image, that were distributed by newsmen to their customers. A means of soliciting a gratuity, newsmen's verses marked the end of the year and the advent of the Christmas season, making an otherwise invisible relationship momentarily visible through the granting of a gift (before the newsman disappeared again). As the *Gentleman's Pocket Magazine* noted, newsmen's verses were designed to 'remind every newspaper reader that the hand that bore it is open to a small boon'.[93] Such single-sheet verses were produced by jobbing printers for the use of not only newsmen but also bellmen (or watchmen) and lamplighters.[94] The tradition dates from at least the early eighteenth century when it was established enough to be adapted for satiric purposes: Narcissus Luttrell owned a copy of 'The State Bell-mans Collection of Verses, for the year 1711' that took aim at contemporary Whig politics.[95] The genre survived well into the nineteenth century. The essay on newsmen in the *Gentleman's Pocket Magazine* of 1829 begins by citing lines from '*Newsmen's Verses*, 1747' and concludes with reference to an example from 1826, while the British Library possesses a collection of newsmen's, lamplighters', and beadles' addresses dating from the 1750s to the 1840s.[96]

The 'bawling newsmen' of *Persuasion* are thus significant in having their own fugitive literary tradition, of which Austen may or may not have been aware. Newsmen's verses combined the work of anonymous hack poets, engravers, and enterprising jobbing printers, and exemplify the capacity of such print to make visible and to constitute a history of otherwise transient and fleeting dimensions of sociality and commerce. Rather than being the antithesis of the novel, the newsman's verse, though subsequently

---

[93] 'The Newsman', 352.   [94] See Rickards and Twyman, *Encyclopedia of Ephemera*, 46–7.
[95] 'The State Bell-mans Collection of Verses, for the year 1711' (London: John Morphew, 1710/11), Eighteenth Century Collections Online, ETSC no. T140664. The notes to the ECCO full citation state: 'Narcissus Luttrell's copy (now in the British Library) also has a MS. date: 1710/11. 24. Febr.'
[96] 'The Newsman', 347. The source of these stanzas was probably *The* READING *and* WINCHESTER *Newsmen's New Year's* VERSES, Jan. 1747', printed in *The Gentleman's Magazine*, 17 (1747), 192; [A collection of broadsides, including a number of Christmas carol-sheets and newsmen's, lamplighters' and beadles' Christmas addresses], BL pressmark 1875.d.8.

'ephemeral' and lost to history, was part of the same cultural continuum: that is, the circulation of knowledge sustained by print in all its myriad forms. Nor did the newsman's verse represent an unmediated popular voice; rather, it was in its own way as artificial and as 'literary' as the novel. The newsman's verse was the product of the same 'moment-centred consciousness' that gave rise to the novel, the ultimate significance of the genre being the possibility that even the most fleeting of human presences and voices could be instantiated (in the root sense of the term) via the 'poetry' of print.

In elaborating a poetics of ephemerality in order to tell a 'tale' of quick time, Austen ensured that *Persuasion* would not be an 'ephemeral production' but an enduring work of literature, making it exemplary of how the early nineteenth-century novel was able to transcend associations with 'trash' by its evocation of what Scott called the 'current of ordinary life'. This was accomplished in not only an aesthetic but also a material sense: by means of the genre of the novel the codex-form book was assimilated into the practices of everyday life, moving from the library to the drawing or work room, carried in pockets, read (and left behind) in coaches, and later in railway carriages and stations. It was through the familiarity of the novel-reading 'habitus' that imaginative literature became something to be 'loved', as Deidre Lynch has argued.[97] However, the novel always retained its essential bookishness, apparent in its occupation of the time of the reader, distracting her from other kinds of quick, transient reading. As much as it remediated the ephemeral textuality of cards, tickets, playbills, and newspapers, acting as a kind of repository, a de facto collection, the very material form of the novel, what Christina Lupton describes as its 'heft' and depth, declared a resistance to the absolute ephemeral, an unwillingness to let time go.[98]

In the specific contexts of 1814, Austen's representation of the world of the newsman inevitably resonated with the kind of questions about the post-war social order evident in the collections of Place and Banks. *Persuasion* has long been recognised as addressing the post-war condition of England by proposing the virtues of the naval 'family' as an alternative to a narcissistic ruling order, wilfully negligent of its social responsibilities and in retreat from active engagement in the wider public sphere, but

---

[97] Lynch, *Loving Literature*.
[98] Christina Lupton, *Reading and the Making of Time in the Eighteenth Century* (Baltimore, MD: Johns Hopkins University Press, 2018), 1, 2. In certain regards, Lupton's study reasserts, in the context of book and media history, the structural dependence of the novel and novel-reading on media forms that are quick, shallow, and not worth the time of reading, i.e. the ephemeral.

attention to the novel's 1814 topicality reveals just how far-reaching this analysis is. Sir Walter Elliot's obsession with the *Baronetage* is consistent with Sarah Sophia Banks's similar preoccupations with title and name: both are dependent on the print trade for substantiation of their attachment to rank. Like Edgeworth in *The Absentee*, Austen highlights the artificiality of social distinction by means of the visiting system. Sir Walter and Elizabeth Elliot's actual disengagement from society is signified by their reliance on the economy of the visiting card: they were 'perpetually having cards left by people of whom they knew nothing' and once they are successful in making the acquaintance of the Dowager Viscountess Dalrymple and her daughter, they arrange their cards 'wherever they might be most visible' (149, 162). Whereas in *Northanger Abbey* the language of cards is an essential part of Catherine Morland's sentimental education, opening doors of opportunity, cards in *Persuasion* perform an empty ritual of exclusivity, representing connections that in Anne's eyes are 'nothing' (162). In this case, the bustle and noise of the streets of Bath, including the bawling newsmen, take on added significance as representing a more vital world out of doors from which Camden Place is estranged (in a way that is similar to the relationship between the Jubilee fair of Hyde Park and the exclusivity of the empty Royal Booth).

Lady Russell is barely aware of the newsmen amongst the cacophonous noises of urban Bath but Austen is. The novelist brings them together in a way that recognises carelessness as a particular feature of a mediatised, modern, busy world, that is carelessness in the sense of lack of care or consideration of others, leading to the invisibility of men such as John Bexley and the need for newsmen to claim the 'boon' of occasional recognition. Equally, though, carelessness can be a kind of independence in the sense of being free from care, what we might call the pleasurable anonymity of the everyday. In this sense Lady Russell's arrival in Bath anticipates the reunion of Anne Elliot and Captain Wentworth at the end of the novel, in 'the comparatively quiet and retired gravel-walk'. Connecting the Royal Crescent with Queen's Square and established in 1771, the gravel walk was secluded from the noisy streets of the city: it was open to the public as a whole for temporary escape from the busy world beyond. Here the couple 'slowly pace the gradual ascent, heedless of every group around them, seeing neither sauntering politicians, bustling house-keepers, flirting girls, nor nursery-maids and children' (261–2). For once in this 'quick' novel, time slows down as Anne Elliot and Captain Wentworth recover their love amongst the 'accidental' democracy of the street, comparable to 'motley groups' of a universal public sphere signified by the history of the frost fair or the 1814 Jubilee. By 'sauntering politicians' Austen was referring to men of leisure of all classes who believed themselves to be entitled to discuss politics in the coffeehouse, the tavern, or here on the gravel walk: their superannuated status is indicated by the fact that they are in the company mainly of women – housekeepers 'bustling', cheeky teenage girls, maids delaying the return to the nursery. If Anne Elliot and Wentworth are 'heedless' of those sharing the gravel walk with them, the crowd is equally oblivious of them, a sign, like Lady Russell's arrival in Bath, of how the commercialisation of culture, of which Bath was the epitome, was dissolving distinctions of status whereby social elites inevitably commanded attention. The genealogy of this scene can be traced back to how the media revolution of the seventeenth century inaugurated the ephemeral 'new present' that was constitutive of modern historicity. It is in the romance of this 'new present' that Austen locates Anne and Captain Wentworth, representing an essentially mediatised consciousness of a present that is simultaneously everything and nothing – that comes and inevitably disappears. As Maurice Blanchot argued, the everyday always 'escapes' and the carelessness of the people with whom Anne Elliot and Wentworth ascend the gravel walk represents a sense of the elusiveness of sociality and the pleasures, in this case, of being 'nothing'. Blanchot also described the everyday as 'the movement by which the individual is held, as though without knowing it, in human anonymity'.[99] The idea of being 'held' resonates with how Wentworth and Anne Elliot are figuratively carried or buoyed by those around them. Rather than the 'everyday' as a sign for the comforting ordinariness of existence, the background noise or hum of what always surrounds us, the everyday of *Persuasion* is finally a time of escape from, as well as into, the plenitude of 'nothing'. The novel tells the tale of 'quick' time, where days come and go, and the most sustaining comfort is being able to walk amongst the careless, ephemeral, democracy of strangers.

---

[99] Blanchot, 'Everyday Speech', 17.

Conclusion

In their account of Romantic poetry as a medium, Celeste Langan and Maureen McLane argue that poetry, unlike the novel, 'had a stronger claim to be considered a supermedial transhistorical venture'.[1] However, the fiction of Austen and Edgeworth suggests that the novel too had aspirations to be a 'supermedium' by incorporating and aestheticising the experience of 'common life'. The society novel in particular achieved this by assimilating the printed ephemera of polite sociability: it remediated the paper filters that facilitated social life in the eighteenth century in order to make the interstices or hyphenations of sociable life, spaces occupied by women in particular, more visible as an appropriate object of fiction. As I suggested previously, the affect of the ephemeral social encounter, the transience of events that flicker to life and disappear, were the common subject of Sarah Sophia Banks and Jane Austen, the former's assemblages of tickets for balls and assemblies and the latter's novels textualising the same phenomenon. The evocation in ephemeral print of 'common life' as a kind of diurnal historiography was the context in which the novel became central to the affective rhythms and routines of human activity, establishing an idea of the everyday as intimate, familiar, and reassuring rather than as something that was estranging in its absolute anonymity or carelessness, something to 'fear' in Blanchot's terms. The materiality of the codex form of the novel, its solidity and tendency to take the reader's time while being portable and adaptable to both private and social life, allowed the novel to remediate the specificity of social and affective experience but also to defend both itself and the reader from the abyss of entropic ephemerality. The novel thus capitalises upon an idea of the everyday that it simultaneously resists. Arguably, however, as a literary form most closely linked with the second printing revolution, with which its 'rise' coincided, the novel never completely escaped its affiliation with ephemera, as

---

[1] Langan and McLane, 'Medium of Romantic Poetry', 255.

indicated by the enduring association of the novel and novel-reading with trashy, 'ephemeral productions', with that which wastes time rather than redeems it.

What of the category of the everyday itself? If printed ephemera and the codex-form book define each other in the course of the eighteenth century and beyond, the category of printed ephemera, the idea of ephemerality, and the activities of the ephemerologists informed the awareness of the everyday as a defining feature of modernity. In *The Ephemeral Eighteenth Century* I have argued that the idea of the everyday is largely a function of media change, having its genesis in the 'new present' defined in the seventeenth century by media such as the news-sheet, retail and commissioned broadsides in general, and the 'stitch'd book'. The impact of this change was mediated in turn by 'gentlemen who made collections' and the para-discipline of ephemerology that, like popular antiquarianism as a whole, was subsumed in the disciplines that emerged from it in the nineteenth century. One of these disciplines, as I have argued, was historical bibliography, indebted to the collectors' method of placing documents 'in tyme' and shaped by attention to the radical contingency of the paper spectrum as a whole, exemplified by the 'wild bibliography' of figures such as Joseph Haslewood. For literary Romanticism, including the novel, ephemeral historicity was formative, both as something from which to make lyric capital and also as something to hold at bay, because of the proximity of ephemerality to anonymous, overwhelmingly inchoate experience.

The activities of the ephemerologists as compilers and systematisers of documents, curious ethnographers of local and national customs, as well as topographical and print historians, also ramified into other disciplines, as Marilyn Butler recognised. John Brewer has acknowledged the origins of the micro-history of everyday life in the work of antiquarians, while cultural studies, media history, and the recent development of media archaeology, for which phenomena such as ballooning and panorama are important, can be linked with the interests and methodologies of Banks, Lysons, Upcott, Haslewood, and others.[2] Indeed, I have suggested, following Jacky Bratton, that one of the reasons why theatre history struggled to assert itself as a legitimate scholarly discipline was its reliance on playbills, tickets, and other kinds of memorabilia that were too closely connected to the ephemerality of the performance event. Finally, I would

---

[2] Brewer, 'Microhistory', 91; Erkki Huhtamo, *Illusions in Motion: Media Archaeology of the Moving Panorama and Related Spectacles* (Cambridge, MA: MIT Press, 2013).

also wish to suggest that ephemerology is part of the genealogy of the materialist cultural history and philosophy of as important a figure as Walter Benjamin, whose *Arcades Project* can be regarded as a symbiosis of the catalogue and the collection, the German term for his system of organising his material, 'das Konvolut', meaning a bundle of papers.

The enduring impact of ephemerology on the humanities is signified by the fact that many of the collections discussed in this book eventually found their way to (or just turned up in) the British Museum and the British Library. Beginning with the ephemera collections of Sir Hans Sloane, the Museum became a repository for the papers collected, systematised, and described by Thomason, Luttrell, Bagford, Banks, Burney Jr, Place, and Lysons, many of which constitute the British Library's important databases today. Many collections still remain invisible, however, 'buried', in Samuel Ayscough's term, as substrates of a substrate – that is, the system of cataloguing based on authorship of the book developed by Panizzi in the nineteenth century, later refined and expanded by the English Short Title Catalogue in the twentieth century but still using ephemera to define the boundaries of print.

The ephemerologists' long-standing commitment to the capacity of print to penetrate and describe the world and to constitute knowledge of its ephemerality is signified in this book by Wood's advertisement for the Indian king, Banks's Omai visiting card and butterfly ball tickets, the Sydney playbill, the 'window' of Place's Jubilee fair poster, or the myriad examples of frost fair ephemera flowing through this period and beyond, like the Thames on which they were momentarily manufactured. While the British Museum library put a halt to acquiring collections of ephemera in the 1890s, ephemerology did not disappear, as indeed it could not, as it marks the necessary place where institutions of knowledge in the humanities, or broadly speaking, the archive, have their commencement.[3] Men and women such as Lysons, Banks, and Place had twentieth-century successors in John Johnson, the history of whose collections and their institutional status initially on the margins of the Bodleian Library into which they were eventually assimilated, places him in a long line of ephemerologists. Johnson was responding to changes in the media in the 1920s, as indeed those who founded the Ephemera Society in the 1970s were also reacting to the media revolutions of the 1960s and the ambitions of higher education and national libraries. In the twenty-first century ephemerality continues to signify concerns about the overflow of

---

[3] Harris, *History*, 403.

information, its evanescence, and questions of what or should be preserved: ephemerality conditions the transformation of written communication in the digital sphere, as much as it did in the second phase of the print era. However, the digital era does not represent the eclipse or decentring of the book in a way that elevates printed ephemera to a status it should have had; nor is the collection as an assemblage of assemblages simply a database *avant la lettre*. Though digital textuality enables us to conceive print culture in a different way that recognises the diversity of the paper spectrum, it is not non-book print without the codex-form book, but something different, the scope and limits of which of which are yet to be fully understood. Ephemerology presents a challenge to the idea that there is no data beyond what can be data-processed because it suggests that there is always beyond social media an absolute ephemeral. On the other hand, however, ephemerology also offers the utopian possibility that the need to process the data of the world could be rendered unnecessary and that the 'thing' – sociality's momentariness – could be realised as itself, in other words, as the impossibly unmediated. John Johnson himself suggested something like this in 1937 when he wrote to a correspondent that his 'little museum' in the printery could 'never have a catalogue. For the catalogue would be as big as itself. Therefore the disposition of the material has got to be its own catalogue and self evident'.[4] The ephemera collection was a kind of anti-catalogue or anti-library, signifying the 'miscellany of the world' that simply is. Johnson, like Banks and the other ephemerologists, were men and women that had no 'fear' of confronting the absolute anonymity that Blanchot claimed was fundamental to everyday life. Their romanticism was the exhilaration of preserving the traces of what was always already lost, in the knowledge that, as Marilyn Butler movingly wrote of popular antiquarianism in 1999: 'the local, particular data provided by the many would always be needed. There were no winners, except the group.'[5]

---

[4] John Johnson to Nicolette Gray, 14 June 1937, Johnson MS c.18 f. 316, Bodleian Library, University of Oxford.
[5] Butler, 'Antiquarianism (Popular)', 338.

Bibliography

Manuscripts and Archives

BL ADD MS 32640 Glossaries of words in the Lincolnshire dialect collected by Sarah Sophia Banks.
BL ADD MSS 34721 A & B, covering the period 1793–1807. Sarah Sophia Banks collection of material on archery.
Bodleian Library Oxford, Papers and Correspondence of John de Monins Johnson.
National Library of Australia. MS 9-Papers of Sir Joseph Banks, 1745–1923 (bulk 1745–1820).
UK National Archives Home Office Papers, 42–19.

Prints and Drawings

BM Department of Prints and Drawings Collections of Sarah Sophia Banks.
BM Department of Prints and Drawings William Blake, Visiting Cards for George Cumberland.

Coins and Medals

BM Department of Coins and Medals Collections of Sarah Sophia Banks.

Newspapers and Journals

British Critic.
Bury and Norwich Post.
Courier.
Daily Advertiser.
Diary, or Woodfall's Register.
European Magazine.
Examiner.
Fraser's Magazine.

Gazetteer.
General Advertiser.
General Evening Post.
Gentleman's Magazine.
Gentleman's Pocket Magazine and Album of Literature and Fine Arts.
Jackson's Oxford Journal.
Kirby's Wonderful and Eccentric Museum.
Lancaster Gazette and General Advertiser.
Leeds Intelligencer.
Lloyd's Evening Post.
London Chronicle.
Mercurius cambro-Britannus, the Brittish Mercury, or, The Welch diurnall communicating remarkable Intelligences and true Newes to awle the whole kingdome ...
Metropolitan Magazine.
Morning Chronicle.
Morning Post.
New Monthly Magazine.
Oracle and Public Advertiser.
Public Advertiser.
Public Ledger.
Star.
Tait's Edinburgh Magazine.
The Times.

Catalogues in Order by Date, Earliest to Latest

Catalogus variorum & insignium librorum instructissimae bibliothecae clarissimi doctissimiq viri Lazari Seaman, S.T.D. quorum auctio habebitur Londini in aedibus defuncti in area & viculo Warwicensi Octobris ultimo / cura Gulielmi Cooper. Londini: Apud Ed Brewster & Guil. Cooper, 1676. Wing/ S2173. Early English Books Online.

A Compleat Catalogue of All the Stitch'd Books and Single Sheets Printed since the Discovery of The Popish Plot (September 1678) to January 1679/80. To which is Added a Catalogue of all His Majesties Proclamations, Speeches, and Declarations with the Orders of the King and Council and what Acts of Parliament have been Published since the Plot. The Continuation is Intended by the Publisher. London: 1680. Wing/ 310:12, Early English Books Online.

General Catalogue of All the Stitch'd Books and Single Sheets &c. Printed the Last Two Years, Commencing from the First Discovery of the Popish Plot (September, 1678) and Continued to Michaelmas Term, 1680. London: J. R., 1680. Wing/ 1671:02. Early English Books Online.

A Complete Collection of Books and Pamphlets Begun in the Year 1640. by the Special Command of King Charles I. of Blessed Memory. London, 1685. Wing (CD-ROM, 1996)/ T995A. Early English Books Online.

A Catalogue of Books, The Library of the late Rev. Dr. Swift. Dublin: printed for George Faulkner, 1745.

Edwards, Anthony. *Catalogue of Books, in Most Branches of Literature.* Cork: Anthony Edwards, 1785.

A Catalogue of the Valuable Library, of Edward Wynne, Esq. London: Leigh and Sotheby, 1786.

Books, Prints, Drawings, Manuscripts, &c. A Catalogue of the Genuine Library of Books, . . . of a Gentleman, Deceased. London: Thomas King, 1797.

A Catalogue of the Curious and Extensive Library of the Late James Bindley, Esq. F. S. A. London: Evans, 1820.

Bibliotheca Histrionica. A Catalogue of the Theatrical and Miscellaneous Library of Mr. John Field. London: Sotheby, 1827.

Catalogue of a Portion of the Very Valuable Library of the Rev. Daniel Lysons, the Duke of Cassano and Another Collection. London: Evans, 1828.

Catalogue of the Library of the Splendid, Curious, and Valuable Library, of the Late Philip Hurd, Esq. London: R. Evans, 1832.

Catalogue of the Curious and Valuable Library of the Late Joseph Haslewood, Esq. F.S.A. London: Evans, 1833.

Catalogue of the Rare and Bijoux Portion . . . from the Library of Mr. J. W. Southgate . . . A Large Assemblage of Broadsides, Old Ballads, Scraps, &c. Collected by the late Isaac Reed Esq . . . London: Southgate, Grimston and Wells, 1833.

Catalogue of a Collection of Miscellaneous Books, Including Many on Angling: The Property of the Late Mr. Boosey. London: Leigh Sotheby, [1841].

Catalogue of Printed Books in the British Museum. Vol. I. London: British Museum, 1841.

Catalogue of the Library of the Late William Upcott, Esq. [London]: Atkins & Andrew, [1846]), 65, BL pressmark 11902.g.44.

Catalogue of the Principal Part of the Library of Dawson Turner, Esq. London: Sotheby & Wilkinson, 1853.

Catalogue of the Pepys Library at Magdalene College Cambridge, Volume III: Prints and Drawings; Part i: General. Compiled by A. W. Aspital. Cambridge: Rowman & Littlefield, 1980.

Other Primary Sources

[A collection of broadsides, cuttings from newspapers, engravings, etc., of various dates, formed by Miss S. S. Banks. Bound in nine volumes] BL pressmark L.R.301.h.3–11.

[A collection of broadsides, including a number of Christmas carol-sheets and newsmen's, lamplighters' and beadles' Christmas addresses], BL pressmark 1875.d.8.

[A collection of extracts from periodicals and newspapers on Chatterton and his work], BL pressmark 1870.c.20.

[A collection of handbills, newspaper cuttings, etc., relating to lotteries between 1802 and 1826, formed by Dawson Turner. With a MS. note by the collector], BL pressmark 8225.bb.78.

A collection of playbills from miscellaneous theatres: Huddersfield-Ledbury 1783–1864, 2 vols., BL pressmark Playbills 291.

[A collection of playbills, notices and press-cuttings dealing with private theatrical performances, 1750–1808], BL pressmark 937.g.96.

'A Dead Wall'. *The Leisure Hour* (18 August 1859): 526–8.

'A Relation of the extraordinary Thunder and Lightning which lately happened in the North of Ireland'. In *Second Continuation Narcissus Luttrell's Popish Plot Catalogues*. Introduced by F. C. Francis. Oxford: Basil Blackwell, 1956.

'A View of the Frost Fair as it Appeared on the Ice on the River Thames Fby 3d 1814,' BM 1880,1113.1760.

Alley, Jerom. *Observations on the Government and Constitution of Great Britain, including a vindication of the both from the aspersions of some late writers, particularly Dr. Price, Dr. Priestley, and Mr. Paine*. Dublin: William Sleater, 1792.

Anon., *Londons Wonder: Being a Most True and positive relation of the taking and killing of a great Whale neer to Greenwich* ... London: Francis Grove, 1658. Wing (2nd edn)/ L2957, Thomason/ E.2134 [2]. Early English Books Online.

[Anon.], 'Waverley; or 'Tis Sixty Years Since'. *Monthly Museum: or, Dublin Literary Repertory of Arts, Science, Literature and Miscellaneous Information* 2 (September 1814): 225–30.

Anon., 'It is thought fit by divers persons of quality, who met on Friday last at *Scriveners Hall*, to advise how just debts may be secured ... to the Parliament. ... This 16 of August, 1644' [London: 1644], Wing (2nd edn)/ I1088, Thomason E.6[18], Early English Books Online.

Association Papers: Part I. Publications printed by special order of the Society for preserving Liberty and Property against Republicans and Levellers, at the Crown and Anchor, in the Strand. Part II. A Collection of tracts, printed at the expence of that society. London: J. Sewell et al., 1793.

An Asylum for Fugitives: Published Occasionally. 2 vols. London: J. Almon, 1776.

Austen, Jane. *Jane Austen's Letters*. Ed. Deirdre le Faye. 4th edn. Oxford: Oxford University Press, 2011.

Austen, Jane. *Northanger Abbey*. Eds. Barbara M. Benedict and Deirdre le Faye. Cambridge, UK: Cambridge University Press, 2006.

Austen, Jane. *Persuasion*. Eds. Janet Todd and Antje Blank. Cambridge, UK: Cambridge University Press, 2006.

Banks, Joseph. *The Letters of Sir Joseph Banks: A Selection, 1768–1820*. Ed. Neil Chambers. London: Imperial College Press, 2000.

Banks, Sir Joseph. *Scientific Correspondence of Sir Joseph Banks, 1765–1820*. Ed. Neil Chambers. 6 vols. London: Pickering & Chatto, 2007.

Banks, Sir Joseph. *Supplementary Letters of Sir Joseph Banks*. Ed. Warren R. Dawson. London: The Trustees of the British Museum, 1962.

Banks, Sir Joseph. *The Banks Letters: A Calendar of the Manuscript Correspondence of Sir Joseph Banks, Preserved in the British Museum, the British Museum (Natural History) and Other Collections in Great Britain.* Ed. Warren R. Dawson. London: British Museum, 1958.
[Birchall, Samuel]. *An Alphabetical List of Provincial Copper-Coins or Tokens.* Leeds: Thomas Gill, 1796.
Boaden, James. *Memoirs of the Life of John Philip Kemble.* 2 vols. in 1 London: Colburn, 1825.
Burke, Edmund. *The Writings and Speeches of Edmund Burke: The French Revolution, 1790–1794.* Ed. Paul Langford. Oxford: Clarendon Press, 1989.
Burney, Frances. *The Court Journals and Letters of Frances Burney.* Vols. III and IV. Ed. Lorna J. Clark. Oxford: Oxford University Press, 2014.
'Charles Mathews, Esq.,' *The Mirror of Literature, Amusement, and Instruction.* 26 (1835): 44–7.
Cowper, William. *The Task and Selected Other Poems.* Ed. James Sambrook. London: Routledge, 1994.
Coleridge, Samuel Taylor. *Collected Letters of Samuel Taylor Coleridge.* Ed. E. L. Griggs. 2 vols. Oxford: Clarendon Press, 1956.
Collins, David. *An Account of the English Colony in New South Wales.* London: Cadell & Davies, 1798.
Crabbe, George. *The News-Paper: A Poem.* London: J. Dodsley, 1785.
Curiosities of Street Literature. London: Reeves and Turner, 1871.
Dibdin, Thomas Frognall. *Bibliomania; or Book Madness.* London: Printed for the author, 1811.
Dibdin, Thomas Frognall. *Reminiscences of a Literary Life.* London: John Major, 1836.
Dickens, Charles. 'Bill-sticking'. *Household Words.* 52 (22 March 1851): 601–6.
Dickens, Charles. *Bleak House.* Ed. Norman Page. Harmondsworth: Penguin, 1971.
Dickens, Charles. *Dombey and Son.* Ed. Alan Horsman. Oxford: Clarendon Press, 1974.
Dickens, Charles. *Martin Chuzzlewit.* Ed. Margaret Cardwell. Oxford: Clarendon Press, 1982.
Dupré, William. *Lexicographica-Neologica Gallica: The Neological French Dictionary.* London: R. Philips, I. and T. Carpenter, and W. Clement, 1801.
Edgeworth, Maria. *Popular Tales.* 3 vols. 4th edn. London: Joseph Johnson, 1811.
Edgeworth, Maria. *The Absentee.* Eds. W. J. McCormack and Kim Walker. Oxford: Oxford University Press, 1988.
Edgeworth, Maria. *The Life and Letters of Maria Edgeworth.* Ed. Augustus Hare. 2 vols. Boston: Houghton Mifflin & Co., 1895.
Evelyn, John. *The Diary of John Evelyn.* Ed. Guy de la Bédoyère. Woodbridge: Boydell & Brewer, 1995.
Farington, Joseph. *The Diary of Joseph Farington.* Eds. Kenneth Garlick and Angus MacIntyre. 16 vols. New Haven, CT: Yale University Press, 1978.

[Feltham, John]. *The Picture of London, for 1804*. London: Richard Phillips, 1804.

For the benefit of J. Butler and W. Bryant: at the Theatre, Sydney on July 30, 1796 will be performed Jane Shore ... [Sydney: George Hughes, Govt. Printer for Theatre, Sydney, 1796], National Library of Australia RBRS N 686.2099441 F692.

Frostiana: or a History of the River Thames, in a Frozen State, with an Account of the Late Severe Frost. London: G. Davis, 1814.

[Jacob, Giles]. *The Poetical Register; or, the lives and characters of the English Dramatick Poets; with an account of their writings. (An Historical Account of the lives and writings of our most considerable English Poets)*. London: E. Curll, 1720/21.

Genest, John. *Some Account of the English Stage, from the Restoration in 1660 to 1830*. 10 vols. Bath: H. E. Carrington, 1832.

Godwin, William. Diary. http://godwindiary.bodleian.ox.ac.uk.

Godwin, William. *History of the Commonwealth of England*. 6 vols. Vol. III. London: Henry Colburn, 1824–28.

Godwin, William. *Political and Philosophical Writings of William Godwin, Volume II: Political Writings II*. Ed. Mark Philp. London: Pickering & Chatto, 1993.

Hartwell Horne, Thomas. *An Introduction to the Study of Bibliography*. 2 vols. London: Cadell and Davies, 1814.

[Haslewood, Joseph]. 'Of Plays, Players, and Play-Houses, with other incidental matter'. 8 vols. BL pressmark 11791 dd. 18.

Haslewood, Joseph. *Some Account of the Life and Publications of the Late Joseph Ritson, Esq*. London: Robert Triphook, 1824.

An Historical Memento, Representing the Different Scenes of Public Rejoicing, which took place the first of August, in St James's and Hyde Parks, London, in Celebration of The Glorious Peace of 1814. London: Edward Orme, 1814.

Holcroft, Thomas. *The Adventures of Hugh Trevor*. Ed. Seamus Deane. Oxford: Oxford University Press, 1978.

Howell, T. J. *A Complete Collection of State Trials*. Vol. XXIII. London: Longman, Hurst, Rees, Orme, and Brown, et al., 1817.

Hunt, Leigh. 'The Play-Bills'. *The Tatler* 12 (17 September 1830): 45.

'JAMES WINSTON, Esq'. *Gentleman's Magazine* 174 (September 1843): 325–6.

'John Fawcett, Esq'. *Gentleman's Magazine*. New series 7 (1837): 550–2.

Johnson, Samuel. *A Dictionary of the English Language*. 2 vols. 2nd edn. London: W. Strahan, 1755.

Johnson, Samuel. *A Dictionary of the English Language*. 10th edn. London: Rivington et al., 1792.

Johnson, Samuel. 'Proposals for the *Harleian Miscellany*. An Account of this Undertaking'. In *Samuel Johnson*. Ed. Donald Greene. Oxford: Oxford University Press, 1984.

[Johnson, Samuel]. *The Rambler. Volume the Sixth*. London: J. Payne, 1752.

Johnson, Samuel. *The Works of Samuel Johnson, Volumes III–V: The Rambler*. Eds. W. J. Bate and Albrecht B. Strauss. New Haven, CT: Yale University Press, 1969.

Luttrell, Narcissus. *A Brief Historical Relation of State Affairs from September 1678 to April 1714*. 6 vols. Oxford: Oxford University Press, 1857.

Malone, Edmund. Ed. *The Critical and Miscellaneous Prose Works of John Dryden*. 3 vols. London: Cadell and Davies, 1800.

Mayhew, Henry. 'Of the Street Sellers of Play-Bills'. *London Labour and the London Poor*. London: George Woodfall, 1851. 287–9.

Mortimer, Thomas. *The Universal Director: Or, the Nobleman and Gentleman's True Guide to the Masters and Professors of the Liberal and Polite Arts and Sciences*. London: J. Coote, 1763.

Nichol, John. *Literary Anecdotes of the Eighteenth Century*. 6 vols. London: John Nichols, 1812.

O. P. Riots. Exhibitions. – Panoramas. – Peace Jubilee and Sundries. 1807–1809. MS Radical Politics and the Working Man in England. Set 59; Vol. I. British Library. Nineteenth Century Collections Online. Gale Cengage.

O. P. Riots. Exhibitions. – Panoramas. – Peace Jubilee and Sundries. 1809–1814. MS Radical Politics and the Working Man in England Set 59; Vol. II. British Library. Nineteenth Century Collections Online. Gale Cengage.

Parliamentary Papers: Consisting of a Complete Collection of Kings Speeches. 3 vols. London: J. Debrett, 1797.

Plato's Advice, a new Song [London?, 1760?]. Eighteenth Century Collections Online. ESTC no. 12150.

Plumptre, James. *James Plumptre's Britain: The Journals of a Tourist in the 1790s*. Ed. Ian Ousby. London: Hutchinson, 1992.

'Progress of a Player', BM, 1948,0214.339.

Pye, Charles. *Provincial Copper Coins or Tokens, issued between the years 1787 and 1796* [London: Charles Pye, 1795].

Rider, William. *A New Universal English Dictionary*. London: W. Griffin for I. Pottinger, 1759.

Savage, William. *A Dictionary of the Art of Printing*. London: Longman, Brown, Green and Longmans, 1841.

Scott, Sir Walter. *The Miscellaneous Prose Works of Sir Walter Scott*. 6 vols. Edinburgh: Cadell, 1827.

[Scott, Walter]. 'ART. IX. *Emma; a Novel. By the Author of Sense and Sensibility, Pride and Prejudice, &c'*. *The Quarterly Review* (October 1815): 188–201.

Scott, Walter. *Heart of Midlothian*. Ed. Tony Inglis. Harmondsworth: Penguin, 1994.

Smith, Charles Manby. *The Little World of London: or, Pictures in Little of London Life*. London: Hall & Virtue, 1857.

Smith, J. T. *A Book for a Rainy Day: or Recollections of the Events of the Last Sixty-Six years*. London: Richard Bentley, 1845.

Southey, Robert. *Life and Correspondence*. Ed. C. C. Southey. 6 vols. London: Longman, Brown, Green & Longmans, 1849.

[Taylor, W.] *This book belongs to W. Taylor's Circulating Library, In Church-street, Kingston Buildings, Bath, where books are to be lent to read at 10s. 6d. at year, 4s. a Quarter, and 2s. a Month, sells all sorts of Bibles, Common-Prayers, &c.*

[...] *gilt and plain Message Cards; Visiting Tickets; and every other Article in the Bookselling or Stationary Branches, at the lowest* Prices. [Bath], [1770?].

Thale, Mary (ed.). *Selections from the Papers of the London Corresponding Society 1792–1799*. Cambridge, UK: Cambridge University Press, 1983.

Theatre-Royal Liverpool ... This present SATURDAY will be performed August 21, 1830, Rowe's celebrated Tragedy of Jane Shore. [Liverpool: Melling and Co., 1830]. Ashford collection of theatre playbills from English theatres from English theatres between 1796 and 1905. National Library of Australia.

'The Newsman'. *Gentleman's Pocket Magazine and Album of Literature and Fine Arts* 1 (1829): 347–52.

The Maid of Kent. 3 vols. London: T. Hookham, 1790.

'The True and Exact Representation of the Wonders upon the Water, During the Last Unparallel'd Frost'. BM 1880, 1113.1770.

'The Solemn Mock Procession of the Pope, Cardinalls, Jesuits, Fryers, Nuns exactly taken as they marcht through the Citty of London November the 17th, 1680'. BM 1849,0315.67; BM 1871,1209.6509.

'The Solemn Mock Procession of the Pope, Cardinalls, Jesuits, Fryers &c. through the City of London, November the 17th, 1679'. BM 1849,0315.69.

The Spectator. Ed. Donald F. Bond. 5 vols. Oxford: Clarendon Press, 1965.

The State Bell-mans Collection of Verses, for the year 1711. London: John Morphew, 1710/11. Eighteenth Century Collections Online. ETSC no. T140664.

The Trial of the Rev. Thomas Fyshe Palmer, Before the Circuit Court of Justiciary, held at Perth, on the 12th and 13th September, 1793. Edinburgh: W. Skirving, 1793.

'To the Right Honourable the House of Commons assembled in Parliament, the humble petition of James Rossington, Clarke'. [London: 1675]. Wing 2nd edn]/ R1995A. Early English Books Online.

Truth and Treason! Or a Narrative of the Royal Procession to the House of Peers, October the 29th, 1795. London: n.p., 1795.

Wallington, Nehemiah. *The Notebooks of Nehemiah Wallington, 1618–1654: A Selection*. Ed. David Booy. Aldershot: Ashgate, 2007.

Walpole, Horace. *Fugitive Pieces in Verse and Prose*. London: Strawberry Hill, 1758.

Wanley, Humfrey. 'An Account of Mr. Bagford's Collections for His History of Printing, by Mr. Humfrey Wanley'. *Philosophical Transactions* 25 (1706–7): 2407–10, [London: B. Walford, 1708].

Wednesday, August 16th 1797, Diversions on Tunbridge-Wells Common ... [Tunbridge Wells: Jasper Sprange, 1797].

Where little wherries once did use to ride ... [London: Printed at Holme's and Broad's Booth, at the sign of the Ship, against Old Swan-Stairs, where is the only real Printing-Press on the frozen Thames. January the 14th, 1715/16]. Eighteenth Century Collections Online. Gale Cengage. ESTC no. T052370.

[Wood, Anthony]. *The Life and Times of Anthony Wood, Antiquary, of Oxford, 1632–1695, Described by Himself.* Ed. Andrew Clark. 5 vols. Oxford: Clarendon Press, 1891.
Wordsworth, William. *The Prelude: The Four Texts (1798, 1799, 1805, 1850).* Ed. Jonathan Wordsworth. Harmondsworth: Penguin, 1995.

Secondary Sources

Ablow, Rachel. *The Feeling of Reading: Affective Experience and Victorian Literature.* Ann Arbor: University of Michigan Press, 2010.
Adorno, Theodor W. *Prisms.* Trans. Samuel Weber and Shierry Weber. Cambridge, MA: MIT Press, 1983.
Alston, R. C. 'A Provincial Printer at Work'. *Factotum* 10 (December 1980): 6–7.
  'The Eighteenth-Century Non-Book: Observations on Printed Ephemera'. In *The Book and Book Trade in Eighteenth-Century Europe.* Eds. Giles von Barber and Bernhard Fabian. Hamburg: Dr. Ernst Hauswedell & Co., 1981. 343–60.
Altick, Richard D. *The Shows of London.* London: Belknap, 1978.
Atherton, Jonathan. 'Rioting, Dissent and the Church in Late Eighteenth Century Britain: The Priestley Riots of 1791'. PhD thesis. University of Leicester, 2012.
'Australians Delight in Canada's Gift of Historic Document'. 2 February 2006. [www.collectionscanada.gc.ca/whats-new/013-301.1-e.html, accessed 1 December 2008].
Baer, Marc. *Theatre and Disorder in Late Georgian London.* Oxford: Clarendon Press, 1992.
Barrell, John. *'Exhibition Extraordinary!!' Radical Broadsides of the mid 1790s.* Nottingham: Trent Editions, 2001.
Barrell, John. *Imagining the King's Death: Figurative Treason, Fantasies of Regicide, 1793–1796.* Oxford: Oxford University Press, 2000.
  'Radicalism, Visual Culture, and Spectacle in the 1790s'. *Romanticism on the Net* 46 (2007): 1–30.
Batey, Charles. 'Johnson, John de Monins (1882–1956)'. Rev. Julie Anne Lambert. *Oxford Dictionary of National Biography.* Oxford University Press, 2004. [www.oxforddnb.com/view/article/34203, accessed 25 January 2017].
Benedict, Barbara M. *Curiosity: A Cultural History of Early Modern Inquiry.* Chicago: University of Chicago Press, 2002.
Benjamin, Walter. *Selected Writings: 1913–1926.* Eds. Marcus Bullock and Michael W. Jennings. Cambridge, MA: Harvard University Press, 1996.
  The Arcades Project. Trans. Howard Eiland and Kevin McLaughlin. Cambridge, MA: Harvard University Press, 1991.
Berg, Maxine and Helen Clifford. 'Selling Consumption in the Eighteenth Century: Advertising and the Trade Card in Britain and France'. *Cultural and Social History* 4:2 (2007): 145–70.

Bewell, Alan. '"On the banks of the South Sea": Botany and Sexual Controversy in the Late Eighteenth Century'. In *Visions of Empire: Voyages, Botany and Representations of Nature*. Eds. David Philip Miller and Peter Hanns Reill. Cambridge, UK. Cambridge University Press, 1996. 173–91.

Birrell, T. A. 'Anthony Wood, John Bagford and Thomas Hearne as Bibliographers'. In *Pioneers in Bibliography*. Eds. Robin Myers and Michael Harris. New Castle, DE: Oak Knoll Press, 1996. 25–39.

Blades, William. *The Enemies of Books*. London: Elliot Stock, 1896.

Blair, Ann M. *Too Much to Know: Managing Scholarly Information before the Modern Age*. Chicago: University of Chicago Press, 2010.

Blair, Ann and Peter Stallybrass. 'Mediating Information, 1450–1800'. In *This Is Enlightenment*. Eds. Clifford Siskin and William Warner. Chicago: University of Chicago Press, 2010. 139–63.

Blanchot, Maurice and Susan Hanson. 'Everyday Speech'. *Yale French Studies* 73 (1987): 12–20.

Bond, Donald F. 'The First Printing of the *Spectator*'. *Modern Philology* 47:3 (1950): 164–77.

Bondeson, Jan. *The London Monster: A Sanguinary Tale*. Philadelphia: University of Pennsylvania Press, 2001.

Boneham, John. 'The Dawson Turner Collection of Printed Ephemera and Great Yarmouth'. *The Electronic British Library Journal* (2014) [www.bl.uk/eblj/2014articles/pdf/ebljarticle132014.pdf] (accessed 2015).

Brack, O. M. and Mary Early. 'Samuel Johnson's Proposals for the "Harleian Miscellany"'. *Studies in Bibliography* 45 (1992): 127–30.

Brant, Clare. '"I Will Carry You with Me on the Wings of Imagination": Aerial Letters and Eighteenth-Century Ballooning'. *Eighteenth-Century Life* 35:1 (2011): 168–87.

'The Progress of Knowledge in the Regions of Air?: Divisions and Disciplines in Early Ballooning'. *Eighteenth-Century Studies* 45:1 (2011): 71–86.

Bratton, Jacky. *New Readings in Theatre History*. Cambridge, UK: Cambridge University Press, 2003.

Brewer, John. 'Microhistory and the History of Everyday Life'. *Cultural and Social History* 7 (2010): 87–109.

Party Ideology and Popular Politics at the Accession of George III. Cambridge, UK: Cambridge University Press, 1976.

Brinkman, Bartholomew. *Poetic Modernism in the Culture of Mass Print*. Baltimore, MD: Johns Hopkins University Press, 2016.

Brown, Bill. 'Introduction: Textual Materialism'. *PMLA* 125:1 (2010): 24–8.

Brown, Stephen. 'James Tytler's Misadventures in the Late Eighteenth-Century Edinburgh Book Trade'. In *Printing Places: Locations of Book Production & Distribution since 1500*. Eds. John Hinks and Catherine Armstrong. New Castle, DE: Oak Knoll Press, 2005. 47–63.

Bryson, Anna. *From Courtesy to Civility: Changing Codes of Conduct in Early Modern England*. Oxford: Oxford University Press, 1998.

Butler, Marilyn. 'Antiquarianism (Popular)'. In *An Oxford Companion to the Romantic Age: British Culture 1776–1832*. Ed. Iain McCalman. Oxford: Oxford University Press, 1999. 328–38.

'Edgeworth, the United Irishmen, and "More Intelligent Treason"'. In *An Uncomfortable Authority: Maria Edgeworth and Her Contexts*. Eds. Heidi Kaufman and Christopher J. Fauske. Newark: University of Delaware Press, 2004. 33–61.

Mapping Mythologies: Countercurrents in Eighteenth-Century British Poetry and Cultural History. Cambridge, UK: Cambridge University Press, 2015.

Maria Edgeworth: A Literary Biography. Oxford: Oxford University Press, 1972.

Calè, Luisa. 'Extra-Illustrations: The Order of the Book and the Fantasia of the Library'. In *The Material Cultures of Enlightenment Arts and Sciences*. Eds. Adriana Craciun and Simon Schaffer. London: Palgrave Macmillan, 2016. 235–54.

Cameron, Hector Charles. *Sir Joseph Banks, K.B. P.R.S: The Autocrat of the Philosophers*. London: Batchworth Press, 1952.

Carroll, Siobhan. *An Empire of Air and Water: Uncolonizable Space in the British Imagination, 1750–1850*. Philadelphia: University of Pennsylvania Press, 2015.

Carter, Harold B. *Sir Joseph Banks 1743–1820*. London: British Museum (Natural History), 1988.

Sir Joseph Banks 1743–1820: A Guide to the Biographical and Bibliographical Sources. London: St Paul's Bibliographies, 1987.

Carter, John and Percy H. Muir (eds.). *Printing and the Mind of Man, a Descriptive Catalogue Illustrating the Impact of Print on the Evolution of Western Civilization during Five Centuries*. New York: Holt, Rinehart, and Wilson, 1967.

Chandler, James. 'Edgeworth and the Lunar Enlightenment'. *Eighteenth-Century Studies* 45:1 (2011): 87–104.

England in 1819: The Politics of Literary Culture and the Case of Romantic Historicism. Chicago: University of Chicago Press, 1998.

Chartier, Roger. *Inscription and Erasure: Literature and Written Culture from the Eleventh to the Eighteenth Century*. Trans. Arthur Goldhammer. Philadelphia: University of Pennsylvania Press, 2007.

Chun, Wendy Hui Kyong. *Programmed Visions: Software and Memory*. Cambridge, MA: MIT Press, 2011.

'The Enduring Ephemeral, or the Future Is a Memory'. *Critical Inquiry* 35 (2008): 148–71.

Clarke, Stephen. '"Lord God! Jesus! What a House!": Describing and Visiting Strawberry Hill'. *Journal for Eighteenth-Century Studies* 33:3 (2010): 357–80.

The Strawberry Hill Press & Its Printing House: An Account and an Iconography. New Haven, CT: The Lewis Walpole Library, 2011.

Clifford, James. *The Predicament of Culture: Twentieth-Century Ethnography, Literature, and Art*. Cambridge, MA: Harvard University Press, 1988.

Clinton, Alan. *Printed Ephemera: Collection Organisation and Access*. London: Clive Bingley, 1981.
Coleman, D. C. *The British Paper Industry 1495–1860: A Study in Industrial Growth*. Oxford: Clarendon Press, 1958.
Coleman, Deirdre. 'Entertaining Entomology: Insects and Insect Performers in the Eighteenth Century'. *Eighteenth-Century Life* 30:3 (2006): 107–34.
Colley, Linda. *Britons: Forging the Nation, 1707–1837*. New Haven, CT: Yale University Press, 1992.
Connolly, Claire. *A Cultural History of the Irish Novel, 1790–1829*. Cambridge, UK: Cambridge University Press, 2012.
Credland, A. G. 'Sarah and Joseph Banks and Archery in the Eighteenth Century'. *Journal of the Society of Archer-Antiquaries* 34 (1991): 42–50.
  'Sarah and Joseph Banks Contd.'. *Journal of the Society of Archer-Antiquaries* 35 (1992): 54–76.
Darnton, Robert. 'What Is the History of Books?' In *The Book History Reader*. Eds. David Finkelstein and Alistair McCleery. London: Routledge, 2002. 9–26.
  '"What Is the History of Books?" Revisited'. *Modern Intellectual History* 4:3 (2007): 499–508.
Daston, Lorraine and Katharine Park. *Wonders and the Order of Nature, 1150–1750*. London: Zone Books, 2001.
Davis, Jim. *Comic Acting and Portraiture in Late-Georgian and Regency England*. Cambridge, UK: Cambridge University Press, 2015.
Davis, Michael T. *London Corresponding Society, 1792–1799*. 6 vols. London: Pickering & Chatto, 2002.
Davis, W. J. and A. W. Waters. *Tickets and Passes of Great Britain and Ireland: Struck or Engraved on Metal, Ivory, etc.* Leamington Spa: Courier Press, 1922.
de Certeau, Michel. *The Practice of Everyday Life*. Trans. Steven Rendall. Berkeley: University of California Press, 1984.
  The Writing of History. Trans. Tom Conley. New York: Columbia University Press, 1988.
DeLanda, Manuel. *A New Philosophy of Society: Assemblage Theory and Social Complexity*. London: Continuum, 2006.
Dewolf Jr, G. P. 'Notes on Making an Herbarium'. *Arnoldia* 28:8–9 (1968): 69–111.
Derrida, Jacques. *Archive Fever: A Freudian Impression*. Trans. Eric Prenowitz. Chicago: University of Chicago Press, 1996.
  'Hostipitality'. *Angelaki: Journal of the Theoretical Humanities* 5:3 (2000): 3–18.
  Of Hospitality: Anne Dufourmantelle Invites Jacques Derrida to Respond. Trans. Rachel Bowlby. Stanford, CA: Stanford University Press, 2000.
  Paper Machine. Trans. Rachel Bowlby. Stanford, CA: Stanford University Press, 2005.

Dierks, Konstantin. 'Letter Writing, Stationery Supplies, and Consumer Modernity in the Eighteenth-Century Atlantic World'. *Early American Literature* 41:3 (2006): 473–94.
Doderer-Winkler, Melanie. *Magnificent Entertainments: Temporary Architecture for Georgian Festivals*. New Haven, CT: Yale University Press, 2013.
Du Toit, Alexander. 'Chalmers, George (*bap.* 1742, *d.* 1825)'. *Oxford Dictionary of National Biography*. Oxford University Press, 2004; online edn, May 2011. [www.oxforddnb.com/view/article/5028, accessed 11 January 2017].
Eaglen, R. J. 'Sarah Sophia Banks and Her English Hammered Coins'. *British Numismatic Journal* 78 (2008): 200–15.
Eagleton, Catherine. 'Collecting African Money in Georgian London: Sarah Sophia Banks and Her Collection of Coins'. *Museum History Journal* 6 (2013): 23–38.
 'Sarah Sophia Banks, Adam Afzelius and a Coin from Sierra Leone'. In *The Material Cultures of Enlightenment Arts and Sciences*. Eds. Adriana Craciun and Simon Schaffer. London: Palgrave Macmillan, 2016. 203–5.
Eisenstein, Elizabeth L. 'An Unacknowledged Revolution Revisited'. *The American Historical Review* 107:1 (2002): 87–105.
 'Reply'. *The American Historical Review* 107:1 (2002): 126–8.
 The Printing Revolution in Early Modern Europe. 2nd edn. Cambridge, UK: Cambridge University Press, 2005. First published 1983.
Elderfield, John (ed.). *Essays on Assemblage*. New York: Museum of Modern Art, 1992.
Eliot, Simon. 'The Reading Experience Database; or, What Are We to Do about the History of Reading?' The Reading Experience Database (RED), 1450–1945. [www.open.ac.uk/Arts/RED/redback.htm, accessed 21 February 2017].
Elliott, Marianne. *Wolfe Tone* 2nd edn. Liverpool: Liverpool University Press, 2012. First published by Yale University Press, 1989.
Ellis, Janice Stagnitto. 'Aloft in a Balloon: Treatment of a Scrapbook of Early Aeronautica Collected by William Upcott, 1783–1840'. *The Book and Paper Group Annual* 16 (1997). [http://cool.conservation-us.org/coolaic/sg/bpg/annual/v16/bp16-02.html, accessed 27 September 2016].
Ellis, Markman. 'Coffee-House Libraries in Mid-Eighteenth-Century London'. *The Library*. Series 7, 10:1 (2009): 3–40.
Ernst, Wolfgang. *Digital Memory and the Archive*. Ed. Jussi Parikka. Minneapolis: University of Minnesota Press, 2013.
Factotum Occasional Paper 4. The First Phase: An Introduction to the Catalogue of the British Library Collections for ESTC. London: British Library, 1984.
Fairbrass, Valerie. '"What Printers Ink Does Each Week for the Theatres": Printing for the Theatre in the Eighteenth and Early Nineteenth Centuries'. *Publishing History* 67 (2010): 39–63.
Favret, Mary A. *War at a Distance: Romanticism and the Making of Modern Wartime*. Princeton, NJ: Princeton University Press, 2010.

Feather, John. *English Book Prospectuses: An Illustrated History*. Newton, PA: Bird & Bull Press, 1984.
Ferdinand, C. Y. *Benjamin Collins and the Provincial Newspaper Trade in the Eighteenth Century*. Oxford: Clarendon Press, 1997.
Fergus, Jan. *Provincial Readers in Eighteenth-Century England*. Oxford: Oxford University Press, 2006.
Ferguson, John Alexander. *Bibliography of Australia, Volume 1: 1784–1830*. Canberra: National Library of Australia, 1975.
Fergusson, Sir James of Kilkerran, *Balloon Tytler*. London: Faber, 1972.
Ferris, Ina. *Book-Men, Book Clubs, and the Romantic Literary Sphere*. Basingstoke: Palgrave Macmillan, 2015.
Fletcher, Ifan Kyrle. 'The Theatre for Collectors'. *Talks on Book Collecting*. London: Cassell and Co., 1952. 85–99.
Fox, Adam. 'Cheap Political Print and Its Audience in Later Seventeenth Century London: The Case of Narcissus Luttrell's "Popish Plot" Collections'. *Scripta Volant, Verba Manent: Schriftkulturen in Europa zwischen 1500 und 1900*. Eds. Alfred Messerli and Roger Chartier. Basel: Schwabe, 2007. 227–42.
Fraser, Angus. 'Turner, Dawson (1775–1858), banker, botanist, and antiquary'. *Oxford Dictionary of National Biography*. Oxford University Press, 23 September 2004. [www.oxforddnb.com/view/article/%2027846, accessed 15 August 2018].
Freeman, Janet Ing. 'Upcott, William (1779–1845)'. *Oxford Dictionary of National Biography*. Oxford University Press, 2004; online edn, 2004. [www.oxforddnb.com/view/article/28005, accessed 28 August 2016].
Freeman, Jude and Roger Wells. 'Jasper Sprange, Printer, of Tunbridge Wells'. In *A Common Tradition: Popular Art of Britain and America*. Eds. Andy Durr and Helen Martin. Exhibition Catalogue. Brighton Festival, 6–24 May 1991. Brighton: Brighton Polytechnic, 1991. 23–34.
Galperin, William. *The History of Missed Opportunities: British Romanticism and the Emergence of the Everyday*. Stanford, CA: Stanford University Press, 2017.
Garber, Marjorie. *The Use and Abuse of Literature*. New York: Pantheon Books, 2011.
Gardiner, Michael. *Critiques of Everyday Life: An Introduction*. London: Routledge, 2000.
Gardner, Victoria E. M. *The Business of News in England, 1760–1820*. Basingstoke: Palgrave Macmillan, 2016.
Garvey, Ellen Gruber. 'Scissoring and Scrapbooks: Nineteenth-Century Reading, Remaking, and Recirculating'. In *New Media, 1740–1915*. Eds. Lisa Gitelman and Geoffrey B. Pingree. Cambridge, MA: MIT Press, 2003. 207–27.
  Writing with Scissors: American Scrapbooks from the Civil War to the Harlem Renaissance. New York: Oxford University Press, 2013.
Gascoigne, John. *Joseph Banks and the English Enlightenment: Useful Knowledge and Polite Culture*. Cambridge, UK: Cambridge University Press, 1994.
George, M. Dorothy. *English Political Caricature to 1792*. 2 vols. Oxford: Clarendon Press, 1959.

Gilmartin, Kevin. *Print Politics: The Press and Radical Opposition in Early Nineteenth-Century England*. Cambridge, UK: Cambridge University Press, 1996.

Gitelman, Lisa. *Paper Knowledge: Towards a Media History of Documents*. Durham, NC: Duke University Press, 2014.

Goldgar, Anne. 'The British Museum and the Virtual Representation of Culture in the Eighteenth Century'. *Albion* 32:2 (2000): 195–231.

Goodman, Kevis. *Georgic Modernity and British Romanticism: Poetry and the Mediation of History*. Cambridge, UK: Cambridge University Press, 2004.

Goodman, Nigel. Ed. *Dawson Turner: A Norfolk Antiquary and His Remarkable Family*. Chichester: Phillimore & Co., 2007.

Goodwin, Gordon. 'Lemon, Robert (1779–1835)'. Rev. G. H. Martin. *Oxford Dictionary of National Biography*. Oxford University Press, 2004; online edn, 2004. [www.oxforddnb.com/view/article/16433, accessed 30 June 2015].

Gowen, David. 'Studies in the History and Function of the British Theatre Playbill and Programme 1654–1914'. DPhil thesis. University of Oxford, 1998.

Grafton, Anthony. 'Codex in Crisis: The Book Dematerializes'. *Worlds Made By Words: Scholarship and Community in the Modern West*. Cambridge, MA: Harvard University Press, 2009. 288–324.

Greenspan, Ezra and Jonathan Rose. 'An Introduction to Book History'. *Book History* 1 (1998): ix–x.

Griffiths, Antony. *The Print in Stuart Britain 1603–1689*. London: British Museum Press, 1998.

Griffiths, Antony and Reginald Williams. *The Department of Prints and Drawings in the British Museum: User's Guide*. London: British Museum Publications, 1987.

Guillory, John. 'Genesis of the Media Concept'. *Critical Inquiry* 36:2 (2010): 321–62.

'The Memo and Modernity'. *Critical Inquiry* 31:1 (2004): 108–32.

Hackwood, Frederick Wm. *William Hone: His Life and Times*. New York: Augustus M. Kelley, 1970. First published 1912.

Halliwell-Phillipps, James Orchard. *A Dictionary of Archaic and Provincial Words, Obsolete Phrases, Proverbs, and Ancient Customs, Volume II: J–Z*. London: John Russell Smith, 1847.

Hansen, David. *Dempsey's People: A Folio of British Street Portraits 1824–1844*. Canberra: National Portrait Gallery, 2017.

'Harper Returns Archival Document to Australia'. Canadian Broadcasting Corporation. 11 September 2007. [www.cbc.ca/news/entertainment/harper-returns-archival-document-to-australia-1.686084, accessed 1 December 2008].

Harris, Michael. 'Printed Ephemera'. In *The Oxford Companion to the Book*. Eds. Michael F. Suarez, S. J. and M. R. Woudhuysen. 2 vols. Vol. I. Oxford: Oxford University Press, 2010. 120–8.

Harris, P. R. *A History of the British Museum Library, 1753–1973*. London: British Library, 1998.

Hartog, François. *Regimes of Historicity: Presentism and Experiences of Time*. Trans. Saskia Brown. New York: Columbia University Press, 2015.
Hayles, N. Katherine. *Writing Machines*. Cambridge, MA: MIT Press, 2002.
Heal, Sir Ambrose. 'Samuel Pepys. His Trade-Cards'. *The Connoisseur* 92 (July–December 1933): 165–71.
Heal, Felicity. *Hospitality in Early Modern England*. Oxford: Oxford University Press, 1990.
Herring, Scott. *The Hoarders: Material Deviance in Modern American Culture*. Chicago: University of Chicago Press, 2014.
Hoag, Elaine. 'The Earliest Extant Australian Imprint, with Distinguished Provenance'. *Script & Print* 31:1 (2007): 5–19.
Horwitz, Henry. 'Luttrell, Narcissus (1657–1732)'. *Oxford Dictionary of National Biography*, Oxford University Press, 2004; online edn, January 2008. [www.oxforddnb.com/view/article/17226, accessed 6 January 2017].
Hudson, Graham. *The Design and Printing of Ephemera in Britain and America 1720–1920*. London: British Library, 2008.
Huhtamo, Erkki. *Illusions in Motion: Media Archaeology of the Moving Panorama and Related Spectacles*. Cambridge, MA: MIT Press, 2013.
Hunter, J. P. '"News, and New Things": Contemporaneity and the Early English Novel'. *Critical Inquiry* 14:3 (1988): 493–515.
Issacharoff, Michael. *Discourse as Performance*. Stanford, CA: Stanford University Press, 1989.
Jackson, H. J. *Romantic Readers: The Evidence of Marginalia*. New Haven, CT: Yale University Press, 2005.
Jacobus, Mary. *Romantic Things: A Tree, a Rock, a Cloud*. Chicago: University of Chicago Press, 2012.
Janković, Vladimir. *Reading the Skies: A Cultural History of English Weather, 1650–1820*. Manchester: Manchester University Press, 2000.
Jenner, Mark. 'Sawney's Seat: The Social imaginary of the London Bog-house c.1660–c.1800'. In *Bellies, Bowels and Entrails in the Eighteenth Century*. Eds. Rebecca Anne Barr, Sylvie Kleiman-Lafon, and Sophie Vasset. Manchester: Manchester University Press, 2018. 101–27.
Jensen, Kristian. *Revolution and the Antiquarian Book: Reshaping the Past, 1780–1815*. Cambridge, UK: Cambridge University Press, 2011.
Jewitt, Llewellynn. *The Life of William Hutton*. London: Frederick Warne, 1869.
Johns, Adrian. 'How to Acknowledge a Revolution'. *The American Historical Review* 107:1 (2002): 106–25.
  The Nature of the Book: Print and Knowledge in the Making. Chicago: Chicago University Press, 1998.
Johnson, John. 'The Development of Printing, Other than Book-Printing'. *The Library*. Series 4, 17 (1936): 22–35.
Jordan, Robert. *The Convict Theatres of Early Australia 1788–1840*. Sydney: Currency Press, 2002.
Junqua, Amélie. 'Unstable Shades of Grey: Cloth and Paper in Addison's Periodicals'. In *The Afterlife of Used Things: Recycling in the Long Eighteenth*

Century. Eds. Ariane Fennetaux, Amélie Junqua, and Sophie Vasset. Abingdon: Routledge, 2015. 184–98.
Kafka, Ben. *The Demon of Writing: Powers and Failures of Paperwork*. New York: Zone Books, 2012.
Kalter, Barrett. *Modern Antiques: The Material Past in England, 1660–1780*. Lewisburg, PA: Bucknell University Press, 2012.
Keen, Paul. *Literature, Commerce, and the Spectacle of Modernity, 1750–1800*. Cambridge, UK: Cambridge University Press, 2012.
  The Crisis of Literature in the 1790s: Print Culture and the Public Sphere. Cambridge, UK: Cambridge University Press, 1999.
Kiessling, Nicolas K. 'The Library of Anthony Wood from 1681 to 1999'. *Bodleian Library Record* 16 (1999): 470–98.
  The Library of Anthony Wood. Oxford: Oxford Bibliographical Society, 2002.
Kirschenbaum, Matthew G. *Mechanisms: New Media and the Forensic Imagination*. Cambridge, MA: MIT Press, 2008.
Klancher, Jon. *Transfiguring the Arts and Sciences: Knowledge and Cultural Institutions in the Romantic Age*. Cambridge, UK: Cambridge University Press, 2013.
  'Wild Bibliography: The Rise and Fall of Book History in Nineteenth-Century Britain'. In *Bookish Histories: Books, Literature, and Commercial Modernity 1700–1900*. Eds. Ina Ferris and Paul Keen. New York: Palgrave Macmillan, 2009. 19–41.
Knight, Jeffrey Todd. *Bound to Read: Compilations, Collections, and the Making of Renaissance Literature*. Philadelphia: University of Pennsylvania Press, 2013.
Knowles, Jane. 'A Tasteful Occupation? The Work of Maria, Elizabeth, Mary Anne, Harriet, Hannah Sarah and Ellen Turner'. In *Dawson Turner: A Norfolk Antiquary and His Remarkable Family*. Ed. Nigel Goodman. Chichester: Phillimore & Co., 2007. 123–40.
Koselleck, Reinhart, *Futures Past: On the Semantics of Historical Time*. Trans. Keith Tribe. New York: Columbia University Press, 1985.
Laird, Mark and Alicia Weisberg-Roberts. Eds. *Mrs. Delany & Her Circle*. New Haven, CT: Yale University Press, 2009.
Lamb, Jonathan. 'Scientific Gusto versus Monsters in the Basement'. *Eighteenth-Century Studies* 42:2 (2009): 309–20.
Langan, Celeste. 'Understanding Media in 1805: Audiovisual Hallucination in *The Lay of the Last Minstrel*'. *Studies in Romanticism* 40 (Spring 2001): 49–70.
Langan, Celeste and Maureen N. McLane. 'The Medium of Romantic Poetry'. In *The Cambridge Companion to British Romantic Poetry*. Eds. James Chandler and Maureen N. McLane. Cambridge, UK: Cambridge University Press, 2008. 239–62.
le Faye, Deirdre. *Jane Austen: A Family Record*. 2nd edn. Cambridge, UK: Cambridge University Press, 2004.
Lefebvre, Henri. *Critique of Everyday Life [1947–1958]*. Trans. John Moore. 3 vols. London: Verso, 1991–2005.

Leis, Arlene. 'Displaying Art and Fashion: Ladies' Pocket-Book Imagery in the Paper Collections of Sarah Sophia Banks'. *Konsthistorisk tidskrift/Journal of Art History* (2013): 1–20.

'Ephemeral Histories: Social Commemoration of the Revolutionary and Napoleonic Wars in the Paper Collections of Sarah Sophia Banks'. In *Visual Culture and the Revolutionary and Napoleonic Wars*. Ed. Satish Padiyar, Philip Shaw, and Phillipa Simpson. London: Routledge, 2017. 183–99.

'Sarah Sophia Banks: Femininity, Sociability and the Practice of Collecting in Late Georgian England'. PhD thesis. University of York, 2013. [http://etheses.whiterose.ac.uk/5794/, accessed 2014].

Lewis, John. *Printed Ephemera: The Changing Uses of Type and Letterforms in English and American Printing*. Ipswich: W. S. Cowell, 1962.

Typography: Design and Practice. London: Barrie and Jenkins, 1978.

Liddle, Dallas. 'The News Machine: Textual Form and Information Function in the London *Times*, 1785–1885'. *Book History* 19 (2016): 132–68.

Lilley, James D. 'Studies in Uniquity: Horace Walpole's Singular Collection'. *ELH* 80:1 (2013): 93–124.

Lloyd, Sarah. *Charity and Poverty in England c. 1680–1820: Wild and Visionary Schemes*. Manchester: Manchester University Press, 2009.

'Ticketing the British Eighteenth Century: "A thing . . . never heard of before"'. *Journal of Social History* 46:4 (2013): 843–71.

'The Religious and Social Significance of Methodist Tickets, and Associated Practices of Collecting and Recollecting, 1741–2017'. *The Historical Journal*, 1–28. doi:10.1017/S0018246X19000244.

Love, Harold. 'The Look of News: Popish Plot Narratives, 1678–1680'. In *The Cambridge History of the Book in Britain, Volume IV: 1557–1695*. Eds. John Barnard and D. F. McKenzie. Cambridge, UK: Cambridge University Press, 2002. 652–6.

Lupton, Christina, *Reading and the Making of Time in the Eighteenth Century*. Baltimore, MD: Johns Hopkins University Press, 2018.

Lynch, Deidre. *Loving Literature: A Cultural History*. Chicago: University of Chicago Press, 2014.

Lynch, Deidre Shauna. 'Canons' Clockwork: Novels for Everyday Use'. In *Bookish Histories: Books, Literature, and Commercial Modernity, 1700–1900*. Eds. Ina Ferris and Paul Keen. Basingstoke: Palgrave Macmillan, 2009. 87–110.

Lynn, Michael. *The Sublime Invention: Ballooning in Europe, 1783–1820*. London: Pickering & Chatto, 2010.

Makepeace, Chris E. *Ephemera: A Book on Its Collection, Conservation and Use*. Aldershot: Gower, 1985.

Mandelbrote, Giles. 'Sloane and the Preservation of Printed Ephemera'. In *Libraries Origins within the Library: The Origins of the British Library's Printed Collections*. Eds. Giles Mandelbrote and Barry Taylor. London: British Library, 2009. 146–68.

Mathias, Peter. *English Trade Tokens: The Industrial Revolution Illustrated*. London: Abelard-Schuman, 1962.
Matthews, William. 'The Lincolnshire Dialect in the Eighteenth Century,' *Notes and Queries* 169 (1935): 398–404.
Maxted, Ian. 'Single Sheets from a County Town: The Example of Exeter'. In *Spreading the Word: The Distribution Networks of Print 1550–1850*. Eds. Robin Myers and Michael Harris. Winchester: St Paul's Bibliographies, 1950. 109–29.
McC. Gatch, Milton. 'John Bagford, Bookseller and Antiquary'. *British Library Journal* 12 (1986): 150–71.
McCalman, Iain. *Radical Underworld: Prophets, Revolutionaries, and Pornographers in London, 1795–1840*. Cambridge, UK: Cambridge University Press, 1988.
McConnell, Anita. 'Newland, Abraham (1730–1807)'. *Oxford Dictionary of National Biography*. Oxford University Press, 2004; online edn, 2004. [www.oxforddnb.com/view/article/20011, accessed 23 January 2015].
McCormick, E. H. *Omai: Pacific Envoy*. Auckland: University of Auckland Press, 1977.
McDowell, Paula. 'Of Grubs and Other Insects: Constructing the Categories of "Ephemera" and "Literature" in Eighteenth-Century British Writing'. *Book History* 15 (2012): 48–70.
  'Mediating Media Past and Present: Toward a Genealogy of "Print Culture" and "Oral Tradition"'. In *This Is Enlightenment*. Eds. Clifford Siskin and William Warner. Chicago: University of Chicago Press, 2010. 229–46.
McGann, Jerome. *A New Republic of Letters: Memory and Scholarship in the Age of Digital Reproduction*. Cambridge, MA: Harvard University Press, 2014.
  The Scholar's Art: Literary Studies in a Managed World. Chicago: University of Chicago Press, 2006.
McKenzie, D. F. *Bibliography and the Sociology of Texts*. London: British Library, 1986.
McKitterick, David. 'Dawson Turner and Book Collecting'. In *Dawson Turner: A Norfolk Antiquary and His Remarkable Family*. Ed. Nigel Goodman. Chichester: Phillimore & Co., 2007. 67–110.
  Print, Manuscript and the Search for Order, 1450–1830. Cambridge, UK: Cambridge University Press, 2003.
McLane, Maureen N. *Balladeering, Minstrelsy, and the Making of British Romantic Poetry*. Cambridge, UK: Cambridge University Press, 2008.
McNulty, Tracy. *The Hostess: Hospitality, Femininity, and the Expropriation of Identity*. Minneapolis: University of Minnesota Press, 2007.
McShane, Angela. 'Ballads and Broadsides'. In *The Oxford History of Popular Print Culture, Volume I: Cheap Print in Britain and Ireland to 1660*. Ed. Joad Raymond. Oxford: Oxford University Press, 2011. 341–62.
Mee, Jon. *Print, Publicity, and Popular Radicalism in the 1790s: The Laurel of Liberty*. Cambridge, UK: Cambridge University Press, 2016.
Melville, Peter. *Romantic Hospitality, and the Resistance to Accommodation*. Waterloo, ON: Wilfrid Laurier University Press, 2007.

Mendle, Michael. 'George Thomason's Intentions'. In *Libraries within the Library: The Origins of the British Library's Printed Collections*. Eds. Giles Mandelbrote and Barry Taylor. London: British Library, 2009. 171–86.
'News and the Pamphlet Culture of Mid-Seventeenth Century England'. In *The Politics of Information in Early Modern Europe*. Eds. Brendan Dooley and Sabrina A. Baron. London: Routledge, 2001. 57–79.
'Preserving the Ephemeral: Reading, Collecting and the Pamphlet Culture of Seventeenth-Century England'. In *Books and Readers in Early Modern England: Material Studies*. Eds. Jennifer Anderson and Elizabeth Sauer. Philadelphia: University of Pennsylvania Press, 2002. 201–16.
Millar, A. H. 'Palmer, Thomas Fyshe (1747–1802), Unitarian Minister and Radical'. *Oxford Dictionary of National Biography*. Oxford: Oxford University Press, 2004; online edn, January 2008. [www.oxforddnb.com/view/article/21220, accessed 2 August 2018].
Milne, Esther. '"Magic Bits of Paste-board": Texting in the Nineteenth Century'. *M/C: A Journal of Media and Culture* 7:1 (2004). [http://journal.media-culture.org.au/0401/02-milne.php, accessed 2014].
Moger, Victoria. *The Favour of Your Company: Tickets and Invitations to London Events and Places of Interest c. 1750–1850*. London: Museum of London in association with The Wynkyn De Worde Society, 1980.
Monteyne, Joseph. *The Printed Image in Early Modern London: Urban Space, Visual Representation, and Social Exchange*. Aldershot: Ashgate, 2007.
Mullini, Roberta. '"With such flourishes as these": The Visual Politics of Charlatans' Handbills in Early Modern London'. *Textus: English Studies in Italy* 22:3 (2009): 553–71.
Muñoz, José Esteban. 'Ephemera as Evidence: Introductory Notes to Queer Acts'. *Women & Performance: A Journal of Feminist Theory* 82 (1996): 5–16.
Murphy, Kevin and Sally O'Driscoll. Eds. *Studies in Ephemera: Text and Image in Eighteenth-Century Print*. Lewisburg, PA: Bucknell University Press, 2013.
Mussell, James. 'The Passing of Print'. *Media History* 18:1 (2011): 77–92.
Nancy, Jean-Luc. *On the Commerce of Thinking: Of Books and Bookstores*. New York: Fordham University Press, 2008.
Newman, Steve. *Ballad Collection, Lyric, and the Canon: The Call of the Popular from the Restoration to the New Criticism*. Philadelphia: University of Pennsylvania Press, 2007.
Noblett, William. 'Cheese, Stolen Paper, and the London Book Trade, 1750–99'. *Eighteenth-Century Life* 38:3 (2014): 100–10.
O'Connell, Sheila. *The Popular Print in England 1550–1850*. London: British Museum, 1999.
Oettermann, Stephan. 'Die fliegenden Plastiken des Johann Karl Enslen/Johann Karl Enslen's Flying Sculptures'. *Daidalos* 37 (15 September 1990): 44–53.
Osborn, James M. 'Reflections on Narcissus Luttrell'. *The Book Collector* 6 (1957): 15–27.

Parrish, Stephen M. 'A Booksellers' Campaign of 1803: Napoleonic Invasion Broadsides at Harvard'. *Harvard Library Bulletin* 8:1 (Winter 1954): 14–26.

Peacey, Jason. *Print and Politics in the English Revolution*. Cambridge, UK: Cambridge University Press, 2013.

Peltz, Lucy. *Facing the Text: Extra-Illustration, Print Culture and Society in Britain, 1769–1840*. San Marino, CA: Huntington Library Press, 2017.

Pemberton, John E. *The National Provision of Printed Ephemera in the Social Sciences: A Report Prepared for the Social Science and Government Committee of the Social Science Research Council*. Coventry: University of Warwick Library, 1971.

Petit, Nicolas. *L'éphémère, l'occasionnel et le non livre à la bibliotheque Sainte-Geneviève*. Paris: Klincksieck, 1997.

Petrucci, Armando. *Public Lettering: Script, Power, and Culture*. Trans. Linda Lappin. Chicago: University of Chicago Press, 1993.

Pincott, Anthony. 'The Book Tickets of Miss Sarah Sophia Banks'. *The Book Plate Journal* 2 (2004): 3–30.

Pincus, Steven. '"Coffee Politicians Does Create": Coffee-Houses and Restoration Political Culture'. *Journal of Modern History* 67 (1995): 807–34.

Piper, Andrew. *Book Was There: Reading in Electronic Times*. Chicago: University of Chicago Press, 2012.

Pollard, A. W. and G. R. Redgrave. *A Short-Title Catalogue of Books Printed in England, Scotland, & Ireland and of English Books Printed Abroad, 1475–1640: A–H*. 2nd edn begun by W. A. Jackson and F. S. Ferguson, completed by Katharine F. Pantzer. London: The Bibliographical Society, 1986.

Pollard, Graham. 'Notes on the Size of the Sheet'. *The Library*. Series 4, 22:2–3 (1941): 105–37.

Price, Leah. 'Getting the Reading Out of It: Paper Recycling in Mayhew's London'. In *Bookish Histories: Books, Literature, and Commercial Modernity, 1700–1900*. Eds. Ina Ferris and Paul Keen. Basingstoke: Palgrave Macmillan, 2009. 148–66.

  How to Do Things with Books in Victorian Britain. Princeton, NJ: Princeton University Press, 2012.

Ramsey, Neil. 'The Grievable Life of the War-Correspondent: The Experience of War in Henry Crabb Robinson's Letters to *The Times*, 1808–1809'. In *Emotions and War: Medieval to Romantic Literature*. Eds. Stephanie Downes, Andrew Lynch, and Katrina O'Loughlin. Basingstoke: Palgrave Macmillan, 2015. 235–50.

Raven, James. *Publishing Business in Eighteenth-Century England*. Woodbridge: Boydell Press, 2014.

  The Business of Books: Booksellers and the English Book Trade 1450–1850. New Haven, CT: Yale University Press, 2007.

Raymond, Joad. *Pamphlets and Pamphleteering in Early Modern Britain*. Cambridge, UK: Cambridge University Press, 2003.

'The Newspaper, Public Opinion, and the Public Sphere in the Seventeenth Century'. In *News, Newspapers and Society in Early Modern Britain*. Ed. Joad Raymond. London: Frank Cass, 1999. 109–40.

Reed, Nicholas. *Frost Fairs on the Frozen Thames*. London: Liliburne Press, 2002.

Register of Ephemera Collections in the United Kingdom, excluding those in the major national collections and others not normally available to the public. Reading: Centre for Ephemera Studies, 2003.

Rickards, Maurice. *Collecting Printed Ephemera*. Oxford: Phaidon/Christie's, 1988.

'The Girl Who Came in from the Garden'. *The Ephemerist*. 53 (June 1986): 148–9.

The Public Notice: An Illustrated History. Melbourne: Wren Publishing, 1973.

This Is Ephemera: Collecting Printed Throwaways. London: David & Charles, 1977.

Rickards, Maurice and Michael Twyman. *The Encyclopedia of Ephemera: A Guide to the Fragmentary Documents of Everyday Life, for the Collector, Curator and Historian*. London: British Library, 2000.

Riley, Noël. *Visiting Card Cases*. Guildford: Lutterworth Press, 1983.

Rimbault, Edward F. *Old Ballads Illustrating the Great Frost of 1683–4 and the Fair on the River Thames*. London: Percy Society, 1844.

Robertson, Frances. *Print Culture: From Steam Press to Ebook*. Abingdon: Routledge, 2013.

Robertson, Patrick Hickman. 'Obituary: Maurice Rickards'. *The Independent*. 20 February 1998. [www.independent.co.uk/news/obituaries/obituary-maurice-rickards-1145817.html, accessed 11 November 2011].

Roe, Michael. 'Mealmaker, George (1768–1808)'. *Australian Dictionary of Biography*. Vol. II. Melbourne University Publishing, 1967; online edn published by National Centre of Biography, Australian National University. [http://adb.anu.edu.au/biography/mealmaker-george-2441/text3253, accessed 3 August 2018].

Rose, R. B. 'The Priestley Riots of 1791'. *Past & Present* 18 (1960): 68–88.

Rosenberg, Daniel. 'Early Modern Information Overload'. *Journal of the History of Ideas* 64: 1 (2003): 1–9.

Rossell, Deac. 'Enslen, Johann Carl (1759–1848)'. In *Encyclopedia of Nineteenth-Century Photography*. Ed. John Hannavy. London: Routledge, 2013. 491–3.

Russell, Gillian. '"An entertainment of oddities": Fashionable Sociability and the Pacific in the 1770s'. In *A New Imperial History: Culture, Identity, and Modernity in Britain and the Empire, 1660–1840*. Ed. Kathleen Wilson. Cambridge, UK: Cambridge University Press, 2004. 48–70.

'Ephemeraphilia: A Queer History,' *Angelaki: Journal of the Theoretical Humanities* 23:1 (2018): 174–86.

'Romantic Militarisation: Sociability, Theatricality, and Military Science in the Woolwich Rotunda, 1814-2013'. In *Tracing War in British Enlightenment and Romantic Culture*. Eds. Neil Ramsey and Gillian Russell. Houndmills: Palgrave Macmillan, 2015. 96–112.

'Sarah Sophia Banks's Private Theatricals: Ephemera, Sociability, and the Archiving of Fashionable Life'. *Eighteenth-Century Fiction* 27:3–4 (Spring–Summer 2015): 535–55.

'The Reading Communities of Collecting: Sale Catalogues, Sociability and Ephemerality, 1676–1862'. *Australian Literary Studies* 29:3 (2014): 15–27.

Women, Sociability and Theatre in Georgian London. Cambridge, UK: Cambridge University Press, 2007.

Russett, Margaret. '*Persuasion*, Mediation'. *Studies in Romanticism* 53:3 (2014): 417–33.

Sandywell, Barry. 'The Myth of Everyday Life: Toward a Heterology of the Ordinary'. *Cultural Studies* 18:2–3 (2004): 160–80.

Schneider, Rebecca, *Performing Remains: Art and War in Times of Theatrical Reenactment*. Abingdon: Routledge, 2011.

Sherbo, Arthur. 'Heber, Richard (1774–1833)'. *Oxford Dictionary of National Biography*. Oxford University Press, 2004; online edn, May 2015. [www.oxforddnb.com/view/article/12854, accessed 13 June 2015].

Sheringham, Michael. *Everyday Life: Theories and Practices from Surrealism to the Present*. Oxford: Oxford University Press, 2006.

Sherman, Stuart. *Telling Time: Clocks, Diaries, and English Diurnal Form, 1660–1785*. Chicago: University of Chicago Press, 1996.

Simmel, Georg. 'The Sociology of Sociability'. In *Simmel on Culture: Selected Writings*. Eds. David Frisby and Mike Featherstone, 120–9. London: Sage, 1997.

Simpson, David. *Romanticism and the Question of the Stranger*. Chicago: University of Chicago Press, 2013.

Siskin, Clifford and William Warner. 'If This Is Enlightenment Then What Is Romanticism?' *European Romantic Review* 22:3 (2011): 281–91.

Siskin, Clifford and William Warner. Eds. *This Is Enlightenment*. Chicago: University of Chicago Press, 2010.

Sloan, Kim (with Andrew Burnett). *Enlightenment: Discovering the World in the Eighteenth Century*. Washington, DC: Smithsonian Books, 2003.

Smith, Chloe Wigston. 'Clothes without Bodies: Objects, Humans, and the Marketplace in Eighteenth-Century It-Narratives and Trade Cards'. *Eighteenth-Century Fiction* 23:2 (2010–11): 347–80.

Smith, Edward. *The Life of Sir Joseph Banks*. London: John Lane, The Bodley Head, 1911.

Stallybrass, Peter. '"Little Jobs": Broadsides and the Printing Revolution'. In *Agent of Change: Print Culture Studies after Elizabeth L. Eisenstein*. Eds. Sabrina Alcorn Baron, Eric N. Lindquist, and Eleanor F. Shevlin. Amherst: University of Massachusetts Press, 2007. 315–41.

Stearn, W. T. *An Introduction to the Species Planatarum and Cognate Botanical Works of Carl Linnaeus*. London: Ray Society, 1957.

Steedman, Carolyn. *An Everyday Life of the English Working Class: Work, Self and Sociability in the Early Nineteenth Century*. Cambridge, UK: Cambridge University Press, 2013.

Dust: The Archive and Cultural History. New Brunswick, NJ: Rutgers University Press, 2002.
Stern, Tiffany. *Documents of Performance in Early Modern England*. Cambridge, UK: Cambridge University Press, 2009.
Stewart, Garrett. *Bookwork: Medium to Object to Concept to Art*. Chicago: University of Chicago Press, 2011.
Stoker, David. 'Disposing of George Thomason's Intractable Legacy 1664–1762'. *The Library*. Series 6, 14 (1992): 337–56.
Sweet, Rosemary. *Antiquaries: The Discovery of the Past in Eighteenth-Century Britain*. London: Hambledon, 2004.
T. B. 'Francis Place'. *Notes and Queries*. Series 3, 9 (March 1866): 191–2.
Tadmor, Naomi. *Family and Friends in Eighteenth Century England: Household, Kinship and Patronage*. Cambridge, UK: Cambridge University Press, 2001.
Tanselle, G. Thomas. 'Some Thoughts on Catalogues'. *The Papers of the Bibliographical Society of America* 102:4 (2008): 573–80.
Taws, Richard. *The Politics of the Provisional: Art and Ephemera in Revolutionary France*. Philadelphia: University of Pennsylvania Press, 2013.
The English Provincial Printer 1700–1800. *British Library Exhibition Notes*. London: British Library, 1983.
The John Johnson Collection: Catalogue of an Exhibition. Oxford: Bodleian Library, 1971.
The John Johnson Collection: An Archive of Printed Ephemera. Chadwyck-Healey-Proquest. [http://johnjohnson.chadwyck.co.uk, accessed 25 January 2017].
The Re:Enlightenment Project. [www.reenlightenment.org, accessed 28 January 2017].
Thomas, Nicholas. *In Oceania: Visions, Artifacts, Histories*. Durham, NC: Duke University Press, 1997.
Thompson, E. P. *The Making of the English Working Class*. London: Victor Gollancz, 1963.
Thornton, Sara. *Advertising, Subjectivity and the Nineteenth-Century Novel: Dickens, Balzac and the Language of the Walls*. Basingstoke: Palgrave Macmillan, 2009.
Tiffany, Daniel. *Toy Medium: Materialism and Modern Lyric*. Berkeley: University of California Press, 2000.
Troide, Lars. 'Burney, Charles (1757–1817)'. *Oxford Dictionary of National Biography*. Oxford University Press, 2004. Eds. H. C. G. Matthew and Brian Harrison; online ed. Lawrence Goldman, January 2008. [www.oxforddnb.com.virtual.anu.edu.au/view/article/4079, accessed 18 June 2014].
Troost, Linda V. 'Archery in the Long Eighteenth Century'. In *British Sporting Literature and Culture in the Long Eighteenth Century*. Ed. Sharon Harrow. Farnham: Ashgate, 2015: 105–24.
Tuite, Clara. 'Maria Edgeworth's Déjà-Voodoo: Interior Decoration, Retroactivity, and Colonial Allegory in *The Absentee*'. *Eighteenth-Century Fiction* 20:3 (2008): 385–413.
  '*Sanditon*: Austen's Pre-post Waterloo'. *Textual Practice* 26:2 (2012): 609–29.

Twyman, Michael. *John Soulby, Printer, Ulverston: A Study of the Work Printed by John Soulby, Father and Son, between 1796 and 1827*. Reading: Museum of English Rural Life, 1966.
'Printed Ephemera'. In *The Cambridge History of the Book in Britain, Volume V: 1695–1830*. Eds. Michael F. Suarez, S. J. and Michael L. Turner. Cambridge, UK: Cambridge University Press, 2009. 66–82.
'The Long Term Significance of Printed Ephemera'. *RBM: A Journal of Rare Books, Manuscripts and Cultural Heritage* 9:1 (2008): 19–57.
Vickery, Amanda. *Behind Closed Doors: At Home in Georgian England*. New Haven, CT: Yale University Press, 2009.
Wahrman, Dror. *Mr. Collier's Letter Racks: A Tale of Art & Illusion at the Threshold of the Modern Information Age*. New York: Oxford University Press, 2012.
Walford, E. 'Visiting Cards'. *Notes and Queries*. 8th series, 6 (11 August 1894): 117.
Wallas, Graham. *The Life of Francis Place 1771–1854*. Rev. edn. London: George Allen & Unwin, 1925. First published 1898.
Waslin, Jane. 'Paper Industry'. In *Australian Encyclopaedia*. Ed. Tony Macdougall. 6th edn. 6 vols. Terrey Hills, New South Wales: Australian Geographic, 1996. VI: 2343–4.
Watt, Tessa. *Cheap Print and Popular Piety 1550–1640*. Cambridge, UK: Cambridge University Press, 1991.
Welberry, David E. 'Foreword' to Friedrick A. Kittler, *Discourse Networks 1800/1900*. Trans. Michael Metteer, with Chris Cullens. Stanford, CA: Stanford University Press, 1990.
Whelan, Kevin. '"The Republic in the Village": The Dissemination and Reception of Popular Political Literature in the 1790s'. In *Books Beyond the Pale: Aspects of the Provincial Book Trade in Ireland before 1850*. Ed. Gerard Long. Dublin: Rare Books Group of the Library Association of Ireland, 1996. 101–40.
Whiting, J. R. S. *Trade Tokens: A Social and Economic History*. Newton Abbot: David & Charles, 1971.
Whyman, Susan E. *Sociability and Power in Late-Stuart England: The Cultural Worlds of the Verneys 1660–1720*. Oxford: Oxford University Press, 1999.
Wood, Frederick T. 'Census of Extant Collections of English Provincial Playbills of the Eighteenth Century'. *Notes and Queries* 190:11 (1946): 222–6.
Wood, Marcus. *Radical Satire and Print Culture 1790–1822*. Oxford: Clarendon Press, 1994.
Woolf, Daniel. 'News, History and the Construction of the Present in Early Modern England'. In *The Politics of Information in Early Modern Europe*. Eds. Brendan Dooley and Sabrina A. Baron. London: Routledge, 2001.
Yale, Elizabeth. *Sociable Knowledge: Natural History and the Nation in Early Modern Britain*. Philadelphia: University of Pennsylvania Press, 2016.
Yale, Elizabeth. 'With Slips and Scraps: How Early Modern Naturalists Invented the Archive'. *Book History* 12 (2009): 1–36.

Yeo, Richard. *Notebooks, English Virtuosi, and Early Modern Science*. Chicago: University of Chicago Press, 2014.

Young, Timothy G. 'Evidence: Toward a Library Definition of Ephemera'. *RBM: A Journal of Rare Books, Manuscripts and Cultural Heritage* 4 (2003): 11–26.

Zwicker, Jonathan. 'Playbills, Ephemera, and the Historical Imagination in Nineteenth-Century Japan'. *The Journal of Japanese Studies* 35:1 (2009): 37–59.

Index

Abercorn, Marquis of, 131
Abree, James, 244
Absentee, The, 27, 204–13, 249
    Anglo-Irish relations, 205, 207
    Arabian Nights in, 209
    archives in, 211–12
    and dockets, 212
    ephemerology of, 27, 211–12
    fashionable sociability in, 207
    hospitality, 207
    military heroism in, 210
    newspapers in, 212–13
    paper instruments in, 208–9
    Pasley's *Essay* in, 209–10
    playbills, 208
    sociability in, 207–8
    and SSB's assemblage, 208
    visiting cards in, 27, 206–9
Account of the National Jubilee, 236
Ackermann, Rudolph, 132, 232
acting profession
    and playbills, 168
Addison, Joseph, 25, 34, 37, 45, 58, 81, 120, 215, *See* Spectator
administration
    and jobbing print, 19
Adorno, Theodor, 150–1
advertisements, 1, 17, 26, 29, 44–5, 77, 86, 163
    and handbills, 45, 48, 237
    lottery, 108–9, 124
    medical, 110
    tickets as, 109
advertising, 17–18, 224
    watch-papers, 219
agents provocateurs, 47
Almack's, 113
almanacs, 17, 63, 65
Alnwick, 108
Alston, R. C., 16–18
America, 46, 49
anonymity
    and handbills in 1790s, 48
antiquarianism, 124, 171, 224–6
    Butler, Marilyn on, 24–5, 254
    popular, 104, 107, 148, 252
    primitive, 174
antiquarians, 24–5
APEC (Asia-Pacific Economic Cooperation), 183
Arabian Nights, 209
Arcades Project, 150–2, 253
archery, 105, 111
    SSB collections, 104–5, 110–12
    Waring, Thomas, 112
archives, 13, 70, 90, 185, 253
    in *The Absentee*, 211–12
    and ballooning, 137
    and centrality of playbills, 172
    Derrida, Jacques on, 73–4
    Edgeworth, 208
    handbills of 1790s, 50
    national, 26, 92
    priceless, 14
    sites of in London, 234
    SSB, 114, 149–50
    UK national, 47
    Walpole, Horace on, 201
art
    exhibitions, 113
    history, 100
    objects, tickets as, 109
    of visiting cards, 192
arts, the, 6, 61
Ashmolean Museum, 30
Asia, East, 193
Asperne, James, 55–6
assemblage, 112–13, 124
    20th century art, 124, 149
    of collections, 254
    DeLanda, Manuel on, 150
    Deleuze, Gilles on, 103, 149
    and SSB, 208
    and visiting cards, 188

assembly rooms, 98, 108, 113, 115, 176
  Norwich, 116
Association for Preserving Liberty and Property, 52–4
  Association Papers, 52–3, 55
associational culture, 26, 46, 69, 77, 86, 104
  documentation of, 173
  and entertainment, 113
  and the Enlightenment, 59
  and ephemerology, 148
  and exchange of information, 120
  and printed ephemera, 22, 80
  and public sphere, 217
  tickets in, 108
  and theatre, 175
  and visiting cards, 187
  and women, 144
Astley's circus, 137, 147, 181
astronomy, 44, 56
Asylum for Fugitives, An (1776), 37
auctions, 17, 68, 75, 95, 98, 203
  library of Narcissus Luttrell, 92
  library of Sara Coleridge, 9
  notices of, 45
  sale catalogues of, 60
  Upcott collections, 60
Austen family at peace celebrations, 240
Austen, Cassandra, 226
Austen, Jane, 21, 27, 115, 204, 226, 251
  Emma, 119, 214, 242
  and the ephemeral, 119
  Mansfield Park, 226
  Northanger Abbey, 197–200
  Persuasion, 27–8, 216, 239–50
  Pride and Prejudice, 119
  The Watsons, 119
Australia
  1796 Sydney playbill *Jane Shore*, 26, 153–4, 177–9, 253
  1796 Sydney playbill *The Busy Body*, 181
  'Botany Bay theatricals', 185
  broadsides, 180
  Collins, David, 179
  convicts, 177, 179
  and Cook, Captain James, 124
    Endeavour Journal, 184
  earliest printing, 26
  First Fleet 1788, 179
  first paper-making mill, 179
  first play performed at, 182
  first printing press, 179
  history of, 181
  Hughes, George, 181
  Hunter, Governor John, 179
  King, Lieutenant-Governor Philip Gidley, 181–3
  National Library of, 26, 157, 184
  New South Wales, 26, 135, 153, 179
  New South Wales General Standing Orders (1802, first book), 180
  newspaper accounts of playbills, 180–1
  Norfolk Island, 182
  playbills from 1800, 179
  Sidaway, Robert, 180
  Sydney Gazette, 179
  Sydney theatre, 180–1
  transportation of 'Scottish Martyrs', 49
  Treasures Gallery, National Library, 184
  UNESCO Memory of the World Register, 184
authorship, 5, 36
autographs, 60
automata, 145
Ayscough, Samuel, 110–11, 147, 253

Baconian empiricism, 25
Bagford, John, 8, 63, 217, 253
ballads, 18, 26, 36, 52, 65, 70, 74, 77, 109, 164, 224
  and accidental reading, 36
  and cheap print, 165
  on 'dead' walls, 163
  and English literature, 36
  frost fair, 219
  as libels, 67
  literature of 'the people', 58, 225
  and 'the popular', 36
  'The royal patient traveller …', 78
  sellers of, 58
  singers of, 53
  as single-sheet publications, 18
  SSB collectanea, 110
  terminology of, 65
  'Two Children in the Wood', 35–6
  and United Irishmen, 210
ballooning, 26, 60, 105, 125, 135, 176, 252
  balloonmania of 1783-84, 114, 230
  Blanchard's 'Grand Aerostatic Balloon', 139
  Charles, Jacques, 135, 139
  and disciplinarity, 143–4
  Enslen, Johann Karl, 147
  and the ephemeral archive, 137
  Lunardi, Vincent, 136–8, 142, 144
  Lynn, Michael on, 144
  and Lysons collection, 142
  and media history, 147
  Montgolfier brothers (Joseph-Michel and Jacques-Étienne), 135, 139

prints, 137
Robert brothers (Anne-Jean and Nicolas-Louis), 135, 139
Sadler's flight at Jubilee of 1814, 223, 230
and sociability, 139
and SSB
　archive, 137–42
　collectanea, 110
subscription tickets, 138
tickets, 138–42, 144
and Tytler, James, 48, 136, 139
　'Edinburgh fire balloon', 139–40
Upcott collection, 143
and women, 129
Zambecarri and Biaggi, 136
balls, 108, 116, 123
Banks, Lady Dorothea, 99, 102
Banks, Sarah Sophia, 10, 26, 35, 66, 98 161, 170, 174, 182, 216, 252, 254
1796 Sydney playbill, 153–61
archery, 104–5, 111–12
archive, 114, 149–50
archivist of sociability, 114–15, 119
and assemblage, 103, 112–13, 124, 208
ballooning archive, 136–42, 148
and Benjamin, Walter, 103, 150–2
book collection, 112
and circle of JB, 119–20
collectanea, 110, 112, 137
collections, 28, 188, 248, See British Library and British Museum
　coins, 114
　cuttings, 124
　fashionable sociability, 129
　funerals of Fox, Pitt and Nelson, 229
　interests, 101, 104
　and JB, 127, 129, 132
　Jubilee of 1814, 231–4, 237–9, 246
　methodology, 112
　prints, 109–10
　Samuel Ayscough article in, 110–12
　tokens, 114
and correspondence networks of JB, 119, 136
and Edgeworth's fiction, 208
and Enlightenment ephemerology, 102
Enslen handbill, 144–5
and ephemera 'books', 112
ephemera of sociable networks, 111
and ephemerality, 120
and ephemerology, 103, 124
fashionable sociability, 26, 103, 114, 201
and feminist historiography, 100
feminist readings of, 128
and Linnaean system, 121–3

and Luttrell, Narcissus, 110
and Lysons, Daniel 104–5
materiality of ephemera, 125
newspaper cuttings, 115
numismatics, 112, 124
private theatricals, 111
'queer' collecting, 103
represented as eccentric, 99, 103
science of ephemerology, 113
sociability, 102, 104, 113, 119, 124–5
subjectivity of, 100, 146
tickets, 102–3, 108, 110, 112, 115–19, 251
　admission, 109, 123, 139
　Bartolozzi specimens, 115
　blank, 124
　bookplates, 109
　'British Balloon', 141
　British Museum, 127–9
　Brooks's Club, 115
　Cipriani specimens, 115
　Damer bookplate, 116
　'Edinburgh fire balloon', 139–40, 149, 151
　Handel commemorations, 115
　Hastings impeachment, 115
　intaglio printing, 109
　Mischianza fete, 114
　Norwich ball, 116–19, 126, 128, 142, 149, 151, 253
　organisation, 121–3
　Pantheon, 115, 142
　for private theatricals, 115
　Ranelagh fete 1803, 132–5
　reader's, 127
　royal booth, Jubilee of 1814, 231, 233, 238
　sent by Sir William Hamilton, 119
　sticklers, 126–7
　trade card, 109
　visiting, 129
　visiting card, 109, 116, 121, 186–7
　women designers of, 115–19
and Turner, Dawson 106–7
visiting cards, 124, 193, 198, 205, 231
　Omai, 151, 193–6, 253
and Walpole, Horace, 105
watch-papers, 219–20
will, 102
and Wood, Anthony, 110
Banks, Sir Joseph, 26, 65, 98–100, 107, 153
British Museum reader's ticket, 127
celebrity of 1770s, 129
correspondence networks, 119
and Dryander, Jonas, 138
early reputation as macaroni, 129
and Endeavour voyage, 129

Banks, Sir Joseph (cont.)
  estate at Revesby Abbey, 105, 135–6
  ex-officio trustee of British Museum, 127
  fashionable sociability, 129–30
  and Franklin, Benjamin, 135–6, 139
  Gillray print of, 129–30
  and Hamilton, Sir William, 119
  installation Knights of Order of the Bath
    1803, 130, 132
  Jubilee of 1814
    ticket for, 231
  Knight of the Garter, 129
  and Linnaean system, 121–3
  and Lysons brothers, 105
  patron of Omai, 193
  portrait by Benjamin West, 129
  President of the Royal Society, 126
  Ranelagh fete 1803
    ticket for, 129–35
  and Turner, Dawson, 106
  visiting tickets, 129
Bankses' home (SSB and JB), No. 32 Soho
    Square, 10, 65, 128, 138, 208, 234
  collections at, 102, 112, 121, 148
  engravers' room, 120, 124
  herbarium, 123
  as a hub of scientific inquiry, 26, 121
  as a 'sociablarium', 123
Baronetage of England (1808), 240, 246, 249
Barrell, John, 160, 164
Bartholomew Fair, 63, 85, 230
Bartolozzi, Francesco, 115, 192
Bath, 28, 244, 246, 249
  Taylor's Circulating Library, 198
  theatre, 157
  theatrical performances, 174
  visiting in, 198
Belfast, 49
belles lettres, 203
bellmen, 247
  verses of, 247
Benedict, Barbara
  *Curiosity A Cultural History of Early Modern
    Inquiry*, 147–9
Benjamin, Walter, 103, 175
  Adorno on, 150–1
  Arcades Project, 150–2, 253
Bermondsey Spa, 145
Berry, Agnes, 116
Bewell, Alan, 130
Bexley, John, 244, 249
Biaggi, Michael, 136
Bible, 192, 223
bibliography, 3, 27, 92, 97, 171, 226
  and ephemera, 63

and ephemerology, 24
  first defined by Thomas Hartwell Horne,
    224
  historical, 96, 252
  Romantic period, 26, 61, 93
  as the 'sociology of texts', 28
  use of term, 216
bibliomania, 96, 171, 224
bibliomaniacs, 77, 172, 222
bibliophiles, 93, 106, 151
  Roxburghe Club, 94
bills, 18, 155, 180, *See* playbills and handbills
  genres of, 18
  lottery, 17
  of mortality, 17, 65
  posting, 17
  sellers of, 180
  shop, 17, 60, 112
binding, 68–9, 95, 192
Bindley, James, 93
Birmingham, 54
  'Church and King' riots of 1791, 46–8
Blagden, Charles, 135–6
Blair, Ann, 13
Blake, William, 192
Blanchot, Maurice, 74, 216, 250, 254
  'Everyday Speech', 31–2
Blomefield, Francis
  *An Essay towards a Topographical History of the
    County of Norfolk* (1739–75), 106
bodies, 192
  handbills on, 46
  prosthesis, 186
  watches on, 220
  and tickets, 109, 116
Bodleian Library, 2, 38, 74, 90, 253
Bonaparte, Napoleon, 216, 226, 239
book history, 3–4, 13, 24, 28
  and centrality of book, 15
  and the 'hidden history' of jobbing print, 19
Book History (journal), 4
book, the
  ascendancy of in eighteenth century, 35
  and the category of ephemera, 4
  contrast with broadsides, 15
  and D. F. McKenzie's 'sociology of texts', 15
  extra-illustrated or grangerized, 62
  pre-eminence of, 6–7
  and title pages, 63
  waning dominance of, 21, 24
bookplates, 105, 109, 116
books, 28, 166, 203, *See* codex-form of
  of 1790s, 210
  and absolute ephemerality, 223
  author-title definition, 147

binding, 68–9
bound, 13
  as commodities, 171
  displacement of sacral, 172
  and ephemera after 1800, 213
  extra-illustrated, 106
  first Australian, 180
  as knowledge, 15
  making, 106
  marketing of, 191
  post-1789, 171–2, 223
  and single sheets, 17, 37–8
  'small or stitched', 66–8, 252
  status of, 33
  and visiting cards, 191
booksellers, 98, 155, 223
  Edwards, 191
  Hookham, 192
  Kearsly, 190
  Rodd, Thomas, 174
  Soulbys, 155
  Sprange, Jasper, 155
bookshops, 35
bookstalls, 98
Botanic Garden, Chelsea, 111
botany, 121, 124
Bourdieu, Pierre, 176
Bowles, Carington (print seller), 137
Brant, Clare, 143, 148
Bratton, Jacky, 173, 175–6, 252
Brewer, John, 252
Britain
  and Ireland, 205
British Critic, 55, 220
British Library, 10, 74, 98, 253
  collection of newsmen's verses, 247
  Eighteenth-Century Short Title Catalogue, 16
  English Short Title catalogue, 16
  Frances Wolfreston collection, 98
  Francis Place collection, 234
  playbill collections, 154, 172
  SSB book collection, 112
  SSB collections, 98–9, 107, 110, 114, 124, 137, 147, 231, 237
British Museum, 28, 65, 74, 85, 90, 95, 120, 127–9, 253
  August Panizzi's *Catalogue* of 1841, 63
  Charles Burney Jr collection, 173, 253
  Daniel Lysons collection, 253
  and 'dead' walls, 163
  Francis Place collection, 235, 253
  frost fair collections, 217, 219
  garden, 128
  George Thomason collection, 253
  JB ex-officio trustee of, 127
  JB reader's ticket, 127
  John Bagford collection, 253
  John Crace collection, 219
  library of Robert Cotton, 111
  Montagu House, 128
  Museum Library, 90, 235
  Narcissus Luttrell collection, 253
  Planta, Joseph, 128
  Sir Hans Sloane collection, 253
  SSB collections, 99, 102, 107, 110–11, 114–15, 121, 137, 148, 173, 231, 253
  tickets, 127–9
  User's Guide (1987), 101
British navy, 108
Brittish Mercury, 71
broadsheets, 12, 18, 20
  and United Irishmen, 210
broadsides, 64, 70, 110
  Australian, 180
  commissioned and retail, 65, 252
  contrast with the book, 15
  definition of, 15
  as libels, 67
  Luttrell collection, 84–5
  newsmen's verses, 247
  and posters, 162
  royal proclamations, 53
  'Sawney in the Boghouse', 81
  terminology, 65
  'The Tall *Indian*-KING', 75, 78
  'To the right honourable the House of Commons', 80
Brooks's Club, 115
Brown, Bill, 24
Brydges, Samuel Egerton, 94
Bunbury, Henry William, 110
bundles, 68–9, 83, 98, 187, 204
  of United Irishmen texts, 210
bureaucracy
  and jobbing print, 19
Burke, Edmund
  Reflections on the Revolution in France, 211
Burke's *Peerage*, 123
Burkitt and Hudson (publishers), 232
Burney collection of newspapers, 173
Burney Jr, Charles (brother of Frances), 111, 172–3, 175, 234, 253
Burney, Frances, 100, 115, 172, 188, 204
Burton, Robert
  Anatomy of Melancholy, 223
Bury and Norwich Post, 227
business
  facilitated by jobbing print, 19
Bute, Earl of, 90

286 Index

Butler, Marilyn, 24–5, 252
  popular antiquarianism, 103, 254
butterfly
  ticket image, 116–19, 253

Cambridge, University of, 66, 172
camera obscura, 145
Canada
  former Prime Minister Harper, 183
  Library of the Parliament of, 183
  National Archives of, 183
  National Library of, 26
card racks, 192
cards, 17, *See* playing, visiting, trade
  invitation, 18
Carlisle House, 113, 129
Carlton House, 240
Carter, Harold, 120, 135
Castlereagh, Lord, 226
catalogues, 63, 75, 191, 253–4, *See* sale catalogues
  library, 104
  Popish Plot, 82–4, 93
cataloguing, 11, 147, 253
Caxton, William, 216
celebrity, 237
censorship, 81, 223
Centlivre, Susannah
  The Busy Body, 180
ceremonies, 110
Chalmers, George, 182
Chalmers, William, 153
Chandler, James, 207, 216
chapbooks, 9, 17, 98
charitable societies, 108
Charles II, king of England, 81, 90
Charleville Castle, 205
Charleville, Countess, 205
Charlotte, queen of England, 130
Chartism, 234
Chatterton, Thomas, 94
Chinese pagoda, 229, 231, 236, 241
Chinoisierie
  Omai visiting card, 193
Chun, Wendy Hui Chong, 7–8
cinema, 23, 147
Cipriani, Giovanni Battista, 115, 192
Clinton, Alan, 11–14, 36, 120
clocks, 243
codex-form book, 3, 33, 43, 52–3, 58, 97, 107, 251–2
  and bibliographical description, 63
  contrast with broadside, 15
  definition of, 15
  and documents, 19

and ephemeral mediality, 21
and ephemeral publications, 224
and handbills, 55
literary value, 28
and Literature, 61
and non-book, 61
and the novel, 205, 248
and posters, 162
and printed ephemera, 58
status of, 171
coffeehouses, 22, 75–6, 88, 98, 104
  owners of as playbill collectors, 173
coins, 60, 104, 110, 114
Coleridge, Samuel Taylor, 9, 27, 153, 168, 177
Coleridge, Sara (daughter of S.T. Coleridge)
  library auction, 9
collectanea, 60, 62, 147
collecting
  'bad' and 'good', 103
collections, 26, 62, 253
  and assemblage, 254
  private, 12
collectors, *See* SSB, Haslewood, Luttrell, Lysons, Thomason, Turner, Upcott, Walpole, Wood
  antiquarian, 24
  Bagford, John, 8, 63
  Burney Jr, Charles, 172–3
  Douce, Francis, 24–5
  of ephemera, 16
  of ephemera in 1960s, 9
  Field, John, 170
  'G. S.', 142
  Grose, Francis, 25
  Kemble, John Philip, 168
  Mathews, Charles, 169
  Miller, William, 72
  of printed ephemera, 25
  Reed, Isaac, 112
  Ritson, Joseph, 94
  Sloane, Sir Hans, 66, 99
  Swift, Jonathan, 68
  Wallington, Nehemiah, 72
  Winston, James, 169, 173
  Wolfreston, Frances, 98
  women, 98
Colley, Linda, 227
Collins, David, 179
commerce, 6, 104
communication, 187
  conversation, 187
  and the ephemeral Enlightenment, 23
  oral, 21, 187, 200

private, 190
  Regency networks of, 208
computers
  databases of, 174–5
  memory of, 7
concerts, 108, 113, 123
Congreve, Sir William, 230–1, 236
Congreve, William, 200
convicts, 177, 179
Cook, Captain James, 124
  Endeavour Journal, 184
  second voyage, 193
copyright, 22
Cork, 19
Cornelys, Teresa
  Carlisle House, 113
coronations
  tickets for, 108
Cotton, Robert, 111
Covent Garden Theatre
  Old Price riots, 235
  playbill collection, 169
Cowper, William, 43
  The Task, 246
Crabbe, George, 43
  'The News-Paper' (1785), 44
Crace, John Gregory, 219
cultural politics, 28
cultural studies, 11, 62, 252
culture
  elite versus popular, 37, 65
  public, 105
Curll, Edmund, 96
customary rights, 235
customs, 56, 104, 148, 252

Daily Advertiser, 195–6
Damer, Anne Seymour, 116
Darnton, Robert, 243
data, 24, 254
  storage of, 175
Davis, G., 238
Davison, William, 108
de Certeau, Michel, 36
'dead' walls, 162–4, 238
  ballads on, 163
  and poetry, 165
  and posters, 167
  site of ephemerality, 163, 215
  The Prelude, 163–4
debating societies, 52, 142
Declaration of the Rights of Man, 211
Defoe, Daniel, 45
DeLanda, Manuel, 150

Delany, Mary, 100
Deleuze, Gilles, 103, 149
Deputy Keeper of the State Paper Office
  Lemon, Robert, 92
Derrida, Jacques, 33, 38, 77, 92, 185
  archives, 73–4
  hospitality, 195–7, 199
  Paper Machine, 13–14
    on book as gathering, 15–16
  paper spectrum, 62, 238
  'priceless archive', 31
  'principle of commencement', 96, 148
Devonshire, Duke of 168
diaries, 42
Dibdin, Thomas Frognall, 69, 77, 55
  Bibliomania, (1811), 69
Dickens, Charles
  Bleak House, 157
  Dombey and Son, 159
  Household Words, 166
  Martin Chuzzlewit, 158–9
dictionaries, 192
Dierks, Konstantin, 191
digital age, 19
  and printed ephemera, 20
digital media, 19
digital texts, 7
digitisation, 90, 175, 184–5
  of Burney collection of newspapers, 173
  of knowledge, 22
disciplinarity, 137, 143–4, 148, 152
  and ephemerology, 100, 148–9, 252
dockets, 19, 121, *See* tickets, terminology of
  absence of in *The Absentee*, 212
  Gascoigne, John on, 212
documents, 12, 25
  in *The Absentee*, 203
  and the book, 19
  Gitelman, Lisa on, 19
  and jobbing printing, 19
  performative force of, 20–1
Dodsley, Robert, 200
doors, 197
doorways, 157
Douce, Francis, 24–5
Downes, John
  Roscius Anglicanus (1708), 176
drama, 3, 165, 215
Drury Lane
  playbill collection, 169
Dryander, Jonas, 123, 138
Dryden, John
  Absalom and Achitophel, 92
  The Medal, 92

Dublin
    theatrical performances, 174
Dundas, Henry, 47

Edgeworth home, 208
Edgeworth, Frances (stepmother of Maria), 205
Edgeworth, Maria, 21, 27, 239, 251
    The Absentee (1812), 27, 188, 204–13, 249
    Belinda (1801), 207
    Popular Tales, 211
    use of visiting cards, 205
Edgeworth, Richard Lovell, 207
Edwards, Anthony, 191
Egypt, 1
eighteenth century, 27
    ideas of ephemerality, 28
Eighteenth Century Collections Online, 44
Eighteenth-Century Short Title Catalogue, 64
Eighteenth-Century Short Title Catalogue (E-CSTC), 16
Eisenstein, Elizabeth L., 5–6
electronic media, 6
Eliot, Simon, 28
Elizabeth I, queen of England, 85
Elliott, Marianne, 210
Ellis, James, 50
Emma, 214
    Walter Scott's review of, 242
Empedocles, 177
Encyclopedia Britannica, 48
Encyclopedia of Ephemera, 10
England
    civil wars, 23, 66, 91
    Commonwealth period, 66
English Short Title Catalogue, 16, 253
engraving, 60, 107
    Bartolozzi, Francesco, 115, 192
    Blake, William, 192
    Cipriani, Giovanni Battista, 115, 192
    intaglio, 14, 192
    portrait, 113
    room at Bankses' home, 120, 124
    visiting cards, 193
Enlightenment
    associational culture, 26, 59, 80
    and ballooning, 138
    British, 62
    continuous with the present, 23
    and diurnal consciousness, 42
    and eighteenth century, 27
    and ephemerology, 27, 66, 100
    inquiry, 188
    knowledge, 6, 66, 207
    mediation, 144
    period, 23
    and print, 246
    science, 26, 66, 108
    Siskin and Warner's 'history of mediations', 22–3
    and sociability, 22
    and theatre history, 176
    and tickets, 114
Enslen, Johann Karl, 144–7
entertainments, 104, 113, 229
entomology, 56
entrepreneurship, 147
Environs of London (1792–96), 105
ephemera
    and 1790s, 57
    after 1800, 213
    20th century descriptions of, 224
    academic study of, 31
    and advertisements, 26
    archive, 74, 77
    assemblage, 112
    and ballads, 26
    and bibliographical description, 63
    and the book, 4, 6–7
    and 'book making', 16
    'books', 26, 64–5, 100, 112, 148, 188, 208
    in Britain since 1960s, 10
    bundles of, 204
    category of, 6, 11, 20, 97
    Centre for Ephemera Studies, University of Reading, 10
    and close reading, 28
    collecting in seventeenth century, 224
    collectors in 1960s, 9
    and continuum of print, 12
    and diurnal consciousness, 42
    Douce and Grose collections, 25
    in entomology, 2, 42
    Ephemera Society, 10, 253
    first sought by collectors, 171
    formation in long eighteenth century, 8
    and handbills in 1790s, 44
    late eighteenth-century meanings, 44
    librarians and, 11
    and library science, 11–13
    and literature, 188
    marginalisation of, 3
    in medicine, 2, 42
    and pamphlets, 26
    political, 83
    and popular culture, 36, 64
    and printing press, 27
    Rickards' definition of, 31, 215
    Rickards' *Encyclopedia of*, 10
    and Romantic period, 27
    and sales catalogues, 76

Samuel Johnson's coinage, 5
and *Short Title Catalogue*, 64
societies, 10
and spectrum of paper, 13
studies, 9
term, 8, 25, 56
and theatre, 26
and tickets, 26
ephemera, printed, 23, 80, 98, 113, 154, 160
and 1790s, 25
accessibility, 29
bibliography, 77
book history definition of, 13
and codex, 20, 58, 167
definition, 3
and Enlightenment mediations, 22–3
and ephemera studies, 3
and the everyday, 33
formation of category, 9–10, 23, 35–6
frost fairs, 28, 253
and hegemonic culture, 10
history of, 27
and jobbing print, 17–20
Jubilee of 1814, 28
and library science, 11–13
as literary art, 161
and literary studies, 14, 28
and literary value, 28
and modernity, 29
non-book print, 17
and the novel, 204–5, 251
Pemberton report on, 11
and 'the people', 65
playbills, 26–7
as a poetics, 20, 177
and popular culture, 61, 225
post 1800, 225
and print culture of eighteenth century, 15
and printing history, 8–9
in prose fiction, 188
public sphere, 104
and public sphere, 230
Raven's definition of, 20
reading, 29
Rickards' definition of, 10
and Romantic period novel, 188
and single-sheets as commodities, 20
and sociability, 22
for Strawberry Hill, 105
term, 23
tickets, 70
and tickets, 22
and typography, 166
Twyman's definition of, 17
what isn't ephemera, 21
what isn't literature, 3
ephemerae
Samuel Johnson's use of, 41–4
ephemerality, 4, 29, 103
absolute ephemerality, 13–14, 65, 223, 242
and Addison, *Spectator* no. 85, 31
beginning in mid-fifteenth century, 5
category of, 6
and category of 'everyday', 28
and centrality of playbills, 172
and 'dead' walls, 163
and digital media, 7
of digitised information, 8, 253
discourse of after French Revolution, 56
discourse of post 1800, 61, 222
'enduring ephemeral', *See* Chun
and Enlightenment mediations, 22–3
ephemeral mediality, 21
and everyday life, 215–16
and exhibition culture, 137
formation in eighteenth century, 8
formative in literary Romanticism, 29
formative in modernism, 29
and *The Harleian Miscellany*, 39
in nineteenth century, 64
and performativity, 20–1
as a poetics, 29, 154, 248
politicised meanings of, 131
politicization of around 1800, 92
and the present, 86
and print culture, 5, 8
and printing press, 27
and regimes of control, 15
and the rise of the poster, 166–7
and SSB, 120
and theatre, 175
and theatre history, 176
trash, 6
ephemerology, 2, 24, 29, 58, 148, 172, 216, 254
of *The Absentee*, 211–12
and bookmaking, 62
and disciplinarity, 148–9
Enlightenment's other science, 26–7, 61, 66
and frost fair print, 218
Georgian, 154
impact on humanities, 253
spatial dimension, 121
and the *Spectator*, 224
and SSB, 100, 103, 113, 124
and Thomason, George, 70
ephemerophiles, 98, 151, 172
Erasmus, 223
Etna, Mount, 177
European Magazine, 55

Evelyn, John, 60, 85–6, 88, 217
everyday life, 6, 215–16, 249, 254
  and ephemerality, 215–16
  and novels, 215
  and orality, 165
  Romantic, 216
everyday, the, 36, 58, 70, 74, 250, 252
  Blanchot on, 31–2
  and ephemera, 31
  in nineteenth century, 28
  and printed ephemera, 32–3
  and 'the popular', 36
  and reading, 29
  study of, 31
Examiner, 236
Exclusion Crisis, 84
Exeter, 18
exhibitions, 17, 45, 123, 137, 176, 235
  Ephemera Society, 10

Facebook, 23
fairground, 176
  booths, 174
Farquhar, George, 200
  The Recruiting Officer, 179
fashion, 138, 143–5, 203
  plates, 203
Favret, Mary, 240–1
Fawcett, John, 169
Feltham, John, 57–8
  The Picture of London (1804), 58
Ferris, Ina, 61, 94
Field, John, 170
  library sale, 170, 174, 224
fireworks, 229–30
First Fleet, 179
flyleaf, 110
food
  readable texts, 34
  wrappings, 35
forms, 18–19
Fox, Adam, 84
Frankenstein, 147
Franklin, Benjamin, 135–6, 139
French Revolution, 48, 171, 211
  and discourse of ephemera and ephmerality, 56
  and mass public, 230
frost fairs, 26, 148, 176, 181, 216, 226, 240, 250, 253, *See Frostiana*
  1683–84, 85–90, 217
  1715–16, 217–18
  1739–40, 217
  1789, 217, 219
  1814, 28, 219–22, 246

  ballads, 219
  Crace collection, 219
  Daniel Lysons collection, 105, 218
  as ephemeral, 222
  Francis Place collection, 237
  handbills, 220–2
  Isaac Reed collection, 218
  Mrs George's collection, 219
  and print, 217–19
  printing press at, 219, 221–2
  and public sphere, 104, 222
  souvenir tickets, 86–7
  tickets, 219–20, 235–6
  watch-papers, 219
  woodcuts, 219
Frostiana, 220–2
  G. Davis (publisher), 231
fugitive literature, 224–5
fugitive print, 25, 54–5, 58–9, 61, 75, 105, 148, 210, 222, 230, 237
  of 1790s, 52
  and handbills, 48
  and Jubilee of 1814, 230
funerals, 109–10
  Fox, Charles James, 105, 110, 114, 229
  Nelson, Horatio, 110, 114, 229
  Pitt, William, 105, 110, 114, 229
Fyshe Palmer, Thomas, 48, 55
  and Ellis, James, 50
  transportation, 51
  trial and conviction, 50

G. S.
  (collector of ballooning), 142
  1841 sale catalogue, 143
Gale Cengage, 173
gambling, 190
gaming clubs, 189
Garber, Marjorie, 3, 21
garlands, 17
Garrick Club, 169
Garrick, David, 60, 173, 176
Gascoigne, John, 121, 212
General Advertiser, 38
General Catalogue, A, 83
General Evening Post, 140
general orders, 179
Genest, John
  account of sale of John Field's library, 174–5
  New Monthly Magazine commentary, 176–7
  Some Account of the English Stage, 174–5
Gentleman's Magazine, 110, 169
  1814 frost fair, 219, 222
  debate between 'JK' and 'AC', 222–4, 234
Gentleman's Pocket Magazine, 244, 247

Index

George III, king of England, 48, 90, 179
  1789 recovery, 110, 114–15
George, Mrs
  frost fair collection, 219
Georgian print culture, 25
Gerrald, Joseph, 49
gift-giving, 102, 120, 188
Gillray, James, 110, 134
  JB as 'great South Sea Caterpillar', 129–30
Gilmartin, Kevin, 222
Ginger, John, 55
Gitelman, Lisa, 7
  on jobbing print and ephemera, 19–20
Glorious Revolution, 223
Godwin, William, 26–7, 53–4
  Caleb Williams, 147
  diary, 189
  History of the Commonwealth of England (1824-28), 90–3
  and Thomason tracts, 90–3
goldbeater's skin, 144–5
Goldgar, Anne, 128
Gordon riots, 46
graffiti, 165
Graham, James, 142
Granger, Rev. James
  Biographical History of England (1769), 62
gravestones, 165
Greenwood, Thomas, 232
Gretton, John
  visiting cards, 190
Grub Street, 42, 95
Guillory, John, 25, 164
Gulston, Eliza B., 116
Gurden, Lilian, 1–2
Gutenberg, Johannes, 5, 217

Habermas, Jürgen, 233
  private sphere, 201
  'town' of culture products, 113
hallways, 199
Hamilton, Sir William, 119
hand press, 23
handbills, 25, 28, 33, 54, 104, 111, 166
  in 1790s, 92, 178, 210
  1814 frost fair, 222
  and anonymity, 48, 54
  in Birmingham riots, 46–8
  and 'dead' walls, 163
  defined as ephemeral 'trash', 226
  in Edgeworth's *Popular Tales*, 211
  Enslen's London debut, 144–5
  first use of term, 45
  frost fair, 226
  and fugitive mediality, 211

fugitive print, 222
Fyshe Palmer, Thomas
  trial and conviction, 50–2
  in Jubilee of 1814, 230, 233, 237–8
  London Corresponding Society, 160
  lottery, 106
  and loyalists, 46, 55–7
Mealmaker, George
  author of Dundee handbill, 50–1
  origins of, 44
  as playbills, 155–6, 159
  and political communication, 46
  and printers, 55
  and radical publishers, 50
  and radicals, 46, 54–5, 57, 159
  size of, 45, 162
  and Thomas Paine, 53
  as tickets, 115
  and trials, 1790s, 50
Tytler, James, 140
  trial and conviction for, 49
  and United Irishmen, 210
  and Unlawful Societies Act, 54–5
  Weir of Horncastle, 126
Handel, George Frederic
  commemorations of 1784, 114–15, 142
handwriting, 109
Harleian Miscellany, The, 38–40, 53, 67, 73, 202
Harley, Robert, first Earl of Oxford, 38
  Harleian library, 202
  Harleian tracts, 202
Harper, Stephen
  former Prime Minister, Canada, 183
Harris, Michael, 4, 43
Haslewood, Joseph, 51, 94–8, 106–7, 151, 172, 175, 223, 225, 252
  The British Bibliographer (1810), 94
  catalogues, 95
  Chatterton collection, 94
  Gentleman's Magazine, 94
  and Luttrell, Narcissus, 95–7, 171
  maker of ephemera books, 171
  making books of ephemera, 94
  'Of Plays, Players and Playhouses', 176
  playbills, 170
  and Ritson, Joseph, 94
  Roxburghe Revels (1834), 94
  and SSB, 110
  unrealised 'History of English theatre', 171
Hastings, Warren
  impeachment trial 1788, 114–15
hawkers, 18, 74, 210, 243, 246
Heber, Richard, 93
heraldry, 104, 112

herbarium, 123–4
    at Bankses' home, 120, 123
higher education, 11, 253
Historical Register, or Edinburgh Monthly Intelligencer, 49
historiography, 171
    diurnal, 42, 72, 210, 251
    theatre, 174
history, 72
    'bill-sticking', 175
    'from below', 11
    of science, 143
    of the year 1814, 28
Hoag, Elaine, 183
Holcroft, Thomas, 173
    Hugh Trevor, 155
homosociality, 76
    female, 116
    male, 93, 98, 113
Hone, William, 34
Hookham, Thomas, 192
Horne, Thomas Hartwell
    Introduction to the Study of Bibliography (1814), 224
hospital
    root meaning, 202
hospitality, 187, 197
    and 'hospital', 202
    polite, 198
    in *The Absentee*, 207
    and visiting cards, 188
Howe, Sir William, 114
Hughes, George, 179–81
Hughes, Jabez, 96
humanities scholarship, 23, 253
Humphrey, Ozias, 60
Hunt, Leigh, 155, 159
Hunter, Governor John, 179–80, 182
Hunter, J. P., 187–8, 215
Hutchinson, Sara, 153
Hutton, William, 47

identity, 14
illuminations, 226
incunabula, 171
indulgences, 5, 171
information, 11, 187
    and ephemerality, 254
    digital, 7
    dissemination of, 22
    networks, 173
    in *The Absentee*, 207
ink, 179, 191
insects, 225
intaglio printing, 109

Intercepted Letter from China, An (1804), 209
internet, 10
invitations, 69, 105, 126, 203
Ireland, 74, 206
    1798 rebellion, 205
    Act of Union, 205
    and Britain, 205
    Catholics, 205
    Cork, 191
    Dublin manners, 209
    Protestants, 205

Jensen, Kristian, 171
    books post-1789, 171–2
jobbing print, 36, 45, 55, 58, 65, 77, 98, 121, 238
    and ballads, 165
    and bureaucracy, 19
    and business, 18
    and construction of knowledge, 19
    and 'dead' walls, 163
    definition of, 17
    and the document, 19
    and ephemera, 17–20
    Gitelman on, 20
    the 'hidden history' of book history, 19
    job house, 17
    and performativity, 21
    playbills, 155
    and playbills, 186
    Raven on, 18–20
    tickets, 108–9
    and tickets, 108
    and typographic revolution, 164
jobbing printers
    newsmen's verses, 247
Johnson, Dorothea, 1, 7
Johnson, John, 1–2, 8–9, 23–4, 29, 35, 38, 74, 253–4
Johnson, John de Monins, *See* Johnson, John
Johnson, Samuel, 4, 25, 27, 30, 33, 37, 49, 60, 73, 176, 223
    'An Account of this Undertaking' (1743), 38–40, 43
    and diurnal historiography, 42
    on ephemerae, 41–4
    essay 191, *The Rambler*, 202–4, 206, 212
    'Essay on the Origin and Importance of Small Tracts and Fugitive Pieces', 38
    fugitive literature, 37–42
    and *The Harleian Miscellany*, 38–40
    The Rambler no. 145 (1751), 40–3
    and visiting cards, 188
Jonson, Ben
    Sejanus, 170

journals, 42, 224
Jubilee of 1814, 28, 110, 114, 227–40, 246, 250
  Account of the National Jubilee, 236
  Bankses' tickets to royal booth, 232
  Chinese pagoda, 229, 231, 236, 241
  and fugitive print, 230
  handbills, 230, 233, 238
  peace festivals, 233
  Place collection, 231, 234–9
  poster for 'Jubilee Printing Office', 238–9
  printing presses, 230, 234
  royal booth, 228, 237–8
  Sadler's balloon flight, 228, 230
  songs, 238
  SSB collection, 231–4, 237–9
  supervision of William Congreve, 230
  Temple of Concord, 229–31
  Temple of Peace, 236
  tickets, 228, 230–1
  watch-papers, 231

Katler, Barrett, 105
Katterfelto, Gustavus, 137, 147
Kean, Edmund, 226
Kearsly, George, 190
Keir, James, 48
Kemble, John Philip, 168, 170
Kentish Post, 244
Keswick
  playbills, 154
Kiessling, Nicolas, 81
King, Lieutenant-Governor Philip Gidley, 153, 181–3
King's Pamphlets, *See* Thomason tracts
King's Theatre, 115
Kingston, Duchess of, 111
Kirby's Wonderful and Eccentric Museum, 221
Kirkgate, Thomas (printer), 105
Kirschenbaum, Matthew, 7
Kittler, Friedrich, 164
Klancher, Jon, 61, 96–7, 172
knowledge, 111, 138
  and Bankses' home, 26
  and codex, 15
  digitisation of, 22
  Enlightenment, 207
  Enlightenment totalities of, 66
  and jobbing print, 19
  proper, 202
  and sociability, 201
Koran, 30–1

labelling, 18
labels, 109, *See* tickets, terminology of
  address, 213

Ladies' Coterie, 113, 129
Lake District, 153
lamplighters, 247
Langan, Celeste, 164, 251
last dying speeches, 17–18, 211
lectures, 17, 108, 229
ledgers, 19
Leeds Intelligencer, 57
legislation
  1790s, 55
    Newspapers Regulation Act 1798, 57
    Seditious Writings Act, 49
    Unlawful Societies Act, 55
Leis, Arlene, 120
leisure, 104
letterpress, 64, 107, 151, 192
letters, 192, 204
Lewis, Charles, 95
Lewis, John, 161
  Printed Ephemera (1962), 9
libel, seditious, 53
libels, 66
  and pamphlets, 67
  terminology of, 67
librarians, 61
  and ephemera, 11
libraries, 13, 35
  circulating, 214
  national, 253
  private, 98
  public, 225
library cataloguing, 147
library sale catalogues, 68
library science, 11, 21, 28
  and ephemera, 11–13
Licensing Act, 6, 81
Liddle, Dallas, 57
Linnaean system, 121–3, 212
Linnean Society, 106
literacy, 191
  political, 52
literary culture, 171, 204
literary heritage, 175
literary history, 26–7, 61, 97, 187
  and ephemerology, 24
  focus on books, 191
  Persuasion, 28
literary studies, 3, 21, 24, 28
  and ephemera, 14, 27–8
  and theatre, 175
literary value, 222
  and printed ephemera, 28
literature, 23, 41, 92
  canon of, 27
  and codex-form book, 61

literature (cont.)
  and ephemera, 3, 188
  fugitive, 25–6, 37–8, 66, 70, 74, 76, 209, 224–5
  'popular', 65
  'serious', 187
  'street', 64
Liverpool
  Theatre Royal, 157
Lloyd, John, 136
Lloyd, Sarah, 126
  'ticket system', 114, 204
  tickets, 108, 151
London, 10, 19, 155, *See* Bankses' home
  Almack's, 113
  and associational culture, 69
  balls in, 116
  Brooks's Club, 115
  Carlisle House, 113
  Charles Dickens on, 166
  'dead' walls in, 162–3
  displaced Irish in, 206
  exhibition culture, 229
  frost fairs, *See* frost fairs
  Jubilee of 1814, 28
  Ladies Coterie, 113
  London Institution, 60
  'Monster', 110, 137, 147
  Pantheon, the, 113, 115, 129
  Seven Dials, 237
  sites of archives, 234
  sociable economy of, 201
  Soho, 10
  Thames, the river, 26
    'a great Whale', 69
  theatrical performances, 174
London Corresponding Society, 46, 52, 160, 234
Long Parliament (1640-1660), 72
longue durée, 148
lotteries, 17, 60, 106
Love, Harold, 84
lower orders, 51, 70, 104, 126–7
Lunar Society, 48, 207
Lunardi, Vincent, 136–9, 142, 144
Lupton, Christina, 248
Luther, Martin, 223
Luttrell, Narcissus, 26, 66, 84–5, 88, 97–8, 103, 106, 112, 148, 160, 176, 223
  broadside, 'Great BRITAINS Wonder', 88
  collecting interests, 187
  collections
    broadsides, 84–5
    dispersal of, 92–3
    frost fair 1683–84, 87–90, 217
    Walter Scott's use of, 93

copy of 'State Bellman's' verses, 247
and frost fair 1683-84, 85
and Haslewood, 95–7
Popish Plot catalogues, 93
and SSB, 110
Lyceum, 145
Lynch, Deidre, 215, 248
Lynn, Michael, 138, 140, 144
Lysons, Daniel, 103–5, 107, 252–3
  catalogue of library, 170
  'Collectanea Dramatica', 170
  collection on ballonmania, 142, 148
  Environs of London (1792–96), 104
  frost fair collections, 218
  part of Banks circle, 105
  Perfect Diurnal of Proceedings, 170
Lysons, Samuel (brother of Daniel), 105

Malone, Edmund, 96
  The Critical and Miscellaneous Prose Works of John Dryden (1800), 92
  use of Luttrell collection, 92
manifestoes, 20
manners, 187, 204, 209, 234
manuscript, 19, 60, 190
Margarot, Maurice, 49
masquerades, 105, 201
mass media, 54, 58
Mathews, Charles, 169, 174, 234
Maudsley, Henry, 230
Maxted, Ian, 18, 36
Mayhew, Henry, 64
  Curiosities of Street Literature, (1871), 64
  London Labour and the London Poor, (1851-52), 64
McGann, Jerome, 22–4
McKenzie, D. F., 4, 15
McKitterick, David, 107
McLane, Maureen N., 164, 251
McLuhan, Marshall, 23
McShane, Angela, 65, 70
Mealmaker, George
  author of Dundee handbill, 50–1
media, 24
  archaeology, 252
  'concept', 244
  digital, 7
  electronic, 6
  innovations around 1800, 164
  studies, 19, 23, 62
  tourism, 168
media history, 27–8, 103, 162, 252
  and ballooning, 147
  and theatre, 175
medicine, 44, 56

Mee, Jon, 220
melodrama, 164
Mendle, Michael, 68, 70, 72, 90
Methodism, 108
methodology, 27
Metropolitan Magazine, 243
microfilm, 90
military
　first public museum, 240
Miller, William, 72, 77, 81
Milne, Esther, 186
Mint, Royal
　and SSB collections, 112
Mischianza (fete), 114
modernism, 29
modernity, 25, 137, 166
Montagu House, 128
Monteyne, Joseph, 85–6
Montgolfier brothers, Charles and Robert, 135
monuments, 165
More, Hannah
　Village Politics, 52
Morning Advertiser, 237
Morning Chronicle, 163, 229, 231
Morning Post, 56, 131, 229
Muñoz, José Esteban, 149
Museum, The
　Walpole's essay in, 200–1

Nancy, Jean-Luc, 20–1, 166
Napoleon, *See* Bonaparte, Napoleon
Nash, John, 229
nation states, 14, 90
natural philosophy
　and sociability, 144
natural wonders, 105
Nelson, Horatio, 228
New Monthly Magazine, 174
　commentary on John Genest, 176–7
New South Wales, 26
news, 71, 92
news sheets, 42, 65, 252
　Perfect Diurnal of Proceedings, 170
newsagents, 244
newsbooks, 70
newsmen, 28, 243–9
　Bexley, John, 244, 249
　newsmen's verse, 247–8
　British Library collection, 247
　and the novel, 247
newspaper cuttings, 107, 110
newspapers, 18, 22, 28, 32, 37, 50, 104, 113, 170, 177, 224
　1790s, 57, 210
　in *The Absentee*, 212–13
　and Austen, 240
　and Darnton's 'communications circuit', 243
　defined as ephemeral 'trash', 226
　as diurnal, 42–3
　lending services, 244
　Newspapers Regulation Act of 1798, 57
　and the novel, 248
　in *Persuasion*, 242
Newton, Richard
　'Progress of a Player', 156
Nicol, George, 130
Northanger Abbey
　visiting, 197–200
　visiting cards, 249
Norwich
　assembly rooms, 116
　ball tickets, 116–19, 126, 128, 142
Notes and Queries, 172
notices, 17
novel, the, 113, 164, 251
　a diurnal form, 42
　and ephemeral mediality, 21
　as a genre, 214–15
　and second printing revolution, 251
　and visiting, 27
novels, 119, 187–8
　as codex-form books, 248
　and ephemeral print, 204–5, 251
　focus of literary history, 191
　and newsmen's verse, 247
　repository of the ephemeral, 248
　Romantic period, 188
　transcending trash, 248
numismatics, 112
nymphs, 145, 147–8

O'Keeffe, John
　The Agreeable Surprise 157
　The Poor Soldier, 180
Oates, Titus, 81
Observations on the Government and Constitution of Great Britain (1792), 56
Old Price Riots, 235, 237
Omai, 151, 193–6
　death of, 195
　and print, 195
　visiting cards of SSB, 193–6, 253
　visiting cards, farewell, 196
opera, 113
opinion, 92
Oracle (newspaper)
　'Copy of a Botany Bay Play Bill', 180–1
orality, 164
　of the everyday, 165
Orme, Edward, 232

Osborne, Thomas, 38
Oxford, 1
  Ashmolean Museum, 90
  Bodleian Library, 2, 38, 74, 90, 253
  and civic sociability, 79
  Merton College, 72
  University of, 1, 66, 74
  University Press, 2

Pacific, 193
Paine, Thomas, 53–4
  Rights of Man, 53, 56
pamphlets, 12, 18, 26, 37, 50, 52, 77
  in 1790s, 210
  and libels, 67
  terminology, 66
Panizzi, August, 64, 253
  Catalogue of Printed Books in the British Museum (1841), 63
panoramas, 145, 164, 235, 252
Pantheon, the, 113, 115, 129, 138, 144, 170, 230
  and elite female sociability, 145
  and Enslen's flying sculptures, 144–7
  ticket for, 142
pantomime, 230
paper, 5, 33, 151, 177, 179, 186
  in *The Absentee*, 207–9
  and Addison's *Spectator* no. 85, 30–1
  currency, 18
  first paper-making mill, Australia, 179
  invention of toilet-paper, 81
  'paperwork', 19
  perishability, 223
  production, 191
  as prosthesis, 14
  scrap, 30–1, 34, 81, 96
  spectrum of and ephemera, 13
  and stationery trade, 191
  tobacco, 31, 35
  types of, 13
  uses of, 13–14
  'war of ideas', 1790s, 25, 33, 210
  waste, 81
  Wiggins Teape, 10
  wrapping, 34, 67
parchment, 5
parliament, 51, 57, 81
Pasley, Charles
  Essay on the Military Police (1810), 209–10
passports, 21
pasteboard, 109, 115, 186–7
patters, 18
PDF (portable document format), 19

peace of 1814, 226–8, 239, *See* also Jubilee of 1814
  as ephemeral, 241
  peace festivals, 226–7, 233
  sociability, 226–7
peace of 1815, 239–40
Peace of Amiens, 117, 130
Peacey, Jason, 70
pedlars, 18, 210
Peerage (Burke's), 123
Pegasus, 145
Pemberton, John E.
  National Provision of Printed Ephemera in the Social Sciences, 11
penny histories, 18, 187
people, the, 24, 233
  and the everyday, 36
  and printed ephemera, 65
Pepys, Samuel, 187
performance studies, 149
performativity
  and ephemerality, 20–1
periodicals, 37, 63, 187, 201, 203–4
periodisation, 23
  and long eighteenth century, 23
  complications of, 27
Perseus, 145
Persuasion, 27, 216, 239–50
  and Debrett's *Baronetage*, 240, 246, 249
  Favret on, 240–1
  and newsmen, 243–8
  newspapers in, 242
  as poetics of ephemerality, 248
  seasons in, 241
  time in, 239–43
  and visiting cards, 249
  and the year 1814, 28, 248–9
petitions, 17, 65
phantasmagoria, 145
Philadelphia, 19, 114
philology, 23–4, 171
philosophy, 150
Piper, Andrew, 7, 15
placards, 167
  election, 224
Place, Francis, 28, 216, 248, 253
  collection on Old Price Riots, 235, 237
  frost fair collection, 237
  frost fair tickets, 235–6
  Jubilee of 1814 collection, 231, 234–9, 246, 253
  member of Westminster Committee, 235
  sociability at 16 Charing Cross, 234
  view of printing press, 238
Planta, Joseph, 128

'Plato's Advice' (song), 236
playbills, 18, 26–8, 58, 76–7, 153, 186, 203
    1796 Sydney *Jane Shore*, 26, 153–4,
        177–9
    after 1803, 161–2
    in *The Absentee*, 208
    and acting profession, 168
    ballads privileged over, 225
    Burney collection of, 234
    centrality of in Georgian archive, 172
    Charles Mathews collection, 169
    collecting, 167
    collection of Charles Burney Jr, 172–3
    Covent Garden collection, 169
    defined as ephemeral 'trash', 226
    in Dickens, Charles, 157–9
    Drury Lane collection, 169
    early modern period, 154
    first collectors, 173
    as handbills, 'house-bills', 155–6, 159, 179
    information on, 156
    James Winston collection, 169
    John Field collection, 170
    and John Genest's *Some Account of the English Stage*, 174
    John Philip Kemble collection, 168
    Joseph Haslewood collection, 170
    Keswick, 154
    mock, 50, 160–1, 164, 181
        'La Guillotine! or George's Head in the Basket', 160–1, 236
    at National Library of Australia, 157
    newspaper accounts of 'Botany Bay Play Bill', 180–1
    and the novel, 248
    and Plumptre, James, 167–8, 215
    as posters, 156
    and printing technology around 1800, 27
    in Romantic period culture, 26
    in Samuel Johnson's essay no. 191, 203–4
    in Scott, Walter, 159
    and Southey, Robert, 157
    Tait's Edinburgh Magazine, 162
    Talfourd, Thomas Noon on, 167
    and theatre history, 252
    as theatre records, 168
    Theatrical Examiner, 162
    and visiting cards, 187
playbooks, 175
playhouses, 155, 179
    1843 relaxation of licensing laws, 176
playing cards, 189–90
plays, 70

pleasure gardens, 108, 113, 170, 176
    Ranelagh, 113
    Vauxhall, 113, 162, 230
Plumptre, James, 157, 167–8, 174
poetics
    of ephemerality, 29, 154, 248
    of print, 20
    of the everyday, 165
poetry, 3, 28, 41, 65, 70, 164, 215, 251
    and 'dead' walls, 165
    and libels, 67
    occasional, 31, 37 110
    Romantic period, 164–5
political clubs, 22
politics
    1790s, 110
Pope, Alexander
    The Rape of the Lock, 145
Popish Plot, 81
    catalogues, 82–4, 93
        A Complete Catalogue, 83
        A General Catalogue, 83
popular entertainment, 174
popular, the, 58, 104 225
    and ballads, 36
Portarlington, Lady, 116
post, 192
    boys, 246
postal system, 22
posters, 15, 26, 156, 166–7, 222, 230
    Jubilee of 1814, 238–9
    on placards, 167
    size of, 162
posting bills, 17
present, the, 71–2, 78. 104
    continuous with Enlightenment and Romanticism, 23
    science of, 107
Priestley, Joseph, 46, 28
Prince Regent, 233, 237
print, 19, 29, 104, 190, *See* fugitive print
    cheap, 58, 65, 92, 109, 163, 165, 225, 233, 237
    continuum of, 12–13
    culture, 5
    Eisenstein on, 5–6
    ephemera as poetics of, 20
    'ephemeralization' of, 6
    and frost fairs, 217–19
    medium of information, 208
    mid-fifteenth century age of, 5
    non-book, 17
    and Omai, 195
    out-of-doors, 58, 159
    and preservation, 5–6

print (cont.)
    post-print age and ephemerality, 7
    radical, 239
    trade, 12, 38, 76
print media, 137, 170
print sellers
    Bowles, Carington, 137
printed ephemera, 166
printers
    Jasper Sprange, Tunbridge Wells, 108
    and handbills, 55
    and playbills, 155
    and Unlawful Societies Act 1799, 54–5
    William Davison, Alnwick, 108
printing
    hand press, 23
    history, 62, 171
    intaglio, 109
    invention of, 164
    letterpress, 109
    second revolution of, 18, 58
    steam press, 216, 246
printing press, 26–7, 179
    earliest products of, 5
    at frost fairs, 86, 219, 221–2
    Place's view of, 238
prints, 138
    'great South Sea Caterpillar', 129–30
    'John Bexley', 244
    'Progress of a Player', 156
    'Sawney in the Boghouse' (1745), 81
private theatricals, 104, 170
    Richmond House 1787-88, 114
    SSB collections, 111
    at Wynnstay, 115
proclamations, 65, 70, 74
    against 'divers wicked and seditious writings', 48
promenading, 113
ProQuest, 2
prose fiction, 3, 119, 187–8
    represenation of ephemera in, 188
    and visiting cards, 27
prospectuses, 90, 112
Public Record Office, 26, 91
public sphere, 19, 26, 70, 103–4, 143, 230
    1790s, 222
    feminized, 114
    and frost fairs, 104, 222
    post-war, 237
    and printed ephemera, 104
    and radicalism, 114

queer theory, 149–50

radical publishers, 50
radicalism, 33, 52
    1790s, 92
    and print, 239
    Wilkite, 46
Raimbach, Abraham, 130–1
Ranelagh
    fete 1803, 129, 132–5
    gardens, 113
Raven, James, 216
    on jobbing print, 18–20
    typographical assuredness, 121
Raymond, Joad, 66
reading, 34
    accidental, 25, 29–30, 34–7, 59, 81, 120, 169, 209, 215
    and playbill collecting, 167
    close, 103, 157, 180
    ephemera, 28
    and everyday life, 29
    fugitive, 114
    handbills, 167
    novels, 215, 248
    posters, 167
    printed ephemera, 29
    Romantic poetry, 164
    superficial, 204
receipts, 18
recipes, 17
Reed, Isaac, 112
    frost fair collections, 218–19
Reeves, John, 52–3, 55
Regency, 233
    communcation networks, 208
    paper economy, 213
    print politics, 222
    public culture, 235
    regulations, 179
    republic of letters, 23, 113, 123, 139
Revesby Abbey, 105
ribbons, 125
Richmond House
    theatricals of 1787–8, 114
Rickards, Maurice, 1, 10
    definition of ephemera, 32, 215
    Encyclopedia of Ephemera, 10
    on typeface, 161
Ridgeway, James, 50
Rights of Man, 53, 56
Ritson, Joseph, 24–5, 94
Rodd, Thomas (bookseller), 174
romances, 98, 187
    penny, 215
Romantic period, 23
    bibliography, 26, 61

and category of ephemera, 27
and codex-form book, 21
ephemeral historicism, 28
fiction, 215
and importance of ephemera, 27
literary culture, 96
media history, 162
mediation, 244
novels, 188
and playbills, 26, 154
poetics of ephemerality, 154
poetry, 164–5, 251
and printed ephemera as a poetics, 177
and wartime, 241
Romanticism
  continuous with the present, 23
  literary, 24, 252
  and poetics of ephemerality, 29
  and Siskin and Warner's 'history of mediations', 22–3
Rowe, Nicholas
  Fair Penitent, 155
  Jane Shore, 153, 157, 177, 180
Roxburghe Club, 94
royal family, 110, 222
royal proclamations, 53
Royal Society, 106, 126, 138
rubbish, 69, 131, 157, 183
rules, 179

Sadler, James, 228, 230
sale catalogues, 63, 95, 98, 148, 237–9
  Anthony Wood collection, 75–8
  'G. S.', 143
  library of Dawson Turner, 106
  library of John Field, 170, 174–5
  library of Jonathan Swift, 68
  library of Philip Hurd, 104
  library of Richard Smith, 69
Samuel, Richardson
  Pamela, 192
Sandwich, Earl of
  patron of Omai, 193
Sappho, 24
Savage, William
  Dictionary of the Art of Printing (1841), 17
Sayers, James, 110
science, 6, 61, 120, 144, 147
  of failure, 148
scientific societies, 22
Scott, Lady Frances, 116
Scott, Walter, 96, 214–15, 242
  Heart of Midlothian, 159
  Life of John Dryden, (1808), 93
  use of Luttrell collection, 93

Waverley (1814), 214
Scottish martyrs, 49
scribal publication, 5
  libels as, 67
scribes, 6
script, 151
seals, 109, 125
seasons, 241
Seditious Writings Act, 49
Selwyn, George, 189
servants, 197, 247
  in *Northanger Abbey*, 199–200
Seven Dials, 237
seventeenth century, 27
Seymour, Lady Charlotte Jane, 123
Shakespeare, William, 24, 112, 174
  first folios, 170
  genius of, 175
  Henry IV, 179
  Richard III, 157, 168, 182
  Stratford-upon-Avon, 168
Shelley, Mary
  Frankenstein, 147
Shelley, P.B
  'England in 1819', 216
Sheridan, Richard Brinsley, 169
Sherman, Stuart, 42, 71
shop bills, 60, 112
shop-fronts, 163
shopping, 113
Short Title Catalogue, 64
shows, 229
Sidaway, Robert, 180–1
Siddons, Sarah, 155
signatures, 14, 109, 125
signwriting, 165
Simmel, Georg
  sociability, 23, 187, 196, 213
single sheets, 43, 91, 107
  and ballads, 18, 26
  and books, 17, 37–8
  and handbills, 45
  indulgences, 5
  and jobbing print, 17
  newsmen's verses, 247
  songs, 18
Siskin, Clifford, 22, 142
  with Warner on 'a history of mediations', 22–3
Skirving, Thomas, 49
Sloane, Sir Hans, 66, 95, 253
Smirke, George, 130
Smith, Edward, 100
Smith, J. T., 99
Smithsonian Institute, 143

sociability, 79, 88, 93, 105, 109, 145, 209, 251
  1790s, 114
  in *The Absentee*, 208
  and ballooning, 139, 147
  Bankses' home, No.32 Soho Square, 121
  of book collecting, 76
  cross-cultural, 207
  elite, 110, 126
  fashionable, 26, 103, 111, 113–15, 129, 131, 138, 193, 200, 204, 207, 237
  history of, 114
  Johnson's essay 191, 203–4
  and knowledge, 201
  literary, 209
  and natural philosophy, 144
  and Order of the Bath, 132
  Place's tailor shop, 234
  and peace of 1814, 226–7
  polite, 103
  and printed ephemera, 22
  of Roxburghe Club, 94
  Simmel on, 23, 187, 196, 213
  as sociable commerce, 190
  social life, 98
  and SSB, 102, 104, 113, 119, 124–5
  SSB as archivist of, 114–15, 119, 154
  and theatre, 176
  and tickets, 72, 123
  and time in *Persuasion*, 242
  virtual, 113, 194
  and visiting, 186
  and visiting cards, 186–8, 192, 196, 203, 206
sociablarium, 123, 142
social media, 254
  of eighteenth century, 21
  and visiting cards, 27
social sciences, 11
  and Pemberton report, 11
society
  polite, 103
Society Islands, 193
Society of the Friends of Liberty, 51
Society of United Irishmen, *See* United Irishmen
sociology, 62, 150
Solander, Daniel, 123
  solander case, 123
soldiers, 210
songs, 18, 50
  1790s, 210
  Jubilee of 1814, 238
  Plato's Advice', 236
  as single sheet publications, 18
  song-sheets, 17
  'Two Children in the Wood', 30, 35–6

Sotheby's auction house
  auction of printed ephemera from library of Sara Coleridge, 9
Soulbys (booksellers), 155
Southey, Robert, 162, 167, 180
  and playbills, 157
souvenirs, 76, 230
  first English secular, 86
  frost fair tickets, 86–7
Spectator, 25, 33, 35, 170
  no. 85, 30, 33–9
    accidental reading, 35
    fugitive literature, 37–8
    and paper, 30–1
    'Two Children in the Wood', 35–6
speculation (card game), 190
Spencer, Earl, 171
Spirit of the Public Journals, The, 56
Sprange, Jasper, 45, 108, 155, 168, 173
squibs, 18, 20, 31
  election, 224
  United Irishmen, 210
stage, the, 175
  as ephemeral, 175
Stallybrass, Peter, 13
State Trials, 50
Stationers' Company, 154
stationery, 19
  trade, 191
Stern, Tiffany, 154
Stockdale, John, 55
Strawberry Hill, 105
street, the, 32, 58, 70, 159
  changing meanings of, 225
Stuart, Caroline (Countess of Portarlington), 205
sublime, the, 242
Swan Theatre, 170
Swift, Jonathan, 68
Sydney Gazette, 179
Symonds, H. D., 50

Tahiti, 129
Tait's Edinburgh Magazine, 162
Talfourd, Thomas Noon, 167
taste, 187, 223
taverns, 22
taxonomy, 129
telephony, 145, 147
Temple of Concord, 229–31
Temple of Peace, 236
text messaging, 27, 186
textual materialism, 28
Thames, the river, 26, 253
  and 'a great Whale', 69
  freezing of 1683–84, 85

Index

thanksgiving services, 227
theatre, 26, 60, 98, 108, 113, 115, 167–70, 234
   and associational culture, 175
   Bath, 157, 167
   'Botany Bay theatricals', 153
   Covent Garden, 235
   Drury Lane, 155, 174, 226
   Dublin, 208
   and ephemerality, 175
   Goodman's Fields, 174
   Haymarket, 174, 181
   illegitimate forms of, 176
   in late Georgian society, 237
   London, 234
   patent, 174
   and playbills, 154–5
   playbills as records, 168
   and sociability, 176
   Swan Theatre, 170
   Sydney, 180–1
   and tickets, 108
theatre history, 27, 62, 170, 177, 252
   and Enlightenment, 176
   and exclusion of ephemerality, 176
   historiography, 174
theatre managers
   as playbill collectors, 173
theatre studies, 62
   'theatre science', 175
Theatric Tourist, 169
Theatrical Examiner, 162
Thickness, Miss, 116
Thomas, Nicholas, 124
Thomason tracts, 26, 68–72, 74, 79, 83, 96, 99, 225
   as 'fugitive', 92
   purchase of, 90
   storage of, 90
   and William Godwin, 90–3
Thomason, George, 26, 66, 69–72, 74–5, 78, 81, 84–5, 90–2, 96, 103, 106, 108, 112, 160, 173, 234, 237
   methodology, 90
Thorne, Robert
   fat face type, 161
tickets, 26, 28–9, 50, 58, 60, 76–7, 86, 109, 124, 175, 177
   admission, 21, 104, 123
   as art objects, 131
   ballads privileged over, 225
   ballooning, 138–42, 144
   and bodies, 109, 116
   'British Balloon', 141
   British Museum, 127–9
   currency of, 126
   defined as ephemeral 'trash', 226
   designed by women, 115–19
   'Edinburgh fire balloon', 139–40
   Enlightenment culture after 1760, 114
   fashionable sociability, 113
   frost fair, 86–7, 217–20, 235–6
   as handbills, 115
   intaglio-printed, 109
   jobbing print, 109
   and jobbing print, 108
   Jubilee of 1814, 228, 230–1, 233
   letterpress printing, 109
   Lloyd on, 108, 151
   lottery, 153
   made of silk, 115
   and Mischianza, 112
   Norwich ball, 116–19, 128, 142
   and the novel, 21, 248
   Pantheon, 142
   'pay', 108
   peace of 1814, 227
   performative work of, 21
   protocols surrounding, 22
   in Samuel Johnson's essay no. 191, 203–4
   and sociability, 72, 123
   social life, 108–9
   'spinning', 108
   SSB collection of, *See* SSB
   status of, 108
   sticklers, 126–7
   terminology of, 108
   theatre, 108
   and theatre history, 252
   in Thomason collection, 70, 72
   ticket system, 114, 204, 233
   visiting cards, 186
   Wood collection, 80
   in Wood collection, 86
time
   diurnal, 42
   in eighteenth century, 247
   and ephemera, 28
   ephemeral, 142
   in *Persuasion*, 216, 239–43
   pocket watch, 42
   and readers, 248
   and reading, 204
   sociability of in *Persuasion*, 242
   'Tyme' and Thomason collection, 90
   war, 241
Times, The, 46, 216, 230, 233, 246
   coverage of Jubilee of 1814, 228–9
tokens, 60, 114
topography, 60, 62
Town and Country Magazine, 129

tracts, 18, 66, 77
  terminology of, 67
trade, 234
  cards, 19, 104–5, 109, 190, 219
  tokens, 104
tradesmen, 109
transport, 105
trash, 64
treaties
  Paris 1814, 226
  Paris 1815, 239
trials, 57, 110
Tuite, Clara, 205
Tunbridge Wells, 45
Turnbull, William (printer), 49
Turner, Dawson, 103, 151, 183
  and book making, 106
  extra-illustration of Blomefield, 106
  library sale-catalogue, 106
  scope of collections, 106–7
  and SSB, 105–7, 110
Twitter, 23
Twyman, Michael, 2
Tyler, Elizabeth (aunt of Robert Southey), 157, 173
type, 179
  Gutenberg's invention of, 5
  moveable, 44
typeface, 26
  Egyptians, 161
  fat face, 161
  neo-classical, 161
  old face, 161
  Rickards, Maurice on, 161
  sans serif, 161
  and technological change, 167
typographic revolution, 179
typography, 14, 124, 218
  Raven on 'typographical assuredness', 19
Tytler, James, 48–9, 136
  convicted under Seditious Writings Act, 49
  as a 'diurnal historiographer', 49
  Encyclopedia Britannica, 48
  and handbill 'To the People and their Friends', 49
  radical politics, 48

UNESCO Memory of the World, 26
United Irishmen, 210
University of Reading
  Centre for Ephemera Studies, 10
Unlawful Societies Act, 54–5
Upcott, William, 60–1, 65, 93, 107, 234, 252
  ballooning collection, 143
urban life, 246

Vauxhall Gardens, 113, 162, 230
vellum, 5
vernacular languages, 104
Victorian era, 23
virtuosos, 102
visiting, 113, 189, 195, 197, 249
  in Bath, 198
  Johnson's essay 191, 202–4
  in *Northanger Abbey*, 197–200
  and the novel, 27
  Walpole essay, 200–2
visiting cards, 27, 104, 109, 186, 200–2
  in *The Absentee*, 206–9
  as art objects, 192
  and assemblage, 188
  card racks, 192
  cases for, 186
  commercialisation of, 190–2
  and cultural value, 202
  elite, 193
  forms of, 189–90
  hallways, 199
  and hospitality, 188
  intaglio, 192
  Johnson's essay 191, 203–4
  in *Northanger Abbey*, 197–200, 249
  Omai, SSB collection, 193–6
  origins of, 189–90
  in *Persuasion*, 249
  and playbills, 187
  printed designs, 192
  and prose fiction, 27
  public view of, 192
  and sociability, 186–8, 192, 196
  SSB collection of, *See* SSB
  supersede oral communication, 200
  and threshold moment, 205
  used by Edgeworth, 205
  virtual sociability of, 203, 206
  Walpole's essay on, 200–2
  widespread by 1740s, 200
visual culture, 148
volunteer movement, 114
von Linné, Carl (Linnaeus), 121

Walford, Edward., 189
Wallington, Nehemiah, 72
walls, 29, 34, 157, *See* 'dead walls'
  posters on, 167
Walpole, Horace, 27, 103, 204
  essay on visiting cards, 200–2, 213
  Fugitive Pieces in Verse and Prose (1758), 200
  and Kirkgate (printer), 105
  Strawberry Hill ephemera, 105
  and visiting cards, 188

Wanley, Humfrey, 63
Waring, Thomas, 112
Warner, William, 22, 144
　with Siskin on 'a history of mediations', 22–3
wars
　between March and June 1815, 240
　English civil, 23, 66, 91
　Revolutionary and Napoleonic, 114, 130, 171, 210, 216
　and technology, 147
watchmen, 247
　in *Persuasion*, 242
watch-papers, 219, 236
　SSB collection, 219–20
Welbery, David, 41
Wellington, Duke of, 226, 238
West, Benjamin
　portrait of Joseph Banks, 129
Westminster Committee, 235
Winston, James, 169, 172–3, 175, 234
　Theatric Tourist, 169
Wolfreston, Frances, 98
women, 115
　and archery, 111
　and ballooning, 144
　as collectors, 98
　of Dawson Turner's family, 106
　designers, tickets, 115–19
　designers, visiting cards, 193, 205
　and entertainment, 113
　and fashion, 145
　of fashion, 203
　and gift giving, 189
　marital status, 118
　and the Pantheon, 145
　and polite associational culture, 129
　and science of the 'present', 107
　and sociability, 145
　and 'sociable' commerce, 102

Wood, Anthony, 26, 66, 72–81, 84–5, 90, 92, 97–8, 103, 105–6, 108, 137, 149, 173
　annotations, 78–9
　Athenae Oxoniensis, (1691-92), 73
　Bibliotheca Oweniana (1684), 77
　collecting interests, 187
　Historia et Antiquitates Universitatis Oxford, (1674), 73
　Popish Plot catalogues, 84
　'To the right honourable the house of commons...', 80
　and sales catalogues, 75–8
　and SSB, 110
　'The royal patient traveller...', 78
　'The Tall *Indian*-KING', 75, 78, 253
　tickets, 79, 86
woodcuts, 219
Woolf, Daniel, 71
word-processing, 185
Wordsworth, William, 27, 166, 177, 209
　The Prelude, 27, 162–5, 167–8
working-classes, 234
World, The, 115
wrappers
　United Irishmen texts, 210
Wright, James
　Historia Histrionica (1699), 176
writing, 12–13, 24, 154, 186
　paraphernalia, 191
Wynne, Edward, 92

Yarmouth
　Dawson Turner collections, 106
year 1814, 28, 242, 249
York, Duke of, 81
Young, Timothy G., 12–13, 18, 40, 224

Zambecarri, Count Francesco, 136
zeppelin airships, 145, 147
zoology, 44, 121, 124

CAMBRIDGE STUDIES IN ROMANTICISM

General Editor
JAMES CHANDLER, University of Chicago

1. *Romantic Correspondence: Women, Politics and the Fiction of Letters*
   MARY A. FAVRET
2. *British Romantic Writers and the East: Anxieties of Empire*
   NIGEL LEASK
3. *Poetry as an Occupation and an Art in Britain, 1760–1830*
   PETER MURPHY
4. *Edmund Burke's Aesthetic Ideology: Language, Gender and Political Economy in Revolution*
   TOM FURNISS
5. *In the Theatre of Romanticism: Coleridge, Nationalism, Women*
   JULIE A. CARLSON
6. *Keats, Narrative and Audience*
   ANDREW BENNETT
7. *Romance and Revolution: Shelley and the Politics of a Genre*
   DAVID DUFF
8. *Literature, Education, and Romanticism: Reading as Social Practice, 1780–1832*
   ALAN RICHARDSON
9. *Women Writing about Money: Women's Fiction in England, 1790–1820*
   EDWARD COPELAND
10. *Shelley and the Revolution in Taste: The Body and the Natural World*
    TIMOTHY MORTON
11. *William Cobbett: The Politics of Style*
    LEONORA NATTRASS
12. *The Rise of Supernatural Fiction, 1762–1800*
    E. J. CLERY
13. *Women Travel Writers and the Language of Aesthetics, 1716–1818*
    ELIZABETH A. BOHLS
14. *Napoleon and English Romanticism*
    SIMON BAINBRIDGE
15. *Romantic Vagrancy: Wordsworth and the Simulation of Freedom*
    CELESTE LANGAN

16. *Wordsworth and the Geologists*
   JOHN WYATT

17. *Wordsworth's Pope: A Study in Literary Historiography*
   ROBERT J. GRIFFIN

18. *The Politics of Sensibility: Race, Gender and Commerce in the Sentimental Novel*
   MARKMAN ELLIS

19. *Reading Daughters' Fictions, 1709–1834: Novels and Society from Manley to Edgeworth*
   CAROLINE GONDA

20. *Romantic Identities: Varieties of Subjectivity, 1774–1830*
   ANDREA K. HENDERSON

21. *Print Politics: The Press and Radical Opposition in Early Nineteenth-Century England*
   KEVIN GILMARTIN

22. *Reinventing Allegory*
   THERESA M. KELLEY

23. *British Satire and the Politics of Style, 1789–1832*
   GARY DYER

24. *The Romantic Reformation: Religious Politics in English Literature, 1789–1824*
   ROBERT M. RYAN

25. *De Quincey's Romanticism: Canonical Minority and the Forms of Transmission*
   MARGARET RUSSETT

26. *Coleridge on Dreaming: Romanticism, Dreams and the Medical Imagination*
   JENNIFER FORD

27. *Romantic Imperialism: Universal Empire and the Culture of Modernity*
   SAREE MAKDISI

28. *Ideology and Utopia in the Poetry of William Blake*
   NICHOLAS M. WILLIAMS

29. *Sexual Politics and the Romantic Author*
   SONIA HOFKOSH

30. *Lyric and Labour in the Romantic Tradition*
   ANNE JANOWITZ

31. *Poetry and Politics in the Cockney School: Keats, Shelley, Hunt and their Circle*
   JEFFREY N. COX

32. *Rousseau, Robespierre and English Romanticism*
   GREGORY DART

33. *Contesting the Gothic: Fiction, Genre and Cultural Conflict, 1764–1832*
   JAMES WATT

34. *Romanticism, Aesthetics, and Nationalism*
   DAVID ARAM KAISER

35. *Romantic Poets and the Culture of Posterity*
   ANDREW BENNETT

36. *The Crisis of Literature in the 1790s: Print Culture and the Public Sphere*
   PAUL KEEN

37. *Romantic Atheism: Poetry and Freethought, 1780–1830*
   MARTIN PRIESTMAN

38. *Romanticism and Slave Narratives: Transatlantic Testimonies*
   HELEN THOMAS

39. *Imagination under Pressure, 1789–1832: Aesthetics, Politics, and Utility*
   JOHN WHALE

40. *Romanticism and the Gothic: Genre, Reception, and Canon Formation, 1790–1820*
   MICHAEL GAMER

41. *Romanticism and the Human Sciences: Poetry, Population, and the Discourse of the Species*
   MAUREEN N. MCLANE

42. *The Poetics of Spice: Romantic Consumerism and the Exotic*
   TIMOTHY MORTON

43. *British Fiction and the Production of Social Order, 1740–1830*
   MIRANDA J. BURGESS

44. *Women Writers and the English Nation in the 1790s*
   ANGELA KEANE

45. *Literary Magazines and British Romanticism*
   MARK PARKER

46. *Women, Nationalism and the Romantic Stage: Theatre and Politics in Britain, 1780–1800*
   BETSY BOLTON

47. *British Romanticism and the Science of the Mind*
   ALAN RICHARDSON

48. *The Anti-Jacobin Novel: British Conservatism and the French Revolution*
   M. O. GRENBY

49. *Romantic Austen: Sexual Politics and the Literary Canon*
   CLARA TUITE

50. Byron and Romanticism
JEROME MCGANN AND JAMES SODERHOLM

51. The Romantic National Tale and the Question of Ireland
INA FERRIS

52. Byron, Poetics and History
JANE STABLER

53. Religion, Toleration, and British Writing, 1790–1830
MARK CANUEL

54. Fatal Women of Romanticism
ADRIANA CRACIUN

55. Knowledge and Indifference in English Romantic Prose
TIM MILNES

56. Mary Wollstonecraft and the Feminist Imagination
BARBARA TAYLOR

57. Romanticism, Maternity and the Body Politic
JULIE KIPP

58. Romanticism and Animal Rights
DAVID PERKINS

59. Georgic Modernity and British Romanticism: Poetry and the Mediation of History
KEVIS GOODMAN

60. Literature, Science and Exploration in the Romantic Era: Bodies of Knowledge
TIMOTHY FULFORD, DEBBIE LEE, AND PETER J. KITSON

61. Romantic Colonization and British Anti-Slavery
DEIRDRE COLEMAN

62. Anger, Revolution, and Romanticism
ANDREW M. STAUFFER

63. Shelley and the Revolutionary Sublime
CIAN DUFFY

64. Fictions and Fakes: Forging Romantic Authenticity, 1760–1845
MARGARET RUSSETT

65. Early Romanticism and Religious Dissent
DANIEL E. WHITE

66. The Invention of Evening: Perception and Time in Romantic Poetry
CHRISTOPHER R. MILLER

67. *Wordsworth's Philosophic Song*
   SIMON JARVIS

68. *Romanticism and the Rise of the Mass Public*
   ANDREW FRANTA

69. *Writing against Revolution: Literary Conservatism in Britain, 1790–1832*
   KEVIN GILMARTIN

70. *Women, Sociability and Theatre in Georgian London*
   GILLIAN RUSSELL

71. *The Lake Poets and Professional Identity*
   BRIAN GOLDBERG

72. *Wordsworth Writing*
   ANDREW BENNETT

73. *Science and Sensation in Romantic Poetry*
   NOEL JACKSON

74. *Advertising and Satirical Culture in the Romantic Period*
   JOHN STRACHAN

75. *Romanticism and the Painful Pleasures of Modern Life*
   ANDREA K. HENDERSON

76. *Balladeering, Minstrelsy, and the Making of British Romantic Poetry*
   MAUREEN N. MCLANE

77. *Romanticism and Improvisation, 1750–1850*
   ANGELA ESTERHAMMER

78. *Scotland and the Fictions of Geography: North Britain, 1760–1830*
   PENNY FIELDING

79. *Wordsworth, Commodification and Social Concern: The Poetics of Modernity*
   DAVID SIMPSON

80. *Sentimental Masculinity and the Rise of History, 1790–1890*
   MIKE GOODE

81. *Fracture and Fragmentation in British Romanticism*
   ALEXANDER REGIER

82. *Romanticism and Music Culture in Britain, 1770–1840: Virtue and Virtuosity*
   GILLEN D'ARCY WOOD

83. *The Truth about Romanticism: Pragmatism and Idealism in Keats, Shelley, Coleridge*
   TIM MILNES

84. *Blake's Gifts: Poetry and the Politics of Exchange*
SARAH HAGGARTY

85. *Real Money and Romanticism*
MATTHEW ROWLINSON

86. *Sentimental Literature and Anglo-Scottish Identity, 1745–1820*
JULIET SHIELDS

87. *Romantic Tragedies: The Dark Employments of Wordsworth, Coleridge, and Shelley*
REEVE PARKER

88. *Blake, Sexuality and Bourgeois Politeness*
SUSAN MATTHEWS

89. *Idleness, Contemplation and the Aesthetic*
RICHARD ADELMAN

90. *Shelley's Visual Imagination*
NANCY MOORE GOSLEE

91. *A Cultural History of the Irish Novel, 1790–1829*
CLAIRE CONNOLLY

92. *Literature, Commerce, and the Spectacle of Modernity, 1750–1800*
PAUL KEEN

93. *Romanticism and Childhood: The Infantilization of British Literary Culture*
ANN WEIRDA ROWLAND

94. *Metropolitan Art and Literature, 1810–1840: Cockney Adventures*
GREGORY DART

95. *Wordsworth and the Enlightenment Idea of Pleasure*
ROWAN BOYSON

96. *John Clare and Community*
JOHN GOODRIDGE

97. *The Romantic Crowd*
MARY FAIRCLOUGH

98. *Romantic Women Writers, Revolution and Prophecy*
ORIANNE SMITH

99. *Britain, France and the Gothic, 1764–1820*
ANGELA WRIGHT

100. *Transfiguring the Arts and Sciences*
JON KLANCHER

101. *Shelley and the Apprehension of Life*
ROSS WILSON

102. *Poetics of Character: Transatlantic Encounters 1700–1900*
SUSAN MANNING

103. *Romanticism and Caricature*
IAN HAYWOOD

104. *The Late Poetry of the Lake Poets: Romanticism Revised*
TIM FULFORD

105. *Forging Romantic China: Sino-British Cultural Exchange 1760–1840*
PETER J. KITSON

106. *Coleridge and the Philosophy of Poetic Form*
EWAN JAMES JONES

107. *Romanticism in the Shadow of War: Literary Culture in the Napoleonic War Years*
JEFFREY N. COX

108. *Slavery and the Politics of Place: Representing the Colonial Caribbean, 1770–1833*
ELIZABETH A. BOHLS

109. *The Orient and the Young Romantics*
ANDREW WARREN

110. *Lord Byron and Scandalous Celebrity*
CLARA TUITE

111. *Radical Orientalism: Rights, Reform, and Romanticism*
GERARD COHEN-VRIGNAUD

112. *Print, Publicity, and Popular Radicalism in the 1790s*
JON MEE

113. *Wordsworth and the Art of Philosophical Travel*
MARK OFFORD

114. *Romanticism, Self-Canonization, and the Business of Poetry*
MICHAEL GAMER

115. *Women Wanderers and the Writing of Mobility, 1784–1814*
INGRID HORROCKS

116. *Eighteen Hundred and Eleven: Poetry, Protest and Economic Crisis*
E. J. CLERY

117. *Urbanization and English Romantic Poetry*
STEPHEN TEDESCHI

118. *The Poetics of Decline in British Romanticism*
JONATHAN SACHS

119. *The Caribbean and the Medical Imagination, 1764–1834: Slavery, Disease and Colonial Modernity*
EMILY SENIOR

120. *Science, Form, and the Problem of Induction in British Romanticism*
DAHLIA PORTER

121. *Wordsworth and the Poetics of Air*
THOMAS H. FORD

122. *Romantic Art in Practice: Cultural Work and the Sister Arts, 1760–1820*
THORA BRYLOWE

123. *European Literatures in Britain, 1815–1832: Romantic Translations*
DIEGO SIGALIA

124. *Romanticism and theatrical experience: Kean, Hazlitt and Keats in the Age of Theatrical News*
JONATHAN MULROONEY

125. *The Romantic Tavern: Literature and Conviviality in the Age of Revolution*
IAN NEWMAN

126. *Print and Performance in the 1820s*
ANGELA ESTERHAMMER

127. *The Italian Idea*
WILL BOWERS

Printed in the United Kingdom by TJ Clays Ltd.